Elements of Economics of Industry: Being the First Volume of Elements of Economics, Volume 1

Alfred Marshall

ELEMENTS OF ECONOMICS

VOL. I.

6

ELEMENTS OF

ECONOMICS OF INDUSTRY

BEING THE FIRST VOLUME OF

ELEMENTS OF ECONOMICS

BY

ALFRED MARSHALL

Professor of Political Economy in the University of Cambridge,
Honorary Fellow of Balliol College, Oxford.

THIRD EDITION

London:

MACMILLAN AND CO., LIMITED.

NEW YORK: THE MACMILLAN COMPANY.

1903

First Edition printed 1892. *Reprinted* 1893, 1894.
Second Edition 1896. *Reprinted* 1898, *January* 1899.
Third Edition, August 1899.
Reprinted 1900, 1901, 1903

PREFACE TO THE THIRD EDITION.

IN the present edition of this volume some matters which had been found difficult by beginners have been omitted, others have been relegated to Appendices, and others again have been explained at greater length than before. Book IV. remains nearly unchanged; and so does Book VI. except Chapters I. II. and XI.; but a considerable part of Books I. II. III. and V. has been rewritten.

A short treatise on economics is apt to ignore many difficulties, and thus to suggest that its conclusions are absolute when they are really only conditional, and that they are universal when really they only apply strictly to a few simple cases. If it avoids this danger by pointing out many difficulties, with which it has no space to deal effectively, the reader may be perplexed. The little *Economics of Industry*, brought out by my wife and myself in 1879, seems to have erred by excess in the first of these directions; and it is perhaps through a reaction that the earlier edition of the present volume erred by excess in the opposite direction. There were indeed several points in the fundamental scheme of Distribution and Exchange, on which I had not made up my own mind in 1879: and, partly for this reason, partly because it was desired to make the book appear simple, difficulties were evaded, and smooth phrases were applied to cover over the jagged ends of broken and incomplete discussions. But, as years went on, I found that pupils even of some ability were misled by the apparently easy and complete solutions which were offered in that little book; and the feeling grew on me that one who has never read any economics at all, is likely to be a more useful man in his generation than one who has read an easy work on economics, and thinks he has mastered the subject sufficiently to be able to derive from it trustworthy guidance in life.

As soon therefore as the way was prepared by the publication of the first volume of my *Principles*, I hastened to compile a small volume designed for beginners, but written frankly without any pretence that a serviceable knowledge of economics can be obtained without great effort. No broad and simple proposition was admitted without some indication of the chief qualifications to which it was liable, and of the dangers of applying it unreservedly to practical problems: a reference was also generally given to a passage in my larger book in which the matter was further studied. No argument was purposely compressed. The intention was that any part of a discussion which appeared unsuitable for a beginner should be omitted altogether, and the rest given in full. But I was hurried, and I failed to carry out my intention completely. It was found afterwards that a part of a study, which was retained, often depended, more than I had noticed at the time, on a part which had been omitted: and whenever that happened, the shortening had made the book not easier but more difficult. This is the fault which I have tried to remove in the present edition. I have been helped by several persons and especially by my wife, by Professor Smart, Professor Flux and Dr Keynes. Even with their generous and great aid, I cannot hope to have noticed every weak spot. But I trust that this edition is more nearly self-contained, and that it is somewhat simpler and less technical than the earlier editions. The allusions to difficulties which lie beyond the limited range of this little volume have been cut down; but not I hope in such a way as to suggest that any short statement of an important economic doctrine can present the whole truth and nothing but the truth.

Balliol Croft, Cambridge,
        July, 1899.

PREFACE TO THE FIRST EDITION.

This volume is an attempt to adapt the first volume of my *Principles of Economics* (Second edition, 1891) to the needs of junior students.

The necessary abridgment has been effected not by systematic compression so much as by the omission of many discussions on points of minor importance and of some difficult theoretical investigations. For it seemed that the difficulty of an argument would be increased rather than diminished by curtailing it and leaving out some of its steps. The argumentative parts of the *Principles* are therefore as a rule either reproduced in full or omitted altogether; reference in the latter case being made in footnotes to the corresponding places in the larger treatise. Notes and discussions of a literary character have generally been omitted.

The influence of trade-unions on wages depends much on the course of foreign trade and on commercial fluctuations; and therefore in the *Principles* all discussion of the subject is postponed to a late stage. But in the present volume, the practical convenience of discussing it in close connection with the main theory of distribution seemed to outweigh the disadvantages of treating it prematurely and in some measure incompletely; and a chapter on *trade-unions* has been added at the end of Book VI.

A few sentences have been incorporated from the *Economics of Industry*, published by my wife and myself in 1879.

Though she prefers that her name should not appear on the title-page, my wife has a share in this volume also. For in writing it, and in writing the *Principles*, I have been aided and advised by her at every stage of the MSS. and the proofs; and thus the pages which are now submitted to the reader are indebted twice over to her suggestions, her judgment and her care.

Dr Keynes, Mr John Burnett and Mr J. S. Cree have read the proofs of the chapter on trade-unions, and have given me helpful advice with regard to it from three different points of view.

18 February, 1892.

CONTENTS.

[Italics are used to give references to definitions of technical terms.]

BOOK I.

PRELIMINARY SURVEY.

BOOK II.

SOME FUNDAMENTAL NOTIONS.

BOOK III.

ON WANTS AND THEIR SATISFACTIONS.

BOOK IV.

THE AGENTS OF PRODUCTION.
LAND, LABOUR, CAPITAL AND ORGANIZATION.

BOOK V.

THE BALANCING OF DEMAND AND SUPPLY.

BOOK VI.

VALUE, OR DISTRIBUTION AND EXCHANGE.

The fourth edition of my "Principles" is that to which references are made in the present volume. But most of them are applicable also to earlier editions.

BOOK I.

PRELIMINARY SURVEY.

CHAPTER I.

INTRODUCTION.

§ 1. POLITICAL ECONOMY, or ECONOMICS, is a study of man's actions in the ordinary business of life; it inquires how he gets his income and how he uses it. It follows the action of individuals and of nations as they seek, by separate or collective endeavour, to increase the material means of their well-being and to turn their resources to the best account. Thus it is on the one side a study of wealth, and on the other, and more important side, a part of the study of man. For man's character has been moulded by his every-day work, and by the material resources which he thereby procures, more than by any other influence unless it be that of his religious ideals; and the great forming agencies of the world's history have been the religious and the economic. Here and there the ardour of the military or the artistic spirit has been for a while predominant: but religious and economic influences have nowhere been displaced from the front rank even for a time; and they have nearly always been more important than all others put together. Religious motives are more intense than economic; but their direct action seldom extends over so large a part of life. For the business by which a person earns his livelihood generally fills his thoughts during by far the greater part of those hours in which his mind is at its best; during them his character is being formed by the way in which he uses his faculties in

Economics is a study of wealth, and a part of the study of man.

Character formed by daily work.

M.   Œ   1

his work, by the thoughts and the feelings which it suggests, and by his relations to his associates in work, his employers or his employés.

And very often the influence exerted on a person's character by the amount of his income is hardly less, if it is less, than that exerted by the way in which it is earned. *Poverty causes degradation.* It makes little difference to the fulness of life of a family whether its yearly income is £1000 or £5000. But it makes a very great difference whether the income is £30 or £150: for with £150 the family has, with £30 it has not, <u>the material conditions of a complete life.</u> It is true that in religion, in the family affections and in friendship, even the poor may find scope for many of those faculties which are the source of the highest happiness. But the conditions which surround extreme poverty, especially in densely crowded places, tend to deaden the higher faculties. Those who have been called the Residuum of our large towns have little opportunity for friendship; they know nothing of the decencies and the quiet, and very little even of the unity of family life; and religion often fails to reach them. No doubt their physical, mental, and moral ill-health is partly due to other causes than poverty, but this is the chief cause.

And in addition to the Residuum there are vast numbers of people both in town and country who are brought up with insufficient food, clothing, and house-room, whose education is broken off early in order that they may go to work for wages, who thenceforth are engaged during long hours in exhausting toil with imperfectly nourished bodies, and have therefore no chance of developing their higher mental faculties. Their life is not necessarily unhealthy or unhappy. Rejoicing in their affections towards God and man, and perhaps even possessing some natural refinement of feeling, they may lead lives that are far less incomplete than those of many who have more material wealth. But, for all that, their poverty is a great and almost unmixed evil to them. Even when they are well, their weariness often amounts to pain, while their pleasures are few; and when sickness comes, the suffering caused by poverty increases tenfold. And though a contented spirit may go far towards reconciling them to these evils, there are others to which it ought not to reconcile them. Overworked and undertaught, weary and careworn, without quiet and without leisure, they have no chance of making the best of their mental faculties.

Although then some of the evils which commonly go with poverty are not its necessary consequences; yet, broadly speaking, "the destruction of the poor is their poverty," and the study of the causes of poverty is the study of the causes of the degradation of a large part of mankind.

§ 2. Slavery was regarded by Aristotle as an ordinance of nature, and so probably was it by the slaves themselves in olden time. The dignity of man was proclaimed by the Christian religion: it has been asserted with increasing vehemence during the last hundred years: but it is only through the spread of education during quite recent times that we are beginning at last to feel the full import of the phrase. Now at last we are setting ourselves seriously to inquire whether it is necessary that there should be any so-called "lower classes" at all: that is, whether there need be large numbers of people doomed from their birth to hard work in order to provide for others the requisites of a refined and cultured life; while they themselves are prevented by their poverty and toil from having any share or part in that life.

Is poverty necessary?

The hope that poverty and ignorance may gradually be extinguished derives indeed much support from the steady progress of the working classes during the present century. The steam-engine has relieved them of much exhausting and degrading toil; wages have risen; education has been improved and become more general; the railway and the printing-press have enabled members of the same trade in

different parts of the country to communicate easily with
one another, and to undertake and carry out broad and far-
seeing lines of policy; while the growing demand for intelligent work has caused the artisan classes to increase so
rapidly that they now outnumber those whose labour is
entirely unskilled. A great part of the artisans have ceased
to belong to the "lower classes" in the sense in which the
term was originally used; and some of them already lead a
more refined and noble life than did the majority of the
upper classes even a century ago.

This progress has done more than anything else to give
practical interest to the question whether it is really impossible
that all should start in the world with a fair chance of
leading a cultured life, free from the pains of poverty and
the stagnating influences of excessive mechanical toil; and
this question is being pressed to the front by the growing
earnestness of the age.

The question cannot be fully answered ·by economic
science; for the answer depends partly on the moral and
political capabilities of human nature; and on these matters
the economist has no special means of information; he must
do as others do, and guess as best he can. But the answer
depends in a great measure upon facts and inferences, which
are within the province of economics; and this it is which
gives to economic studies their chief and their highest interest.

§ 3. It might have been expected that a science, which
Reasons why deals with questions so vital for the well-being of
Economics is
in the main of mankind, would have engaged the attention of
recent growth. many of the ablest thinkers of every age, and be
now well advanced towards maturity. But the bearing of
economics on the higher well-being of man has been over-
looked; and it has not received that share of attention which
its importance and its difficulty require.

Its progress has been hindered also by the fact that many

of those conditions of industrial life, and of those methods of production, distribution and consumption, with which modern economic science is concerned, are constantly changing, and that their present forms are only of recent date[1].

§ 4. It is often said that the modern forms of business are distinguished from the earlier by being more competitive. But this account is not quite satis- *Competition.* factory. The strict meaning of competition seems to be the racing of one person against another, with special reference to bidding for the sale or purchase of anything. This kind of racing in business is no doubt both more intense and more widely extended than it used to be: but it is only a secondary, and one might almost say, an accidental consequence from the fundamental characteristics of modern business.

There is no one term that will express these characteristics adequately. They are, as we shall presently see, a certain independence and habit of choosing one's own course for one-self, a self-reliance; a deliberation and yet a promptness of choice and judgment, and a habit of forecasting the future and of shaping one's course with reference to distant aims. They may and often do cause people to compete with one another; but on the other hand they may tend, and just now indeed they are tending, in the direction of co-operation and combination of all kinds good and evil. But these tendencies towards collective ownership and collective action are quite

---

[1] It is indeed true that the change in substance is in some respects not so great as the change in outward form; and much more of modern economic theory than at first appears can be adapted to the conditions of backward races. But the changes in form have hindered writers of each successive age from deriving much benefit from the work of their predecessors. Modern economic conditions however, though very complex, are in many ways more definite than those of earlier times: business is more clearly marked off from other concerns of life; the rights of individuals as against others and as against the community are more sharply defined; and above all the emancipation from custom, and the growth of free activity, of constant forethought and restless enterprise have given a new precision and interest to the study of value.

different from those of earlier times, because they are the
result not of custom, not of any passive drifting into association with one's neighbours, but of free choice by each
individual of that line of conduct which after careful deliberation seems to him the best suited for attaining his ends,
whether they are selfish or unselfish.

Further the term "competition" not only fails to go to
the root of the matter, and thus errs by defect; it also errs
by excess. For it has gathered about it evil savour, and has
come to imply a certain selfishness and indifference to the
well-being of others. Now it is true that there is less deliberate selfishness in early than in modern forms of industry;
but there is also less deliberate unselfishness. It is the delibe-
rateness, and not the selfishness, that is the characteristic of
the modern age.

Custom in a primitive society extends the limits of the

Man is not more selfish than he was,
family, and prescribes certain duties to one's
neighbours which fall into disuse in a later civilization; but it also prescribes an attitude of
hostility to strangers. In a modern society the obligations of
family kindness become more intense, though they are concentrated on a narrower area; and neighbours are put more
nearly on the same footing with strangers. In ordinary dealings with both of them the standard of fairness and honesty
is lower than in some of the dealings of a primitive people
with their neighbours, but it is much higher than in their
dealings with strangers. Thus it is the ties of neighbourhood
alone that have been relaxed. The ties of family are in
many ways stronger than before; family affection leads to
much more self-sacrifice and devotion than it used to do.
And again sympathy with those who are strangers to us is a
growing source of a kind of deliberate unselfishness that never
existed before the modern age. That country which is the
birthplace of modern competition devotes a larger part of its
income than any other to charitable uses, and spent twenty

millions on purchasing the freedom of the slaves in the West Indies. In every age poets and social reformers have tried to stimulate the people of their own time to a nobler life by enchanting stories of the virtues of the heroes of old. But neither the records of history nor the contemporary observation of backward races, when carefully studied, give any support to the doctrine that man is on the whole harder and harsher than he was, or that he was ever more willing than he is now to sacrifice his own happiness for the benefit of others in cases where custom and law have left him free to choose his own course. Among races whose intellectual capacity seems not to have developed in any other direction, and who have none of the originating power of the modern business man, there will be found many who show an evil sagacity in driving a hard bargain in a market even with their neighbours. No traders are more unscrupulous in taking advantage of the necessities of the unfortunate than the corn-dealers and money-lenders of the East.

Again, the modern era has undoubtedly given new openings for dishonesty in trade. The advance of nor more dishonest. knowledge has discovered new ways of making things appear other than they are, and has rendered possible many new forms of adulteration. The producer is now far removed from the ultimate consumer; and his wrong-doings are not visited with the prompt and sharp punishment which falls on the head of a person who, being bound to live and die in his native village, plays a dishonest trick on one of his neighbours. The opportunities for knavery are certainly more numerous than they were; but there is no reason for thinking that people avail themselves of a larger proportion of such opportunities than they used to do. On the contrary, modern methods of trade imply habits of trustfulness on the one side and a power of resisting temptation to dishonesty on the other, which do not exist among a backward people. Instances of simple truth and personal fidelity are met with under all social conditions : but those who have tried to establish a business of modern type in a backward country find that they can scarcely ever depend on the native population for filling posts of trust. Adulteration and fraud in trade were rampant in the middle ages to an extent that is surprising when we consider the difficulties of wrong doing without detection at that time.

The term "competition" is then not well suited to describe the special characteristics of industrial life in the modern age. We need a term that does not imply any moral qualities, whether good or evil, but which indicates the undisputed fact that modern business is characterized by more self-reliant habits, more forethought, more deliberate and free choice. There is not any one term adequate for this purpose : but

Economic Freedom. FREEDOM OF INDUSTRY AND ENTERPRISE, or more shortly, ECONOMIC FREEDOM, points in the right direction, and may be used in the absence of a better.

Of course this deliberate and free choice may lead to a certain departure from individual freedom, when co-operation or combination seems to offer the best route to the desired end. The questions how far these deliberate forms of association are likely to destroy the freedom in which they had their origin, and how far they are likely to be conducive to the public weal, will occupy a large share of our attention towards the end of this treatise.

CHAPTER II.

THE GROWTH OF FREE INDUSTRY AND ENTERPRISE.

§ 1. THE growth of Economic Freedom has been slow and fitful. Early civilizations were necessarily Early civili-
in warm climates because no great advance in zations.
culture can be made except where there is a considerable surplus above the bare necessaries of life; and Influence of
in a cold climate man's whole energies are ab- climate.
sorbed in providing these necessaries, unless he is aided by accumulated wealth and knowledge. But a warm climate lowers energy and in consequence the great body of workers in the old civilizations of the East were of a submissive and unenterprising character; and were kept to their work by the discipline of the ruling castes. These ruling castes had generally come at no distant date from a more bracing climate, either in mountainous regions or in the distant North. They devoted themselves to war, to political and sacerdotal functions, and sometimes to art; but they avoided manual work, and left that to serfs and slaves. The manual labour classes scarcely even conceived the idea of freedom; but looked to custom as the great protector against arbitrary oppression. It is true that some customs were very cruel; Influence of
but if customs were merely cruel they speedily custom.
destroyed the lower classes and therefore also the upper classes who rested on them. And in consequence those races which have had a long history are also those whose customs have on the whole been kindly, and the good largely predominates over the evil in the records of the influence of custom on moral as well as physical well-being.

There is much to be learnt even now from the ideals of
the life of the free citizen which were thought
out by the best minds among the Greeks and
Romans. But those ideals started from the
assumption that the free man should avoid all hard and
depressing toil, and leave that for slaves. The great body of
the workers were in slavery, and there were no high ideals
of life for them. Thus even the best thought of Greece and
Rome left on one side the central problem of our age : it
never even inquired how far it might be possible for those
who bore the chief burden of the world's work to lead lives
worthy of man ; it certainly did not pioneer the path of
modern industry. Later on the Christian faith
in the brotherhood of all men did something to
lighten the lot of the poor. But it was often a form of
words rather than a living power to govern men's actions :
and the ruling classes kept the main body of the people in a
serfdom, which was not always happy.

Ancient Greece and Rome.

The Middle Ages.

Freedom had more scope in the great trading and industrial towns ; from them the leadership in
economic progress passed, about four hundred
years ago, to Holland and other countries ; and
nearly two hundred years ago the first place among the
leaders fell to England.

Transition to modern industry.

The English had always been vigorous, but they had not
always been industrious ; and it was long before they showed
much power of making new inventions, and of organizing
work so as to make it effective. But England offered an
asylum from religious persecution to the protestant artisans
of the Continent, who were also generally the ablest, the most
inventive, and most stedfast. Their instruction gave England
the right lines on which to work. She derived stimulus from
the trade across the Atlantic and Pacific Oceans, which
followed the discovery of America and of the route round
the Cape : for she was better situated than any other country

for this trade; and the work suited well the temper of her people. America and Asia alike offered markets for simple manufactures made in large quantities on the same pattern. Thus she began to grow in wealth; and she gradually applied her energies more and more to manufacturing on a large scale. One invention followed another in rapid succession. She used water power, and afterwards steam power to take off some of the most wearisome work from the hands of men and women, and to increase production; and in a way things went well with her[1].

But there was another side to the picture. Up to the eighteenth century the wages of labour had been much under the influence of custom; and what competition there was for employment was mostly confined to a small area; a town or a few villages in the same neighbourhood. But the new industry in the latter half of the eighteenth century began to attract artisans and labourers from all parts of England to the manufacturing districts.

At first there were few large factories. Capitalists

---

[1] The quarter of a century beginning with 1760 saw improvements follow one another in manufacture even more rapidly than in agriculture. During that period the transport of heavy goods was cheapened by Brindley's canals, the production of power by Watt's steam-engine, and that of iron by Cort's processes of puddling and rolling, and by Roebuck's method of smelting it by coal in lieu of the charcoal that had now become scarce; Hargreaves, Crompton, Arkwright, Cartwright and others invented, or at least made economically serviceable, the spinning jenny, the mule, the carding machine, and the power-loom; Wedgwood gave a great impetus to the pottery trade that was already growing rapidly; and there were important inventions in printing from cylinders, bleaching by chemical agents, and in other processes. A cotton factory was for the first time driven directly by steam-power in 1785, the last year of the period. The beginning of the nineteenth century saw steam-ships and steam printing-presses, and the use of gas for lighting towns. Railway locomotion, telegraphy and photography came a little later. Our own age has seen numberless improvements and new economies in production, prominent among which are those relating to the production of steel, the telephone, the electric light, and the gas-engine; and the social changes arising from material progress are in some respects more rapid now than ever. But the groundwork of the changes that have happened since 1785 was chiefly laid in the inventions of the years 1760 to 1785.

distributed their orders to a great number of small masters scattered over the country wherever there was water-power to be had; they themselves *undertaking* the risks of buying the raw material and selling the manufactured goods. It was only when steam-power began to displace water-power that the size of the factories increased rapidly. But, both in its earlier and its later forms, the new movement tended to release the bonds that had bound nearly everyone to live in the parish in which he was born; and it developed free markets. The working classes became more migratory, and more accustomed to try to sell their labour in the best market, wherever it could be found, while the employers also ranged far a-field in their search for workers.

§ 2. Thus the new organization of industry added vastly to production; but it was accompanied by some great evils. Which of these evils was unavoidable we cannot tell. For just when the change was moving most quickly, England was stricken by a combination of calamities almost unparalleled in history. They were the cause of a great part—it is impossible to say of how great a part—of the sufferings that are commonly ascribed to the sudden outbreak of unrestrained competition. The loss of her great colonies was quickly followed by the great French war, which cost her more than the total value of the accumulated wealth she had at its commencement. An unprecedented series of bad harvests made bread fearfully dear. And worse than all, a method of administration of the poor law was adopted which undermined the independence and vigour of the people.

The new organization accompanied by great evils.

The first part of this century therefore saw free enterprise establishing itself in England under unfavourable circumstances, its evils being intensified, and its benefits being lessened by external misfortunes.

The old trade customs and gild regulations were unsuitable to the new industry. In some places they were abandoned by common consent: in others they were successfully upheld for a time. But it was a fatal success; for the new industry, incapable of flourishing under the old bonds, left those places for others where it could be more free. Then the workers turned to Government for the enforcement of old laws of Parliament prescribing the way in which the trade should be carried on, and even for the revival of the regulation of prices and wages by justices of the peace.

Attempts to maintain old regulations.

These efforts could not but fail. The old regulations had been the expression of the social, moral and economic ideas of the time; they had been felt out rather than thought out; they were the almost instinctive result of the experience of generations of men who had lived and died under almost unchanged economic conditions. In the new age changes came so rapidly that there was no time for this. Each man had to do what was right in his own eyes, with but little guidance from the experience of past times; those who endeavoured to cling to old traditions were quickly supplanted.

The new race of manufacturers consisted chiefly of those who had made their own fortunes, strong, ready, enterprising men: who, looking at the success obtained by their own energies, were apt to assume that the poor and the weak were to be blamed rather than to be pitied for their misfortunes. Impressed with the folly of those who tried to bolster up economic arrangements which the stream of progress had undermined, they were apt to think that nothing more was wanted than to make competition perfectly free and let the strongest have their way. They glorified individualism, and were in no hurry to find a modern substitute for the social and industrial bonds which had kept men together in earlier times.

Meanwhile misfortune had reduced the total net income of the people of England. In 1820 a tenth of it was absorbed in paying the mere interest on the National Debt. The goods that were cheapened by the new inventions were chiefly manu-

Influence of war, heavy taxes and dearness of food. factured commodities of which the working man was but a small consumer: but the Corn-Laws prevented him from getting cheaply the bread on which he often spent three-fourths of his little wages. He had to sell his labour in a market in which the forces of supply and demand would have given him a poor pittance even if they had worked freely. But he had not the full advantage of economic freedom; he had no efficient union with his fellows; he had neither the knowledge of the market, nor the power of holding out for a reserve price, which the seller of commodities has, and he was urged on to work and to let his family work during long hours and under unhealthy conditions. This reacted on the efficiency of the working population, and therefore on the net value of their work, and therefore it kept down their wages. The employment of children during excessive hours began in the seventeenth century, and remained grievous till after the repeal of the corn laws.

But after the workmen had recognized the folly of attempting to revive the old rules regulating industry, there was no longer any wish to curtail the freedom of enterprise. The sufferings of the English people at their worst were never comparable to those which had been caused by the want of

The new system saved England from French armies. freedom in France before the Revolution; and it was argued that, had it not been for the strength which England derived from her new industries, she would probably have succumbed to a foreign military despotism, as the free cities had done before her. Small as her population was she at some times bore almost alone the burden of war against a conqueror in control of nearly all the resources of the Continent; and at other times subsidized larger, but poorer countries in the struggle against him. Rightly or wrongly, it was thought at the time that Europe might have fallen permanently under the dominion of France, as she had fallen in an earlier age under that of Rome, had not the free energy of English industries supplied the sinews of war against the common foe. Little was therefore heard in complaint against the excess of free enterprise, but much against that limitation of it which prevented Englishmen from obtaining food from abroad in return for the manufactures which they could now so easily produce.

And even trades-unions, which were then beginning that brilliant though chequered career which has been more full of interest and instruction than almost anything else in English history, passed into the phase of seeking little from authority except to be left alone. They had learnt by bitter experience the folly of attempting to enforce the old rules by which Government had directed the course of industry; and they had as yet got no far-reaching views as to the regulation of trade by their own action: their chief anxiety was to increase their own economic freedom by the removal of the laws against combinations of workmen.

§ 3. It has been left for our own generation to perceive all the evils which arose from this sudden increase of economic freedom. Now first are we getting to understand the extent to which the capitalist employer, untrained to his new duties, was tempted to subordinate the wellbeing of his workpeople to his own desire for gain; now first are we learning the importance of insisting that the rich have duties as well as rights in their individual and in their collective capacity; now first is the economic problem of the new age showing itself to us as it really is. This is partly due to a wider knowledge and a growing earnestness. But however wise and virtuous our grandfathers had been, they could not have seen things as we do; for they were hurried along by urgent necessities and terrible disasters.

Dangers of a sudden increase of freedom.

But we must judge ourselves by a severer standard. For we are not now struggling for national existence; and our resources have not been exhausted by great wars: on the contrary our powers of production have been immensely increased;

The nation is richer, and need not sacrifice everything to production.
and, what is at least as important, the repeal of the Corn Laws and the growth of steam communication have enabled a largely increased population to obtain sufficient supplies of food on easy terms. The average money income of the people has more than doubled; while the price of almost all important commodities except animal food and house-room has fallen by one-half or even further. It is true that even now, if wealth were distributed equally, the total production of the country would only suffice to provide necessaries and the more urgent comforts for the people[1], and that as things are, many have barely the necessaries of life. But the nation has grown in wealth, in health, in education and in morality; and we are no longer compelled to subordinate almost every other consideration to the need of increasing the total produce of industry.

In particular during the present generation this increased prosperity has made us rich and strong enough to impose new restraints on free enterprise; some temporary material loss being submitted to for the sake of a higher and greater ultimate gain. But these new restraints are different from the old. They are imposed not as a means of class domination; but with the purpose of defending the weak, and especially children and the mothers of children, in matters in which they are not able to use the forces of competition in their own defence. The aim is to devise, deliberately and promptly, remedies adapted to the quickly changing circumstances of modern industry; and thus to obtain the good,

[1] The average income per head in the United Kingdom which was about £15 in 1820 is about £37 now; i.e. it has risen from about £75 to £185 per family of five; and its purchasing-power in terms of commodities is nearly as great as that of £400 in 1820. There are not a few artisans' families, the total earnings of which exceed £185, so that they would lose by an equal distribution of wealth: but even they have not more than is required to support a healthy and many-sided life.

without the evil, of the old defence of the weak that in other ages was gradually evolved by custom. And by the aid of the telegraph and the printing-press, of representa- tive government and trade associations, it is possible for the people to think out for them- selves the solution of their own problems. The growth of knowledge and self-reliance has given them that true self-controlling freedom, which enables them to impose of their own free will restraints on their own actions; and the problems of collective production, collective ownership and collective consumption are entering on a new phase.

The influence of the telegraph and printing-press.

Projects for great and sudden changes are now, as ever, foredoomed to fail, and to cause reaction. We are still unable to move safely, if we move so fast that our new plans of life altogether outrun our instincts. It is true that human nature can be modified; new ideals, new opportunities and new methods of action may, as history shows, alter it very much even in a few generations. This change in human nature has perhaps never covered so wide an area and moved so fast as in the present generation. But still it is a growth, and therefore gradual; and changes of our social organization must wait on it, and therefore they must be gradual too.

But though they wait on it, they may always keep a little in advance of it, promoting the growth of our higher social nature by giving it always some new and higher work to do, some practical ideal towards which to strive. Thus gradually we may attain to an order of social life, in which the common good overrules individual caprice, even more than it did in the early ages before the sway of individualism had begun. But unselfishness then will be the offspring of deliberate will, though aided by instinct individual freedom then will develop itself in collective freedom;—a happy contrast to the old

Movement towards higher forms of collectivism.

M. 2

order of life, in which individual slavery to custom caused collective slavery and stagnation, broken only by the caprice of despotism or the caprice of revolution.

We have been looking at this movement from the English point of view. But other nations are taking their share in it. America faces new practical difficulties with such intrepidity and directness that she is already contesting with England the leadership in economic affairs; she supplies many of the most instructive instances of the latest economic tendencies of the age, such as the growing democracy of trade and industry, and the development of speculation and trade combination in every form, and she will probably before long take the chief part in pioneering the way for the rest of the world. Nor is Australia showing less signs of vigour than her elder sister; she has indeed some advantage over the United States in the greater homogeneity of her people.

On the Continent the power of obtaining important results by free association is less than in English speaking countries; and in consequence there is less resource and less thoroughness in dealing with industrial problems. But their treatment is not quite the same in any two nations: and there is something characteristic and instructive in the methods adopted by each of them; particularly in relation to the sphere of governmental action. In this matter Germany is taking the lead. It has been a great gain to her that her manufacturing industries developed later than those of England; and she has been able to profit by England's experience and to avoid many of her mistakes.

CHAPTER III.

THE SCOPE OF ECONOMICS.

§ 1.   Economics is a study of men as they live and move and think in the ordinary business of life.   It is The chief motives of business life have a money measure. a study of real men, not of fictitious men, or "economic men."   But it concerns itself chiefly with those motives which affect, most powerfully and most steadily, man's conduct in the business part of his life.   Everyone who is worth anything carries his higher nature with him into business ; and, there as elsewhere, he is influenced by his personal affections, by his conceptions of duty and his reverence for high ideals.   But, for all that, the steadiest motive to business work is the desire for the pay which is the material reward of work.   The pay may be on its way to be spent selfishly or unselfishly, for noble or base ends ; and here the variety of human nature comes into play.   But the motive is supplied by a definite amount of £. s. d. : and it is this definite and exact money measurement of the steadiest motives in business life, which has enabled economics far to outrun every other branch of the study of man.   Just as the chemist's fine balance has made chemistry more exact than most other physical sciences ; so this economist's balance, rough and imperfect as it is, has made economics more exact than any other branch of social science. But of course economics cannot be compared with the exact physical sciences : for it deals with the ever changing and subtle forces of human nature.

In fact the economist only does in a more patient and thoughtful way, and with greater precautions, what everybody is always doing every day in ordinary life. He does not attempt to weigh the real value of the higher affections of our nature against those of our lower : he does not balance the love for virtue against the desire for agreeable food.

Economics follows the practice of ordinary discourse. He estimates the incentives to action by their effects just in the same way as people do in common life. He follows the course of ordinary conversation, differing from it only in taking more precautions to make clear the limits of his knowledge as he goes. These precautions are laborious, and make some people think that economic reasonings are artificial. But the opposite is the fact. For he does but bring into prominence those assumptions and reservations, which everyone makes unconsciously every day.

For instance, if we find a man in doubt whether to spend a few pence on a cigar, or a cup of tea, or on riding home instead of walking home, then we may follow ordinary usage, and say that he expects from them equal gratifications. Again if we find that the desires to secure either of two gratifications will induce men in similar circumstances each to do just an hour's extra work, or will induce men in the same rank of life and with the same means each to pay a shilling for it, we then may say that those gratifications are equal.

Next suppose that the person, whom we saw doubting between several little gratifications for himself, had thought after a while of a poor invalid whom he would pass on his way home, and had spent some time in making up his mind whether he would choose a physical gratification for himself, or would do a kindly act and rejoice in another's joy. As his desires turned now towards the one, now the other, there would be change in the quality of his mental states. But the economist treats them in the first instance merely as motives to action, which are shown to be evenly balanced, since they are measured by the same sum of money. A study of these money values is only the starting-point of economics : but it is the starting-point.

§ 2. Again the desire to earn a shilling is a much stronger motive to a poor man with whom money is scarce than to a rich one. A rich man, in doubt whether to spend a shilling on a single cigar, is weighing against one another smaller pleasures than a poor man, who is doubting whether to spend a shilling on a supply of tobacco that will last him for a month. The clerk with £100 a year will walk to business in a heavier rain than the clerk with £300 a year ; for if the poorer man spends the money, he will suffer more from the want of it afterwards than the richer would. The gratification that is measured in the poorer man's mind by sixpence is greater than that measured by it in the richer man's mind.

These difficulties can however be avoided. For if we take averages sufficiently broad to cause the personal peculiarities of individuals to counterbalance one another, the money which people of equal incomes will give to obtain a benefit or avoid an injury is a sufficiently accurate measure of the benefit or the injury. *Allowance for the different utilities of money to rich and poor.* If there are a thousand families living in Sheffield and another thousand in Leeds, each with about £100 a-year, and a tax of £1 is levied on all of them, we may be sure that the injury which the tax will cause in Sheffield is very nearly equal to that which it will cause in Leeds: and similarly anything that increased all the incomes by a £1 would give command over very nearly the same amount of additional happiness in the two towns.

Thus "money" or "general purchasing power" or "command over material wealth," is the centre around which economic science clusters ; this is so, not because money or material wealth is regarded as the main aim of human effort, nor even as affording the main subject-matter for the study of the economist, *Economic motives are not exclusively selfish.*

but because in this world of ours it is the one convenient means of measuring human motive on a large scale; and if the older economists had made this clear, they would have escaped many grievous misrepresentations. The splendid teachings of Carlyle and Ruskin as to the right aims of human endeavour and the right uses of wealth, would not then have been marred by bitter attacks on economics, based on the mistaken belief that that science had no concern with any motive except the selfish desire for wealth, or even that it inculcated a policy of sordid selfishness.

CHAPTER IV.

ECONOMIC LAWS.

§ 1. THIS brings us to consider *Economic Laws.* Every cause has a tendency to produce some definite result if nothing occurs to hinder it. Thus gravitation tends to make things fall to the ground : but when a balloon is full of gas lighter than air, the pressure of the air will make it rise in spite of the tendency of gravitation to make it fall. The law of gravitation states how any two things attract one another ; how they tend to move towards one another, and will move towards one another if nothing interferes to prevent them. The law of gravitation is therefore a statement of tendencies.

Nearly all laws of science are statements of tendencies.

It is a very exact statement—so exact that mathematicians can calculate a Nautical Almanac that will show the moments at which each satellite of Jupiter will hide itself behind Jupiter. They make this calculation for many years beforehand ; and navigators take it to sea, and use it in finding out where they are. Now there are no economic tendencies which act as steadily and can be measured as exactly as gravitation can : and consequently there are no laws of economics which can be compared for precision with the law of gravitation.

The exact laws of simple sciences.

§ 2. Let us then look at a science less exact than astronomy. The science of the tides explains how the tide rises and falls twice a day under the action of the sun and the moon : how there are strong tides at new and full moon, and weak tides at the

The inexact laws of complex sciences.

moon's first and third quarter; and how the tide running up
into a closed channel, like that of the Severn, will be very
high; and so on. Thus, having studied the lie of the land
and the water all round the British isles, people can calculate
beforehand when the tide will *probably* be at its highest on
any day at London Bridge, or at Gloucester; and how high it
will be there. They have to use the word *probably*; which
the astronomers do not need to use when talking about the
eclipses of Jupiter's satellites. Why is that? The reason is
that though many forces act upon Jupiter and his satellites,
each one of them acts in a definite manner which can be
predicted beforehand. But no-one knows enough about the
weather to be able to say beforehand how it will act: and
a heavy downpour of rain in the Thames valley or a strong
north-east wind in the German Ocean may make the tides
at London Bridge differ a good deal from what had been
expected.

§ 3. The laws of economics are to be compared with the
laws of the tides rather than with the simple
and exact law of gravitation. For the actions of
men are so various and uncertain, that the best
statement of tendencies that we can make in a
science of human conduct, must needs be inexact and faulty.
This might be urged as a reason against making any statements at all on the subject; but to do that would be almost
to abandon life. Life is human conduct and the thoughts
that grow up around it. By the fundamental impulses of our
nature we all—high and low, learned and unlearned—are in
our several degrees constantly striving to understand the
courses of human action, and to shape them for our purposes
—whether selfish or unselfish, whether noble or ignoble. And
since we *must* form to ourselves some notions of the tendencies
of human action, our choice is between forming those notions
carelessly and forming them carefully. The harder the task,
the greater the need for steady patient inquiry; for turning to

The science of man is complex and its laws are inexact.

account the experience that has been reaped by the more advanced physical sciences; and for framing as best we can well thought-out estimates, or provisional laws, of the tendencies of human action.

§ 4. Our plan of work is then this :—We study the actions of individuals, but study them in relation to social life. We take as little notice as possible of individual peculiarities of temper and character. We watch the conduct of a whole class of people—sometimes the whole of a nation, sometimes only those living in a certain district, more

The individual regarded as a member of an industrial group.

often those engaged in some particular trade at some time and place : and by the aid of statistics, or in other ways, we ascertain how much money on the average the members of the particular group we are watching, are just willing to pay as the price of a certain thing which they desire, or how much must be offered to them to induce them to undergo a certain effort or abstinence that they dislike. The measurement of motive thus obtained is not indeed perfectly accurate; for if it were, economics would rank with the most advanced of the physical sciences; and not, as it actually does, with the least advanced.

But yet the measurement is accurate enough to enable experienced persons to forecast fairly well the extent of the results that will follow from changes in which motives of this kind are chiefly concerned. Thus, for instance, they can estimate very closely the payment that will be required to produce an adequate supply of labour of any grade, from the lowest to the highest, for a new trade which it is proposed to start in any place. And, when they visit a factory of a kind that they have never seen before, they can tell within a shilling or two a week what any particular worker is earning, by merely observing how far his is a skilled occupation and what strain it involves on his physical, mental and moral faculties.

And, starting from simple considerations of this kind, they can go on to analyse the causes which govern the local distribution of different kinds of industry, the terms on which people living in distant places exchange their goods with one another, and so on. They can explain and predict the ways in which fluctuations of credit will affect foreign trade, or again the extent to which the burden of a tax will be shifted from those on whom it is levied on to those for whose wants they cater, and so on.

In all this economists deal with man as he is : not with an abstract or "economic" man; but a man of flesh and blood;

Economists deal mainly with one side of life but not the life of a fictitious being.

one who shapes his business life to a great extent with reference to egoistic motives; but also one who is not above the frailties of vanity or recklessness, and not below the delight of doing his work well for its own sake; who is not below the delight of sacrificing himself for the good of his family, his neighbours, or his country, nor below the love of a virtuous life for its own sake.

§ 5. Thus then a law of social science, or a *Social Law*, is a statement of social tendencies; that is, a

Definition of 'law,' 'social,'

statement that a certain course of action may be expected under certain conditions from the members of a social group.

Economic laws, or statements of economic tendencies, are

and 'economic.'

social laws relating to branches of conduct in which the strength of the motives chiefly concerned can be measured by a money price.

Corresponding to the substantive "law" is the adjective "legal." But this term is used in connection with "law" in the sense of an ordinance of government; not in connection with scientific laws of relation between cause and effect. The adjective used for this purpose is derived from "norma," a term which is nearly equivalent to "law"; and we say that the course of action which may be expected under certain conditions from the members of an industrial group is the *normal* action of the members of that Normal action. group relatively to those conditions.

Normal action is not always morally right; very often it is action which we should use our utmost efforts to stop. For instance, the normal condition of many of the very poorest inhabitants of a large town is to be devoid of enterprise, and unwilling to avail themselves of the opportunities that may offer for a healthier and less squalid life elsewhere; they have not the strength, physical, mental and moral, required for working their way out of their miserable surroundings. The existence of a considerable supply of labour ready to make match-boxes at a very low rate is normal in the same way that a contortion of the limbs is a normal result of taking strychnine. It is one result, a deplorable result, of the action of those laws which we have to study.

The earlier English economists paid almost exclusive attention to the motives of individual action. But it must not be forgotten that economists, Motives to collective action. like all other students of social science, are concerned with individuals chiefly as members of the social organism. As a cathedral is something more than the stones of which it is built, as a person is something more than a series of thoughts and feelings, so the life of society is something more than the sum of the lives of its individual members. It is true that the action of the whole is made up of that of its constituent parts; and that in most economic problems the best starting-point is to be found in the motives that affect the individual, regarded not indeed as an isolated atom, but as a member of some particular trade or industrial group; but it is also true, as German writers have well urged, that economics has a great and an increasing concern in motives connected with the collective ownership of property and the collective pursuit of important aims. Many new kinds of voluntary association are growing up under the influence of other motives besides that of pecuniary gain ; and the Co-operative movement in particular is opening to the economist new opportunities of measuring motives whose action it had seemed impossible to reduce to any sort of law[1].

[1] For a continuation of this subject see Appendix A on *Methods of Study*.

·

CHAPTER V.

SURVEY OF THE WORK TO BE DONE.

§ 1. THE laws, or statements of tendency, with which we shall be chiefly concerned in this volume, are those relating to man's Wants and their satisfac- tion, to the Demand for wealth and its Consump- tion (Book III) ; to its Production, especially under the modern organization of industry (Book IV) ; to some of those general relations between the demand for a thing, and the difficulty of providing a supply of it which govern Value (Book V) ; and (Book VI) to Exchange in relation to the Distribution of the income of the nation between those who work with their heads or hands, those who store up capital to provide machinery and other things that will make labour more efficient, and landowners ; or which is nearly the same thing the broad features of the problem of wages, profits and rent.

Tendencies studied in Books III—VI.

The present volume deals mainly with the Economics of Industry. A later volume will deal with the Economics of Trade and Finance. It will discuss systems of money, credit and banking ; the organization of markets, the relation between wholesale and retail prices ; foreign trade ; taxes and other ways and means of collective action ; and lastly public responsibilities and the general functions of collective action in economic affairs, whether through the Government, through the form of opinion, or through voluntary co-operation.

§ 2. Economics is thus taken to mean a study of the economic aspects and conditions of man's political, social and private life; but more especially of his social life. The aims

Aims of the
economist. of the study are to gain knowledge for its own sake, and to obtain guidance in the practical conduct of life, and especially of social life; the need for such guidance was never so urgent as now.

It would indeed be a mistake to be always thinking

His first duty
is to discover
truth. of the practical purposes of our work, and planning it out with direct reference to them. For by so doing we are tempted to break off each line of thought as soon as it ceases to have immediate bearing on that particular aim which we have in view at the time: the direct pursuit of practical aims leads us to group together bits of all sorts of knowledge, which have no connection with one another except for the immediate purposes of the moment, and throw but little light on one another. Our mental energy is spent in going from one to another; nothing is thoroughly thought out; no real progress is made. The grouping, therefore, which is best for the purposes of science is that which collects together all those facts and reasonings which are similar to one another in nature: so that the study of each may throw light on its neighbour.

And yet it may be well to have before us at starting

But the direc-
tions of his
search are
indicated by
urgent social
problems. some tolerably clear notion of the practical problems which supply the chief motive to the study of the modern economist. Many of them do not lie quite within the range of his science, and none of them can be fully answered by mere science: the ultimate resolve must always lie with conscience and common sense. But the following are some of the chief issues which are of special urgency in England in our own generation, and to which economics can contribute some important material of carefully arranged facts and well considered arguments:—

How should we act so as to increase the good and diminish

the evil influences of economic freedom, both in its ultimate results and in the course of its progress? If the first are good and the latter evil, but those who suffer the evil do not reap the good, how far is it right that they should suffer for the benefit of others?

Taking it for granted that a more equal distribution of wealth is to be desired, how far would this justify changes in the institutions of property, or limitations of free enterprise even when they would be likely to diminish the aggregate of wealth? In other words, how far should an increase in the income of the poorer classes and a diminution of their work be aimed at, even if it involved some lessening of national material wealth? How far could this be done without injustice, and without slackening the energies of the leaders of progress? How ought the burdens of taxation to be distributed among the different classes of society?

Ought we to rest content with the existing forms of division of labour? Is it necessary that large numbers of the people should be exclusively occupied with work that has no elevating character? Is it possible to educate gradually among the great mass of workers a new capacity for the higher kinds of work; and in particular for undertaking co-operatively the management of the businesses in which they are themselves employed?

What are the proper relations of individual and collective action in a stage of civilization such as ours? How far ought voluntary association in its various forms, old and new, to be left to supply collective action for those purposes for which such action has special advantages? What business affairs should be undertaken by society itself acting through its Government, imperial or local? Have we, for instance, carried as far as we should the plan of collective ownership and use of open spaces, of works of art, of the means of instruction and amusement, as well as of those material requisites of a civilized life, the supply of which requires united action, such as gas and water, and railways?

When Government does not itself directly intervene, how far should it allow individuals and corporations to conduct their own affairs as they please? How far should it regulate the management of railways and other concerns which are to some extent in a position of monopoly, and again of land and other things the quantity of which cannot be increased by man? Is it necessary to retain in their full force all the existing rights of property; or have the original necessities for which they were meant to provide, in some measure passed away?

Are the prevailing methods of using wealth entirely justifiable? What scope is there for the moral pressure of social opinion in constraining and directing individual action in those economic relations in which the rigidity and violence of Government interference would be likely to do more harm than good?

In what respect do the duties of one nation to another in economic matters differ from those of members of the same nation to one another?

BOOK II.

SOME FUNDAMENTAL NOTIONS.

CHAPTER I.

INTRODUCTORY.

§ 1. SINCE Economics is the study of man's actions in the ordinary affairs of life, it needs to borrow more than other sciences do from common experience. Its reasonings must therefore be expressed in language that is intelligible to the general public; it must endeavour to conform itself to the familiar terms of everyday life, and, so far as possible, to use them as they are commonly used.

Difficulties of definition in economics.

But unfortunately almost every word in common use has several shades of meaning, and therefore needs to be interpreted by the context. Economists must take, as the standard use of their words, that which seems most in harmony with every day usage in the market place; and they must add a little special interpretation wherever it is necessary. For by this means only can they say exactly what they want to say without perplexing the general reader.

CHAPTER II.

WEALTH.

§ 1. Our difficulties begin at once. "Wealth" is really the same word as well-being: but in its common use it means only material possessions of different kinds. Further "a wealthy man" is a person who has a great deal of wealth: and so economists have sometimes been blamed for speaking of the "wealth" of the labourer. It is argued that as he is not wealthy, he cannot properly be said to possess wealth. But this objection must be set aside: and we must persist in saying that the cottager's furniture, and other household goods constitute his little stock of wealth.

This word "goods" is a useful one. A man's goods are commonly understood to be his material posses-
Goods. sions. But the word is often used more broadly; as when we say it is a great good to a man to be able to find recreation in reading or music after his day's work is done. This use of the word has been adopted by economists of other countries: it is practically very convenient; and it is sufficiently in accordance with popular usage in this country for us to adhere to it.

Thus then *Goods* are all desirable things, all things that satisfy human wants.

All wealth consists of things that satisfy wants, directly or indirectly. All wealth therefore consists of desirable things or "goods"; but not all goods are reckoned as wealth. The affection of friends, for instance, is a very important element of well-being, but it is not ever reckoned as wealth, except by a poetic licence. Let us begin by classifying goods, and then consider which of them should be accounted as elements of wealth.

Desirable things are Material, or Personal and Non-material. *Material* goods consist of useful material things, and of all rights to hold, or use, or derive benefits from material things, or to receive them at a future time.

Classification of goods.

Thus they include the physical gifts of nature, land and water, air and climate; the products of agriculture, mining, fishing, and manufacture; buildings, machinery, and imple-ments; mortgages and other bonds; shares in public and private companies, all kinds of monopolies, patent-rights, copyrights; also rights of way and other rights of usage. Lastly, opportunities of travel, access to good scenery, museums, &c., ought, strictly speaking, to be reckoned under this head.

A man's *non-material* goods fall into two classes. One consists of his own qualities and faculties for action and for enjoyment; such for instance as that faculty of deriving recreation from reading or music, to which we have just referred. All these lie within himself and are called *in-ternal*. The second class are called *external* because they consist of relations beneficial to him with other people. Such, for instance, were the labour dues and personal services of various kinds which the ruling classes used to require from their serfs and other dependents. But these have passed away; and the chief instances of such relations beneficial to their owner now-a-days are to be found in the good will and business connection of traders and professional men.

Again, goods may be *transferable* or *non-transferable*. Every thing that can be bought or sold is of course transferable. But a person's "internal" faculties for action and enjoyment are non-transferable. A successful tradesman or medical prac-titioner may sell the goodwill of his business. But at first, at all events, the business will not be as good to the new comer as it was to him; because part of his business connection depended on personal trust in him; and that was non-transferable.

Those goods are *free*, which are not appropriated and are afforded by Nature without requiring the effort of man. The land in its original state was a free gift of nature. But in settled countries it is not a free good from the point of view of the individual. Wood is still free in some Brazilian forests: the fish of the sea are free generally: but some sea fisheries are jealously guarded for the exclusive use of members of a certain nation, and may be classed as national property. Oyster beds that have been planted by man are not free in any sense. Those that have grown naturally are free in every sense if they are not appropriated: if they are private property, they are still free gifts from the point of view of the nation; but, since the nation has allowed its rights in them to become vested in individuals, they are not free from the point of view of the individual; and the same is true of private rights of fishing in rivers. The wheat grown on free land and the fish caught in free fisheries are not free: for they have been acquired by labour.

§ 2. When a man's *wealth* is spoken of simply, and without any interpretation clause in the context, it is

Wealth.

to be taken to consist of two classes of goods.

In the first class are those material goods to which he has (by law or custom) private rights of property. These include not only such things as land and houses, furniture and machinery, and other material things which may be in his single private ownership; but also any shares in public companies, bonds, mortgages and other obligations which he may hold requiring others to pay money to him. On the other hand, the debts which he owes to others may be regarded as negative wealth; and they must be subtracted from his total possessions before his true Net wealth can be found. It is perhaps hardly necessary to say that services and other goods, which pass out of existence in the same instant that they come into it, do not contribute to the stock of wealth, and may therefore be left out of our account.

In the second class are those of his non-material goods which are external to him, and serve directly as the means of enabling him to acquire material goods. Thus it excludes all his own personal qualities and faculties, even those which enable him to earn a living. But it includes his business or professional practice, and especially that "goodwill," which can be transferred by sale to a new comer.

It is true that, pursuing the lines indicated by Adam Smith and followed by most continental economists, we might define *Personal Wealth* so as to include **Personal wealth.** all those energies, faculties, and habits which directly contribute to making people industrially efficient. But confusion would be caused by using the term "wealth" simply when we desire to include a person's industrial qualities. For this purpose it will be best to use the more explicit phrase "material and personal wealth." "Wealth" simply should *always* mean external wealth only.

§ 3. We have still to take account of those of a man's goods which are common to him with his neighbours; and which therefore it would be a needless trouble to mention when comparing his wealth with theirs. But these goods may be important for some purposes, and especially for comparisons between the economic conditions of distant places or distant times.

They consist of the benefits which he derives from being a member of a certain State or community. They include civil and military security, and the right and opportunity to make use of public property and institutions of all kinds, such as roads and gaslight; and they include rights to justice or to a free education, &c. The townsman and the countryman have each of them for nothing many advantages which the other either cannot get at all, or can get only at great expense. Other things being equal, one person has more real wealth in its broadest sense than another, if the place in which the former lives has a better climate, better roads, better water, more wholesome drainage, and cheaper and better newspapers, and places of amusement and instruction. House-room, food and clothing, which would be insufficient in a cold climate, may be abundant in a warm climate: on the other hand, that warmth which lessens men's physical needs, and makes them rich with but a slight provision of material wealth, makes them poor in the energy that procures wealth.

Many of these things are *collective goods*; *i.e.* goods which are not in private ownership. And this brings us to consider wealth from the Social, as opposed to the Individual point of view.

Collective goods.

The most obvious forms of such wealth are public material property of all kinds, such as roads and canals, buildings and parks, gasworks and waterworks; though unfortunately many of them have been secured not by public savings, but by pnblic borrowings, and there is the heavy "negative" wealth of a large debt to be set against them.

The Thames has added more to the wealth of England than all its canals, and perhaps even than all its railroads. And, though the Thames is a free gift of nature, except in so far as its navigation has been improved, while the canal is the work of man, we ought for many purposes to reckon the Thames a part of England's wealth. Again, German economists delight to insist that the organization of a free and well-ordered State is an element of national wealth.

National wealth includes the individual as well as the collective property of its members. And in estimating the aggregate sum of their individual wealth, we may save some trouble by omitting all debts and other obligations due to one member of a nation from another. For instance, so far as the English national debt and the bonds of an English railway are owned within the nation, we can adopt the simple plan of counting the railway itself as part of the national wealth, and neglecting Government and railway bonds altogether. But we still have to deduct for those bonds, &c., issued by the English Government or by private Englishmen, and held by foreigners; and to add for those foreign bonds, &c., held by Englishmen.

§ 4. The notion of *Value* is intimately connected with that of Wealth; and a little may be said about it here. "The word *value*" says Adam Smith "has two different meanings, and sometimes expresses the utility of some particular object and sometimes the power of purchasing other goods which the possession of that object conveys." But experience has shown that it is not well to use the word in the former sense.

Value.

The value, that is the exchange value, of one thing in terms of another at any place and time, is the amount of that second thing which can be got there and then in exchange for the first. Thus the term value is relative, and expresses the relation between two things at a particular place and time.

Civilized countries generally adopt gold or silver or both as money. Instead of expressing the values of lead and tin, and wood, and corn and other things in terms of one another, we express them in terms of money in the first instance; and call the value of each thing thus expressed its *price*. If we know that a ton of lead will exchange for fifteen sovereigns at any place and time, while a ton of tin will exchange for ninety sovereigns, we say that their prices then and there are £15 and £90 respectively, and we know that the value of a ton of tin in terms of lead is six tons then and there.

The price of every thing rises and falls from time to time and place to place; and with every such change the purchasing power of money changes so far as that thing goes. If the purchasing power of money rises with regard to some things, and at the same time falls equally with regard to equally important things, its general purchasing power (or its power of purchasing things in general) has remained stationary. This phrase conceals some difficulties, which we must study later on. But meanwhile we may take it in its popular sense, which is sufficiently clear; and we may throughout this volume neglect possible changes in the general purchasing power of money. Thus the price of anything will be taken as representative of its exchange value relatively to things in general, or in other words as representative of its general purchasing power.

CHAPTER III.

PRODUCTION. CONSUMPTION. LABOUR. NECESSARIES.

§ 1. MAN cannot create material things. In the mental and moral world indeed he may produce new *Man can pro-* ideas; but when he is said to produce material *duce only* things, he really only produces useful results or *utilities* "utilities"; or, in other words, his efforts and sacrifices result in changing the form or arrangement of matter to adapt it better for the satisfaction of wants. All that he can do in the physical world is either to re-adjust matter so as to make it more useful, as when he makes a log of wood into a table; or to put it in the way of being made more useful by nature, as when he puts seed where the forces of nature will make it burst out into life.

It is sometimes said that traders do not produce: that while the cabinet-maker produces furniture, the furniture-dealer merely sells what is already produced. But there is no scientific foundation for this distinction. They both produce utilities, and neither of them can do more: the furniture-dealer moves and re-arranges matter so as to make it more serviceable than it was before, and the carpenter does nothing more. The sailor or the railway-man who carries coal above ground produces a further utility, just as much as the miner who carries it underground; the dealer in fish helps to move on fish from where it is of comparatively little use to where it is of greater use, and the fisherman does no more. It is true that there are often more traders than are necessary to do the work; and whenever that is the case, there is waste. But there is also waste if there are two men to a plough which can be well worked by one man: in both cases all those who are at work are productive; though they may produce but little.

Consumption may be regarded as negative production.

**and can con-
sume only
utilities.** Just as man can produce only "utilities," so he can consume nothing more. He can produce services and other immaterial products, and he can consume them. But as his production of material products is really nothing more than a rearrangement of matter which gives it new utilities; so his consumption of them is nothing more than a disarrangement of matter, which lessens or destroys its utilities. Often indeed when he is said to consume things, he does nothing more than to hold them for his use, while, as Senior says, they "are destroyed by those numerous gradual agents which we call collectively *time*." As the "producer" of wheat is he who puts seed where Nature will make it grow, so the "consumer" of pictures, of curtains and even of a house or a yacht does little to wear them out himself; but he holds them and uses them while time wastes them.

§ 2.   All labour is directed towards producing some effect.

**Nearly all
labour is in
some sense
productive.** For though some exertions are taken merely for their own sake, as when a game is played for amusement, they are not counted as labour. Jevons well defined *labour* as any exertion of mind or body undergone partly or wholly with a view to some good other than the pleasure derived directly from the work. If we had to make a fresh start it would be best to regard all labour as productive except that which failed to promote the aim towards which it was directed, and so produced no utility. And, on the whole, "Productive" when used by itself as a technical term leads to more trouble than it is worth. "Productive of" really means "that which produces"; and the only safe course is to finish the phrase, and say straight out what it is that is produced. For instance we may speak of labour as *productive of material wealth, of necessaries*, &c.

§ 3.   This brings us to consider the term Necessaries.

It is common to divide wealth into Necessaries, Comforts and Luxuries; the first class including all things required to meet wants which *must* be satisfied, while the latter consist of things that meet wants of a less urgent character. But here again there is a troublesome ambiguity. When we say that a want *must* be satisfied, what are the consequences which we have in view if it is not satisfied? Do they include death? Or do they extend only to the loss of strength and vigour? In other words, are Necessaries the things which are necessary for life, or those which are necessary for efficiency?

The older use of the term Necessaries was limited to those things which were sufficient to enable the labourers, taken one with another, to support themselves and their families. But we now recognise that a distinction must be made between the necessaries for efficiency and the necessaries for existence; and that there is for each rank of industry, at any time and place, a more or less clearly defined income which is necessary for merely sustaining its members; while there is another and larger income which is necessary for keeping it in full efficiency.

Necessaries for existence, and for efficiency.

Thus in the South of England population has increased during the present century at a fair rate, allowance being made for migration. But the efficiency of labour, which in earlier times was as high as that in the North of England, has sunk relatively to the North; so that the low-waged labour of the South is often dearer than the more highly paid labour of the North. This indicates that the labourers in the South have had the bare necessaries for existence and the increase of numbers, but they have not had the necessaries for efficiency.

It may be true that the wages of any industrial class might have sufficed to maintain a higher efficiency, if they had been spent with perfect wisdom. But every estimate of necessaries must be relative to a given place and time; and unless there be a special interpretation clause to the contrary, it may be assumed that the wages will be spent with just that amount of wisdom, forethought, and unselfishness, which prevails in fact among the industrial class under discussion. With this understanding we may say that the income of any class in the ranks of industry is below its *necessary* level, when any increase in their income would in the course of time produce a more than proportionate increase in their efficiency. Consumption may be economized by a change of habits; but any stinting of necessaries is wasteful.

The necessaries for the efficiency of an ordinary agricultural or of an unskilled town labourer and his family, in England in this generation, may be said to consist of a well-drained dwelling with several rooms, warm clothing, with some changes of under-clothing, pure water, a plentiful supply of cereal food, with a moderate allowance of meat and milk, and a little tea, &c., some education and some recreation; and lastly, sufficient freedom for his wife from other work to enable her to perform properly her maternal and her household duties. If in any district unskilled labour is deprived of any of these things, its efficiency will suffer in the same way as that of a horse that is not properly tended, or a steam-engine that has an inadequate supply of coals. All consumption up to this limit is strictly productive consumption: any stinting of this consumption is not economical, but wasteful.

In addition, perhaps, some consumption of alcohol and tobacco, and some indulgence in fashionable dress are in many places so habitual, that they may be said to be *conventionally necessary*, since in order to obtain them, the average man and woman will sacrifice some things which are necessary for efficiency. Their wages are therefore less than are practically necessary for efficiency, unless they provide not only for what is strictly necessary consumption, but include also a certain amount of conventional necessaries.

Conventional necessaries.

CHAPTER IV.

CAPITAL. INCOME.

§ 1. It is customary to divide the stock of goods which constitutes wealth into that which is and that which is not capital. But the purposes for which the division is wanted are many and various; and in consequence the term Capital has many uses both in the language of the market-place and in the writings of economists. In fact there is no other part of economics in which the temptation is so strong to invent a completely new set of terms. But this would throw the science out of touch with real life. We must therefore take the ordinary usages of the term as the foundation of our account; and add such explanations, as are required to give to our use of the term some measure of clearness and precision.

Adam Smith said that a person's capital is *that part of his stock from which he expects to derive an income;* and in fact each use of the term capital has corresponded more or less closely to one of the uses of the term Income; and there is an advantage in studying the two terms Capital and Income together.

Capital yields income.

In a primitive community no distinction is made between capital and other forms of wealth: each family is nearly self-sufficing, and provides most of its own food and clothing and even household furniture. Only a very small part of the income, or comings in, of the

Income in its broad use.

family are in the form of money; when one thinks of their income at all, one reckons in the benefits which they get from their cooking utensils just as much as those which they get from their plough : one draws no distinction between their capital and the rest of their accumulated stock, to which the cooking utensils and plough alike belong.

But with the growing use of money in common life the notion of income has been more and more confined to those comings in which are in the form of money; or else—like the free use of a house, the free coals, gas, water, &c., of some employees—take the place of things on which most people spend a part of their money-income.

'Trade capital' corresponds to 'money-income.'

In harmony with this meaning of Income, the language of the market-place commonly regards a man's capital as that part of his wealth which he devotes to acquiring an income in the form of money; or, more generally, to acquisition by means of trade. It may be convenient sometimes to speak of this as his *Trade capital*; which may be defined to consist of those things which a person uses in his trade, such as the factory and the business plant of a manufacturer; that is, his machinery, his raw material, any food, clothing, and house-room that he may hold for the use of his employees, and the goodwill of his business. And of course we must add to the things in his possession those to which he has a right and from which he is drawing income : including loans which he has made on mortgage or in other ways, and all the command over capital which he may hold in the form of shares of railway companies, &c., and again of money which he may keep with his banker. On the other hand debts owed by him must be deducted from his capital. This may be taken as the standard use of *Capital* for the purposes of business life.

§ 2. But a broader use is needed when we come to regard capital from the point of view, not of the individual, but of Society as a whole; or, in other

Social capital.

words, when we seek for a definition of capital in general, or *Social Capital*.

The chief difference relates to land, and other free gifts of nature.   The balance of usage and convenience   land is is in favour of reckoning rights to land as part of   omitted. individual capital.   But when regarding capital from the social point of view it is best to put under separate heads those of the nation's resources which were made by man, and those which were not; and to separate the capital which is the result of labour and saving from those things which nature has given freely.

This plan is well adapted for the main purposes of the economist.   For indeed his chief concern with capital in general, or social ·capital, is when he is considering the way in which the three agents of production, land (*i.e.* natural agents), labour and capital, contribute to producing the national income (or the *National Dividend*, as it will be called later on); and the way in which this is distributed among the three agents.

This fact points further to the convenience of keeping up a close relation between our uses of the terms Capital and Income from the point of view of society as we did from that of the individual.   But of course income is now to be treated more broadly and not strictly limited to that which takes the form of money.   All wealth is designed to yield what in pure theory may be called an In-come of benefit or gain in some form or other; and the language of the market-place, while refusing to admit so broad a use of the term Income as that, commonly includes a certain number of forms of income, other than money income.

This use is exemplified in the rules of the income-tax commissioners, who count in everything which is commonly treated in a business fashion; even though it may happen, like a dwelling-house inhabited by its owner, to yield its income of comfort directly.   That is done partly because of

the practical importance of house-room, and partly because
the real income from it can easily be separated off and estimated.

In the present treatise therefore, capital in general, *i.e.*
capital regarded from the social point of view, will be taken
to consist of those kinds of wealth, other than the free gifts
of nature, which yield income that is generally reckoned as
such in common discourse: together with similar things in
public ownership, such as government factories.

Thus it will include all things held for trade purposes,
whether machinery, raw material or finished goods; theatres
and hotels, home farms and houses: but not furniture or
clothes owned by those who use them. For the former are,
and the latter are not commonly regarded by the world at
large as yielding income.

§ 3. It is troublesome to have to use the word Capital
in two senses so different as those of the two
preceding sections. But it cannot be helped.
The use of the word to mean Trade-capital is well
adapted for many purposes of economic inquiry,
as well as for the practical needs of business.
And it is so firmly established in the market-place that there
would be no wisdom in an attempt to dislodge it.

Relation
between
different
uses of the
term Capital.

But the second use of the word to mean "Social capital" is
equally necessary in its place. That use, or one differing from
it only in small matters of detail, has been the chief use of
the term in their most important discussions by the economists
of all countries from the dawnings of economic science till
now. And it is very often used by business men and statesmen in broad discussions of public well-being; so it also is
indispensable.

In ordinary conversation people are apt to pass from one
use of the word to the other, without noticing the change.
This causes confusion, which can sometimes be set right at
once, by someone's breaking in and asking "are you speaking

of capital in a broader sense than before," or "in a narrower sense" as the case may be. But the economist cannot afford to run the risk of confusions of this kind. He must always make quite sure that he knows what he means himself; and he must not trust to someone's interrupting him and asking him to explain himself. And this makes it seem as though he were introducing new difficulties that are not met with in common conversation. But that is not the case. He does not make new difficulties. He merely brings into prominence some that are latent in every day discourse. The trouble of examining them in a good light is worth what it costs; for it saves constant confusion of thought.

Finally it should be remarked that though there is no perfectly clear and consistent tradition as to the verbal definition of capital; there is a clear tradition that we should use the term Wealth in preference to Capital when our attention is directed to the relations in which the stock of useful things stands to general well-being, to methods of consumption, and to pleasures of possession: and that we should use the term Capital when our attention is directed to those attributes of productiveness and prospectiveness, which attach to all the stored-up fruits of human effort, but are more prominent in some than in others. We should speak of Capital when considering things as agents of production; and we should speak of Wealth when considering them as results of production, as subjects of consumption and as yielding pleasures of possession[1].

[1] These differences of opinion among economists as to the best definition of capital seem very confusing. But they are of much less importance practically than appears at first sight. For instance, whatever definition of capital be taken, it is true that a general increase of capital augments the demand for labour and raises wages: and, whatever definition be taken, it is not true that all kinds of capital act with equal force in this direction, or that it is possible to say how great an effect any given increase in the total amount of capital will have in raising wages, without specially inquiring as to the particular form which the increase has taken. This inquiry is the really important part of the work: it has to be made, and it is made by all careful writers in very much the same manner, and it comes to the same result, whatever be the definition of capital with which we have started.

§ 4.   Capital has been classed as *consumption capital*, and *auxiliary* or *instrumental capital*.   It seems necessary to retain this distinction because it is often used.   But it is not a good one : no clear line of division can be drawn between the two classes.   The general notion of the distinction which the terms are designed to suggest, can however be gathered from the following approximate definitions.

Consumption capital consists of goods in a form to satisfy wants directly; that is, goods which afford a direct sustenance to the workers, such as food, clothes, house-room, &c.

Consumption capital.

Auxiliary, or *instrumental*, *capital* is so called because it consists of all the goods that aid labour in production.   Under this head come tools, machines, factories, railways, docks, ships, &c.; and raw materials of all kinds.

Auxiliary capital.

But of course a man's clothes assist him in his work and are instrumental in keeping him warm; and he derives a direct benefit from the shelter of his factory as he does from the shelter of his house.

Next we may follow Mill in distinguishing *circulating capital* "which fulfils the whole of its office in the production in which it is engaged, by a single use," from *fixed capital* "which exists in a durable shape and the return to which is spread over a period of corresponding duration."

Circulating and fixed capital.

Sometimes again we have to distinguish certain forms of capital as *specialized*; because, having been designed for use in one trade, they cannot easily be diverted to another.

Specialized capital.

Both of these distinctions correspond to differences in degree, not to hard and sharp lines of division.

§ 5.   To return to Income.   If a person is engaged in business, he is sure to have to incur certain outgoings for raw material, the hire of labour, &c.   And, in that case, his true or *Net Income* is found by deducting from his gross income the outgoings that belong to its production. Net income.

Now anything that a person does, for which he is paid directly or indirectly in money, helps to swell his money income; while no services that he performs for himself are reckoned as adding to his nominal income. Thus a woman who makes her own clothes, or a man who digs in his own garden or repairs his own house, is earning income just as would the dressmaker, gardener or carpenter who might be hired to do the work.

It would be a great convenience if there were two words available: one to represent a person's total income and another his money income, *i.e.* that part of his total income which comes to him in the form of money. For scientific purposes it would be best that the word income when occurring alone should always mean total real income. But as this plan is inconsistent with general usage we must, whenever there is any danger of misunderstanding, say distinctly whether the term is to be taken in its narrower or its broader use.

In this connection we may introduce a term of which we shall have to make frequent use hereafter. Net advan-
The need for it arises from the fact that every tages.
occupation involves other disadvantages besides the fatigue of the work required in it, and every occupation offers other advantages besides the receipt of money wages. The true reward which an occupation offers to labour has to be calculated by deducting the money value of all its disadvantages from that of all its advantages; and we may describe this true reward as the *Net Advantages* of the occupation.

§ 6. The income derived from wealth has many forms. It includes all the various benefits which a person derives from the ownership of wealth whether he uses it as capital or not. Thus it includes the benefits which he gets from the use of his own piano, equally with those which a piano dealer would win by letting out a piano on hire. And it includes,

4—2

as a special case, the money income which is derived from capital. This income is most easily measured when it takes
Interest of capital.
the form of a payment made by a borrower for the use of a loan for, say, a year; it is then expressed as the ratio which that payment bears to the loan, and is called *Interest*.

This is one of a group of notions, which we shall need to study carefully hereafter, but of which provisional definitions may conveniently be introduced here.

When a man is engaged in business, his *Profits* for the
Profits,
year are the excess of his receipts from his business during the year over his outlay for his business; the difference between the value of his stock and plant at the end and at the beginning of the year being taken as part of his receipts or as part of his outlay, according as there has been an increase or decrease of value. What re-
Earnings of Management,
mains of his profits after deducting interest on his capital at the current rate may be called his *Earnings of undertaking or management*.

The income derived from the ownership of land and other
Rent.
free gifts of nature is commonly called *Rent*; and the term is sometimes stretched, so as to include the income derived from houses and other things the supply of which is limited and cannot quickly be increased.

§ 7. Social Income may be estimated by adding together
Social income.
the incomes of the individuals in the society in question, whether a nation or any other larger or smaller group of persons. But to reckon it directly is for most purposes simplest and best. Everything that is produced in the course of a year, every service rendered, every fresh utility brought about is a part of the national income.

Thus it includes the benefit derived from the advice of a physician, the pleasure got from hearing a professional singer, and the enjoyment of all other services which one person may be hired to perform for another. It includes the services rendered not only by the omnibus driver, but also by the coachman who drives a private carriage. It includes the services of the domestic servant who makes or mends or cleans a carpet or a dress, as well as the results of the work of the upholsterer, the milliner, and the dyer.

We must however be careful not to count the same thing twice. If we have counted a carpet at its full value, we have already counted the values of the yarn and the labour that were used in making it; and these must not be counted again[1].

[1] Suppose however a landowner with an annual income of £10,000 hires a private secretary at a salary of £500, who hires a servant at wages of £50. It may seem that if the incomes of all these three persons are counted in as part of the net income of the country, some of it will be counted twice over, and some three times. But this is not the case. The landlord transfers to his secretary, in return for his assistance, part of the purchasing power derived from the produce of land; and the secretary again transfers part of this to his servant in return for his assistance. The farm produce the value of which goes as rent to the landlord, the assistance which the landlord derives from the work of the secretary, and that which the secretary derives from the work of the servant are independent parts of the real net income of the country; and therefore the £10,000 and the £500 and the £50 which are their money measures, must all be counted in when we are estimating the income of the country. But if the landlord makes an allowance of £500 a year to his son, that must not be counted as an independent income; because no services are rendered for it, and it would not be assessed to the Income-tax.

BOOK III.

ON WANTS AND THEIR SATISFACTION.

CHAPTER I.

INTRODUCTORY.

In Book III. we are to make a short provisional study of wants and their satisfaction; or, to express nearly the same thing in other words, of demand and consumption.

This subject has been somewhat neglected by economists till recently; partly because science seemed to have little to say upon it, beyond what is the common property of all sensible people who have had a large experience of life. But in recent years economics has borrowed much from the exact habits of thought and expression of the older physical sciences; and, when these were applied to state clearly how the demand for a thing is to be measured, they were found to open up at once new aspects of the main problems of economics. The theory of demand is yet in its infancy; but we can already see that it may be possible to collect and arrange statistics of consumption in such a way as to throw light on difficult questions of great importance to public well-being.

And while the progress of the science is giving us a new power, the spirit of the age is giving us a new motive for this inquiry. It is urging us to pay ever closer attention to the

Scope of Book III.

question whether our increasing wealth may not be made to go further than it does in promoting the general well-being; and this again compels us to examine how far the exchange value of any element of wealth, whether in collective or individual use, represents accurately the addition which it makes to happiness and well-being.

We will begin this Book with a short study of the variety of human wants, considered in their relation to human efforts and activities. For the progressive nature of man is one whole. There is a special need to insist on this just now, because the reaction against the comparative neglect of the study of wants by the earlier economists shows signs of being carried to the opposite extreme. It is important still to assert the great truth on which they dwelt somewhat too exclusively; viz. that while wants are the rulers of life among the lower animals, it is to changes in the forms of efforts and activities that we must turn when in search for the keynotes of the history of mankind.

CHAPTER II.

WANTS IN RELATION TO ACTIVITIES.

§ 1. HUMAN wants and desires are countless in number and very various in kind. The uncivilized man indeed has not many more needs than the brute animal; but every step in his progress upwards increases the variety of them together with the variety in his method of satisfying them. Thus though the brute and the savage alike have their preferences for choice morsels, neither of them cares much for change for its own sake. As, however, man rises in civilization, as his mind becomes developed, and even his animal passions begin to associate themselves with mental activities, his wants become rapidly more subtle and more various; and in the minor details of life he begins to desire change for the sake of change, long before he has consciously escaped from the yoke of custom. The first great step in this direction comes with the art of making a fire: gradually he gets to accustom himself to many different kinds of food and drink cooked in many different ways; and before long, monotony begins to become irksome to him; and he finds it a great hardship when accident compels him to live for a long time exclusively on one or two kinds of food.

Wants are progressive.

As a man's riches increase his food and drink become more various and costly; but his appetite is limited by nature, and when his expenditure on food is extravagant it is more often to gratify the desires of hospitality and display than to indulge his own senses.

Desire for food;

But, as Senior says :—"Strong as is the desire for variety, it is weak compared with the desire for distinc- for distinction; tion: a feeling which if we consider its univer- sality and its constancy, that it affects all men and at all times, that it comes with us from the cradle and never leaves us till we go into the grave, may be pronounced to be the most powerful of human passions." This great half-truth is well illustrated by a comparison of the desire for choice and various food with that for choice and various dress.

§ 2. That need for dress which is the result of natural causes varies with the climate and the season of year, and a little with the nature of a person's and for costly dress. occupations. But in dress conventional wants overshadow those which are natural. For instance in England now a well-to-do labourer is expected to appear on Sunday in a black coat and, in some places, in a silk hat; though these would have subjected him to ridicule but a short time ago; and in all the lower ranks of life there is a constant increase both in that variety and expensiveness which custom requires as a minimum, and in that which it tolerates as a maximum; and the efforts to obtain distinction by dress are extending themselves throughout the lower grades of English Society.

But in the upper grades, though the dress of women is still various and costly, that of men is simple and inexpensive as compared with what it was in Europe not long ago, and is to-day in the East. For those men who are most truly distinguished on their own account, have a natural dislike to seem to claim attention by their dress; and they have set the fashion[1].

---

[1] A woman may display wealth, but she may not display only her wealth, by her dress; or else she defeats her ends. She must also suggest some distinction of character as well as of wealth: for though her dress may owe more to her dressmaker than to herself, yet there is a traditional assumption that, being less busy than man with external affairs, she can give more time to taking thought as to her dress. Even under the sway of modern fashions, to be "well dressed"—not "expensively dressed"—is a reasonable minor aim

§ 3.   House-room satisfies the imperative need for shelter

House-room. from the weather : but that need plays very little

part in the effective demand for house-room.   For though a small but well-built cabin gives excellent shelter, its stifling atmosphere, its necessary uncleanliness, and its want of the decencies and the quiet of life are great evils.   It is not so much that they cause physical discomfort as that they tend to stunt the faculties, and limit people's higher activities.   With every increase in these activities the demand for larger house-room becomes more urgent[1].

And therefore relatively large and well appointed house-room is, even in the lowest social ranks, at once a "necessary for efficiency[2]," and the most convenient and obvious way of advancing a material claim to social distinction.   And even in those grades in which everyone has house-room sufficient for the higher activities of himself and his family, a yet further and almost unlimited increase is desired as a requisite for the exercise of many of the higher social activities.

§ 4.   It is again the desire for the exercise and develop-

Wants which develop activities. ment of activities, spreading through every rank of society, which leads not only to the pursuit of

science, literature and art for their own sake, but to the rapidly increasing demand for the work of those who pursue them as professions.   This is one of the most marked characteristics of our age ; and the same may be said of the growing desire for those amusements, such as athletic games

---

for those who desire to be distinguished for their faculties and abilities; and this will be still more the case if the evil dominion of the wanton vagaries of fashion should pass away.   For to arrange costumes beautiful in themselves, various and well-adapted to their purposes is an object worthy of high endeavour; it belongs to the same class, though not to the same rank in that class, as the painting of a good picture.

[1] It is true that many active minded working men prefer cramped lodgings in a town to a roomy cottage in the country; but that is because they have a strong taste for those activities for which a country life offers little scope.

[2] See above Book II. ch. III. § 3.

and travelling, which develop activities, rather than indulge any sensuous craving[1].

For indeed the desire for excellence for its own sake, is almost as wide in its range as the lower desire for distinction. As that graduates down from the ambition of those who may hope that their names will be in men's mouths in distant lands and in distant times, to the hope of the country lass that the new ribbon she puts on for Easter may not pass unnoticed by her neighbours; so the desire for excellence for its own sake graduates down from that of a Newton, or a Stradivarius, to that of the fisherman who, even when no one is looking and he is not in a hurry, delights in handling his craft well, and in the fact that she is well built and responds promptly to his guidance. Desires of this kind exert a great influence on the Supply of the highest faculties and the greatest inventions; and they are not unimportant on the side of Demand. For a large part of the demand for the most highly skilled professional services and the best work of the mechanical artisan, arises from the delight that people have in the training of their own faculties, and in exercising them by aid of the most delicately adjusted and responsive implements.

Desire for excellence.

Speaking broadly therefore, although it is man's wants in the earliest stages of his development that give rise to his activities, yet afterwards each new step upwards is to be regarded rather as the development of new activities giving rise to new wants, than that of new wants giving rise to new activities.

Relation of Wants to Activities.

We see this clearly if we look away from healthy conditions of life, where new activities are constantly being developed, and watch the West Indian negro using his new

[1] As a minor point it may be noticed that those drinks which stimulate the mental activities are largely displacing those which merely gratify the senses. The consumption of tea is increasing very fast while that of alcohol is stationary; and there is in all ranks of society a diminishing demand for the grosser and more immediately stupefying forms of alcohol.

freedom and wealth not to get the means of satisfying new wants, but in idle stagnation that is not rest; or again look at that rapidly lessening part of the English working classes, who have no ambition and no pride or delight in the growth of their faculties and activities, and spend on drink whatever surplus their wages afford over the bare necessaries of a squalid life.

CHAPTER III.

GRADATIONS OF DEMAND.

§ 1. THE terms Utility and Want are closely related. The utility of a thing to a person is measured by the extent to which it satisfies his wants at the time. And wants are here reckoned simply with regard to their volume and intensity. If judged by an ethical or prudential standard, solid food may be more useful than whiskey of equal price, and warm underclothing than a new evening dress. But if a person prefers the whiskey or the evening dress, then it satisfies the greater want, it has the greater "utility," for him or her. No doubt this use of the term Utility might mislead those not accustomed to it; but that seldom occurs in practice.

The term Utility.

We have just seen that each several want is limited, and that with every increase in the amount of a thing which a man has, the eagerness of his desire to obtain more diminishes; until it yields place to the desire for some other thing, of which perhaps he hardly thought so long as his more urgent wants were still unsatisfied. Everyone says now and then to himself—I have had so much of this that I do not care to buy any more. If it were cheaper I might buy a little more; but I do not care enough for it to buy more at a price as high as is charged for it. In other words, the additional benefit which a person derives from a given increase of his stock of anything, diminishes with the growth of the stock that he already has. This statement of a fundamental tendency of

The law of satiable wants or diminishing utility.

human nature may be called the *law of satiable wants* or *of diminishing utility.*

Suppose, for instance, that tea of a certain quality is to be had at 2*s.* per lb. A person might be willing to give 10*s.* for a single pound once a year rather than go without it altogether; while if he could have any amount of it for nothing he would perhaps not care to use more than 30 lbs. in the year. But as it is, he buys perhaps 10 lbs. in the year; that is to say, the difference between the satisfaction which he gets from buying 9 lbs. and 10 lbs. is enough for him to be willing to pay 2*s.* for it: while the fact that he does not buy an eleventh pound, shows that he does not think that it would be worth an extra 2*s.* to him.

Such facts as these come within the daily experience of everybody. They illustrate the rule that the *total utility* of
Total utility. a thing to any one (that is, the total satisfaction or benefit it yields him) generally increases with every increase in his stock of it; but yet does not increase as fast as his stock increases. If a number of equal additions be made to his stock, one after another, the additional benefit which he derives from any one will be less than from the previous one. In other words, if his stock of it increases at a uniform rate, the benefit which he derives from it increases at a diminishing rate.

To return to our purchaser of tea. The market price of 2*s.* a pound measures the utility to him of the tea which lies at the margin, or terminus or end of his purchases; and this introduces us to one of those few technical terms which are indispensable; because the notions which they express are ever recurring in the business of life; while yet there are no words in ordinary use which represent them well.

We may call that part of the commodity which a person
Marginal purchase. is only just induced to purchase his *marginal purchase*; because he is on the margin of doubt whether it is worth his while to incur the outlay required

to obtain it. And the utility of his marginal purchase may be called the *marginal utility* of the commodity **Marginal** to him. Or, if instead of buying it, he makes **utility.** the thing himself, then its marginal utility is the utility of that part which he thinks it only just worth his while to make. If the price which a purchaser of tea is just willing to pay for any pound be called his *demand price,* **Marginal** then 2s. is his *marginal demand price.* And **demand price.** our law may be worded :—

The larger the amount of a thing that a person has, the less will, *other things being equal,* be the price which he will pay for a little more of it : or, in other words, the less will be his marginal demand for it. The condition "other things being equal" must not be allowed to drop out of sight. If, for instance, his income were suddenly increased, he would be likely to buy more of a thing, even though he had a good stock of it already.

§ 2. Next we have to take account of the fact that, as people say, "a shilling is worth much more to **The marginal** a poor man than to a rich one." We have **utility of** already[1] noticed, for instance, that a clerk with **money varies.** £100 a-year will walk to his business in a much heavier rain than the clerk with £300 a-year ; for a threepenny omnibus fare measures a greater benefit, or utility to the poorer man than to the richer. If the poorer man spends the money, he will suffer more from the want of it afterwards than the richer would. The benefit that is measured in the poorer man's mind by threepence, is greater than that measured by it in the richer man's mind. If the richer man rides a hundred times in the year and the poorer man twenty times, then the benefit of the hundredth ride which the richer man is only just induced to take is measured to him by threepence ; and the benefit of the twentieth ride which the poorer man

---

[1] Book i. Ch. iii. § 1.

is only just induced to take is measured to him by threepence. For each of them the marginal benefit or utility is measured by threepence; but it is greater in the case of the poorer man than in that of the richer.

So when tea, sold at 2s. a pound, is drunk by different people some of whom are richer than others, then 2s. a pound will measure the utility, or benefit, to each one of them of the tea that lies at the margin or terminus or end of his or her purchases. But while one will drink twenty pounds a year, another will make shift with six; and the benefit of the marginal purchase will be much greater to the latter than to the former. If the price of this kind of tea fell to 1s. 8d., a poor person who was enabled to buy an extra seventh pound of it, would derive more benefit from the change than a richer one would from adding another pound, or perhaps even another two or three pounds to his or her already large consumption. Thus we may say generally that every increase in a person's resources increases the price which he is willing to pay for any given benefit. And in the same way every diminution of his resources diminishes the price that he is willing to pay for any benefit.

To obtain complete knowledge of a person's demand for anything, we should have to ascertain how much of it he would be willing to purchase at each of the prices at which it is likely to be offered. Thus for instance we may find that he would buy

A person's Demand for anything.

6 lbs. at 50d. per lb.	10 lbs. at 24d. per lb.
7 „ 40 „	11 „ 21 „
8 „ 33 „	12 „ 19 „
9 „ 28 „	13 „ 17 „

If corresponding prices were filled in for all intermediate amounts we should have an exact statement of his demand, and the complete list may be called his *demand schedule*[1].

[1] We may here introduce the first of a series of simple diagrams designed to illustrate economic theory. *Those who wish may omit the whole series;* for the

§ 3. When we say that a person's demand for anything increases, we mean that he will buy more of it than he would before at the same price, and that he will buy as much of it as before at a higher price.

That is to say, a general increase in his demand is an increase throughout the whole list of prices at which he is willing to purchase different amounts of it; and not merely that he is willing to buy more of it at the current price[1].

Increase in a person's demand.

reasoning in the text is always complete in itself and does not depend on them. They do but express familiar facts in a new language which is terse and precise, and will be found helpful by those readers who are inclined towards it.

Such a demand schedule may be translated, on a plan now coming into familiar use, into a curve that may be called his *demand curve*. Let Ox and Oy be drawn the one horizontally, the other vertically. Let an inch measured along Ox represent 10 lb. of tea, and an inch measured along Oy represent 40d.

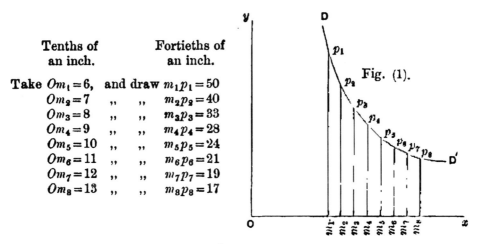

Tenths of an inch.			Fortieths of an inch.
Take $Om_1 = 6$,	and draw		$m_1 p_1 = 50$
$Om_2 = 7$	,,	,,	$m_2 p_2 = 40$
$Om_3 = 8$	,,	,,	$m_3 p_3 = 33$
$Om_4 = 9$	,,	,,	$m_4 p_4 = 28$
$Om_5 = 10$	,,	,,	$m_5 p_5 = 24$
$Om_6 = 11$	,,	,,	$m_6 p_6 = 21$
$Om_7 = 12$	,,	,,	$m_7 p_7 = 19$
$Om_8 = 13$	,,	,,	$m_8 p_8 = 17$

Fig. (1).

m_1 being on Ox and $m_1 p_1$ being drawn vertically from m_1; and so for the others. Then $p_1 p_2 \dots p_8$ are points on his Demand Curve for tea; or as we may say DEMAND POINTS. If we could find demand points in the same manner for every possible quantity of tea we should get the whole continuous curve DD' as shown in the figure.

[1] Geometrically it is represented by raising his demand curve, or, what comes to the same thing, moving it to the right, with perhaps some modification of its shape; or in other words by raising his demand schedule.

For some discussion of the uses of the term Demand by Mill and Cairnes, see *Principles* III. III. 4.

§ 4. So far we have looked at the demand of a single

Demand of a individual. And in the particular case of such a
market. thing as tea, the demand of a single person is
fairly representative of the general demand of a whole market :
for the demand for tea is a constant one ; and, since it can be
purchased in small quantities, every variation in its price is
likely to affect the amount which he will buy. But even
among those things which are in constant use, there are
many for which the demand on the part of any single individual cannot vary continuously with every small change in
price, but can move only by great leaps. For instance, a
small fall in the price of hats or watches will not affect the
action of everyone, but it will induce a few persons, who were
in doubt whether or not to get a new hat or a new watch, to
decide in favour of doing so.

In large markets, however, where rich and poor, old and
young, men and women, persons of all varieties of tastes,
temperaments and occupations are mingled together, every
fall, however slight, in the price of a commodity in general
use, will, other things being equal, increase the total sales of
it ; just as an unhealthy autumn increases the mortality of a
large town, though many persons are uninjured by it.

Let us however return to the demand for tea. The
aggregate demand in the place is the sum of the demands
of all the individuals there. Some will be richer and some
poorer than the individual consumer whose demand schedule
we have just written down ; some will have a greater and
others a smaller liking for tea than he has. Let us suppose
that there are in the place a million purchasers of tea, and
that their average consumption is equal to his at each several
price. Then the demand of that place is represented by the
same schedule as before, if we write a million pounds of tea
instead of one pound[1].

---

[1] The demand is represented by the same curve as before, only an inch

There is then one general *Law of Demand* :—The greater the amount to be sold, the smaller must be the price at which it is offered in order that it may find purchasers ; or, in other words, the amount demanded increases with a fall in price, and diminishes with a rise in price.

Law of Demand.

There will not be any uniform relation between the fall in price and the increase of demand. A fall of one-tenth in the price may increase the sales by a twentieth or by a quarter, or it may double them. But as the numbers in the left-hand column of the demand schedule increase, those in the right-hand column will always diminish.

The price will measure the marginal utility of the commodity to each purchaser *individually*: we cannot speak of price as measuring marginal utility *in general*, because the wants and circumstances of different people are different.

§ 5. The demand prices in our list are those at which various quantities of a thing can be sold in a market *during a given time and under given conditions.* If the conditions vary in any respect the prices will probably require to be changed; and this has constantly to be done when the desire for anything is materially altered by a variation of custom, or by a cheapening

Growth of a rival commodity.

measured along Ox now represents ten million pounds instead of ten pounds. And a formal definition of the Demand curve for a market may be given thus:—The demand curve for any commodity in a market during any given unit of time is the locus of demand points for it. That is to say, it is a curve such that if from any point P on it, a straight line PM be drawn perpendicular to Ox, PM represents the price at which purchasers will be forthcoming for an amount of the commodity represented by OM.

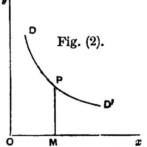

Fig. (2).

It must be remembered that the demand schedule gives the prices at which various quantities of a thing can be sold in a market during a given time and under given conditions. If the conditions vary in any respect the figures of the schedule will probably require to be changed.

of the supply of a rival commodity, or by the invention of a new one. For instance, the list of demand prices for tea is drawn out on the assumption that the price of coffee is known; but a failure of the coffee harvest would raise the prices for tea. The demand for gas is liable to be reduced by an improvement in electric lighting; and in the same way a fall in the price of a particular kind of tea may cause it to be substituted for an inferior but cheaper variety.

Our next step will be to consider the general character of demand in the cases of some important commodities ready for immediate consumption. We shall thus be continuing the inquiry made in the preceding chapter as to the variety and satiability of wants; but we shall be treating it from a rather different point of view, viz. that of price-statistics.

CHAPTER IV.

THE ELASTICITY OF WANTS.

§ 1. We have seen that the only universal law as to a person's desire for a commodity is that it dimi- nishes, other things being equal, with every in- Elasticity of demand crease in his supply of that commodity. But this diminution may be slow or rapid. If it is slow the price that he will give for the commodity will not fall much in conse- quence of a considerable increase in his supply of it; and a small fall in price will cause a comparatively large increase in his purchases. But if it is rapid, a small fall in price will cause only a very small increase in his purchases. In the former case his willingness to purchase the thing stretches itself out a great deal under the action of a small inducement: the elasticity of his wants, we may say, is great. In the latter case the extra inducement given by the fall in price causes hardly any extension of his desire to purchase: the elasticity of his demand is small. If a fall in price from say 16d. to 15d. per lb. of tea would much increase his purchases, then a rise from 15d. to 16d. would much diminish them: when the demand is elastic for a fall in price, it is elastic also for the opposite rise.

As with the demand of one person so with that of a whole market. And we may say generally:—The *elasticity of demand* in a market is great or small according as the amount demanded increases much or little for a given fall in price, and diminishes much or little for a given rise in price.

§ 2. The price which is so high relatively to the poor man as to be almost prohibitive, may be scarcely felt varies with different incomes. by the rich; the poor man for instance never tastes wine, but the very rich man may drink as much of it as he has a fancy for, without giving himself a thought of its cost. We shall therefore get the clearest notion of the law of the elasticity of demand, by considering one class of society at a time. Of course there are many degrees of richness among the rich, and of poverty among the poor; but for the present we may neglect these minor subdivisions.

When the price of a thing is very high relatively to any class, they will buy but little of it; and in some cases custom and habit may prevent them from using it freely even after its price has fallen a good deal. But such cases, though not infrequent, will not form the general rule, and anyhow as soon as it has been taken into common use, any considerable fall in its price will cause a great increase in the demand for it. The elasticity of demand will be great for high prices, and great or at least considerable for medium prices, but it will decline as the price falls; and gradually fade away if the fall goes so far that satiety level is reached.

The level at which "very high" prices end and "high" prices begin, is of course different for different classes, and so is the level at which "low" prices end and "very low" prices begin. Varieties in detail arise from the fact that there are some commodities with which people are easily satiated, and others—chiefly things used for display—for which their desire is almost unlimited [1].

§ 3. There are some things the current prices of which Illustrations. in this country are "very low" relatively even to the poorer classes; such are for instance salt, and many kinds of savours and flavours, and also cheap medicines.

---

[1] The figures in Ch. iii. § 4 show a small elasticity in the demand for tea, and a diminution in the total outlay on it as its price falls. To illustrate the general rule that the total outlay is largest for prices neither very high, nor very low, we might suppose 2 pounds to be bought at 50 pence, 4 at 40, 8 at 30, 14 at 24, 17 at 20, 20 at 17, 24 at 14, 27 at 12, 30 at 9, 40 at 5, 50 at 3; so that the total outlay would be 200 pence for a very high price, rising to 340 pence for medium prices and falling again to 150 for a very low price. But see *Principles*, III. iv. 2.

It is doubtful whether any fall in price would induce a considerable increase in the consumption of these.

The current prices of meat, milk and butter, wool, tobacco, imported fruits, and of ordinary medical attendance, are such that every variation in price makes a great change in the consumption of them by the working classes, and the lower half of the middle classes; but the rich would not much increase their own personal consumption of them however cheaply they were to be had. In other words the direct demand for these commodities is very elastic on the part of the working and lower middle classes, though not on the part of the rich. But the working class is so numerous that their consumption of such things as are well within their reach is much greater than that of the rich; and therefore the aggregate demand for all things of the kind is very elastic. A little while ago sugar belonged to this group of commodities: but its price in England has now fallen so far as to be low relatively even to the working classes, and the demand for it is therefore not elastic.

The current prices of wall-fruit, of the better kinds of fish and other moderately expensive luxuries are such as to make the consumption of them by the middle class increase much with every fall in price; in other words the middle class demand for them is very elastic: while the demands on the part of the rich and on the part of the working class is much less elastic, the former because it is already nearly satiated, the latter because the price is still too high.

The current prices of such things as rare wines, fruit out of season, highly skilled medical and legal assistance, are so high that there is but little demand for them except from the rich: but what demand there is has in most cases considerable elasticity. And in fact much of the demand for the more expensive kinds of food is really a demand for the means of obtaining social distinction, and is almost insatiable.

§ 4. The case of necessaries is exceptional. When the
Demand for   price of wheat is very high, and again when it
necessaries.   is very low, the demand has very little elasticity :
at all events if we assume that wheat, even when scarce, is the
cheapest food for man ; and that, even when most plentiful,
it is not consumed in any other way. We know that a fall in
the price of the quartern loaf from 6d. to 4d. has scarcely any
effect in increasing the consumption of bread. With regard
to the other end of the scale it is more difficult to speak with
certainty, because there has been no approach to a scarcity in
England since the repeal of the corn laws. But, availing ourselves of estimates made in a less happy time, we may suppose that deficits in the supply of 1, 2, 3, 4, or 5 tenths would
cause a rise in price of 3, 8, 16, 28, or 45 tenths respectively.
Much greater variations in prices indeed than this have not
been uncommon. Thus wheat sold in London for ten shillings
a bushel in 1335, but in the following year it sold for ten
pence.

There may be even more violent changes than this in the
price of a thing which is not necessary, if it is perishable and
the demand for it is inelastic : thus fish may be very dear one
day, and sold for manure two or three days later.

Water is one of the few things the consumption of which
we are able to observe at all prices from the very highest
down to nothing at all. At moderate prices the demand for
it is very elastic. But the uses to which it can be put are
capable of being completely filled : and as its price sinks towards zero the demand for it loses its elasticity. Nearly the
same may be said of salt. Its price in England is so low that
the demand for it as an article of food is very inelastic : but
in India the price is comparatively high and the demand is
comparatively elastic.

The price of house-room on the other hand has never
fallen very low except when a locality is being deserted by
its inhabitants. Where the condition of society is healthy,

and there is no check to general prosperity, there seems always to be an elastic demand for house-room, on account both of the real conveniences and the social distinction which it affords. The desire for those kinds of clothing which are not used for the purpose of display, is satiable: when their price is low the demand for them has scarcely any elasticity.

§ 5. When trying to ascertain how the purchases of a commodity are affected by changes in its price, we meet with several difficulties. We must take account of changes in the purchasing power of money which are a source of confusion in all statistics of prices. And we must allow for changes in fashion, and taste and habit, for the opening out of new uses of a commodity, for the discovery or improvement or cheapening of other things that can be applied to the same uses with it. *Causes that obscure the influence of price on demand.*

And further we must remember that time is required to enable a rise in the price of a commodity to exert its full influence on consumption. Time is required for consumers to become familiar with substitutes that can be used instead of it, and perhaps for producers to get into the habit of producing them in sufficient quantities. Time may be also wanted for the growth of habits of familiarity with the new commodities and the discovery of methods of economizing them. *Slowness of the growth of new habits.*

For instance when wood and charcoal became dear in England, familiarity with coal as a fuel grew slowly, fireplaces were but slowly adapted to its use, and an organized traffic in it did not spring up quickly even to places to which it could be easily carried by water: the invention of processes by which it could be used as a substitute for charcoal in manufacture went even more slowly, and is indeed hardly yet complete. Again, when in recent years the price of coal became very high, a great stimulus was given to the invention of economies in its use especially in the production of iron and steam; but few of these inventions bore much practical fruit till after the high price had passed away. Again, when a new line of tramways or of suburban railways is opened, even those who live near the line do not get into the habit of making the most of its assistance at once; and a good deal more time elapses before many of those whose places of business are near one end of the line change their homes so as to live near the other end. Again, when petroleum first became plentiful few people were ready to use it freely; gradually petroleum and petroleum lamps have become familiar to all classes of society: too much influence would therefore be attributed to the fall in price which has occurred since then, if it were credited with all the increase of consumption[1].

[1] The demand for things of a higher quality depends much on sensibility: some people care little for a refined flavour in their wine provided they can get plenty of it: others crave a high quality, but are easily satiated. In the ordinary working class districts the inferior and the better joints are sold at nearly the same price: but some well paid artisans in the north of England have developed a liking for the best meat, and will pay for it nearly as high a price as can be got in the west end of London, where the price is kept artificially high by the necessity of sending the inferior joints away for sale elsewhere. Use also gives rise to acquired distastes as well as to acquired tastes.

Generally speaking those things have the most elastic demand, which are capable of being applied to many different uses. Water for instance is needed first as food, then for cooking, then for washing of various kinds and so on. When there is no special drought, but water is sold by the pailful, the price may be low enough to enable even the poorer classes to drink as much of it as they are inclined, while for cooking they sometimes use the same water twice over, and they apply it very scantily in washing. The middle classes will perhaps not use any of it twice for cooking; but they will make a pail of water go a good deal further for washing purposes than if they had an unlimited supply at command. When water is supplied by pipes, and charged at a very low rate by meter, many people use as much of it even for washing as they feel at all inclined to do; and when the water is supplied not by meter but at a fixed annual charge; and is laid on in every place where it is wanted, the use of it for every purpose is carried to the full satiety limit.

CHAPTER V.

THE CHOICE BETWEEN DIFFERENT USES OF THE SAME THING. IMMEDIATE AND DEFERRED USES.

§ 1. THE primitive housewife finding that she has a limited number of hanks of yarn from the year's shearing, considers all the domestic wants for clothing and tries to distribute the yarn between them in such a way as to contribute as much as possible to the family well-being. She will think she has failed if, when it is done, she has reason to regret that she did not apply more to making, say socks, and less to vests. That would mean that she had miscalculated the points at which to suspend the making of socks and vests respectively; that she had gone too far in the case of vests, and not far enough in that of socks; and that therefore at the points at which she actually did stop, the utility of yarn turned into socks was greater than that of yarn turned into vests. But if, on the other hand, she hit on the right points to stop at, then she made just so many socks and vests that she got an equal amount of good out of the last bundle of yarn that she applied to socks, and the last she applied to vests. This illustrates a general principle, which may be expressed thus :—

Distribution of means between different uses.

If a person has a thing which he can put to several uses, he will distribute it between these uses in such a way that it has the same marginal utility in all. For if it had a greater marginal utility in one use than another, he would gain by taking away some of it from the second use and applying it to the first.

One great disadvantage of a primitive economy, in which there is but little free exchange, is that a person may easily have so much of one thing, say wool, that, when he has applied it to every possible use, its marginal utility in each use is low: and at the same time he may have so little of some other thing, say wood, that its marginal utility for him is very high. Meanwhile some of his neighbours may be in great need of wool, and have more wood than they can turn

Difficulties of barter.

to good account. If each gives up that which has for him the lower utility and receives that which has the higher, each will gain by the exchange. But to make such an adjustment by barter, would be tedious and difficult.

The difficulty of barter is indeed not so very great where there are but a few simple commodities, each of which can be adapted by domestic work to several uses; the weaving wife and the spinster daughters adjusting rightly the marginal utilities of the different uses of the wool, while the husband and the sons do the same for the wood.

§ 2. But when commodities have become very numerous

The need for money.

and highly specialized, there is an urgent need for the free use of money, or general purchasing power; for that alone can be applied easily in an unlimited variety of purchases. And in a money-economy, good management is shown by so adjusting the margins of suspense on each line of expenditure that the marginal utility of a shilling's worth of goods on each line shall be the same.

Thus for instance the clerk who is in doubt whether to ride to town, or to walk and have some little extra indulgence at his lunch, is weighing against one another the (marginal) utilities of two different modes of spending his money. And

A chief use of domestic accounts.

when an experienced housekeeper urges on a young couple the importance of keeping accounts carefully, a chief motive of the advice is that they may avoid spending impulsively a great deal of money on furniture and other things; for, though some quantity of these is really needful, yet, when bought lavishly, they do not give high (marginal) utilities in proportion to their cost. And when the young pair look over their year's budget at the end of the year, and find perhaps that it is necessary to curtail their expenditure somewhere, they compare the (marginal) utilities of different items, weighing the loss of utility that would result from taking away a pound's expenditure here, with that which they would lose by taking it away there: they strive to adjust their parings down so that the aggregate loss of utility may be as little as possible.

§ 3.   The different uses between which a commodity is distributed need not all be present uses; some may be present and some future.   A prudent person will endeavour to distribute his means between all their several uses **Balancing of** present and future in such a way that they will **future benefits** have in each the same marginal utility.   But, in **against present.** estimating the present marginal utility of a distant source of benefit to him, a twofold allowance must be made; firstly, for its uncertainty[1]; and secondly, for the difference in the value to him of a distant as compared with a present benefit[2].

If people regarded future benefits as equally desirable with similar and equal benefits at the present **Future bene-** time, they would probably endeavour to dis- **fits are "dis-** tribute their pleasures evenly throughout their **counted" at different rates** lives.   They would therefore generally be willing **by different** to give up a present pleasure for the sake of an **people.** equal pleasure in the future, provided they could be certain of having it.   But in fact human nature is so constituted that in estimating the "present value" of a future benefit most

---

[1] This is an *objective* property which all well-informed persons would estimate in the same way.

[2] This is a *subjective* property which different people would estimate in different ways according to their individual characters, and their circumstances at the time.

people generally make a second deduction from its future value, in the form of what we may call a "discount," that increases with the period for which the pleasure is deferred. One will reckon a distant benefit at nearly the same value which it would have for him if it were present; while another who has less power of realizing the future, less patience and self-control, will care comparatively little for any benefit that is not near at hand.

Many people derive from the mere feeling of ownership a stronger satisfaction than they derive from ordinary pleasures in the narrower sense of the term: for example, the delight in the possession of land will often induce people to pay for it so high a price that it yields them but a very poor return on their investment. There is a delight in ownership for its own sake; and there is a delight in ownership on account of the distinction it yields. Sometimes the latter is stronger than the former, sometimes weaker; and perhaps no one knows himself or other people well enough to be able to draw the line quite certainly between the two[1].

[1] The rates at which different people discount the future affect not only their tendency to save, as the term is ordinarily understood, but also their tendency to buy things which will be a lasting source of pleasure rather than those which give a stronger but more transient enjoyment; to buy a new coat rather than to indulge in a drinking bout, or to choose simple furniture that will wear well, rather than showy furniture that will soon fall to pieces. And further, the same person will discount future pleasures at different rates at different times, according to his mood.

CHAPTER VI.

VALUE AND UTILITY.

§ 1. WE may now turn to consider how far the price, which is actually paid for a thing, represents the satisfaction that arises from its possession. This is a subject on which economic science has very little to say, but that little is of some importance.

Price and Utility.

We have already seen that the price which a person pays for a thing, can never exceed, and seldom comes up to that which he would be willing to pay rather than go without it : so that the gratification which he gets from its purchase generally exceeds that which he gives up in paying away its price; and he thus derives from the purchase a surplus of satisfaction. The excess of the price which he would be willing to pay rather than go without the thing, over that which he actually does pay, is the economic measure of this surplus satisfaction. It has some analogies to a rent, but is perhaps best called *Consumer's Surplus.*

Consumers' Surplus.

It is obvious that the Consumer's Surpluses derived from some commodities are much greater than from others.   There are many comforts and luxuries of which the prices are very much below those which many people would pay rather than go entirely without them ; and which therefore afford a very great Consumer's Surplus.   Good instances are matches, salt, a penny newspaper, or a postage-stamp.

We are apt to underrate the benefits which we derive from the opportunities afforded to us by our surroundings, or, as the Germans say, from the *Conjuncture* of circumstances around us. We take it for granted that we can buy a newspaper with several thousand lines of news in it for a penny: and we seldom consider that if we would pay (say) a shilling rather than be deprived of our newspaper, the opportunity of buying it for a penny gives us a surplus benefit of eleven pence a day.

This notion is of great importance for the higher work of the economic student. But it involves many difficulties, and is apt to be misunderstood and misapplied by the beginner: and therefore, what little is said of it in the present treatise, may be relegated to Appendix B.

§ 2. The notion itself in some vague form or other is constantly present with us. This is another instance in which the daily language of ordinary life, while sufficient for many practical purposes, is not quite exact and complete; so that on examination it is found to suggest more than appears at first sight.

Thus, for instance, it is a common saying that the real value of things to us is not gauged by the price we pay for them: that, though we spend for instance much more on tea than on salt, yet salt is of greater real value to us; and that this would be clearly seen, if we were entirely

As regards a single person.

deprived of it. This argument is but thrown into precise form, when it is said that we cannot trust the marginal utility of a commodity to indicate its total utility: on the ground that though, when a person spends sixpence on a quarter of a pound of tea instead of on a stone of salt, he does so because he prefers the tea: yet he would not prefer the tea if he did not know that he could easily get whatever salt he needed for his more urgent requirements.

Again, if the real value of anything were being discussed with reference, not to a single individual, but to people in general, it would naturally be assumed that a shilling's worth of gratification to one Englishman might be taken as equivalent with a shilling's worth to another, "to start with," and "until cause to the contrary were shown." But every one would know that this was a reason- *or as regards people in general.* able course only on the supposition that the consumers of tea and those of salt belonged to the same classes of people; and included people of every variety of temperament. And if, instead of comparing tea and salt, which are both used largely by all classes, we had compared either of them with champagne or pineapples, this assumption could not have been made even for a first rough guess. In earlier generations many statesmen, and even some economists, neglected to make adequate allowance for considerations of this class, especially when constructing schemes of taxation; and their words or deeds seemed to imply a want of sympathy with the sufferings of the poor; though more often they were due simply to want of thought.

On the whole however it happens that by far the greater number of the events with which economics deals, affect in about equal proportions all the different classes of society; so that if the money measures of the happiness caused by two events are equal, there is not in general any very great difference between the amounts of the happiness in the two cases. And it is on account of this fact that the exact measurement of the Consumers' Surplus in a market has already much theoretical interest, and may become of high practical importance [1].

§ 3. There is another need for caution when estimating the dependence of well-being upon material wealth. Not only does a person's happiness often depend more on his own physical, mental *Allowance for collective wealth.* and moral health than on the external conditions of his wellbeing: but even among these conditions many that are of chief importance for his real happiness are apt to be omitted from an inventory of his wealth. Some are free gifts of

M.   [1] Compare p. 21.   6

nature; and these might indeed be neglected without great harm if they were always the same for everybody; but in fact they vary much from place to place. More of them however are elements of collective wealth which are often omitted from the reckoning of individual wealth; but which become important when we compare different parts of the modern civilized world, and even more important when we compare our own age with earlier times.

An increase of income nearly always causes pleasure; but the new enjoyments which it provides often lose quickly much of their charm. Partly this is the result of familiarity; which makes people cease to derive much pleasure from accustomed comforts and luxuries, though they suffer great pain from their loss. Partly it is due to the fact that with increased riches there often comes either the weariness of age, or at least an increase of nervous strain, and perhaps habits of living that lower physical vitality and diminish the capacity for pleasure.

Value of leisure and rest, In every civilized country there have been some followers of the Buddhist doctrine that a placid serenity is the highest ideal of life; that it is the part of the wise man to root out of his nature as many wants and desires as he can; that real riches consist not in the abundance of goods but in the paucity of wants. At the other extreme are those who maintain that the growth of new wants and desires is always beneficial because it stimulates people to increased exertions. They seem to have made the mistake, as Mr Herbert Spencer says, of supposing that life is for working, instead of working for life.

Value of work for its own sake. The truth seems to be that as human nature is constituted, man rapidly degenerates unless he has some hard work to do, some difficulties to overcome; and that some strenuous exertion is necessary for physical and moral health. The fulness of life lies in the development and activity of as many and as high faculties as possible. There is intense pleasure in the ardent pursuit of any aim, whether it be success in business, the advancement of art and science, or the improvement of the condition of one's fellow-beings. The highest constructive work of all kinds must often alternate between periods of over-strain and periods of lassitude and stagnation; but for ordinary people, for those who have no strong ambitions, whether of a lower or a higher kind, a moderate income earned by moderate and fairly steady work offers the best opportunity for the growth of those habits of body, mind and spirit in which alone there is true happiness.

There is some misuse of wealth in all ranks of society. And though speaking generally, we may say that every increase in the income of the working classes adds to the fulness and nobility of human life, because it is used chiefly in the satisfaction of real wants; yet even among the artisans in England, and perhaps still more in new countries, there are signs of the growth of that unwholesome desire for wealth as a means of display which has been the chief bane of the well-to-do classes in every civilized country. Laws against luxury have been futile; but it would be a gain if the moral sentiment of the community could *The higher uses of wealth.* induce people to avoid all sorts of display of individual wealth. There are indeed true and worthy pleasures to be got from wisely ordered magnificence: but they are at their best when free from any taint of personal vanity on the one side, and envy on the other; as they are when they centre round public buildings, public parks, public collections of the fine arts, and public games and amusements. So long as wealth is applied to provide for every family the necessaries of life and culture, and an abundance of the higher forms of enjoyment for collective use, so long the pursuit of wealth is a noble aim; and the pleasures which it brings are likely to increase with the growth of those higher activities which it is used to promote.

When the necessaries of life are once provided, everyone

should seek to increase the beauty of things in his possession rather than their number or their magnificence. An improvement in the artistic character of furniture and clothing trains the higher faculties of those who make them, and is a source of growing happiness to those who use them. But if instead of seeking for a higher standard of beauty, we spend our growing resources on increasing the complexity and intricacy of our domestic goods, we gain thereby no true benefit, no lasting happiness. The world would go much better if everyone would buy fewer and simpler things, and would take trouble in selecting them for their real beauty being careful of course to get good value in return for his outlay, but preferring to buy a few things made well by highly paid labour rather than many made badly by low paid labour. But we are exceeding the proper scope of the present Book; the discussion of the influence on general well-being which is exerted by the mode in which each individual spends his income is one of the more important of those applications of economic science to the art of living which will find their place at the end of the Treatise.

BOOK IV.

THE AGENTS OF PRODUCTION.
LAND, LABOUR, CAPITAL AND ORGANIZATION.

CHAPTER I.

INTRODUCTORY.

§ 1. THE agents of production are commonly classed as Land, Labour and Capital.

By "Land" is meant not merely land in the strict sense of the word, but the whole of the material and the forces which Nature gives freely for man's aid, in land and water, in air and light and heat[1]. "Land" is, in a certain sense, a fixed quantity; and we shall have to examine the causes which limit its yield of produce to the labour and capital applied to it. *Chapters II, III.*

The amount of labour available for any work depends partly upon the number of people able and ready to do the work, and partly on their willingness to exert themselves, and these are very elastic quantities. We shall see how they are affected by the wages, or other reward available for the work: how high wages enable parents to bring up a large proportion of their children to full age, well nourished in mind and body. And we shall gradually inquire (for the question can only be opened out *Chapters IV, V, VI.*

[1] See below, p. 87.

in the present Book) how children and adults drift from occupations that hold out small attractions to others that are not more difficult and hold out greater.

We shall look at the growth of wealth, which when considered as an agent of production, is called Capital[1]. We shall see how it is affected by that "balancing of future benefits against present"; which has already been noticed[2] as controlling people's willingness to forego immediate pleasure and to provide machinery, buildings, ships, railways, and to make labour more efficient in the future.

Chapter VIII.

Then we shall make some study of division of labour and industrial organization generally, and inquire how they increase the efficiency of labour.

Chapters IX—XIII.

Thus we shall prepare the way for an inquiry into the causes that govern the Supply price of anything. For as the price, required to attract purchasers for any given amount of a commodity, was called the Demand price for that amount; so the price required to call forth the exertion necessary for producing any given amount of a commodity, may be called the *Supply price* for that labour. In Book V, we shall add up the supply prices of all the different things needed to make a commodity, and call the sum of them the supply price of that commodity. Then we shall set against this the corresponding demand price for it; and we shall see how the relations between the two govern value.

Supply Price.

Books III and IV lead up to Book V.

[1] See above p. 49.　　　[2] See p. 77.

CHAPTER II.

THE FERTILITY OF LAND.

§ 1. THE agents of production, other than labour, are described as land and capital: those material things which owe their usefulness to human labour being classed under capital, and those which owe nothing to it being classed as land. The distinction is obviously a loose one: for bricks are but pieces of earth slightly worked up; and the soil of old settled countries has for the greater part been worked over many times by man, and owes to him its present form. There is however a scientific principle underlying the distinction. While man has no power of creating matter, he creates utilities by putting things into a useful form[1]; and the utilities made by him can be increased in supply if there is an increased demand for them: they have a supply price. But there are other utilities over the supply of which he has no control; they are given as a fixed quantity by nature and have therefore no supply price. The term "land" has been extended by economists so as to include the permanent sources of these utilities[2]; whether they are found in land, as the term is commonly used, or in seas and rivers, in sunshine and rain, in winds and waterfalls.

When we have inquired what it is that marks off land from those material things which we regard as products

Land.

[1] See Book II. Chapter III.
[2] In Ricardo's famous phrase "the original and indestructible powers of the soil."

of the land, we shall find that the fundamental attribute of land is its extension. The right to use a certain area of the earth's surface is a primary condition of anything that man can do; it gives him room for his own actions, with the enjoyment of the heat and the light, the air and the rain which nature assigns to that area; and it determines his distance from, and in a great measure his relations to, other things and other persons.

Some parts of the earth's surface contribute to production chiefly by the services which they render to the navigator: others are chiefly of value to the miner; others—though this selection is made by man rather than by nature—to the builder. But when the productiveness of land is spoken of our first thoughts turn to its agricultural use.

§ 2. To the agriculturist an area of land is the means of supporting a certain amount of vegetable, and perhaps ultimately of animal life. He can by sufficient labour make almost any land bear large crops. He can prepare the soil mechanically and chemically for whatever crops he intends to grow next. He can adapt his crops to the nature of the soil and to one another; selecting such a rotation that each will leave the land in such a state, and at such a time of year, that it can be worked up easily and without loss of time into a suitable seed bed for the coming crop. He can even permanently alter the nature of the soil by draining it, or by mixing with it other soil that will supplement its deficiencies[1].

Man's power of altering the character of the soil.

---

[1] Mechanically, the soil must be so far yielding that the fine roots of plants can push their way freely in it; and yet it must be firm enough to give them a good hold. The action of fresh air and water and of frosts are nature's tillage of the soil; but man gives great aid in this mechanical preparation of the soil. The chief purpose of his tillage is to enable the soil to hold plant roots gently but firmly, and to enable the air and water to move about freely in it. Even when he manures the ground he has this mechanical preparation in view. For farmyard manure benefits clay soils by subdividing them and making them lighter and more open, no less than by enriching them chemically; while to sandy soils it gives a much needed firmness of texture, and helps them,

The greater part of the soil in old countries owes much of its character to human action; all that lies just below the surface has in it a large element of capital, the produce of man's past labour: the inherent properties of the soil, the free gifts of nature, have been largely modified; partly robbed and partly added to by the work of many generations of men.

But it is different with that which is above the surface. Every acre has given to it by nature an annual income of heat and light, of air and moisture; and over these man has but little control. He may indeed alter the climate a little by extensive drainage works or by planting forests, or cutting them down. But, on the whole, the action of the sun and the wind and the rain are an annuity fixed by nature for each plot of land. Ownership of the land gives possession of this annuity: and it also gives the space required for the life and action of vegetables and animals; the value of this space being much affected by its geographical position.

mechanically as well as chemically, to hold the materials of plant food which would otherwise be quickly washed out of them.

Chemically the soil must have the inorganic elements that the plant wants in a form palatable to it. The greater part of the bulk of the plant is made up of so-called "organic compounds"; that is, compounds of carbon chiefly with oxygen, hydrogen and nitrogen; and of these it obtains by far the greater part from air and water. Only a small fraction (somewhere about a twentieth on an average) of its dry bulk consists of mineral matter that it cannot get except from the soil. And as most soils have given them by nature at least some small quantities of all the mineral substances that are necessary for plant life, they can support some sort of vegetation without human aid. Often however they have but very scanty provision of one or two necessary elements; and then man can turn a barren into a very fertile soil by adding a small quantity of just those things that are needed; using in most cases either lime in some of its many forms, or those artificial manures which modern chemical science has provided in great variety.

We may then continue to use the ordinary distinction
Original and between the original or inherent properties,
artificial pro- which the land derives from nature, and the
perties of land. artificial properties which it owes to human
action; provided we remember that the first include the
space-relations of the plot in question, and the annuity that
nature has given it of sunlight and air and rain; and that in
many cases these are the chief of the inherent properties of
the soil. It is chiefly from them that the ownership of
agricultural land derives its peculiar significance, and the
Theory of Rent its special character. But the question how
far the fertility of any soil is due to the original properties
given to it by nature, and how far to the changes in it made
by man, cannot be fully discussed without taking account of
the kind of produce raised from it.

CHAPTER III.

THE FERTILITY OF LAND, CONTINUED. THE LAW OF DIMINISHING RETURN.

§ 1. *The law of* (or *statement of tendency to*) *diminishing return* as applied to land is :—

An increase in the capital and labour applied in the cultivation of land causes *in general* a less than proportionate increase in the amount of produce raised.

The law of diminishing return.

We learn from history and by observation that every agriculturist in every age and clime desires to have the use of a good deal of land; and that when he cannot get it freely, he will pay for it, if he has the means. If he thought that he would get as good results by applying all his capital and labour to a very small piece, he would not pay for any but a very small piece.

When land that requires no clearing is to be had for nothing, every one uses just that quantity which he thinks will give his capital and labour the largest return. His cultivation is "extensive," not "intensive." He does not aim at getting many bushels of corn from each acre; he tries to get as large a total crop as possible with a given expenditure of seed and labour; and therefore he sows as many acres as he can manage to bring under a light cultivation. Of course he may go too far: he may spread his work over so large an area that he would gain by concentrating his capital and labour on a smaller

It is based on general experience.

space; and under these circumstances if he could get command over more capital and labour so as to apply more to each acre, the land would give him an *Increasing Return;* that is, an extra return larger in proportion than it gives to his present expenditure. But if he has made his calculations rightly, he is using just so much ground as will give him the highest return; and he would lose by concentrating his capital and labour on a smaller area. If he had command over more capital and labour and were to apply more to his present land, he would gain less than he would by taking up more land ; he would get a *Diminishing Return,* that is, an extra return smaller in proportion than he gets for the last applications of capital and labour that he now makes, provided of course that there is meanwhile no perceptible improvement in his agricultural skill. As his sons grow up they will have more capital and labour to apply to land; and in order to avoid obtaining a Diminishing Return, they will want to cultivate more land. But perhaps by this time all the neighbouring land is already taken up, and in order to get more they must buy it or pay a rent for the use of it, or migrate where they can get it for nothing.

This tendency to a Diminishing Return was the cause of Abraham's parting from Lot, and of most of the migrations of which history tells. And wherever the right Its relation to migrations. to cultivate land is much in request, we may be sure that the tendency to a Diminishing Return is in full operation. Were it not for this tendency every farmer could save nearly the whole of his rent by giving up all but a small piece of his land, and bestowing all his capital and labour on that. If all the capital and labour which he would in that case apply to it, gave as good a return in proportion.as that which he now applies to it, he would get from that plot as large a produce as he now gets from his whole farm, and would make a net gain of all his rent save that of the little plot that he retained.

It may be conceded that the ambition of farmers often leads them to take more land than they can properly manage. But when we say that a farmer would gain by applying his capital and labour to a smaller area, we do not necessarily mean that he would get a larger gross produce; we may mean only that the saving in rent would more than counter-balance any probable diminution of the total returns that he got from the land. If a farmer pays a fourth of his produce as rent, he would gain by concentrating his capital and labour on less land, provided the extra capital and labour applied to each acre gave anything more than three-fourths as good a return in proportion as he got from his earlier expenditure.

Its relation to modern farming.

Again, it may be granted that much land, even in a country as advanced as England, is so unskilfully cultivated that it could be made to give more than double its present gross produce if twice the present capital and labour were applied to it skilfully. Very likely those are right who maintain that if all English farmers were as able, wise and energetic as the best are, they might profitably apply twice the capital and labour that is now applied. Assuming rent to be one fourth of the present produce, they might get seven hundredweight of produce for every four that they now get: it is conceivable that with still more improved methods they might get eight hundredweight, or even more. But this does not prove that, *as things are*, further capital and labour could obtain from land an Increasing Return. The fact remains that, taking farmers as they are, with the skill and energy which they actually have, we find as the result of universal observation that there is not open to them a short road to riches by giving up a great part of their land, by concentrating all their capital and labour on the remainder, and saving for their own pockets the rent of all but that remainder. The reason why they cannot do this is told in the Law of Diminishing Return.

It is important to remember that the Return to capital
and labour of which the Law speaks, is measured
by the *amount* of the produce raised independently
of any changes that may meanwhile take place in
the *price* of produce; such, for instance, as might
occur if a new railway had been made in the neighbourhood,
or a new town population had grown up close by. Such
changes will be of vital importance when we come to draw
inferences from the Law of Diminishing Return, and particularly
when we discuss the pressure of increasing population
on the means of subsistence. But they have no bearing on
the Law itself, because that has to do not with the value of
the produce raised, but only with its amount.

The Law relates to the amount of the produce.

We may now formulate the limitations which were implied
under the words "in general" in our provisional statement
of the Law. The Law is a statement of a tendency
which may indeed be held in check for a time by improvements
in the arts of production and by the fitful course of the
development of the full powers of the soil; but which must
ultimately become irresistible if the demand for produce
should increase without limit. Our final statement of the
Law may then be divided into two parts, thus:—

Firstly, although an improvement in the arts of agriculture
may raise the return which land generally
affords to any given amount of capital and
labour; and although the capital and labour
already applied to any piece of land may have been so inadequate
for the development of its full powers, that some
further expenditure on it even with the existing arts of
agriculture would give a more than proportionate return;
yet these conditions are rare in an old country: and, except
when they are present, the application of increased capital
and labour to land will add a less than proportionate amount
to the produce raised, unless there be meanwhile an increase
in the skill of the individual cultivator. Secondly, whatever

Final statement of the Law.

may be the future developments of the arts of agriculture, a continued increase in the application of capital and labour to land must ultimately result in a diminution of the extra produce which can be obtained by a given extra amount of capital and labour.

§ 2. Making use of a term suggested by James Mill, we may regard the capital and labour applied to land as consisting of equal successive *Doses*[1]. As we have seen, the return to the first few doses may perhaps be small and a greater number of doses may get a larger proportionate return; the return to successive doses may even in exceptional cases alternately rise and fall. But our law states that sooner or later (it being always supposed that there is meanwhile no change in the arts of cultivation) a point will be reached after which any further dose will obtain a less proportionate return than the preceding doses. *A Dose of capital and labour.*

The dose which only just remunerates the cultivator may be said to be the *marginal dose*, and the return to it the *marginal return*. If there happens to be in the neighbourhood land that is cultivated but only just pays its expenses, and so gives no surplus for rent, we may suppose this dose applied to it. We can then say that the dose applied to it is applied to land on the *margin of cultivation*, and this way of speaking has the advantage of simplicity. But it is not necessary for the argument to suppose that there is any such land: what we want to fix our minds on is the return to the marginal dose: whether it happens to be applied to poor land or to rich does not matter; all that is necessary is that it *Marginal dose, marginal return, margin of cultivation.*

---

[1] The phrase *a Dose of Capital and Labour* may be taken provisionally to mean £1 of outlay distributed according to the exigencies of the case between the hire of labour, the payment for the use and the wear and tear of capital, and lastly for management. Some difficulties connected with the phrase are discussed in a Note at the end of *Principles*, IV. III.

should be the last dose which can profitably be applied to that land[1].

When we speak of the marginal, or the "last" dose applied to the land, we do not mean the last in time, we mean that dose which is on the margin of profitable expenditure; that is, which is applied so as just to give the ordinary returns to the capital and labour of the cultivator, without affording any surplus. To take a concrete instance, we may suppose a farmer to be thinking of sending the hoers over a field once more; and after a little hesitation he decides that it is worth his while, but only just worth his while to do it. The dose of capital and labour spent on doing it, is then the last dose in our present sense, though there are many doses still to be applied in reaping the crop. Of course the return to this last dose cannot be separated from the others; but we ascribe to it all that part of the produce which we believe would not have been produced if the farmer had decided against the extra hoeing. Since the return to the marginal dose (it does not matter · whether the dose is applied to poor land or rich) just remunerates the cultivator, it follows that he will be just remunerated for the whole of his capital and labour by as many times the marginal return as he has applied doses in all. Whatever he gets in excess of this is the *Surplus Produce* of the land. This surplus is retained by the cultivator if he owns the land himself[2].

The marginal dose not necessarily the last in time.

Surplus Produce.

---

[1] Ricardo was well aware of this: though he did not emphasize it enough. Those opponents of his doctrine who have supposed that it has no application to places where all the land pays a rent, have mistaken the nature of his argument.

[2] Let us seek a graphical illustration. If on any given field there were expended a capital of £50, a certain amount of produce would be raised from it: a certain amount larger than the former would be raised if there were expended on it a capital of £51. The difference between these two amounts may be regarded as the produce due to the fifty-first pound; and if we suppose the capital to be applied in successive doses of £1 each we may speak of this difference as the produce due to the fifty-first dose. Let the doses be repre-

(This Surplus Produce may, under certain conditions, become the rent which the owner of the land can Its relation to rent. exact from the tenant for its use. But, as we shall see hereafter, the full rent of a farm in an old country is made up of three elements: the first being due to the value of the soil as it was made by Nature; the second to improvements made in it by man; and the third, which is often the most important of all, to the growth of a dense and rich population, and to facilities of communication by public roads, railroads, &c.)

In an old country it is seldom possible to discover what was the original state of the land before it was first cultivated. The results of some of man's work are for good and evil fixed in the land; they cannot be distinguished from the results of nature's work, but must be counted with them. The line of division between nature's work and man's work is blurred, and must be drawn more or less arbitrarily. But for most purposes it is best to regard the first difficulties of coping with nature as pretty well conquered before we begin to reckon the farmer's cultivation. Thus the returns that we

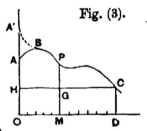

Fig. (3).

sented in order by successive equal divisions of the line *OD*. Let there now be drawn from the division of this line representing the fifty-first dose *M*, a line *MP* at right angles to *OD*, in thickness equal to the length of one of the divisions, and such that its length represents the amount of the produce due to the fifty-first dose. Suppose this done for each separate division up to that corresponding to the last dose which it is found profitable to put on the land. Let this last dose be the 110th at *D*, and *DC* the corresponding return that only just remunerates the farmer. The extremities of such lines will lie on a curve *APC*. The gross produce will be represented by the sum of these lines: i.e. since the thickness of each line is equal to the length of the division on which it stands, by the area *ODCA*. Let *CGH* be drawn parallel to *DO*, cutting *PM* in *G*; then *MG* is equal to *CD*; and since *DC* just remunerates the farmer for one dose, *MG* will just remunerate him for another: and so for all the portions of the thick vertical lines cut off between *OD* and *HC*. Therefore the sum of these, that is, the area *ODCH*, represents the share of the produce that is required to remunerate him; while the remainder, *AHGCPA*, is the Surplus Produce, which under certain conditions becomes the rent.

M. ·7

count as due to the first doses of capital and labour are
generally the largest of all, and the tendency of the return to
diminish shows itself at once.   Having English agriculture
chiefly in view, we may fairly take, as Ricardo did, this as the
typical case[1].

§ 3.   There is no absolute measure of the richness or
fertility of land.   Even if there be no change in
the arts of production, a mere increase in the
demand for produce may invert the order in
which two adjacent pieces of land rank as regards fertility.   The one which gives the smaller produce,
when both are uncultivated, or when the cultivation of both
is equally slight, may rise above the other and justly rank
as the more fertile when both are cultivated with equal
thoroughness.   In other words, many of those lands which are
the least fertile when cultivation is merely extensive, become
among the most fertile when cultivation is intensive.

*Order of rela-
tive fertility
may change
with circum-
stances.*

It has been well said that as the strength of a chain is
that of its weakest link, so fertility is limited by that element
in which it is most deficient.   Those who are in a hurry, will
reject a chain which has one or two very weak links, however
strong the rest may be; and prefer to it a much slighter
chain that has no flaw.   But if there is heavy work to be
done, and they have time to make repairs, they will set the
larger chain in order, and then its strength will exceed that
of the other.   In this we find the explanation of much that
is apparently strange in agricultural history.

The first settlers in a new country generally avoid land
which does not lend itself to immediate cultivation.   They are often repelled by the very
luxuriance of natural vegetation, if it happens
to be of a kind that they do not want.   They do not care to

*Favourite
soils of early
settlers.*

---

[1] That is, we may substitute (fig. 3) the dotted line BA' for BA and
regard $A'BPC$ as the typical curve for the return to capital and labour applied
in English agriculture.

plough land that is at all heavy, however rich it might become if thoroughly worked. They will have nothing to do with water-logged land. They generally select light land which can easily be worked with a double plough, and then they sow their seed broadly, so that the plants when they grow up may have plenty of light and air, and may collect their food from a wide area.

We cannot then call one piece of land more fertile than another till we know something about the skill and enterprise of its cultivators, and the amount of capital and labour at their disposal; and till we know whether the demand for produce is such as to make intensive cultivation profitable with the resources at their disposal. If it is, those lands will be the most fertile which give the highest average returns to a large expenditure of capital and labour; but if not, those will be the most fertile which give the best returns to the first few doses. The term fertility has no meaning except with reference to the special circumstances of a particular time and place.

Fertility is relative to place and time.

§ 4. But further, the order of fertility of different soils is liable to be changed by changes in the methods of cultivation and in the relative values of different crops. Thus when at the end of last century Mr Coke showed how to grow wheat well on light soils by preparing the way with clover, they rose relatively to clay soils; and now though they are still sometimes called from old custom "poor," some of them have a higher value, and are really more fertile, than much of the land that used to be carefully cultivated while many of the light soils were left in a state of nature.

As there is no absolute standard for fertility, so there is none of good cultivation. The best cultivation in the richest parts of the Channel Islands, for instance, involves a lavish expenditure of capital and labour on each acre: for they are near good markets and have a monopoly of an equable and early climate. If left to

Good cultivation a relative term.

nature, the land would not be very fertile; for, though it has many virtues, it has two weak links (being deficient in phosphoric acid and potash). But, partly by the aid of the abundant seaweed on its shores, these links can be strengthened, and the chain thus becomes exceptionally strong. Intense, or as it is ordinarily called in England "good" cultivation, will thus raise £100 worth of early potatoes from a single acre. But an equal expenditure per acre by the farmer in Western America would ruin him; relatively to his circumstances it would not be good, but bad cultivation[1].

§ 5. The statement of the Law of Diminishing Return by Ricardo and other English economists in the earlier half of this century, was inexactly worded. They stated that the first settlers in a new country invariably chose the richest lands, and that as population increased, poorer and poorer soils were gradually brought under cultivation, speaking carelessly as though there were an absolute standard of fertility. But as we have already seen, where land is free, everyone chooses that which is best adapted for his own purpose, and that which will give him, all things considered, the best return for his capital and labour. He looks out, therefore, for land that can be cultivated at once, and passes by land that has any weak links in the chain of its elements of fertility, however strong it may be in some other links. But besides having to avoid malaria, he must think of his communication with his markets and the base of his resources; and in some cases the need for security against the attacks of enemies and wild beasts outweighs all other considerations. It is therefore not to be expected that the lands which were first chosen, should turn out always to be those which ultimately come to be regarded as the most fertile.

---

[1] The changes in the relative fertilities of different kinds of land, which result from changes in the arts of production and the general economic condition of the people are examined a good deal more fully and with the aid of graphic illustrations in *Principles*, IV. III. 3, 4.

The isolated farmer suffers many hardships, which diminish as a village grows up near him ; and when that expands into a large industrial centre, his gain is much greater. All his produce will be worth more ; some things which he used to throw away will fetch a good price. He will find new openings in dairy farming and market gardening ; and with a larger range of produce he will make use of rotations that keep his land always active without denuding it of any of the elements that are necessary for its fertility. But here we are passing away from the causes which determine the *amount* of a farmer's produce, to those which determine its exchange value in terms of the things offered for it by the neighbouring industrial population. We are passing away from the explanation of the law of diminishing return and beginning to study its applications.

Even when cultivation has reached a stage after which each successive dose applied to a field would get a less *amount* of return than the preceding dose, it may be possible for an increase in the population to cause a more than proportional increase in the means of subsistence derived from it. The evil day is indeed only deferred : but it is deferred. The growth of population, if not checked by other causes, must ultimately be checked by the difficulty of obtaining raw produce ; but in spite of the Law of Diminishing Return, the pressure of population on the means of subsistence may be restrained for a long time to come by the opening up of new fields of supply, by the cheapening of railway and steamship communication, and by the growth of organization and knowledge.

In the following chapters we shall have much to say about the evil effects of local congestions of population in making it difficult to get fresh air and light, and in some cases fresh water. Again, natives of New England who have gone to the fertile plains of the West, would often be willing to barter part of their heavy crops for the pure water which the barren

granite soil of their old homes supplied ; and even in England
there are many places, particularly at the sea-side, which are
kept poor by the want of drinking water.

§ 6. In river-fisheries, the extra returns to additional
doses of capital and labour show a rapid diminution. As to
the sea, opinions differ. Its volume is vast, and fish are very
prolific ; and it may be true, as some think, that a practically
unlimited supply can be drawn from the sea without appreciably affecting the numbers that remain.

The produce of mines again, among which may be
reckoned quarries and brickfields, is said to

*The return
from fisheries
and mines.* conform to the Law of Diminishing Return;
but this statement is misleading. The produce
of the field is something other than the soil ; for the field,
properly cultivated, retains its fertility, but the produce of
the mine is part of the mine itself. The supply of agricultural
produce and of fish is a perennial stream ; mines are as it
were Nature's reservoir. The more nearly a reservoir is
exhausted, the greater is the labour of pumping from it ; but
if one man with one pump could pump it out in ten days,
ten men with ten pumps could pump it out in one day:
and when once empty, it would yield no more. So the mines
that are being opened this year might just as easily have been
opened many years ago : if the plans had been properly laid
in advance, and the requisite specialized capital and skill got
ready for the work, ten years' supply of coal might have been
raised in one year without any increased difficulty ; and when
a vein had once given up its treasure, it could produce no more.

There is, however, increasing difficulty in obtaining a
further supply of minerals, except in so far as we obtain
increased power over Nature's stores through improvements
in the arts of mining, and through better knowledge of the
contents of the earth's crust ; and there is no doubt that,
other things being equal, the continued application of capital
and labour to mines will result in a diminishing rate of yield.

CHAPTER IV.

THE GROWTH OF POPULATION.

§ 1. MAN is the chief means of the production of that wealth of which he is himself the ultimate aim; and it seems best to make at this stage some study of the growth of population in numbers, in strength and in character.

In the animal and vegetable world the growth of numbers is governed simply by the tendency of individuals to propagate their species on the one hand, and on the other hand by the struggle for life which thins out vast numbers of the young before they arrive at maturity. In the human race alone the conflict of these two opposing forces is complicated by the influences of forethought and self-control, of prudence and a sense of duty.

The study of the growth of population is often spoken of as though it were a modern one; but in a more or less vague form it has occupied the attention of thoughtful men in all ages of the world. We may however confine ourselves here to some account of its most famous student, Malthus, whose *Essay on the Principle of Population* is the starting point of all modern speculations on the subject[1].

His reasoning consists of three parts which must be kept distinct. The first relates to the supply of labour. By a careful study of facts he proves that every people of whose history we have a trustworthy record, has been so prolific that the growth of its numbers would have been rapid and continuous if it had not been checked either

Malthus.

---

[1] First edition 1798: he published a much enlarged and improved edition in 1803. The history of the Doctrine of Population, and of its connection with the practical needs of different nations at different times, is sketched in *Principles*, IV. III. 1, 2.

by a scarcity of the necessaries of life, or some other cause, that is, by disease, by war, by infanticide, or lastly by voluntary restraint.

His second position relates to the demand for labour. Like the first it is supported by facts, but by a different set of facts. He shows that up to the time at which he wrote no country (as distinguished from a city, such as Rome or Venice,) had been able to obtain an abundant supply of the necessaries of life after its territory had become very thickly peopled. The produce which Nature returns to the work of man is her effective demand for population : and he shows that up to this time a rapid increase in population, when already thick, had not led to a proportionate increase in this demand.

Thirdly, he draws the conclusion that what had been in the past, was likely to be in the future ; and that the growth of population would be checked by poverty or some other cause of suffering, unless it were checked by voluntary restraint. He therefore urges people to use this restraint, and, while leading lives of moral purity, to abstain from very early marriages.

The changes which the course of events has introduced into the doctrine of population relate chiefly to the second and third steps of his reasoning. We have already noticed that the English economists of the earlier half of this century overrated the tendency of an increasing population to press upon the means of subsistence. It was indeed not their fault that they could not foresee the vast developments of steam transport by land and by sea, which have enabled Englishmen of the present generation to obtain the products of the richest lands of the earth at comparatively small cost. But the fact that Malthus did not foresee these changes makes the second and third steps of his argument antiquated in form ; though they are still in a great measure valid in substance. We may then proceed to state the doctrine of population in its modern form.

§ 2. The growth in numbers of a people depends firstly on the "natural increase," that is, the excess of their births over their deaths; and secondly on migration. Natural increase and migration.

The number of births depends chiefly on habits relating to marriage. The age of marriage varies with the climate, being earlier in warm climates than in cold; but in every case the longer marriages are postponed beyond the age that is natural to the climate, the smaller is the birth-rate. Given the climate, the average age of marriage depends chiefly on the ease with which young people can establish themselves, and support a family according to the standard of comfort that prevails among their friends and acquaintances; and therefore it is different in different stations of life. Causes affecting the age of marriage.

In the middle classes a man's income seldom reaches its maximum till he is forty or fifty years old; and the expense of bringing up his children is heavy and lasts for many years. The artisan earns nearly as much at twenty-one as he ever does, unless he rises to a responsible post, but he does not earn much before he is twenty-one: his children are likely to be a considerable expense to him till about the age of fifteen; unless they are sent into a factory, where they may pay their way at a very early age; and lastly the unskilled labourer earns nearly full wages at eighteen, while his children begin to pay their own expenses very early. In consequence, the average age at marriage is highest among the middle classes: it is low among the artisans and lower still among the unskilled labourers. Variations in different classes.

Unskilled labourers, when not so poor as to suffer actual want and not restrained by any external cause, have seldom, if ever, shown a lower power of increase than that of doubling in thirty years; that is, of multiplying a million-fold in six hundred years, a billion-fold in twelve hundred: and hence it might be inferred *a priori* that their increase has never gone on without restraint for any considerable time. This inference is confirmed by the teaching of all history. Throughout Europe during the Middle Ages, and in some parts of it even up to the present time, unmarried labourers have usually slept in the farm-house or with their parents; while a

Hindrances to early marriage in stationary rural districts.

married pair have generally required a house for themselves: when a village has as many hands as it can well employ, the number of houses is not increased, and young people wait as best they can. There are many parts of Europe even now in which custom, exercising almost the force of law, prevents more than one son in each family from marrying; he is generally the eldest, but in some places the youngest: if any other son marries, he must leave the village. When great material prosperity, and the absence of all extreme poverty are found in old-fashioned corners of the Old World, the explanation generally lies in some such custom as this with all its evils and hardships.

§ 3.   In this respect the position of the hired agricultural labourer has changed very much. The towns are now always open to him and his children; and if he betakes himself to the New World he is likely

Influence of peasant properties.

to succeed better than any other class of emigrants. But the gradual rise in the value of land and its growing scarcity are tending to check the increase of population in some districts in which the system of peasant properties prevails; especially those in which there is not much enterprise for opening out new trades or for emigration, and parents feel that the social position of their children will depend on the amount of their land.

On the other hand there seem to be no conditions more favourable to the rapid growth of numbers than those of the agricultural districts of new countries. Land is to be had in abundance, railways and steamships carry away the produce of the land; and they bring back in exchange implements of advanced types, and many of the comforts and luxuries of life. The "farmer," as the peasant proprietor is called in America, finds therefore that a large family is not a burden, but an assistance to him. He and they live healthy out-of-door lives; there is nothing to check, but everything to stimulate the growth of numbers. The natural increase is aided by immigration; and thus, in spite of the fact that some classes of the inhabitants of large cities in America are, it is said, reluctant to have many children, the population has increased sixteen-fold in the last hundred years.

§ 4. The growth of population in England has a more clearly defined history than that in the United Kingdom, and we shall find some interest in noticing its chief movements. Population in England.

The restraints on the increase of numbers during the Middle Ages were the same in England as else-where. In England as elsewhere the religious orders were a refuge to those for whom no estab-lishment in marriage could be provided; and religious celibacy while undoubtedly acting in some measure as an independent check on the growth of population, is in the main to be regarded rather as a method in which the broad natural forces tending to restrain population expressed themselves, than as an addition to them. Infectious and contagious diseases, both endemic and epidemic, were caused by dirty habits of life, which were even worse in England than in the South of Europe; and famines were caused by the failures of good harvests and the difficulties of communication, though this evil was less in England than elsewhere. Country life was, as elsewhere, rigid in its habits; young people found it difficult to establish themselves until some other married pair had passed from the scene and made a vacancy in their own parish; for, though artisans and domestic retainers moved about a good deal, migration was seldom thought of by an agricultural labourer. Restraints during Middle Ages.

In the latter half of the seventeenth and the first half of
the eighteenth century the central government
exerted itself to hinder the adjustment of the
supply of population in different parts of the
country to the demand for it by Settlement Laws, which
made any one chargeable to a parish who had resided there
forty days, but ordered that he might be sent home by force
at any time within that period. Landlords and farmers were
so eager to prevent people from getting a "settlement" in
their parish that they put great difficulties in the way of
building cottages, and sometimes even razed them to the
ground. In consequence the agricultural population of England was stationary during the hundred years ending with
1760; while the manufactures were not yet sufficiently
developed to absorb large numbers. This retardation in the
growth of numbers was partly caused by, and partly a cause
of, a rise in the standard of living; a chief element of which
was an increased use of wheat in the place of inferior grains
as the food of the common people.

Seventeenth and eighteenth centuries.

From 1760 onwards those who could not establish themselves at home found little difficulty in getting employment
in the new manufacturing or mining districts, where the
demand for workers often kept the local authorities from
enforcing the removal clauses of the Settlement Act. To
these districts young people resorted freely, and the birth-
rate in them became exceptionally high; but so did the death-
rate also; the net result being a fairly rapid growth of population. At the end of the century, when Malthus wrote his
Essay, the Poor Law again began to influence the age of marriage, but this time in the direction of making it unduly early.

The sufferings of the working classes caused by a
series of famines and by the French War made
some measure of relief necessary; and the need of
large bodies of recruits for the army and navy was an additional inducement to tender-hearted people to be somewhat

*The nine-
teenth cen-
tury.*

liberal in their allowances to a large family, with the practical effect of making the father of many children often able to procure more indulgences for himself without working than he could have got by hard work if he had been unmarried or had only a small family. Those who availed themselves most of this bounty, were naturally the laziest and meanest of the people, those with least self-respect and enterprise. So although there was in the manufacturing towns a fearful mortality, particularly of infants, the quantity of the people increased fast; but its quality improved little, if at all, till the passing of the New Poor Law in 1834. Since that time the rapid growth of the town population has, as we shall see in the next Chapter, tended to increase mortality; but this has been counteracted by the growth of temperance, of medical knowledge, of sanitation and of general cleanliness. Emigration has increased, the age of marriage has been slightly raised, and a somewhat less proportion of the whole population are married; but, on the other hand, the ratio of births to a marriage has risen; the net result being that population has grown nearly steadily.

§ 5. Early in this century, when wages were low and wheat was dear, the working classes generally spent more than half their income on bread: and consequently a rise in the price of wheat diminished marriages very much among them: that is, it diminished very much the number of marriages by banns. But it raised the income of many members of the well-to-do classes, and therefore often increased the number of marriages by license. Since however these were but a small part of the whole, the net effect was to lower the marriage-rate. But as time went on, the price of wheat fell and wages rose, till now the working classes spend on the average less than a quarter of their incomes on bread; and in consequence the chief influence on the marriage-rate is exercised, not by the price of wheat, but by variations of commercial prosperity.

Modern causes affecting marriage-rate.

Since 1873 though the average real income of the population of England has indeed been increasing, its rate of increase has been less than in the preceding years. But meanwhile there has been a great fall of prices, and consequently a great fall in the money-incomes of many classes of society; and people are governed in their calculations as to whether they can afford to marry or not, more by the money income which they expect to be able to get, than by elaborate calculations of changes in its purchasing power. The standard of living therefore among the working classes has been rising rapidly, perhaps more rapidly than at any other time in English history: their household expenditure measured in money has remained about stationary, and measured in goods has increased very fast. The English marriage-rate fell from 8·8 per 1000 in 1873, to 7·1 in 1886, the lowest rate that has occurred since civil registration began; but it has somewhat risen again since then.

[1] The latter half of *Principles* IV. iv. contains a good many statistical tables relating to the growth of population in England, and to a comparison of the birth, death, and marriage-rates of different countries of the Western world. It is seen that the marriage-rate is generally highest where the number of early marriages is the greatest; and so also is the fecundity of marriages. The general mortality is high wherever the birth-rate is high.

CHAPTER V.

THE HEALTH AND STRENGTH OF THE POPULATION.

§ 1. WE have next to consider the conditions on which depend health and strength, physical, mental and moral. They are the basis of industrial effici- ency, on which the production of material wealth depends; while on the other hand the chief importance of material wealth lies in the fact that, when wisely used, it increases the health and strength, physical, mental and moral of the human race.

The basis of industrial efficiency.

In many occupations industrial efficiency requires little else than physical vigour; that is, muscular strength, a good constitution and energetic habits. In estimating muscular, or indeed any other kind of strength for industrial purposes, we must take account of the number of hours in the day, of the number of days in the year, and the number of years in the lifetime, during which it can be exerted. But with this precaution we can measure a man's muscular exertion by the number of feet through which his work would raise a pound weight, if it were applied directly to this use; or in other words by the number of "foot pounds" of work that he does[1].

Physical strength.

---

[1] This measure can be applied directly to most kinds of navvies' and porters' work, and indirectly to many kinds of agricultural work. In a controversy that was waged after the great agricultural lock-out as to the relative efficiency of unskilled labour in the South and North of England, the most trustworthy measure was found in the number of tons of material that a man would load into a cart in a day.

In backward countries, particularly where there is not much use of horses or other draught animals, a great part of men's and women's work may be measured fairly well by the muscular exertion involved in it. But in England less than one-sixth of the industrial classes are now engaged on work of this kind; while the force exerted by steam-engines alone is more than twenty times as much as could be done by the muscles of all Englishmen.

Although the power of sustaining great muscular exertion

General vigour.

seems to rest on constitutional strength and other physical conditions, yet even it depends also on force of will, and strength of character. Energy of this kind, which may perhaps be taken to be the strength of the man, as distinguished from that of his body, is moral rather than physical; but yet it depends on the physical condition of nervous strength[1]. This strength of the man himself, this resolution, energy and self-mastery, or in short this "vigour" is the source of all progress: it shows itself in great deeds, in great thoughts and in the capacity for true religious feeling.

§ 2. In discussing the growth of numbers a little has been said incidentally of the causes which determine length of life: but they are in the main the same as those which determine constitutional strength and vigour, and they will occupy our attention again in the present chapter.

The first of these causes is the climate. A warm climate

Influence of climate.

is not altogether hostile to high intellectual and artistic work: but it prevents people from being able to endure very hard exertion of any kind continued for a long time.

Climate has also a large share in determining the neces-

The necessaries of life.

saries of life; the first of which is food. Food must supply the nitrogenous and other elements that

---

[1] This must be distinguished from nervousness, which, as a rule, indicates a general deficiency of nervous strength; though sometimes it proceeds from nervous irritability or want of balance.

are required to build up growing tissues and to repair the waste of the body. It must also afford heat, some of which can be converted into muscular force; and for this purpose carbonaceous food, when it can be properly digested, is the cheapest[1]. Much also depends on the proper preparation of food, and a skilled housewife with ten shillings a week to spend on food will often do more for the health and strength of her family than an unskilled one with twenty. The great infant mortality among the poor is largely due to the want of care and judgment in preparing their food; and those who do not entirely succumb to this want of motherly care often grow up with enfeebled constitutions. Even in London in the seventeenth and eighteenth centuries the mortality was eight per cent. greater when corn was dear than when it was cheap: and though the increase of wealth and of charity and the constant supply of cheap foreign corn has caused the worst effects of hunger to cease, yet the want of fitting food is still a frequent cause of that general weakening of the system which renders it unable to resist disease.

We have already seen that the necessaries for efficiency vary with the nature of the work to be done, but we must now examine this subject a little more closely.

As regards muscular work in particular, there is a close connection between the supply of food that a man has, and his available strength. If the work is intermittent, as that of some dock labourers, a cheap but nutritious grain diet is sufficient. But for very heavy continuous strain, such as is involved in puddlers' and the hardest navvies' work, food is required which can be digested and assimilated even when the body is tired. This quality is still more essential in the food of the higher grades of labour which involve increased nervous strain, though the quantity required is generally small.

Other material necessaries.

[1] The nitrogenous elements are most easily got from animal food. They exist also in vegetable foods; but not in a form that is so easily digested.

M. 8

After food, the next necessaries of life and labour, are clothing, house-room and firing; when they are deficient, the mind becomes torpid, and ultimately the physical constitution is undermined.

§ 3. Next come three closely allied conditions of vigour, Hope, freedom namely, hopefulness, freedom, and change. All and change. history is full of the record of inefficiency caused in varying degrees by slavery, serfdom, and other forms of civil and political oppression and repression. Freedom and hope increase not only man's willingness but also his power for work; physiologists tell us that a given exertion consumes less of the store of nervous energy if done under the stimulus of pleasure than of pain: and without hope there is no enterprise. Security of person and property are two conditions of this hopefulness and freedom; but security always involves restraints on freedom, and it is one of the most difficult problems of civilization to discover how to obtain the security, which is a condition of freedom, without too great a sacrifice of freedom itself.

Changes of work, of scene, and of personal associations bring new thoughts, call attention to the imperfections of old methods, stimulate a "divine discontent," and in every way develop creative energy. A shifting of places enables the more powerful and original minds to find full scope for their energies and to rise to important positions: whereas those who stay at home are often over much kept in their places. Few men are prophets in their own land; neighbours and relations are generally the last to pardon the faults and to recognize the merits of those who are less docile and more enterprising than those around them. It is doubtless chiefly for this reason that in almost every part of England a disproportionately large share of the best energy and enterprise is to be found among those who were born elsewhere.

Freedom so far has been regarded as freedom from external bonds. But that higher freedom, which comes of self-mastery, is an even more important condition for the highest work. The elevation of the ideals of life on which this depends, is due on the one side to political and economic causes, and on the other to personal and religious influences; among which the influence of the mother in early childhood is supreme.

§ 4. Bodily and mental health and strength are much influenced by occupation[1]. At the beginning of this century the conditions of factory work were *Influence of occupation.* needlessly unhealthy and oppressive for all, and especially for young children. But Factory and Education Acts have removed the worst of these evils from factories; though many of them still linger about domestic industries and the smaller workshops. Infant mortality also is diminishing, though there remains much room for improvement in this direction.

The higher wages, the greater intelligence, and the better medical facilities of townspeople should cause infant mortality to be much lower among them than in the country. But it is generally higher, especially where there are many mothers who neglect their family duties in order to earn money wages.

In almost all countries there is a constant migration towards the towns. The large towns and especially London absorb the very best blood from *Town life.* all the rest of England; the most enterprising, the most highly gifted, those with the highest *physique* and the strongest characters go there to find scope for their abilities. But by the time their children and children's children have grown up

---

[1] The rate of mortality is low among ministers of religion and schoolmasters; among the agricultural classes, and in some other industries such as those of wheelwrights, shipwrights and coal-miners. It is high in lead and tin mining, in file-making and earthenware manufacture. But neither these nor any other regular trade show as high a rate of mortality as is found among London general labourers and costermongers; while the highest of all is that of servants in inns. Such occupations are not directly injurious to health, but they attract those who are weak in physique and in character and they encourage irregular habits.

8—2

without healthy play, and without fresh air, there is little trace left of their original vigour[1].

There is perhaps no better use of public and private money than in providing public parks and playgrounds in large cities, in contracting with railways to increase the number of the workmen's trains run by them, and in helping those of the working classes who are willing to leave the large towns to do so, and to take their industries with them; while money spent on reducing the cost of living in large towns by building workmen's houses at a loss or in other ways, is likely to do almost as much harm as good, and sometimes even more. If the numbers of the working classes in the large towns are reduced to those whose work must be carried on there, the scarcity of their labour will enable them to command high wages; and therefore if sanitary laws and rules against overcrowding are rigidly enforced, and space enough is secured to provide opportunities of healthy play for their children, those who live in large towns will have a better chance of leaving a healthy progeny behind them; and meanwhile some check will be given to the migration from the country to the towns.

§ 5. In the earlier stages of civilization natural selection and competition made it the rule that those, who were strongest and most vigorous, left the largest progeny behind them. It is to this cause, more than any other, that the progress of the

[1] This is seen even in trades that require but little muscular strength; only a very small proportion of those artisans to whom London owes its pre-eminence as a centre of highly skilled work come from parents who were born there; and there are scarcely any whose grandparents were born there.

The death-rate of large towns gives no just indication of their effect on the health and vigour of the people; chiefly because many of the town influences which lower vigour do not appreciably affect mortality. Other reasons are that the immigrants into towns are generally picked lives and in the full strength of youth; and that young people whose parents live in the country generally go home to die. The mortality of females in London between the ages of fifteen and thirty-five is for this reason abnormally low.

human race, as of all other forms of life, is due; and though in the later stages of civilization the upper classes have commonly married late, and in consequence have had fewer children than the working classes, this has. been compensated for by the fact that among the working classes

Nature's tendency to weed out the weak and cause the strong to survive

themselves the old rule has held; and the vigour of the nation that is tending to be damped out among the upper classes is thus replenished by the fresh stream of strength that is constantly welling up from below. But in France for a long time, recently in America, and to a less extent in England, there has been some tendency for the abler and more intelligent part of the working class population to avoid having large families ; and this is a source of great danger.

There are increasing reasons for fearing, that though the progress of medical science and sanitation is saving from death a continually increasing number of the children of those who are feeble physically

is often counteracted by man.

and mentally; yet meanwhile those who are strong, are tending to defer their marriages and in other ways to limit the number of children whom they leave behind them. The causes are partly selfish and partly unselfish; and the former probably do less harm than the latter; for perhaps it is best for the world that hard and frivolous people should leave but few descendants of their own type. But some people marry late, and have few children, in consequence of a desire to secure as good a social position as possible for themselves and their children. This desire contains many elements that fall short of the highest ideals of human aims, and in some cases, a few that are distinctly base; but after all it has been one of the chief factors of progress, and those who are affected by it include many of the best and strongest of the race. Such persons, having a high sense of duty, are specially likely to be influenced by the doctrine that large families are injurious to

the world and that they can do better for a small than for a
large family.

There are other considerations of which account ought to
Practical con- be taken; but so far as the points discussed in
clusion.   this chapter are concerned, it seems *primâ facie*
advisable that people should not bring children into the world,
till they can see their way to giving them at least as good an
education both physical and mental as they themselves had;
and that it is best to marry moderately early provided there
is sufficient self-control to keep the family within the requisite
bounds without transgressing moral laws. The general adoption of these principles of action, combined with an adequate
provision of fresh air and of healthy play for our town
populations, could hardly fail to cause the strength and vigour
of the race to improve. And we shall presently find reasons
for believing that if the strength and vigour of the race
improves, the increase of numbers will not for a long time
to come cause a diminution of the average real income of the
people.

Thus then the progress of knowledge, and in particular
The forces of of medical science, the ever-growing activity and
good and evil. wisdom of Government in all matters relating to
health, and the increase of material wealth, all tend to lessen
mortality and to increase health and strength, and to lengthen
life. On the other hand, vitality is lowered and the death-
rate raised by the rapid increase of town life, and by the
tendency of the higher strains of the population to marry
later and to have fewer children than the lower. If the
former set of causes were alone in action, but so regulated as
to avoid the danger of over-population, it is probable that
man would quickly rise to a physical and mental excellence
far superior to any that the world has yet known; while if
the latter set acted unchecked, he would speedily degenerate.
As it is, the two sets hold one another very nearly in balance,
the former slightly preponderating. While the population

of England continues to increase, those who are out of health in body or mind are certainly not an increasing part of the whole; and the rest are much better fed and clothed, and with a few exceptions are stronger than they were.

It is sometimes urged that the death-rate in some large towns, and especially in London, is not as high as might have been anticipated if town life is really injurious to health and vigour.   But this argument seems untrustworthy, partly because many of the town influences which lower vigour, do not much affect mortality; and partly because the majority of immigrants into the towns are in the full strength of youth, and of more than average energy and courage; while young people whose parents live in the country generally go home when they become seriously ill.

It is not to be concluded from this that the race is degenerating physically, nor even that its nervous strength is on the whole decaying.   On the contrary the opposite is plainly true of those boys and girls who are able to enter freely into modern outdoor amusements, who frequently spend holidays in the country and whose food, clothing and medical care are abundant, and governed by the best modern knowledge.   But until quite recently the children of the working classes in large towns have had a bad time: and it is doubtful whether the recent diminution of their hours of labour, the advances of sanitation and medical science, improvement of their food and clothing, of their education and even in some cases their playgrounds quite make up for the evils inherent in town life[1].

[1] Manchester and other very large towns are not now growing as fast as they were doing earlier in this century.   Not only are the centres of such towns more and more taken up by warehouses and other buildings which are occupied in the day time by people who live in the suburbs; but further, the medium sized towns and spreading industrial districts are growing fast partly at the expense of very large towns.   This change seems likely to be hastened by the growing cheapness and efficiency of the electrical transmission of force.

CHAPTER VI.

INDUSTRIAL TRAINING.

§ 1. HAVING discussed the causes which govern the growth of a numerous and vigorous population, we have next to consider the training that is required to develop its industrial efficiency.

Very backward races are unable to keep on at any kind

Unskilled labour a relative term.

of work for a long time; and even the simplest form of what we regard as unskilled work is skilled work relatively to them; for they have not the requisite assiduity, and they can acquire it only by a long course of training. But where education is universal, an occupation may fairly be classed as unskilled, though it requires a knowledge of reading and writing. Again, in districts in which manufactures have long been domiciled, a habit of responsibility, of carefulness and promptitude in handling expensive machinery and materials becomes the common property of all; and then much of the work of tending machinery is said to be entirely mechanical and unskilled, and to call forth no human faculty that is worthy of esteem. But in fact it is probable that not one-tenth of the present populations of the world have the mental and moral faculties, the intelligence, and the self-control that are required for it: perhaps not one half could be made to do the work well by steady training for two generations. Even of a manufacturing population only a small part are capable of doing many of the tasks that appear at first sight to be entirely monotonous. Machine-weaving, for instance, simple as it seems, is divided into higher and lower grades; and most of those who work in the lower grades have not "the stuff in them" that is required for weaving with several colours. And the differences are even greater in industries that deal with hard materials, wood, metals, or ceramics.

Some kinds of manual work require long-continued practice in one set of operations, but these cases are not very common, and they are becoming rarer: for machinery is constantly taking over work that requires manual skill of this kind. It is indeed true that a general command over the use of one's fingers is a very important element of industrial efficiency; but this is the result chiefly of nervous strength, and self-mastery. It is of course developed by training, but the greater part of this may be of a general character and not special to the particular occupation; just as a good cricketer soon learns to play tennis well, so a skilled artisan can often move into other trades without any great and lasting loss of efficiency.

Manual skill that is so specialized, as to be wholly incapable of being transferred from one occupation to another, is becoming steadily less and less important. Putting aside for the present the faculties of artistic perception and artistic creation, we may say that what makes one occupation higher than another, what makes the workers of one town or country more efficient than those of another, is chiefly a superiority in general sagacity and energy which is not specialized to any one trade.

To be able to bear in mind many things at a time, to have everything ready when wanted, to act promptly and show resource when anything goes wrong, to accommodate oneself quickly to changes in details of the work done, to be steady and trustworthy, to have always a reserve of force which will come out in emergency, these are the qualities

which make a great industrial people. They are not peculiar
to any occupation, but are wanted in all; and if they cannot
always be easily transferred from one trade to other kindred
trades, the chief reason is that they require to be supplemented by some knowledge of materials and familiarity with
special processes.

We may then use the term *general ability* to denote

General and
Specialized
ability.

those faculties and that general knowledge and
intelligence which are in varying degrees the
common property of all the higher grades of
industry: while that manual dexterity and that acquaintance
with particular materials and processes which are required for
the special purposes of individual trades may be classed as
specialized ability.

§ 2.   General ability depends largely on the surroundings

Influence of
the home.

of childhood and youth. In this the first and far
the most powerful influence is that of the mother.
Next comes the influence of the father, of other children, and
in some cases of servants. As years pass on the child of the
working man learns a great deal from what he sees and hears
going on around him; and when we enquire into the advantages for starting in life which children of the well-to-do
classes have over those of artisans, and which these in their
turn have over the children of unskilled labourers, we shall
have to consider these influences of home more in detail.
But at present we may pass to consider the more general influences of school education.

Little need be said of general education; though the in-

School.

fluence even of that on industrial efficiency is
greater than it appears. It is true that the
children of the working classes must very often leave school,
when they have but learnt the elements of reading, writing,
arithmetic and drawing; and it is sometimes argued that part
of the little time spent on these subjects would be better
given to practical work. But the advance made during

school-time is important not so much on its own account, as for the power of future advance which a school education gives. Reading and writing afford the means of that wider intercourse which leads to breadth and elasticity of mind, and which is enabling the working man of to-day to be as capable a citizen as was the country gentleman of last century[1].

§ 3. Technical education used to mean little more than imparting that manual dexterity and that ele- Technical mentary knowledge of machinery and processes, education. which an intelligent lad quickly picks up for himself when his work has begun; though if he has learnt it beforehand, he can perhaps earn a few shillings more at starting than if he had been quite ignorant. But such so-called education does not develop faculties; it rather hinders them from being developed. A lad, who has picked up the knowledge for himself, has educated himself by so doing; and he is likely to make better progress in the future than one who has been taught in a school of this old-fashioned kind. Technical education is however outgrowing its mistakes; and is aiming, firstly, at giving a general command over the use of eyes and fingers[2] (though there are signs that this work is being taken over by general education, to

---

[1] It is true that learning to spell does not educate the faculties to any considerable extent, and that the time spent on it is nearly wasted. If spelling and pronunciation could be brought into harmony in the English language, as they are in most other languages, children would, it has been estimated, be able to read fluently a year earlier than they can now.

[2] According to the best English opinions, technical education for the higher ranks of industry should keep the aim of developing the faculties almost as constantly before it as general education does. It should rest on the same basis as a thorough general education, but should go on to work out in detail special branches of knowledge for the benefit of particular trades. Our aim should be to add the scientific training in which the countries of Western Europe are ahead of us to that daring and restless energy and those practical instincts, which seldom flourish unless the best years of youth are spent in the workshop; recollecting always that whatever a youth learns for himself by direct experience in well-conducted works, teaches him more and stimulates his mental activity more than if it were taught him by a master in a technical school with model instruments.

which it properly belongs); and secondly at imparting artistic skill and knowledge, and methods of investigation, which are useful in particular occupations, but are seldom properly acquired in the course of practical work.

The old apprenticeship system is not exactly suited to modern conditions and it has fallen into disuse; but a substitute for it is wanted. So many and various are the branches of any great modern industry that it would be impossible for the employers to undertake, as they used to do, that every youth committed to their care should learn all; and indeed a lad of ordinary ability would be bewildered by the attempt. But the employer might bind himself to see that the apprentice is thoroughly taught in the workshop all the subdivisions of one great division of his trade, instead of letting him learn only one of these subdivisions, as too often happens now. The apprentice's training would then often be as broad as if he had been taught the whole of the trade as it existed a few generations ago; and it might be supplemented by a theoretical knowledge of all branches of the trade, acquired in a technical school.

Apprentice-ships.

§ 4. It is true that there are many kinds of work which can be done as efficiently by an uneducated as by an educated workman: and that the higher branches of education are of little direct use except to employers and foremen and a comparatively small number of artisans. But a good education confers great indirect benefits even on the ordinary workman. It stimulates his mental activity; it fosters in him a habit of wise inquisitiveness; it makes him more intelligent, more ready, more trustworthy in his ordinary work; it raises the tone of his life in working hours and out of working hours; it is thus an important means towards the production of material wealth; at the same time that, regarded as an end in itself, it is inferior to none of those which the production of material wealth can be made to subserve.

Indirect benefits of a good education.

We must however look in another direction for a part, perhaps the greater part, of the immediate economic gain which the nation may derive from an improvement in the general and technical education of the mass of the people. We must look not so much at those who stay in the rank and file of the working classes, as at those who rise from a humble birth to join the higher ranks of skilled artisans, to become foremen or employers, to advance the boundaries of science, or possibly to add to the national wealth in art and literature.

The laws which govern the birth of genius are inscrutable. It is probable that the percentage of children of the working classes, who are endowed with natural abilities of the highest order, is not so great as that of the children of people, who have attained

At present much natural ability runs to waste.

or have inherited a higher position in society. But since the manual labour classes are four or five times as numerous as all other classes put together, it is not unlikely that more than half the best natural genius that is born into the country belongs to them ; and of this a great part is fruitless for want of opportunity. There is no extravagance more prejudicial to the growth of national wealth than that wasteful negligence which allows genius that happens to be born of lowly parentage to expend itself in lowly work. No change would conduce so much to a rapid increase of material wealth as an improvement in our schools, and especially those of the middle grades; provided it is combined with an extensive system of scholarships, which will enable the clever son of a working man to rise gradually from school to school till he had the best theoretical and practical education which the age can give[1].

§ 5. Most parents are willing enough to do for their children what their own parents did for them ; and perhaps even to go a little beyond it, if they find themselves among

[1] The influence exerted on national prosperity by education of all kinds general, technical and artistic, is now attracting increased attention, and England is setting herself to profit by the experiences of other countries in this matter.

neighbours who happen to have a rather higher standard.

Sacrifices of parents for the education of their children. But to do more than this requires, in addition to the moral qualities of unselfishness and a warmth of affection that are perhaps not rare, a certain habit of mind which is as yet not very common. It requires the habit of distinctly realizing the future, and of regarding a distant event as of nearly the same importance as if it were close at hand,—a habit which is at once a chief product and a chief cause of civilization, and is seldom fully developed except among the middle and upper classes of the more cultivated nations.

Industrial grades. Mill was so much impressed by the difficulties that beset a parent in the attempt to bring up his son to an occupation widely different in character from his own, that he said[1]:—"So complete, indeed, has hitherto been the separation, so strongly marked the line of demarcation, between the different grades of labourers, as to be almost equivalent to an hereditary distinction of caste; each employment being chiefly recruited from the children of those already employed in it, or in employments of the same rank with it in social estimation, or from the children of persons who, if originally of a lower rank, have succeeded in raising themselves by their exertions. The liberal professions are mostly supplied by the sons of either the professional or the idle classes: the more highly skilled manual employments are filled up from the sons of skilled artisans or the class of tradesmen who rank with them: the lower classes of skilled employments are in a similar case; and unskilled labourers, with occasional exceptions, remain from father to son in their pristine condition. Consequently the wages of each class have hitherto been regulated by the increase of its own population, rather than that of the general population of the country."

But he goes on, "The changes, however, now so rapidly taking place in usages and ideas are undermining all these

---

[1] Book II. ch. XIV. § 2.

distinctions;" and, since he wrote, the broad lines of division which he pointed out have been almost obliterated by the rapid action of those causes which, as we saw earlier in the chapter, are reducing the amount of skill and ability required in some occupations and increasing it in others.

Divisions between grades are fading away.

We cannot any longer regard different occupations as distributed among four great planes; but we may perhaps think of them as resembling a long flight of steps of unequal breadth, some of them being so broad as to act as landing stages. Or even better still we might picture to ourselves two flights of stairs, one representing the "hard-handed industries" and the other "the soft-handed industries;" because the vertical division between these two is in fact as broad and as clearly marked as the horizontal division between any two grades.

But though parents generally bring up their children to occupations in their own grade, and therefore the total supply of labour in any grade in one generation is in a great measure determined by the numbers in

Provisional conclusion.

that grade in the preceding generation, yet within the grade itself there is greater mobility. If the advantages of any one occupation in it rise above the average, there is a quick influx of youth from other occupations into the grade. The vertical movement from one grade to another is seldom very rapid or on a very large scale; but, when the advantages of a grade have risen relatively to the difficulty of the work required of it, many small streams of labour, both youthful and adult, will begin to flow towards it; and though none of them may be very large, they will together have a sufficient volume to satisfy before long the increased demand for labour in that grade.

We must defer to a later stage a fuller discussion of the obstacles which the conditions of any place and time oppose to the free mobility of labour, and also of the inducements which they offer to anyone to change his occupation or to bring up his son to an occupation different from his own. But we have seen enough to conclude that, other things being equal, an increase in the earnings that are to be got by labour increases its rate of growth; or, in other words, a rise in its demand price increases the supply of it. If the state of knowledge, and of social and domestic habits be given, then the vigour of the population, and both the numbers and vigour of any trade in particular, may be said to have a supply price in this sense, that there is a certain level of the demand price which will keep them stationary; that a higher price would cause them to increase, and that a lower price would cause them to decrease. The same proposition holds true as to the numbers of population as a whole in nearly all countries. But the influence of economic causes on the growth of numbers is very uncertain in its action especially where, as in France, all but the very poorest classes lay great store on the inheritance of family property.

During these three chapters we have discussed the supply of labour mainly as a means towards the production of material wealth. But here, as in every other economic inquiry, we must bear in mind that the only aim of that production is the development of the people in numbers, in health, in strength, in happiness and above all in character.

CHAPTER VII.

THE GROWTH OF WEALTH.

§ 1. The earliest forms of wealth were probably imple- *Early forms of* ments for hunting and fishing, and personal orna- *wealth.* ments; and, in cold countries, clothing and huts.
As numbers thickened and the people settled down to agriculture, cultivated land took the first place in the inventory of wealth; and that part of the value of the land which was due to improvements (among which wells held a conspicuous place) became the chief element of capital, in the narrower sense of the term. Next in importance came houses, domesticated animals, and in some places boats and ships; but the implements of production whether for use in agriculture or in domestic manufactures remained for a long time of little value. During all this time the only trade that used very expensive implements was the trade of carrying goods by water: the weavers' looms, the husbandman's ploughs and the blacksmith's anvils were of simple construction and were of little account beside the merchant's ships. But in the eighteenth century England inaugurated the era of expensive implements.

The implements of the English farmer had been rising slowly in value for a long time; but the progress *Modern forms* was quickened in the eighteenth century. After *of wealth.* a while the use first of water power and then of steam power caused the rapid substitution of expensive machinery for inexpensive hand tools in one department of production after another. As in earlier times the most expensive implements were ships and, in some cases, canals for navigation and irrigation; so now they are the means of locomotion in general—railways and tramways, canals, docks and ships, telegraph and telephone systems and water-works: even gas-works might almost come under this head, on the ground that a great part of their plant is devoted to distributing the gas. After these come mines and iron and chemical works, ship-building yards, printing-presses, and other large factories full of expensive machinery. And, on whichever side we look, we find that the progress and diffusion of knowledge are constantly leading to the adoption of new processes and new machinery, which economize human effort on condition that some of the effort is spent a good while before the attainment of the ultimate ends to which it is directed.

As civilization progresses, man develops new wants, and new and more expensive ways of gratifying them. There seems to be no good reason for believing that we are anywhere near a stationary state in which there will be no new important wants to be satisfied; in which there will be no more room for profitably investing present effort in providing for the future; and in which the accumulation of wealth will cease to have any reward. The whole history of man shows that his wants expand with the growth of his wealth and knowledge. And with the growth of openings for the investment of capital there is a constant increase in that surplus of production over the necessaries of life, which gives the power to save.

§ 2. The habit of distinctly realizing the future and providing for it has developed itself slowly and
Slow growth of the habit of providing for the future.
fitfully in the course of man's history. Travellers tell us of tribes who might double their resources and enjoyments without increasing their total labour, if they would only apply a little in advance the means that lie within their power and their knowledge; as, for instance, by fencing in their little plots of vegetables against the intrusion of wild animals.

But even this apathy is perhaps less strange than the wastefulness that is found now among some classes in our own country. Cases are not rare of men who alternate between earning two or three pounds a week and being reduced to the verge of starvation: the utility of a shilling to them when they are in employment is less than that of a penny when they are out of it, and yet they never attempt to make provision for the time of need. At the opposite extreme there are misers, in some of whom the passion for saving borders on insanity; while, even among peasant proprietors and some other classes, we meet not unfrequently with people who carry thrift so far as to stint themselves of necessaries, and to impair their power of future work. Thus they lose every way: they never really enjoy life; while the income which their stored-up wealth brings them is less than they would have got from the increase of their earning power, if they had invested in themselves the wealth that they have accumulated in a material form.

In India, and to a less extent in Ireland, we find people who do indeed abstain from immediate enjoyment and save up considerable sums with great self-sacrifice, but spend all their savings in lavish festivities at funerals and marriages. They make intermittent provision for the near future, but scarcely any permanent provision for the distant future: the great engineering works by which their productive resources have been so much increased, have been made chiefly with the capital of the much less self-denying race of Englishmen.

Thus the causes which control the accumulation of wealth differ widely in different countries and different ages. They are not quite the same among any two races, and perhaps not even among any two social classes in the same race. They depend much on social and religious sanctions; and it is remarkable how, when the binding force of custom has been in any degree loosened, differences of personal character will cause neighbours brought up under like conditions to differ from one another more widely and more frequently in their habits of extravagance or thrift than in almost any other respect.

§ 3.　The thriftlessness of early times was in a great measure due to the want of security that those who
made provision for the future would enjoy it:
only those, who were already wealthy, were strong
enough to hold what they had saved; the laborious and self-
denying peasant who had heaped up a little store of wealth
only to see it taken from him by a stronger hand, was a
constant warning to his neighbours to enjoy their pleasure
and their rest when they could.　The border country between
England and Scotland made little progress so long as it was
liable to incessant forays; there was very little saving by the
French peasants in the last century when they could escape
the plunder of the tax-gatherer only by appearing to be poor,
or by Irish cottiers, who, on many estates, even a generation
ago, were compelled to follow the same course in order to
avoid the landlords' claims of exorbitant rents.

Security as a
condition of
saving.

Insecurity of this kind has nearly passed away from the
civilized world.　But we are still suffering in England from
the effects of the Poor-law which ruled at the beginning of
the century, and which introduced a new form of insecurity
for the working classes.　For it arranged that part of their
wages should, in effect, be given in the form of poor relief;
and that this should be distributed among them in inverse
proportion to their industry and thrift and forethought, so
that many thought it foolish to make provision for the future.
The traditions and instincts, which were fostered by that evil
experience, are even now a great hindrance to the progress of
the working classes; and the principle which nominally at
least underlies the present Poor-law, that the State should
take account only of destitution and not at all of merit, acts
in the same direction though with less force.

Insecurity of this kind also is being diminished: the
growth of enlightened views as to the duties of the State and
of private persons towards the poor, is tending to make it

every day more true that those who have helped themselves, and endeavoured to provide for their own future, will be cared for by society better than the idle and the thoughtless. But the progress in this direction remains slow, and there is much to be done yet.

Again, modern methods of business have brought with them opportunities for the safe investment of capital in such ways as to yield a revenue to persons who have no good opportunity of engaging in any business,—not even in that of agriculture, where the land will under some conditions act as a trustworthy savings-bank[1]. These new opportunities have induced some people who would not otherwise have attempted it to put by something for their own old age. And, what has had a still greater effect on the growth of wealth, it has rendered it far easier for a man to provide a secure income for his wife and children after his death: for, after all, family affection is the main motive of saving.

§ 4. That men labour and save chiefly for the sake of their families and not for themselves, is shown by the fact that they seldom spend, after they have retired from work, more than the income that comes in from their savings, preferring to leave their stored-up wealth intact for their families; while in this country alone twenty millions a year are saved in the form of insurance policies and are available only after the death of those who save them.

The chief motive of saving is family affection.

A man can have no stronger stimulus to energy and enterprise than the hope of rising in life, and leaving his family to start from a higher round of the social ladder than that on which he began. It may even give him an overmastering passion which reduces to insignificance the desire for ease, and for all ordinary pleasures, and sometimes even destroys in him the finer sensibilities and nobler aspirations. But, as is shown by the marvellous growth of wealth in America during

---

[1] Other influences exerted by modern methods of business on the growth of wealth are noticed in *Principles* VI. VII. 5.

the present generation, it makes him a mighty producer and accumulator of riches; unless indeed he is in too great a hurry to grasp the social position which his wealth will give him. For his ambition may then lead him into as great extravagance as could have been induced by an improvident and self-indulgent temperament.

The greatest savings are made by those who have been brought up on narrow means to stern hard work, who have retained their simple habits, in spite of success in business, and who nourish a contempt for showy expenditure and a desire to be found at their death richer than they had been thought to be. This type of character is frequent in the quieter parts of old but vigorous countries, and it was very common among the middle classes in the rural districts of England for more than a generation after the pressure of the great French war and the heavy taxes that lingered in its wake.

§ 5. Next, as to the sources of accumulation. The power to save depends on an excess of income over necessary expenditure; and this is greatest among the wealthy. In this country, most of the larger incomes, but only a few of the smaller, are chiefly derived from capital. And, early in the present century, the commercial classes in England had much more saving habits than either the country gentlemen or the working classes. These causes combined to make English economists of the last generation regard savings as made almost exclusively from the profits of capital.

The source of accumulation is surplus income. Profits.

But even in modern England rent and the earnings of professional men and of hired workers are an important source of accumulation: and they have been the chief source of it in all the earlier stages of civilization. Moreover the middle, and especially the professional classes, have always denied themselves much in order to invest capital in the education of their children; while a great part of the wages of the working classes is invested in the physical

Rent and earnings.

health and strength of their children.   The older economists took too little account of the fact that human faculties are as important a means of production as any other kind of capital ; and we may conclude, in opposition to them, that any change in the distribution of wealth which gives more to the wage receivers and less to the capitalists is likely, other things being equal, to hasten the increase of material production, and that it will not perceptibly retard the storing-up of material wealth. Of course other things would not be equal, if the change were brought about by violent methods which gave a shock to public security.   But a slight and temporary check to the accumulation of material wealth need not necessarily be an evil, even from a purely economic point of view, if, being made quietly and without disturbance, it provides better opportunities for the great mass of the people, increases their efficiency, and develops in them such habits of self-respect as to result in the growth of a much more efficient race of producers in the next generation.   For then it may do more in the long-run to promote the growth of even material wealth than great additions to our stock of factories and steam-engines.

A people among whom wealth is well distributed, and who have high ambitions, are likely to accumulate a great deal of public property ; and the savings made in this form alone by some well-to-do demo- *Public accumulations of democracies.* cracies form no inconsiderable part of the best possessions which our own age has inherited from its predecessors.   The growth of the co-operative movement in all its many forms, of building societies, friendly societies, trades unions, of working men's savings-banks &c., shows that, even so far as the immediate accumulation of material *Co-operation.* wealth goes, the resources of the country are not, as the older economists assumed, entirely lost when they are spent in paying wages[1].

[1] It must however be admitted that what passes by the name of public property is often only nothing more than private wealth borrowed on a mort-

§ 6. The sacrifice of present pleasure for the sake of future, has been called *abstinence* by economists. But this term has been misunderstood: for the greatest accumulators of wealth are very rich persons, some of whom live in luxury, and certainly do not practise abstinence in that sense of the term in which it is convertible with abstemiousness. What economists meant was that, when a person abstained from consuming anything which he had the power of consuming, with the purpose of increasing his resources in the future, his abstinence from that particular act of consumption increased the accumulation of wealth. Since, however, the term is liable to be misunderstood, it is better to say that the accumulation of wealth is generally the result of a postponement of enjoyment, or of a *waiting* for it[1].

Interest is the reward of waiting.

This willingness to wait is generally increased by a rise in the rate of interest which is the reward of waiting. Conversely a fall in the rate of interest generally lowers the margin at which a person finds it just not worth while to give up present pleasures for the sake of those future pleasures that are to be secured by saving some of his means. It will therefore generally cause people to consume a little more now, and to make less provision for future enjoyment. But this rule is not without exception.

Influence of changes in the rate of interest on saving.

For indeed Sir Josiah Child remarked two centuries ago, that in countries in which the rate of interest is high, merchants "when they have gotten great wealth, leave trading" and lend out their money at interest, "the gain thereof being so easy, certain and great; whereas in other countries where interest is at a lower rate, they continue merchants from generation to generation, and enrich themselves and the state."

gage of future public revenues. Municipal gas-works for instance are not generally the results of public accumulations. They were built with wealth saved by private persons, and borrowed on public account.

[1] A further study of the nature of sacrifice involved in waiting is made in *Principles* IV. VIII. 8, 9.

And it is as true now, as it was then, that many men retire from business when they are yet almost in the prime of life, and when their knowledge of men and things might enable them to conduct their business more efficiently than ever. Again, as Mr Sargant has pointed out, if a man has decided to go on working and saving till he has provided a certain income for his old age, or for his family after his death, he will find that he has to save more if the rate of interest is low than if it is high. Suppose, for instance, that he wishes to provide an income of £400 a year on which he may retire from business, or to insure £400 a year for his wife and children after his death: if then the current rate of interest is 5 per cent., he need only put by £8,000 or insure his life for £8,000; but if it is 4 per cent., he must save £10,000 or insure his life for £10,000.

It is then possible that a continued fall in the rate of interest may be accompanied by a continued increase in the yearly additions to the world's capital. But none the less is it true that a fall in the distant benefits to be got by a given amount of working and waiting for the future does tend on the whole to diminish the provision which people make for the future; or in more modern phrase, that a fall in the rate of interest tends to check the accumulation of wealth. For though with man's growing command over the resources of nature, he may continue to save much even with a low rate of interest; yet, while human nature remains as it is, every fall in that rate is likely to cause many more people to save less than to save more than they would otherwise have done.

To sum up:—The accumulation of wealth is governed by a great variety of causes: by custom, by habits of self-control and realizing the future, and above all by the power of family affection. Security is a necessary condition for it, and the progress of knowledge and intelligence furthers it in many ways.

A rise in the rate of interest, or demand price for saving, tends to increase the volume of saving. For in spite of the fact that a few people who have determined to secure an income of a certain fixed amount for themselves or their family will save less with a high rate of interest than with a low rate, it is a nearly universal rule that a rise in the rate increases the *desire* to save; and it often increases the *power* to save, or rather it is often an indication of an increased efficiency of our productive resources.

It must however be recollected that the annual investment of wealth is a small part of the already existing stock, and that therefore the stock would not be increased perceptibly in any one year by even a considerable increase in the annual rate of saving[1].

[1] The following table is compiled chiefly from data collected by Mr Giffen.

Country and Author of Estimate.	Land. £ million.	Houses, &c. £ million.	Farm-capital. £ million.	Other wealth. £ million.	Total wealth. £ million.	Wealth per cap. £
ENGLAND.						
1690 (Gregory King)	180	45	25	70	320	58
1812 (Colquhoun) .	750	300	143	653	1,846	180
1885 (Giffen) . . .	1,333	1,700	382	3,012	6,427	315
UNITED KINGDOM.						
1812 (Colquhoun) .	1,200	400	228	208	2,736	160
1865 (Giffen) . . .	1,864	1,031	620	2,598	6,113	200
1875 (Giffen) . . .	2,007	1,420	668	4,453	8,548	260
1885 (Giffen) . . .	1,691	1,927	522	5,897	10,037	270
UNITED STATES.						
1880 (Census) . .	2,040	2,000	480	4,208	8,728	175
FRANCE.						
1878 (de Foville) .	4,000	1,000	560	2,440	8,000	215
ITALY.						
1884 (Pantaleoni) .	1,160	360			1,920	65

The series of bad harvests and the difficulty of importing food during the great war at the beginning of this century impoverished the people of England, but nearly doubled the nominal value of the land of England. Since then free trade, the improvements in transport, the opening of new countries and other causes have lowered the nominal value of that part of the land which is devoted to agriculture, but have added much to the real wealth of the people.

CHAPTER VIII.

INDUSTRIAL ORGANIZATION.

§ 1. WRITERS on social science from the time of Plato downwards have delighted to dwell on the in- *The doctrine* creased efficiency which labour derives from or- *that organiza-* ganization. Adam Smith gave a vivid descrip- *tion increases* tion of the advantages of the division of labour; *much to bio-* he pointed out how they render it possible for *logy.* increased numbers to live in comfort on a limited territory; and he argued that the pressure of population on the means of subsistence tends to weed out those races who through want of organization or for any other cause are unable to turn to the best account the advantages of the place in which they live. Before two more generations had elapsed Malthus' historical account of man's struggle for existence set Darwin thinking as to the effects of the struggle for existence in the animal world. Since that time biology has more than repaid her debt; and economists have learnt much from the profound analogies which have been discovered between industrial organization on the one side and the physical organization of the higher animals on the other. The development of the organism, whether social or physical, involves a greater subdivision of functions between its separate parts on the one hand, and on the other a more intimate connection between them. Each part gets to be less and less self-sufficient, to depend for its well-being more and more on other parts, so that no change can take place in any part of a highly-developed organism without affecting others also.

This increased subdivision of functions, or "differentia-

tion" as it is called, manifests itself with regard to industry
in such forms as the division of labour, and the
development of specialized skill, knowledge and
machinery : while "integration," that is, a
growing intimacy and firmness of the connections between the
separate parts of the industrial organism, shows itself in such
forms as the increase of security of commercial credit, and of
the means and habits of communication by sea and road, by
railway and telegraph, by post and printing-press. This leads
us to consider the main bearings in economics of the law that
the struggle for existence causes those organisms to multiply
which are best fitted to derive benefit from their environment.

Differentiation and Integration.

This law is often misunderstood; and taken to mean that
those organisms tend to survive which are *best
fitted to benefit* the environment. But this is not
its meaning. It states that those organisms tend
to survive which are *best fitted to utilize* the environment for
their own purposes. Now those that utilize the environment
most, may turn out to be those that benefit it most. But it
must not be assumed in any particular case that they are
thus beneficial, without special study of that case.

The law of struggle for survival.

§ 2. Adam Smith was aware that competition did not
always cause the survival of those businesses and
those methods of business which were most advantageous to society; and though he insisted on
the general advantages of that minute division
of labour and of that subtle industrial organization which were being developed with unexampled rapidity
in his time, yet he was careful to indicate points in which
the system failed, and incidental evils which it involved.
But many of his followers were less careful. They were not
contented with arguing that the new industrial organization
was obtaining victories over its rivals in every direction,
and that this very fact proved that it met a want of the

*Harmonies and discords between indi-
vidual and col-
lective inter-
ests.*

times, and had a good balance of advantages over disadvantages: but they went further and applied the same argument to all its details; they did not see that the very strength of the system as a whole enabled it to carry along with it many incidents which were in themselves evil. For a while they fascinated the world by their romantic accounts of the flawless proportions of that "natural" organization of industry which had grown from the rudimentary germ of self-interest. They depicted each man selecting his daily work with the sole view of getting for it the best pay he could, but with the inevitable result of choosing that in which he could be of most service to others. They argued for instance that, if a man had a talent for managing business, he would be surely led to use that talent for the benefit of mankind: that meanwhile a like pursuit of their own interests would lead others to provide for his use such capital as he could turn to best account; and that his own interest would lead him so to arrange those in his employment that everyone should do the highest work of which he was capable, and no other.

This "natural organization of industry" had a fascination for earnest and thoughtful minds; it prevented them from seeing and removing the evil that was intertwined with the good in the changes that were going on around them; and it hindered them from inquiring whether many even of the broader features of modern industry may not be transitional, having indeed good work to do in their time, as the caste system had in its time: but like it chiefly serviceable in leading the way towards better arrangements for a happier age[1].

---

[1] Physical peculiarities acquired by parents during their life-time are seldom, if ever, transmitted. But the children of those who lead healthy lives physically and morally are perhaps born with a firmer fibre than others, and certainly are more likely to be well nourished, well trained, to acquire wholesome instincts, and to have that self-respect which is a mainspring of progress.

CHAPTER IX.

INDUSTRIAL ORGANIZATION, CONTINUED. DIVISION OF LABOUR. THE INFLUENCE OF MACHINERY.

§ 1. THE first condition of an efficient organization of industry is that it should keep everyone employed at such work as his abilities and training fit him to do well, and should equip him with the best machinery and other appliances for his work. We shall confine ourselves to the division of labour between different classes of operatives, with special reference to the influence of machinery. In the following chapter we shall consider the reciprocal effects of division of labour and localization of industry; in a third chapter we shall inquire how far the advantages of division of labour depend upon the aggregation of large capitals into the hands of single individuals or firms, or, as is commonly said, on production on a large scale; and lastly, we shall examine the growing specialization of the work of business management.

Plan of this and the two following chapters.

Everyone is familiar with the fact that "practice makes perfect," that it enables an operation, which at first seemed difficult, to be done after a time with comparatively little exertion, and yet much better than before; and physiology in some measure explains this fact.

Practice makes perfect.

Adam Smith pointed out that a lad who had made nothing but nails all his life could make them twice as quickly as a firstrate smith who only took to nailmaking occasionally. Anyone who has to perform exactly

Illustrations.

the same set of operations day after day on things of exactly the same shape, gradually learns to move his fingers exactly as they are wanted, by almost automatic action and with greater rapidity than would be possible if every movement had to wait for a deliberate instruction of the will. One familiar instance is seen in the tying of threads by children in a cotton mill. Again, in a clothing or a boot factory, a person who sews, whether by hand or machinery, just the same seam on a piece of leather or cloth of just the same size, hour after hour, day after day, is able to do it with far less effort and far more quickly than a worker with much greater quickness of eye and hand, and of a much higher order of general skill, who was accustomed to make the whole of a coat or the whole of a boot.

Again, in the wood and the metal industries, if a man has to perform exactly the same operations over and over again on the same piece of material, he gets into the habit of holding it exactly in the way in which it is wanted, and of arranging the tools and other things which he has to handle in such positions that he is able to bring them to work on one another with the least possible loss of time and of force in the movements of his own body. Accustomed to find them always in the same position and to take them in the same order, his hands work in harmony with one another almost automatically: and, as he becomes more practised, his expenditure of nervous force diminishes even more rapidly than his expenditure of muscular force.

But when the action has thus been reduced to routine, it has nearly arrived at the stage at which it can be taken over by machinery. The chief difficulty to be overcome is that of getting the machinery to hold the material firmly in exactly the position in which the machine tool can be brought to bear on it in the right way, and without wasting too much time in taking grip of it. But this can generally be contrived when it is worth

The provinces of manual labour and of machinery.

while to spend some labour and expense on it ; and then the whole operation can often be controlled by a worker who, sitting before a machine, takes with the left hand a piece of wood or metal from a heap and puts it in a socket, while with the right he draws down a lever, or in some other way sets the machine tool at work, and finally with his left hand throws on to another heap the material which has been cut or punched or drilled or planed exactly after a given pattern. Thus machinery constantly supplants that purely manual skill, the attainment of which was, even up to Adam Smith's time, the chief advantage of division of labour. But, at the same time, it increases the scale of manufactures and makes them more complex ; and, on the whole, increases the opportunities for division of labour of all kinds, and especially in the matter of business management.

§ 2. The powers of machinery to do work that requires too much accuracy to be done by hand are perhaps best seen

Interchange-
able Parts.
in some branches of the metal industries in which the system of Interchangeable Parts is being rapidly developed. It is only after long training and with much care and labour that the hand can make one piece of metal accurately to resemble or to fit into another : and after all the accuracy is not perfect. But this is just the work which a well made machine can do most easily and most perfectly. For instance, if sowing and reaping machines had to be made by hand, their first cost would be very high ; and when any part of them was broken, it could be replaced only at great cost by sending the machine back to the manufacturer or by bringing a highly skilled mechanic to the machine. But as it is, the manufacturer keeps in store many facsimiles of the broken part, which were made by the same machinery, and are therefore interchangeable with it. A farmer in the North-West of America, perhaps a hundred miles away from any good mechanic's shop, can yet use complicated machinery with confidence ; since he knows that by telegraphing the

number of the machine and the number of any part of it which he has broken, he will get by the next train a new piece which he can himself fit into its place. The importance of this principle of interchangeable parts has been but recently grasped; there are however many signs that it will do more than any other to extend the use of machine-made machinery to every branch of production, including even domestic and agricultural work.

The influences which machinery exerts over the character of modern industry are well illustrated in the *The watch-* manufacture of watches. A few years ago the *making trade.* chief seat of this business was in French Switzerland; where the subdivision of labour was carried far, though a great part of the work was done by a more or less scattered population. There were about fifty distinct branches of trade, each of which did one small part of the work. In almost all of them a highly specialized manual skill was required, but very little judgment; the earnings were generally low, because the trade had been established too long for those in it to have anything like a monopoly, and there was no difficulty in bringing up to it any child with ordinary intelligence. But this industry is now yielding ground to the American system of making watches by machinery, which requires very little specialized manual skill. In fact the machinery is becoming every year more and more automatic, and is getting to require less and less assistance from the human hand. But the more delicate the machine's power, the greater is the judgment *Machinery in-* and carefulness which is called for from those *creases the de-* who see after it. Take for instance a beautiful *mand for gene-* *ral intelli-* machine which feeds itself with steelwire at one *gence;* end, and delivers at the other tiny screws of exquisite form; it displaces a great many operatives who had indeed acquired a very high and specialized manual skill, but who lived sedentary lives, straining their eyesight through microscopes, and finding in their work very little scope for any faculty

M. 10

except a mere command over the use of their fingers. But
the machine is intricate and costly, and the person who minds
it must have an intelligence, and an energetic sense of responsibility, which go a long way towards making a fine character;
and which, though more common than they were, are yet
sufficiently rare to be able to earn a very high rate of pay.
No doubt this is an extreme case; and the greater part of the
work done in a watch factory is much simpler. But much
of it requires higher faculties than the old system did, and
those engaged in it earn on the average higher wages; at the
same time that it has already brought the price of a trustworthy watch within the range of the poorest classes of the
community, and it is showing signs of being able soon to ac-
complish the very highest class of work.

Those who finish and put together the different parts of a
watch must always have highly specialized skill:
but most of the machines which are in use in a
watch factory, are not different in general character from those which are used in any other of
the lighter metal trades: in fact many of them are mere
modifications of the turning lathes and of the slotting, punch-
ing, drilling, planing, shaping, milling machines and a few
others, which are familiar to all engineering trades. This is a
good illustration of the fact that while there is a constantly
increasing subdivision of labour, many of the lines of division
between trades which are nominally distinct are becoming
narrower and less difficult to be passed. In old times it would
have been very small comfort to watch-makers, who happened
to be suffering from a diminished demand for their wares,
to be told that the gun-making trade was in want of extra
hands; but most of the operatives in a watch factory would
find machines very similar to those with which they were
familiar, if they strayed into a gun-making factory or sewing-
machine factory, or a factory for making textile machinery.
A watch factory with those who worked in it could be con-

*and weakens
barriers be-
tween different
trades.*

verted without any overwhelming loss into a sewing-machine factory: almost the only condition would be that no one should be put to work in the new factory which required a higher order of general intelligence, than that to which he was already accustomed[1].

§ 3. We may now pass to consider the effects which machinery has in relieving that excessive muscular strain which a few generations ago was the common lot of more than half the working men even in such a country as England. The most marvellous instances of the power of machinery are seen in large iron-works, and especially in those for making armour plates, where the force to be exerted is so great that man's muscles count for nothing, and where every movement, whether horizontal or vertical, has to be effected by hydraulic or steam force; man merely standing by ready to govern the machinery and clear away ashes or perform some such secondary task.

Machinery relieves the strain on human muscles.

Machinery of this class has increased our command over nature, but it has not directly altered the character of man's work very much; for that which it does he could not have done without it. But in other trades machinery has lightened man's labours. The house-carpenters, for instance, make things of the same kind as those used by our forefathers, with much less toil for themselves. They now give themselves chiefly to those parts of the task which are most pleasant and most interesting; while in every country town and almost every village there are found steam mills for sawing, planing and moulding, which relieve them of that grievous fatigue which not very long ago used to make them prematurely old[2].

---

[1] The changes in the methods of printing are almost as instructive as those in watch-making. They are traced in *Principles* IV. IX. 5.

[2] The jack-plane, used for making smooth large boards for floors and other purposes, was the worst enemy of the carpenter. All but specially skilled men were compelled to spend a great part of their time with the jack-plane, and this brought on heart-disease, making them as a rule old men by the time they

New machinery, when just invented, generally requires a

Machinery great deal of care and attention. But the work
takes over mo- of its attendant is always being sifted; that
notonous work which is uniform and monotonous is gradually
taken over by the machine, which thus becomes steadily more
and more automatic and self-acting; till at last there is nothing for the hand to do, but to supply the material at certain
intervals and to take away the work when finished. There
still remains the responsibility for seeing that the machinery
is in good order and working smoothly; but even this task is
often made light by the introduction of an automatic movement, which brings the machine to a stop the instant anything
goes wrong.

Nothing could be more narrow or monotonous than the
occupation of a weaver of plain stuffs in the old time. But
now one woman will manage four or more looms, each of
which does many times as much work in the course of the
day as the old hand-loom did; and her work is much less
monotonous and calls for much more judgment than his did.
So that for every hundred yards of cloth that are woven, the
purely monotonous work done by human beings is probably
not a twentieth part of what it was.

As Roscher says, it is monotony of life much more than

and lessens monotony of work that is to be dreaded: mono-
monotony of tony of work is an evil of the first order only
life. when it involves monotony of life. Now when a

---

were forty. But now those who become prematurely old through overwork
are to be found almost exclusively among the professional classes, among
those engaged in the more anxious kinds of business, and in some agricultural
districts in which the rate of wages is still very low and the people are habitu-
ally underfed. Adam Smith tells us that "workmen, when they are liberally
paid, are very apt to overwork themselves and to ruin their health and constitution in a few years. A carpenter in London, and in some other places, is
not supposed to last in his utmost vigour above eight years....Almost every
class of artificers is subject to some particular infirmity occasioned by excessive application to their peculiar species of work." *Wealth of Nations*, Book I.
Chapter VII.

person's employment requires much physical exertion, he is fit for nothing after his work; and unless his mental faculties are called forth in his work, they have little chance of being developed at all. But the nervous force is not very much exhausted in the ordinary work of a factory, at all events where there is not excessive noise, and where the hours of labour are not too long. The social surroundings of factory life stimulate mental activity in and out of working hours; and even those factory workers, whose occupations are seemingly the most monotonous, have more intelligence and mental resource than has been shown by the English agricultural labourer, whose employment has more variety. It is true that the American agriculturist is an able man, and that his children rise rapidly in the world. But partly because land has been plentiful, and he has generally owned the farm that he cultivates, he has had better social conditions than the English; he has always had to think for himself, and has long had to use and to repair complex machines. The English agricultural labourer has had many great disadvantages to contend with; but is steadily improving his position.

§ 4. We may next consider what are the conditions under which the economies in production arising from division of labour can best be secured. It is obvious that the efficiency of specialized machinery or specialized skill is but one condition of its economic use; the other is that sufficient work should be found to keep it well employed. As Babbage pointed out, in a large factory "the master manufacturer by dividing the work to be executed into different processes, each requiring different degrees of skill or force, can purchase exactly that precise quantity of both which is necessary for each process; whereas if the whole work were executed by one workman that person must possess sufficient skill to perform the most difficult and sufficient strength to execute the most laborious of the operations into which the

Specialization of skill and machinery cannot be carried far unless the scale of production is large.

work is divided." The economy of production requires not only that each person should be employed constantly in a narrow range of work, but also that, when it is necessary for him to undertake different tasks, each of these tasks should be such as to call forth as much as possible of his skill and ability. Just in the same way the economy of machinery requires that a powerful turning-lathe when specially arranged for one class of work should be kept employed as long as possible on that work; and if after all it is necessary to employ it on other work, that should be such as to be worthy of the lathe, and not such as could have been done equally well by a much smaller machine.

Many of those economies in the use of specialized skill and machinery which are commonly regarded as within the reach of very large establishments, do not depend on the size of individual factories. Some depend on the aggregate production of the kind in the neighbourhood; while others again, especially those connected with the growth of knowledge and the progress of the arts, depend chiefly on the aggregate volume of production in the whole civilized world. And here we may introduce two technical terms. We may divide the economies arising from an increase in the scale of production of any kind of goods, into two classes. Those which we have been discussing may be called *Internal Economies;* because they are dependent on the resources of the individual houses of business engaged in it, on their internal organization and on the efficiency of their management. We have next to examine those *External economies* which arise from the general development of an industry and especially from the concentration of many businesses of a similar character in particular localities: or, as is commonly said, from the Localization of Industry.

External and Internal Economies.

151

CHAPTER X.

INDUSTRIAL ORGANIZATION CONTINUED. THE CONCENTRA-
TION OF SPECIALIZED INDUSTRIES IN PARTICULAR
LOCALITIES.

§ 1. IN an early stage of civilization every place had to depend on its own resources for most of the heavy wares which it consumed; unless indeed it happened to have special facilities for water carriage. But the slowness with which customs changed, made it easy for producers to meet the wants of consumers with whom they had little communication; and it enabled comparatively poor people to buy a few expensive goods from a distance, in the security that they would add to the pleasure of festivals and holidays during a life-time, or perhaps even during two or three life-times. Consequently the lighter and more expensive articles of dress and personal adornment, together with spices and some kinds of metal implements used by all classes, and many other things for the special use of the rich, often came from astonishing distances.

Many various causes have led to the localization of industries, but the chief have been physical; such as the character of the climate and the soil, or the existence of mines and quarries in the neighbourhood, or within easy access by land or water. Thus metallic industries have generally been either near mines or in places where fuel was cheap. The iron industries in England first sought those districts in which charcoal was plentiful, and afterwards they went to the neighbourhood of

Primitive forms of localized industries.

Various origins of localized industries.

collieries. Staffordshire makes many kinds of pottery, all the materials of which are imported from a long distance; but she has cheap coal and excellent clay for making the heavy "*seggars*" or boxes in which the pottery is placed while being fired. Straw plaiting has its chief home in Bedfordshire, where straw has just the right proportion of silex to give strength without brittleness; and Buckinghamshire beeches have afforded the material for the Wycombe chairmaking. The Sheffield cutlery trade is due chiefly to the excellent grit of which its grindstones are made.

Another chief cause has been the patronage of a court. The rich folk there assembled make a demand for goods of specially high quality; and this attracts skilled workmen from a distance, and educates those on the spot. Thus the mechanical faculty of Lancashire is said to be due to the influence of Norman smiths who were settled at Warrington by Hugo de Lupus in William the Conqueror's time. And the greater part of England's manufacturing industry before the era of cotton and steam had its course directed by settlements of Flemish and Huguenot artisans; many of which were made under the immediate direction of Plantagenet and Tudor kings. These immigrants taught us how to weave woollen and worsted stuffs, though for a long time we sent our cloths to the Netherlands to be fulled and dyed. They taught us how to cure herrings, how to manufacture silk, how to make lace, glass, and paper, and to provide for many other of our wants.

§ 2. When an industry has once thus chosen a locality for itself, it is likely to stay there long: so great

Advantages of localized industries. Hereditary skill;

are the advantages which people following the same skilled trade get from near neighbourhood to one another. The mysteries of the trade become no mysteries; but are as it were in the air, and children learn many of them unconsciously. Good work is rightly appreciated; inventions and improvements in machinery, in processes and the general organization of the business have their merits promptly discussed; if one man starts a new idea it is taken up by others and combined with suggestions of their own, and thus becomes the source of further new ideas. And presently subsidiary trades grow up in the _{subsidiary} neighbourhood, supplying it with implements and _{trades;} materials, organizing its traffic, and in many ways conducing to the economy of its material.

Again, the economic use of expensive machinery can sometimes be attained in a very high degree in a _{specialized} district in which there is a large aggregate pro- _{machinery;} duction of the same kind, even though no individual capital employed in the trade be very large. For subsidiary industries devoting themselves each to one small branch of the process of production, and working it for a great many of their neighbours, are able to keep in constant use machinery of the most highly specialized character; and to make it pay its expenses, though its original cost may have been high, and its rate of depreciation very rapid.

Again, in all but the earliest stages of economic development a localized industry gains a great advantage _{local market} from the fact that it offers a constant market for _{for skill.} skill. Employers are apt to resort to any place where they are likely to find a good choice of workers with the special skill which they require; while men seeking employment naturally go to places where they expect to find a good market for their skill, in consequence of the presence of many employers who require its aid. The owner of an isolated factory is often put to great shifts for want of some special skilled labour which has suddenly run short; and a skilled workman, when thrown out of employment in it, has no easy refuge.

On the other hand a localized industry has some disadvantages as a market for labour if the work done in it is chiefly of one kind, such for instance as can be done only by strong men. In those iron districts in which there are no

textile or other factories to give employment to women and
children, wages are high and the cost of labour
dear to the employer, while the average money
earnings of each family are low. But the remedy
for this evil is obvious, and is found in the growth
in the same neighbourhood of industries of a supplementary
character. Thus textile industries are constantly found con-
gregated in the neighbourhood of mining and engineering
industries, in some cases having been attracted by almost
imperceptible steps; in others, as for instance at Barrow,
having been started deliberately on a large scale in order to
give variety of employment in a place where previously there
had been but little demand for the work of women and
children.

But there may be too exten-sive a demand for one kind of labour.

The advantages of variety of employment are combined
with those of localized industries in some of our manufacturing
towns, and this is a chief cause of their continued growth.
But on the other hand the value which the central sites of a
large town have for trading purposes, enables them to command much higher ground-rents than the situations are worth
for factories, even when account is taken of this combination
of advantages : and there is a similar competition for dwelling
space between the employés of the trading houses, and the
factory workers. The result is that factories now congregate
in the outskirts of large towns and in manufacturing districts
in their neighbourhood rather than in the towns themselves.

A district which is dependent chiefly on one industry is
liable to extreme depression, in case of a falling-
off in the demand for its produce, or of a failure
in the supply of the raw material which it uses.
This evil again is in a great measure avoided by
those large towns, or large industrial districts in
which several distinct industries are strongly developed. If one of them fails for a time, the others are likely
to support it in many ways, chiefly indirect; one of these

Different in-dustries in the same neigh-bourhood mitigate each other's depres-sions.

being that they keep in heart the local shopkeepers, who are thus enabled to continue their assistance longer than they otherwise could, to the workpeople in those trades that happen to be depressed.

It is instructive to study the influence of improved means of communication on the character of England's industries. The agricultural population has di- Changes in the minished relatively to the rest, though not so fast distribution of England's in- as is commonly supposed. Manufacture employs dustries. a rather smaller proportion of the population than it did a generation ago. But there has been a great increase in industries in which the progress of invention has done little towards economizing effort, and which meet growing demands: the chief of these are education, domestic service, building, dealing, and transport by road.

CHAPTER XI.

INDUSTRIAL ORGANIZATION, CONTINUED. PRODUCTION ON A LARGE SCALE.

§ 1. THE advantages of production on a large scale are best shown in manufacture; under which head
Manufacture is typical for our present purpose. we may include all businesses engaged in working up material into forms in which it will be adapted for sale in distant markets. The characteristic of manufacturing industries which makes them offer generally the best illustrations of the advantages of production on a large scale, is their power of choosing freely the locality in which they will do their work. They are thus contrasted on the one hand with agriculture and other extractive industries (mining, quarrying, fishing etc.), the geographical distribution of which is determined by nature; and on the other hand with industries that make or repair things to suit the special needs of individual consumers, from whom they cannot be far removed, at all events without great loss.

The chief advantages of production on a large scale are
Economy of material. economy of skill, economy of machinery and economy of materials: but the last of these is rapidly losing importance relatively to the other two. It is true that an isolated workman often throws away a number of small things which would have been collected and turned to good account in a factory; but waste of this kind can scarcely occur in a localized manufacture even if it is in the hands of small men; and there is not very much of it in any branch

of industry in modern England, except agriculture and domestic cooking[1].

But small factories are still placed under a great disadvantage, even in a localized industry, by the growing variety and expensiveness of machinery. For in Specialized machinery. a large establishment there are often many expensive machines each made specially for one small use. Each of them requires space in a good light, and thus stands for something considerable in the rent and general expenses of the factory; and independently of interest and the expense of keeping it in repair, a heavy allowance must be made for depreciation in consequence of its being probably improved upon before long. A small manufacturer must therefore have many things done by hand or by imperfect machinery, though he knows how to have them done better and cheaper by special machinery, if only he could find constant employment for it.

But next, a small manufacturer may not always be acquainted with the best machinery for his purpose. Improvements in machinery. It is true that if the industry in which he is engaged has been long established on a large scale, his machinery will be well up to the mark, provided he can afford to buy the best in the market. In agriculture and the cotton industries for instance, improvements in machinery are devised almost exclusively by machine makers; and they are accessible to all, at any rate on the payment of a royalty for patent right. But this is not the case in industries that are as yet

---

[1] No doubt many of the most important advances of recent years have been due to the utilizing of what had been a waste product; but this has been generally due to a distinct invention, either chemical or mechanical, the use of which has been indeed promoted by minute subdivision of labour, but has not been directly dependent on it.

Again, it is true that when a hundred suits of furniture, or of clothing, have to be cut out on exactly the same pattern, it is worth while to spend great care on so planning the cutting out of the boards or the cloth, that only a few small pieces are wasted. But this is properly an economy of skill; one planning is made to suffice for many tasks, and therefore can be done well and carefully.

in an early stage of development or are rapidly changing their form; such as the chemical industries, the watchmaking industry and some branches of the jute and silk manufactures; and in a host of trades that are constantly springing up to supply some new want or to work up some new material.

There are however some trades in which the advantages which a large factory derives from the economy of machinery almost vanish as soon as a moderate size has been reached. For instance in cotton spinning, and calico weaving, a comparatively small factory will hold its own and give constant employment to the best known machines for every process : so that a large factory is only several parallel smaller factories under one roof; and indeed some cotton-spinners, when enlarging their works, think it best to add a weaving department. In such cases the large business gains little or no economy in machinery; but even then it generally saves something in building, particularly as regards chimneys, in the economy of steam power, and in the management and repairs of engines and machinery. This last point is of rather more importance than appears at first sight; and large works even though they produce nothing but soft goods, have generally well-organized carpenters' and mechanics' shops, which not only diminish the cost of repairs, but have the important advantage of preventing delays from accidents to the plant.

Akin to these last, there are a great many advantages Buying and which a large factory, or indeed a large business selling. of almost any kind, nearly always has over a small one. A large business buys in great quantities and therefore cheaply; it pays low freights and saves on carriage in many ways, particularly if it has a railway siding. It often sells in large quantities, and thus saves itself trouble; and yet at the same time it gets a good price, because it offers conveniences to the customer by having a large stock from which he can select and at once fill up a varied order; while its reputation gives him confidence. It can spend large sums on advertising by commercial travellers and in other ways; its agents give it trustworthy information on trade and personal matters in distant places, and its own goods advertise one another.

Many of these economies in the matter of buying and selling can be secured by a large trading house, which puts out its work to be done by small manufacturers or by workpeople at their own homes. So far therefore they do not tell in the direction of destroying small manufacturers, but rather of limiting the character of the work of business management done by them; as we shall see more fully in the next chapter.

Alliance between large traders and small producers.

Next, with regard to the economy of skill. Everything that has been said with regard to the advantages which a large establishment has in being able to afford highly specialized machinery applies equally with regard to highly specialized skill. It can contrive to keep each of its employés constantly engaged in the most difficult work of which he is capable, and yet so to narrow the range of his work that he can attain the facility and excellence which come from long-continued practice. This economy gives a practical supremacy to large factories in industries which offer much scope for it, if the work cannot be subdivided among many small factories on the plan described in the last chapter.

Specialized skill.

§ 2. The head of a large business can reserve all his strength for the broadest and most fundamental problems of his trade: he must indeed assure himself that his managers, clerks and foremen are the right men for their work, and are doing their work well; but beyond this he need not trouble himself much about details. He can keep his mind fresh and clear for thinking out the most difficult and vital problems of his business; for studying the broader movements of the markets, the yet undeveloped results of current events at home and abroad; and for contriving how to improve

The large manufacturer can give himself wholly to broad questions of policy.

the organization of the internal and external relations of his business.

For much of this work the small employer has not the time if he has the ability; he cannot take so broad a survey of his trade, or look so far ahead; he must often be content to follow the lead of others. And he must spend much of his time on work that is below him; for if he is to succeed at all, his mind must be in some respects of a high quality, and must have a good deal of originating and organizing force; and yet he must do much routine work.

On the other hand the small employer has advantages of his own. The master's eye is everywhere; there is no shirking by his foremen or workmen, no divided responsibility, no sending half-understood messages backwards and forwards from one department to another. He saves much of the book-keeping, and nearly all of the cumbrous system of checks that are necessary in the business of a large firm; and the gain from this source is of very great importance in trades which use the more valuable metals and other expensive materials.

The small manufacturer can save in superintendence,

And though he must always remain at a great disadvantage in getting information and in making experiments, yet in this matter the general course of progress is on his side. For External economies are constantly growing in importance relatively to Internal in all matters of trade-knowledge: newspapers, and trade and technical publications of all kinds are perpetually scouting for him and bringing him much of the knowledge he wants—knowledge which a little while ago would have been beyond the reach of anyone who could not afford to have well-paid agents in many distant places. Again, it is to his interest also that the secrecy of business is on the whole diminishing, and that the most important improvements in method seldom remain secret for long after they have passed from the experimental stage. It is to his advantage

and he gains much from the modern diffusion of trade-knowledge.

that changes in manufacture depend less on mere rules of thumb and more on broad developments of scientific principle; and that many of these are made by students in the pursuit of knowledge for its own sake, and are promptly published in the general interest. Although therefore the small manufacturer can seldom be in the front of the race of progress, he need not be far from it, if he has the time and the ability for availing himself of the modern facilities for obtaining knowledge. But it is true that he must be exceptionally strong if he can do this without neglecting the minor but necessary details of the business.

The advantages which a large business has over a small one are conspicuous in manufacture, because, as we have noticed, it has special facilities for concentrating a great deal of work in a small area. But there is a strong tendency for large establishments to drive out small ones in many other industries; in particular the retail trade is being transformed, and the small shopkeeper is losing ground daily. Large firms are gaining rapidly in the Transport Industries, to a less extent in mining and very little if at all in agriculture[1].

Trade and transport, mining, agriculture.

[1] The small shopkeeper has special facilities for bringing his goods to the door of his customers; for humouring their several tastes; and for knowing enough of them individually to be able safely to sell on credit. But the importance of these advantages is diminishing. Meanwhile cycles, tramways &c. are making it easier for customers to visit large central establishments for the purchase of those goods which it is important to select from a large and varied stock and one which is constantly renewed with changing fashions; while groceries and other goods of which the small shopkeeper could keep a fair supply are conveniently obtained by a written order from the price list of shops or stores which turn over their stock rapidly and keep everything fresh. See *Principles* IV. xi. 6, 7.

CHAPTER XII.

INDUSTRIAL ORGANIZATION, CONTINUED. BUSINESS MANAGEMENT.

§ 1. BUSINESS may be taken to include all provision for
the wants of others which is made in the ex-
Business
management
has many
forms.
pectation of payment direct or indirect from those
who are to be benefited. It is thus contrasted
with the provision for our own wants which each
of us makes for himself, and with those kindly services which
are prompted by family affection and the desire to promote
the well-being of others.

Even in modern England we find now and then a village
Primitive
methods.
artisan who adheres to primitive methods, and
makes things on his own account for sale to his
neighbours; managing his own business and undertaking all
its risks[1]. But such cases are rare: and in the greater part
The modern
undertaker.
of the business of the modern world the task of
so directing production that a given effort may
be most effective in supplying human wants has to be broken
up and given into the hands of a specialized body of employers, or to use a more general term, of business men. They
"adventure" or "undertake" its risks; they bring together
the capital and the labour required for the work; they arrange
or "engineer" its general plan, and superintend its minor
details. Looking at business men from one point of view we

[1] The most striking instances of an adherence to old-fashioned methods of
business are supplied by the learned professions; for a physician or a solicitor
manages as a rule his own business and does all its work.

may regard them as a highly skilled industrial grade, from another as middlemen intervening between the manual worker and the consumer.

There are some kinds of business men who undertake great risks, and exercise a large influence over the welfare both of the producers and of the consumers of the wares in which they deal, but who are not to any considerable extent direct employers of labour. *Subdivision of the tasks of undertaking and superintendence.* For instance some Manchester warehousemen give themselves to studying the movements of fashion, the markets for raw materials, the 'general state of trade, of the money market and of politics, and all other causes that are likely to influence the prices of different kinds of goods during the coming season; and after employing, if necessary, skilled designers to carry out their ideas, they give out to manufacturers in different parts of the world contracts for making the goods on which they have determined to risk their capital. And in the clothing trades and some others, we see a revival of what has been called the "house industry," which prevailed long ago in the textile *House industries.* industries; that is, the system in which large undertakers give out work to be done in cottages and very small workshops to persons who work alone or with the aid of some members of their family, or who perhaps employ two or three hired assistants. In remote villages in almost every county of England agents of large undertakers come round to give out to the cottagers partially prepared materials for goods of all sorts, but especially clothes such as shirts and collars and gloves; and take back with them the finished goods. It is however in the great capital cities of the world, and in other large towns, especially old towns, where there is a great deal of unskilled and unorganized labour, with a somewhat low physique and morale, that the system is most fully developed, especially in the clothing trades, which employ two hundred thousand people in London alone, and in the cheap furniture

11—2

trades. There is a continual contest between the factory and the domestic system, now one gaining ground and now the other: for instance just at present the growing use of sewing-machines worked by steam power is strengthening the position of the factories in the boot trade; while factories and workshops are getting an increased hold of the tailoring trade. On the other hand the hosiery trade is being tempted back to the dwelling-house by recent improvements in hand knitting machines; and it is possible that new methods of distributing power by gas and petroleum and electric engines may exercise a like influence on many other industries.

Or there may be a movement towards intermediate plans, **Sheffield trades.** similar to those which are largely followed in the Sheffield trades. Many cutlery firms for instance put out grinding and other parts of their work, at piece-work prices, to working men who rent the steam power which they require, either from the firm from whom they take their contract or from someone else: these workmen sometimes employing others to help them, sometimes working alone.

Thus there are many ways in which those who undertake the chief risks of buying and selling may avoid the trouble of housing and superintending those who work for them. They all have their advantages; and when the workers are men of strong character, as at Sheffield, the results are on the whole not unsatisfactory. But unfortunately it is often the weakest class of workers, those with the least resource and the least self-control who drift into work of this kind. The elasticity of the system which recommends it to the undertaker, is really the means of enabling him to exercise, if he chooses, an undesirable pressure on those who do his work.

For while the success of a factory depends in a great measure on its having a set of operatives who adhere steadily to it, the capitalist who gives out work to be done at home has an interest in retaining a great many persons on his books; he is tempted to give each of them a little employment occasionally and play them off one against another; and this he can easily do because they do not know one another, and cannot arrange concerted action[1].

§ 2. When the profits of business are under discussion they are generally connected in people's minds with the employer of labour: "the employer" is often taken as a term practically coextensive with the receiver of business profits. But the instances which we have just considered are sufficient to illustrate the truth that the superintendence of labour is but one side, and often not the most important side of business work; and that the employer who undertakes the whole risks of his business really performs two entirely distinct services on behalf of the community, and requires a twofold ability.

The faculties required in the ideal manufacturer.

The ideal manufacturer, for instance, if he makes goods not to meet special orders but for the general market, must, in his first rôle as merchant and organizer of production, have a thorough knowledge of *things* in his own trade. He must have the power of forecasting the broad movements of production and consumption, of seeing where there is an opportunity for supplying a new commodity that will meet a real want or improving the plan of producing an old commodity. He must be able to judge cautiously and undertake risks boldly; and he must of course understand the materials and machinery used in his trade.

But secondly in this rôle of employer he must be a natural leader of *men*. He must have a power of first choosing his assistants rightly and then trusting them fully; of interesting them in the business and of getting them to trust him, so as to bring out whatever enterprise and power of origination there is in them; while he himself exercises a general control over everything, and preserves order and unity in the main plan of the business.

[1] The subject of this section is studied a good deal more fully in *Principles* IV. XII. 1—4.

The abilities required to make an ideal employer are so great and so numerous that very few persons can exhibit them all in a very high degree. Their relative importance however varies with the nature of the industry and the size of the business; and while one employer excels in one set of qualities, another excels in another; <u>scarcely any two owe their success to exactly the same combination of advantages. Some men make their way by the use of none but noble qualities, while others owe their prosperity to qualities in which there is very little that is really admirable except sagacity and strength of purpose.</u>

Such then being the general nature of the work of business management, we have next to inquire what opportunities different classes of people have of developing business ability; and, when they have obtained that, what opportunities they have of getting command over the capital required to give it scope.

§ 3. The son of a man already established in business

The son of a business man starts with many advantages, starts with so many advantages that we might expect business men to constitute a sort of caste; dividing out among their sons the chief posts of command, and founding hereditary dynasties, which ruled certain branches of trade for many generations together. But it is not so.

A man who gets together a great business by his own efforts has probably been brought up by parents of strong but also with disadvantages. earnest character, and educated by their personal influence and by struggle with difficulties in early life. But his children, at all events if they were born after he became rich, and in any case his grandchildren, are perhaps left a good deal to the care of domestic servants who are not of the same strong fibre as the parents by whose influence he was educated. And while his highest ambition was probably success in business, they are likely to be at least equally anxious for social distinction.

For a time indeed all may go well. His sons find a firmly established trade connection, and what is perhaps even more important, a well-chosen staff of subordinates with a generous interest in the business. By mere assiduity and caution, availing themselves of the traditions of the firm, they may hold together for a long time. But when a full generation has passed, when the old traditions are no longer a safe guide, and when the bonds that held together the old staff have been dissolved, then the business almost invariably falls to pieces unless it is practically handed over to the management of new men who have meanwhile risen to partnership in the firm.

But in most cases his descendants arrive at this result by a shorter route. They prefer an abundant income coming to them without effort on their part, to one which though twice as large could be earned only by incessant toil and anxiety; and they sell the business to private persons or a joint-stock company; or they become sleeping partners in it; that is sharing in its risks and in its profits, but not taking part in its management: in either case the active control over their capital falls chiefly into the hands of new men.

§ 4. The oldest and simplest plan for renovating the energies of a business is that of taking into partnership some of its ablest employés. Or again two or more people may combine their resources for a large and difficult undertaking. In such cases there is often a distinct partition of the work of management: in manufactures for instance one partner will sometimes give himself almost exclusively to the work of buying raw material and selling the finished product, while the other is responsible for the management of the factory: and in a trading establishment one partner will control the wholesale and the other the retail department. In these and other ways private partnership is capable of adapting itself to a great variety of problems: it is very strong and very elastic; it has played a great part in the past, and it is full of vitality now.

Private partnerships.

§ 5.   But from the end of the Middle Ages to the present time there has been in some classes of trades a movement **Joint-stock companies.** towards the substitution of public joint-stock companies, the shares of which can be sold to anybody in the open market, for private companies, the shares in which are not transferable without the leave of all concerned. The effect of this change has been to induce people, many of whom have no special knowledge of trade, to give their capital into the hands of others employed by them : and there has thus arisen a new distribution of the various parts of the work of business management.

The ultimate undertakers of the risks incurred by a joint-stock company are the shareholders; but as a rule they do not take much active part in engineering the business and controlling its general policy; and they take no part in superintending its details. After the business has once got out of the hands of its original promoters, the control of it is left chiefly in the hands of Directors; who, if the company is a very large one, probably own but a very small proportion of its shares, while the greater part of them have not much technical knowledge of the work to be done. They are not generally expected to give their whole time to it; but they are supposed to bring wide general knowledge and sound judgment to bear on the broader problems of its policy; and at the same time to make sure that the "Managers" of the company are doing their work thoroughly. To the Managers and their assistants is left a great part of the work of engineering the business, and the whole of the work of superintending it: but they are not required to bring any capital into it; and they are supposed to be promoted from the lower ranks to the higher according to their zeal and ability. Since the joint-stock companies in the United Kingdom have an aggregate income of £100,000,000, and do a tenth of the business of all kinds that is done in the country, they offer very large opportunities to men with natural talents for business management, who have not inherited any material capital, or any business connection.

Joint-stock companies have great elasticity and can expand themselves without limit when the work to which they have set themselves offers a wide scope; and they are gaining ground in nearly all directions. But they have one great source of weakness in the absence of any adequate knowledge of the business on the part of the shareholders who undertake its chief risks; though a few of the larger shareholders often exert themselves to find out what is going on; and are thus able to exercise an effective and wise control over the general management of the business[1]. It is a strong proof of the marvellous growth in recent times of a spirit of honesty and uprightness in commercial matters, that the leading officers of great public companies yield as little as they do to the vast temptations to fraud which lie in their way. If they showed an eagerness to avail themselves of opportunities for wrong-doing at all approaching that of which we read in the commercial history of earlier civilizations, their wrong uses of the trust imposed in them would have been on so great a scale as to prevent the development of this democratic form of business. There is every reason to hope that the progress of trade morality will continue, and that it will be aided in the future as it has been in the past, by a diminution of trade secrecy

The system rendered workable only by the modern growth of business morality.

---

[1] It is true that the head of a large private firm undertakes the chief risks of the business, while he intrusts many of its details to others; but his position is secured by his power of forming a direct judgment as to whether his subordinates serve his interests faithfully and discreetly. If those to whom he has intrusted the buying or selling of goods for him take commissions from those with whom they deal, he is in a position to discover and punish the fraud. If they show favouritism and promote incompetent relations or friends of their own, or if they themselves become idle and shirk their work, or even if they do not fulfil the promise of exceptional ability which induced him to give them their first lift, he can discover what is going wrong and set it right. But in all these matters the great body of the shareholders of a joint-stock company are, save in a few exceptional instances, almost powerless.

and by increased publicity in every form ; and thus collective and democratic forms of business management may be able to extend themselves safely in many directions in which they have hitherto failed, and may far exceed the great services they already render in opening a large career to those who have no advantages of birth.

The same may be said of the undertakings of Governments

Government undertakings. imperial and local : they also may have a great future before them, but up to the present time the tax-payer who undertakes the ultimate risks has not generally succeeded in exercising an efficient control over the businesses, and in securing officers who will do their work with as much energy and enterprise as is shown in private establishments. The problem of Government undertakings involves however many complex issues, into which we cannot inquire here.

§ 6. The system of Co-operation aims at avoiding the

Co-operative association. evils of these two methods of business management. In that ideal form of Co-operative Society, for which many still fondly hope, but which as yet has been scantily realized in practice, a part or the whole of those shareholders who undertake the risks of the business are themselves employed by it. The employés, whether they contribute towards the material capital of the business or not, have a share in its profits, and some power of voting at the general meetings at which the broad lines of its policy are laid down, and the officers appointed who are to carry that policy into effect. They are thus the employers and masters of their own managers and foremen ; they have fairly good means of judging whether the higher work of engineering the business is conducted honestly and efficiently, and they have the best possible opportunities for detecting any laxity or incompetence in its detailed administration. And lastly they render unnecessary some of the minor work of superintendence that is required in other establishments ; for their own pecuniary interests and the pride they take in the success of their own business make each of them averse to any shirking of work either by himself or by his fellow workmen.

But unfortunately the system has very great difficulties of its own. For human nature being what it is, the employés themselves are not always the best possible masters of their own foremen and managers; jealousies and frettings at reproof are apt to act like sand, that has got mixed with the oil in the bearings of a great and complex machinery. And in particular, since the hardest work of business management is generally that which makes the least outward show, those who work with their hands are apt to underrate the intensity of the strain involved in the highest work of engineering the business, and to grudge its being paid for at anything like as high a rate as it could earn elsewhere. And in fact the managers of a Co-operative Society seldom have the alertness, the inventiveness and the ready versatility of the ablest of those men who have been selected by the struggle for survival, and have been trained by the perfectly free and unfettered responsibility of private business. Partly for these reasons the co-operative system has seldom been carried out in its entirety; and its partial application has so far attained its highest success in the task of retailing commodities consumed by working men—a task in which it has special advantages. But *bonâ fide* co-operative production is now at last making excellent progress.

Its difficulties in the task of business management.

Those working-men indeed whose tempers are strongly individualistic, and whose minds are concentrated almost wholly on their own affairs, will perhaps always find their quickest and most congenial path to material success by commencing business as small independent "undertakers," or by working their way upwards in a private firm or a public company. But co-operation has a special charm for those in whose tempers the social element is stronger, and who desire not to separate themselves from

It may outgrow some of these.

their old comrades, but to work among them as their leaders. Its aspirations may in some respects be higher than its practice; but it undoubtedly does rest in a great measure on ethical motives. The true co-operator combines a keen business intellect with a spirit full of an earnest Faith; and some co-operative societies have been served excellently by men of great genius both mentally and morally—men who for the sake of the Co-operative Faith that is in them, have worked with great ability and energy, and with perfect uprightness, being all the time content with lower pay than they could have got as business managers on their own account or for a private firm. Men of this stamp are more common among the officers of co-operative societies than in other occupations; and though they are not very common even there, yet it may be hoped that the diffusion of a better knowledge of the true principles of co-operation, and the increase of general education are every day fitting a larger number of co-operators for the complex problems of business management.

Meanwhile many partial applications of the co-operative principle are being tried under various conditions,

Profit Sharing. each of which presents some new aspect of business management. Thus under the scheme of Profit-Sharing, a private firm while retaining the unfettered management of its business, pays its employés the full market rate of wages whether by Time or Piece-work, and agrees in addition to divide among them a certain share of any profits that may be made above a certain fixed minimum; it being hoped that the firm will find a material as well as a moral reward in the diminution of friction, in the increased willingness of their employés to go out of their way to do little things that may be of great benefit comparatively to the firm, and lastly in attracting to themselves workers of more than average ability and industry[1].

[1] In Schloss' *Methods of Remuneration* the relation of Profit sharing to co-operation and other forms of "Gain sharing" is well shown.

Other partial co-operative schemes are doing good work in various degrees. For instance the Oldham Cotton Mills are really joint-stock companies: but among their shareholders are many working men who have a special knowledge of the trade, though not many of their own employés. There is a larger element of co-operation in the Productive establishments, owned by the main body of Co-operative Stores, through their agents, the Co-operative Wholesale Societies. Here the Scotchmen are in advance; in the English Society the workers as such have as yet no direct share either in the management or in the profits of the works.

Other forms of partial Co-operation.

But we must not pursue this inquiry further now: enough has been said to show that the world is only just beginning to be ready for the higher work of the co-operative movement in its many different forms. It may therefore be reasonably expected to attain a much larger success in the future than in the past; and to offer excellent opportunities for working-men to practise themselves in the work of business management, to grow into the trust and confidence of others, and gradually rise to posts in which their business abilities will find scope.

Hopes for the future.

§ 7. In speaking of the difficulty that a working-man has in rising to a post in which he can turn his business ability to full account, the chief stress is commonly laid upon his want of capital: but this is not always his chief difficulty. For instance the co-operative distributive societies have accumulated a vast capital, on which they find it difficult to get a good rate of interest; and which they would be rejoiced to lend to any set of working-men who could show that they had the capacity for dealing with difficult business problems. Co-operators who have firstly a high order of business ability and probity, and secondly the "personal capital" of a great reputation among their fellows for these qualities, will have no difficulty in

The rise of the working-man hindered by his want of capital;

getting command of enough material capital for a considerable undertaking: the real difficulty is to convince a sufficient number of those around them that they have these rare qualities. And the case is not very different when an individual endeavours to obtain from the ordinary sources the loan of the capital required to start him in business.

It is true that in almost every business there is a constant increase in the amount of capital required to make a fair start; but there is a much more rapid increase in the amount of capital which is owned by people who do not want to use it themselves, and are so eager to lend it out that they will accept a constantly lower and lower rate of interest for it. Much of this capital passes into the hands of bankers and others, people of keen intellect and restless energy; people who have no class prejudices and care nothing for social distinctions; and who would promptly lend it to anyone of whose business ability and honesty they were convinced. To say nothing of the credit that can be got in many businesses from those who supply the requisite raw material or stock in trade, the opportunities for direct borrowing are now so great that an increase in the amount of capital required for a start in business is no very serious obstacle in the way of a person who has once got over the initial difficulty of earning a reputation for being likely to use it well.

But perhaps a greater, though not so conspicuous, hindrance to the rise of the working man is the growing complexity of business. The head of a business has now to think of many things about which he never used to trouble himself in earlier days; and these are just the kind of difficulties for which the training of the workshop affords the least preparation. Against this must be set the rapid improvement of the education of the working man not only at school, but what is more important, in after life by newspapers, and from the work of co-operative societies and trades unions, and in other ways.

and even more by the growing complexity of business.

About three-fourths of the whole population of England belong to the wage-earning classes; and at all events when they are well fed, properly housed and educated, they have their fair share of that nervous strength which is the raw material of business ability. Without going out of their way they are all consciously or unconsciously competitors for posts of business command. The ordinary workman, if he shows ability, generally becomes a foreman, from that he may rise to be a manager, and to be taken into partnership with his employer. Or having saved a little of his own he may start one of those small shops which still can hold their own in a working man's quarter, stock it chiefly on credit, and let his wife attend to it by day, while he gives his evenings to it. In these or in other ways he may increase his capital till he can start a small workshop, or factory. Once having made a good beginning, he will find the banks eager to give him generous credit. He must have time; and since he is not likely to start in business till after middle age he must have a long as well as a strong life; but if he has this and has also "patience, genius and good fortune" he is pretty sure to command a large capital before he dies. In a factory those who work with their hands, have better opportunities of rising to posts of command than the book-keepers and many others to whom social tradition has assigned a higher place. But in trading concerns it is otherwise; what manual work is done in them has as a rule no educating character, while the experience of the office is better adapted for preparing a man to manage a commercial than a manufacturing business.

There is then on the whole a broad movement from below upwards. Perhaps not so many as formerly rise at once from the position of working-men to that of employers: but there are more who get on sufficiently far to give their sons a good chance of attaining to the highest posts. The complete rise is not so very often accomplished in one generation; it is more often spread over

A rapid rise not an unmixed benefit.

two; but the total volume of the movement upwards is probably greater than it has ever been. And it may be remarked in passing that it is better for society as a whole that the rise should be distributed over two generations. The workmen who at the beginning of this century rose in such large numbers to become employers were seldom fit for posts of command: they were too often harsh and tyrannical; they lost their self-control, and were neither truly noble nor truly happy; while their children were often haughty, extravagant, and self-indulgent, squandering their wealth on low and vulgar amusements, having the worst faults of the older aristocracy without their virtues. The foreman or superintendent who has still to obey as well as to command, but who is rising and sees his children likely to rise further, is in some ways more to be envied than the small master. His success is less conspicuous, but his work is often higher and more important for the world, while his character is more gentle and refined and not less strong. His children are well-trained; and if they get wealth, they are likely to make a fairly good use of it.

§ 8. When a man of great ability is once at the head of an independent business, whatever be the route by which he has got there, he will with moderate good fortune, soon be able to show such evidence of his power of turning capital to good account as to enable him to borrow in one way or another almost any amount that he may need; and on the other hand a man with small ability in command of a large capital, speedily loses it: he may perhaps be one who could and would have managed a small business with credit, and left it stronger than he had found it: but if he has not the genius for dealing with great problems, the larger it is the more speedily will he break it up.

Adjustment of capital to business ability.

These two sets of forces, the one increasing the capital at the command of able men, and the other destroying the capital that is in the hands of weaker men, bring about the result that there is a far more close correspondence between the ability of business men and the size of the businesses which they own than at first sight would appear probable. And when we consider all the many routes, by which a man of great natural business ability can work his way up high in some private firm or public company, we may conclude that wherever there is work on a large scale to be done in such a country as England, the ability and the capital required for it are pretty sure to be speedily forthcoming.

Further, just as industrial skill and ability are getting every day to depend more and more on the broad faculties of judgment, promptness, resource, carefulness and steadfastness of purpose—faculties which are not specialized to any one trade, but which are more or less useful in all—so it is with regard to business ability. In fact business ability consists more of these general and non-specialized faculties than do industrial skill and ability in the lower grades: and the higher the grade of business ability the more various are its applications.

Since then business ability in command of capital moves with great ease horizontally from a trade which is overcrowded to one which offers good openings for it: and since it moves with great ease vertically, the abler men rising to the higher posts in their own trade, we see, even at this early stage of our inquiry, some good reasons for believing that in modern England the supply of business ability in command of capital accommodates itself, as a general rule, to the demand for it; and thus has a fairly defined supply price.

Supply price of business ability in command of capital.

Finally, we may regard this supply price of business ability in command of capital as composed of three elements. The first is the supply price of capital; the second is the supply price of business ability and energy; and the third is the supply price of that organization by which the appropriate business ability and the requisite capital are brought together.

M.

The price of the first of these three elements is "Interest;"
Net and Gross Earnings of Management. we may call the price of the second taken by itself "*Net* Earnings of Management," and that of the second and third taken together "*Gross* Earnings of Management."

The last few years have seen a marked increase in the relative force of very large businesses in certain industries. The change has not been brought about by new principles in business organization, so much as by the development of processes and methods in manufacture and mining, in transport and banking, which are beyond the reach of any but very large capitals; by the increase in the scope and functions of markets, and in the technical facilities for handling large masses of goods. But the change is important: and it will be fully investigated in Volume II., in connection with and in dependence on a study of the modern organization of markets for credit and for goods.

CHAPTER XIII.

CONCLUSION. THE LAW OF INCREASING IN RELATION TO
THAT OF DIMINISHING RETURN.

§ 1. AT the beginning of this Book we saw how the extra
Return of raw produce which Nature affords to
an increased application of capital and labour, **Relation of the later Chapters of this Book to the earlier.**
other things being equal, tends in the long run
to diminish. In the remainder of the Book and
especially in the last four chapters we have looked at the other
side of the shield, and seen how man's power of productive
work increases with the volume of the work that he does.
Considering first the causes that govern the supply of labour,
we saw how every increase in the physical, mental, and
moral vigour of a people makes them more likely, other
things being equal, to rear to adult age a large number of
vigorous children. Turning next to the Growth of Wealth we
observed how every increase of wealth tends in many ways to
make a greater increase more easy than before. And lastly
we saw how every increase of wealth and every increase in the
numbers and intelligence of the people increased the facilities
for a highly developed Industrial Organization, which in its
turn adds much to the collective efficiency of capital and
labour.

Looking more closely at the economies arising from an
increase in the scale of production of any kind of goods, we
found that they fell into two classes—those dependent on the
general development of the industry and those dependent on
the resources of the individual houses of business engaged in
it and the efficiency of their management; that is, into *external*
and *internal* economies.

We saw how these latter economies are liable to constant
fluctuations so far as any particular house is concerned, and
therefore when we speak of the normal cost of production of
any class of goods we must suppose them to be produced by a
firm that is fairly representative of the whole body of pro-
A Representa-   ducers of those goods.   Our Representative firm
tive firm.   must be one which has had a fairly long life, and
fair success, which is managed with normal ability, and which
has normal access to the economies, External and Internal,
which belong to that aggregate volume of production[1].

The general argument of the present Book shows that an
increase in the aggregate volume of production of anything
will generally increase the size, and therefore the Internal
economies possessed by this Representative firm; and that it
will always increase the External economies to which such a
firm has access; and that thereby the firm will be enabled to
manufacture at a less proportionate cost of labour and sacrifice than before.

In other words we say broadly that while the part which
The Laws of   Nature plays in production conforms to the Law
Increasing Re- of Diminishing Return, the part which man plays
turn,   conforms to the *Law of Increasing Return,*
which may be stated thus:—An increase of capital and
labour leads generally to an improved organization, which
increases the efficiency of the work of capital and labour.

Therefore in those industries which are not engaged in
raising raw produce an increase of capital and labour generally gives a return increased more than in proportion; and
further this improved organization tends to diminish or even
override any increased resistance which Nature may offer to
raising increased amounts of raw produce.   If the actions of
the Laws of Increasing and Diminishing Return are balanced
and of Con-   we have the *Law of Constant Return* and an
stant Return.   increased produce is obtained by labour and
sacrifice increased just in proportion.

For the two tendencies towards Increasing and Diminishing Return press constantly against one another. In the production of wheat and wool, for instance, the latter tendency has almost exclusive sway in an old country, which cannot import freely[1]. In turning the wheat into flour, or the wool into blankets, an increase in the aggregate volume of production brings some new economies, but not many; for the trades of grinding wheat and making blankets are already on so great a scale that any new economies that they may attain are more likely to be the result of new inventions than of improved organization. In a country however in which the blanket trade is but slightly developed, these latter may be important; and then it may happen that an increase in the aggregate production of blankets diminishes the proportionate difficulty of manufacturing by just as much as it increases that of raising the raw material. In that case the actions of the Laws of Diminishing and of Increasing Return would just neutralize one another; and blankets would conform to the Law of Constant Return. But in most of the more delicate branches of manufacturing, where the cost of raw material counts for little, and in most of the modern transport industries the Law of Increasing Return acts almost unopposed.

§ 2. Our discussion of the character and organization of industry taken as a whole tends to show that an increase in the volume of labour causes in general, other things being equal, a more than proportionate increase in the total efficiency of labour. But we must not forget that other things may not be equal. The increase of numbers may be accompanied by more or less general adoption of unhealthy and enervating habits of life in over-crowded towns. Or it may have started badly, outrunning the material resources of the people, causing them with imperfect appliances to make excessive demands on the soil;

Subject to certain conditions,

[1] As regards the struggle of the two tendencies in agriculture, compare above Book IV. Ch. III. § 5.

and so to call forth the stern action of the Law of Diminishing Return as regards raw produce, without having the power of minimizing its effects : having thus begun with poverty, an increase in numbers may go on to its too frequent consequences in that weakness of character which unfits a people for developing a highly organized industry.

All this and more may be granted, and yet it remains true that the collective efficiency of a people with a given average of individual strength and skill may increase more than in proportion to their numbers. If they can for a time escape from the pressure of the Law of Diminishing Return by importing food and other raw produce ; if their wealth, not being consumed in great wars, increases at least as fast as their numbers ; and if they avoid habits of life that would enfeeble them ; then every increase in their numbers is likely *for the time* to be accompanied by a more than proportionate increase in their power of obtaining material goods. For it enables them to secure the many various economies of specialized skill and specialized machinery, of localized industries and production on a large scale : it enables them to have increased facilities of communication of all kinds ; while the very closeness of their neighbourhood diminishes the expense of time and effort involved in every sort of traffic between them, and gives them new opportunities of getting social enjoyments and the comforts and luxuries of culture in every form. It is true that against this must be set the growing difficulty of finding solitude and quiet and even fresh air. This deduction is a weighty one; but there still remains a balance of good.

Taking account of the fact that an increasing density of population generally brings with it access to new social enjoyments we may give a rather broader scope to this statement and say :—An increase of population accompanied by an equal increase in the material sources of enjoyment and aids to

an increase of numbers may be accompanied by a more than proportionate increase of collective efficiency.

production is likely to lead to a more than proportionate increase in the aggregate income of enjoyment of all kinds; provided firstly, an adequate supply of raw produce can be obtained without great difficulty, and secondly there is no such overcrowding as causes physical and moral vigour to be impaired by the want of fresh air and light and of healthy and joyous recreation for the young.

The accumulated wealth of civilized countries is at present growing faster than the population: and though it may be true that the wealth per head would increase somewhat faster if the population did not increase quite so fast; yet as a matter of fact an increase of population is likely to continue to be accompanied by a more than proportionate increase of the material aids to production: and in England *at the present time*, with easy access to abundant foreign supplies of raw material, an increase of population is accompanied by a more than proportionate increase of the means of satisfying human wants other than the need for light, fresh air, &c. It must however be remembered that England's foreign supplies of raw produce may at any time be checked by changes in the trade regulations of other countries, and may be almost cut off by a great war; while the naval and military expenditure which would be necessary to make the country fairly secure against this last risk, would appreciably diminish the benefits that she derives from the action of the Law of Increasing Return[1].

The effects of a growth of numbers must be distinguished from those of a growth of wealth.

---

[1] The Englishman Mill bursts into unwonted enthusiasm when speaking of the pleasures of wandering alone in beautiful scenery: and many American writers give fervid descriptions of the growing richness of human life as the backwoodsman finds neighbours settling around him, as the backwoods settlement developes into a village, the village into a town, and the town into a vast city.

BOOK V.

THE BALANCING OF DEMAND AND SUPPLY.

CHAPTER I.

ON MARKETS.

§ 1. In later stages of our work we shall be much occupied with the balancing of those economic forces of growth and decay, which have been discussed in the last few chapters in connection with the rise and fall of business firms. But for the present, we must turn to a simpler sort of balancing or equilibrium, resembling rather that of a weight suspended by an elastic string, or of several balls resting in a bowl. The present Book is given to a general inquiry into the balancing of the forces of Demand and Supply, these terms being used in their broadest sense: that is, as hinted at the end of the first chapter of Book IV., it is a bringing together of the chief notions of that Book and of Book III.

§ 2. When demand and supply are spoken of in relation to one another, it is of course necessary that the markets to which they refer should be the same. **Definition of a Market.**
As Cournot says, " Economists understand by the term *Market,* not any particular market-place in which things are bought and sold, but the whole of any region in which buyers

and sellers are in such free intercourse with one another that the prices of the same goods tend to equality easily and quickly." Or again as Jevons says:—"Originally a market was a public place in a town where provisions and other objects were exposed for sale; but the word has been generalized, so as to mean any body of persons who are in intimate business relations and carry on extensive transactions in any commodity. A great city may contain as many markets as there are important branches of trade, and these markets may or may not be localized. The central point of a market is the public exchange, mart or auction rooms, where the traders agree to meet and transact business. In London the Stock Market, the Corn Market, the Coal Market, the Sugar Market, and many others are distinctly localized; in Manchester the Cotton Market, the Cotton Waste Market, and others. But this distinction of locality is not necessary. The traders may be spread over a whole town, or region of country, and yet make a market, if they are, by means of fairs, meetings, published price lists, the post office or otherwise, in close communication with each other."

Thus the more nearly perfect a market is, the stronger is the tendency for the same price to be paid for the same thing at the same time in all parts of the market: but of course if the market is large, allowance must be made for the expense of delivering the goods to different purchasers; each of whom must be supposed to pay in addition to the market price a special charge on account of delivery[1].

§ 3. In applying economic reasonings in practice it is often difficult to ascertain how far the movements **Boundaries of** of supply and demand in any one place are influ- **a market.** enced by those in another. It is clear that the general tendency of the telegraph, the printing press and steam traffic is

---

[1] Thus it is common to see the prices of bulky goods quoted as delivered "free on board" (f.o.b.) any vessel in a certain port, each purchaser having to make his own reckoning for bringing the goods home.

to extend the area over which such influences act and to increase their force. The whole Western World may, in a sense, be regarded as one market for many kinds of stock exchange securities, for the more valuable metals, and to a less extent for wool and cotton and even wheat; proper allowance being made for expenses of transport, in which may be included taxes levied by any customs houses through which the goods have to pass. For in all these cases the expenses of transport, including customs duties, are not sufficient to prevent buyers from all parts of the Western World from competing with one another for the same supplies.

There are many special causes which may widen or narrow the market of any particular commodity: but nearly all those things for which there is a very wide market are in universal demand, and capable of being easily and exactly described. Thus for instance cotton, wheat, and iron satisfy wants that are urgent and nearly universal. They can be easily described, so that they can be bought and sold by persons at a distance from one another and at a distance also from the commodities. If necessary, samples can be taken of them which are truly representative: and they can even be "graded," as is the actual practice with regard to grain in America, by an independent authority; so that the purchaser may be secure that what he buys will come up to a given standard, though he has never seen a sample of the goods which he is buying, and perhaps would not be able himself to form an opinion on it if he did.

General conditions of a wide market for a thing. Suitability for grading.

Commodities for which there is a very wide market must also be such as will bear a long carriage: they must be somewhat durable, and their value must be considerable in proportion to their bulk. A thing which is so bulky that its price is necessarily raised very much when it is sold far away from the place in which it is produced, must as a rule have a narrow market. The market for common

Portability.

bricks for instance is practically confined to the near neighbourhood of the kilns in which they are made: they can scarcely ever bear a long carriage by land to a district which has any kilns of its own. But bricks of certain exceptional kinds have a market extending over a great part of England.

§ 4. Let us then consider more closely the markets for things which satisfy in an exceptional way these conditions of being in general demand, cognizable and portable. They are, as we have said, stock exchange securities and the more valuable metals.

Any one share or bond of a public company, or any bond of a government is of exactly the same value as any other of the same issue; and it can make no difference to any purchaser which of the two *Stock exchange securities.* he buys. Some securities, principally those of comparatively small mining, shipping, and other companies, require local knowledge, and are not very easily dealt in except on the stock exchanges of provincial towns in their immediate neighbourhood. But the whole of England is one market for the shares and bonds of a large English railway. In ordinary times a dealer will sell, say, Midland Railway shares, even if he has not them himself; because he knows they are always coming into the market, and he is sure to be able to buy them.

But the strongest case of all is that of securities which are called "international," because they are in request in every part of the globe. They are the bonds of the chief governments, and of very large public companies such as those of the Suez Canal and the New York Central Railway. For bonds of this class the telegraph keeps prices at almost exactly the same level in all the stock exchanges of the world. If the price of one of them rises in New York or in Paris, in London or in Berlin, the mere news of the rise tends to cause a rise in other markets; and if for any reason the rise is delayed, that particular class of bonds is likely soon to be offered for sale in the high priced market under telegraphic orders from the other markets, while dealers in the first market will be making telegraphic purchases in other markets. These sales on the one hand, and purchases on the other, strengthen the tendency which the price has to seek the same level everywhere[1].

Stock exchanges then are the pattern on which markets have been, and are being formed for dealing in many kinds of produce which can be easily and exactly described, are portable and in general demand. The material commodities however which possess these qualities in the highest degree are gold and silver. For that very reason they have been chosen by common consent for use as money, to represent the value of other things; and the world-market for them is most highly organized.

The world-market for the precious metals.

At the opposite extremity to international stock-exchange securities and the more valuable metals are, firstly, things which must be made to order to suit particular individuals, such as well-fitting clothes; and secondly, perishable and bulky goods, such as fresh vegetables, which can seldom be profitably carried long distances. The first can scarcely be said to have a wholesale market at all; the conditions by which their price is determined are those of retail buying and selling, and the study of them may be postponed[2].

Thus the character of the markets varies with the area of Space over which they extend : but it varies even more with

---

[1] It is a characteristic fact that securities which are part of large issues are preferred on the Stock exchange.

[2] A man may not trouble himself much about small retail purchases: he may give half a crown for a packet of paper in one shop which he could have got for two shillings in another. But it is otherwise with wholesale prices. A manufacturer cannot sell a ream of paper for six shillings while his neighbour is selling it at five. For those whose business it is to deal in paper know almost exactly the lowest price at which it can be bought, and will not pay more than this. The manufacturer has to sell at about the market price, that is at about the price at which other manfacturers are selling at the same time.

the length of Time of which account is taken; and we shall find that if the period is short, the supply is limited to the stores which happen to be at hand: if the period is longer, the supply will be influenced by the cost of producing the commodity in question; and if the period is very long, this cost will be influenced by the cost of producing the labour and the material things required for producing the commodity. We shall consider in the next chapter those temporary equilibria of demand and supply, in which the cost of producing the commodity exerts either no influence or merely an indirect influence.

At a later stage we shall have to combine the difficulties with regard to time on the side of supply with those on the side of demand, of which something has already been said [1].

[1] Book III. Ch. IV. § 5.

CHAPTER II.

TEMPORARY BALANCE OF DEMAND AND SUPPLY.

§ 1. THE simplest case of balance, or equilibrium, between
desire and effort is found when a person satisfies
one of his wants by his own direct work. When
a boy picks blackberries for his own eating, the
action of picking may itself be pleasurable for a while; and
for some time longer the pleasure of eating may be more than
enough to repay the trouble of picking. But after he has
eaten a good deal, the desire for more diminishes; while the
task of picking begins to bring weariness; which may indeed
be caused more by monotony than by fatigue. Equilibrium
is reached, when at last his eagerness to play and his disincli-
nation for the work of picking counterbalance the desire for
eating. The satisfaction which he can get from picking
fruit has arrived at its *maximum :* for up to that time every
fresh picking has added more to his pleasure than it has
taken away; and after that time any further picking would
take away from his pleasure more than it would add.

In a casual bargain that one person makes with another,
as for instance when two backwoodsmen barter a rifle for a
canoe, there is seldom anything that can properly be called
an equilibrium of supply and demand: there is probably a
surplus of satisfaction on either side; for probably the one

*Equilibrium
between desire
and effort.*

would be willing to give something besides the rifle for the canoe, if he could not get the canoe otherwise; while the other would in case of necessity give something besides the canoe for the rifle.

We may put aside as of little practical importance a class of dealings which has been much discussed. They relate to pictures by old masters, rare coins and other things, which cannot be "graded" at all. The price at which each is sold, will depend much on whether any rich persons with a fancy for it happen to be present at its sale. If not, it will probably be bought by dealers who reckon on being able to sell it at a profit; and the variations in the price for which the same picture sells at successive auctions, great as they are, would be greater still if it were not for the steadying influence of professional purchasers.

§ 2. Let us then turn to the ordinary dealings of modern life; and take an illustration from a corn-market in a country town, and let us assume for the sake of simplicity that all the corn in the market is of the same quality. The amount which each farmer or other seller offers for sale at any price is governed by his own need for money in hand, and by his calculation of the present and future conditions of the market with which he is connected. There are some prices which no seller would accept, some which no one would refuse. There are other intermediate prices which would be accepted for larger or smaller amounts by many or all of the sellers. Everyone will try to guess the state of the market and to govern his actions accordingly. Let us suppose that in fact there are not more than 600 quarters, the holders of which are willing to accept as low a price as 35s.; but that holders of another hundred would be tempted by 36s.; and holders of yet another three hundred by 37s. Let us suppose also that a price of 37s. would tempt buyers for only 600 quarters; while another hundred could be sold at 36s., and yet another

two hundred at 35*s.*   These facts may be put out in a table
thus :—

At the price	Holders will be willing to sell	Buyers will be willing to buy
37*s.*	1000 quarters,	600 quarters.
36*s.*	700 ,,	700 ,,
35*s.*	600 ,,	900 ,,

Of course some of those who are really willing to take
36*s.* rather than leave the market without selling, will not
show at once that they are ready to accept that price.   And
in like manner buyers will fence, and pretend to be less eager
than they really are.   So the price may be tossed hither and
thither like a shuttlecock, as one side or the other gets the
better in the "higgling and bargaining" of the market.   But
unless they are unequally matched; unless, for instance, one side
is very simple or unfortunate in failing to gauge the strength of
the other side, the price is likely to be never very far from 36*s.*;
and it is nearly sure to be pretty close to 36*s.* at the end of the
market.   For if a holder thinks that the buyers will really
be able to get at 36*s.* all that they care to take at that price,
he will be unwilling to let slip past him any offer that is
well above that price.

Buyers on their part will make similar calculations; and
if at any time the price should rise considerably above 36*s.*
they will argue that the supply will be much greater than
the demand at that price: therefore even those of them who
would rather pay that price than go unserved, wait; and by
waiting they help to bring the price down.   On the other
hand, when the price is much below 36*s.*, even those sellers
who would rather take the price than leave the market with
their corn unsold, will argue that at that price the demand
will be in excess of the supply: so they will wait, and by
waiting help to bring the price up.

The price of 36*s.* has thus some claim to be called the true equilibrium price : because if it were fixed on at the beginning, and adhered to throughout, it would exactly equate demand and supply (i.e. the amount which buyers were willing to purchase at that price would be just equal to that for which sellers were willing to take that price); and because every dealer who has a perfect knowledge of the circumstances of the market expects that price to be established. If he sees the price differing much from 36s. he expects that a change will come before long, and by anticipating it he helps it to come quickly.

§ 3.   We have already used the term "demand price"[1] to denote the price at which buyers can be found for any given amount of a thing in a market. Thus in this market 37s. is the demand price for 600 quarters; 36s. for 700 and so on. We have introduced a corresponding term "supply price"[2] to denote the price which holders of a commodity will be willing to take for any given amount. Thus in this market 35s. is the supply price for 600 quarters, 36s. for 700 ; and so on.

Transition to normal prices.

We have next to enquire what causes govern supply-prices, that is prices which dealers are willing to accept for different amounts. In the present chapter we have looked at the affairs of only a single day; and have supposed the stocks offered for sale to be already in existence. But of course these stocks are dependent on the amount of wheat sown in the preceding year; and that, in its turn, was largely influenced by the farmers' guesses as to the price which they would get for it in this year. This is the point at which we have to work in the next chapter.

[1] Book III. Ch. III. § 1.
[2] Book IV. Ch. I.

CHAPTER III.

BALANCING OF NORMAL DEMAND AND SUPPLY.

§ 1. WE have noticed that even in the corn-exchange of a country town on a market-day the equilibrium price is affected by calculations of the future relations of production and consumption; while dealings for future delivery already predominate in the leading corn-markets of America and Europe, and are rapidly weaving into one web all the leading threads of trade in corn throughout the whole world. If it is thought that the growers of any kind of grain in any part of the world have been losing money, and are likely to sow a less area for a future harvest, far-seeing dealers argue that prices are likely to rise as soon as that harvest comes into sight. Thus anticipations of that rise exercise an influence on present sales for future delivery, and that in its turn influences cash prices; so that these prices are indirectly affected by estimates of the expenses of producing further supplies. But in this and the following chapters we are specially concerned with movements of price ranging over still longer periods than those for which the most far-sighted dealers in futures generally make their reckoning.

Transition from market to normal price.

§ 2. We may revert to the discussion of the analogy between the supply price and the demand price of a commodity at the point at which we left it at the end of the last chapter. We there noticed that corresponding to the demand price at which any amount of a commodity would find purchasers in a market, there is a supply price at which that amount would be offered for sale by producers or their agents. We have to take account of

The account of supply price carried a little further.

the fact that the production of the commodity will probably require many different kinds of labour and the use of capital in many forms. The exertions of all the different kinds of labour that are directly or indirectly involved in making it; together with the abstinences or rather the waitings required for saving the capital used in making it: all these efforts and sacrifices together will be called its *Real Cost of Production.* The sums of money, that have to be paid for these efforts and sacrifices, will be called either its *Money Cost of Production,* or, (for shortness) its *Expenses of Production.* They are the prices which have to be paid in order to call forth an adequate supply of the efforts and waitings that are required for making it; or, in other words, they are its supply price[1].

Real and Money Cost of Production.

Expenses of Production.

The raw material, machinery, labour, &c., that are required for making a commodity may be called its *Factors of Production.* Its expenses of production when any given amount of it is produced are thus the supply prices of the corresponding quantities of its factors of production. And the sum of these is the supply price of that amount of the commodity.

Factors of Production.

§ 3. It must not be forgotten that trading expenses enter into the expenses of production in almost every case; and that in some cases they are a very large part of the whole. For instance, the supply price of wood in the neighbourhood of Canadian forests often consists almost exclusively of the price of the labour of lumber men: but the supply price of Canadian deal

Relative importance of different elements of Cost of Production.

---

[1] Mill and some other economists have followed the practice of ordinary life in using the term Cost of Production in two senses, sometimes to signify the difficulty of producing a thing, and sometimes to signify the outlay of money that has to be incurred in order to induce people to overcome this difficulty and produce it. But by passing from one use of the term to the other without giving explicit warning, they have led to many misunderstandings and much barren controversy.

in the wholesale London market consists in a large measure of
freights; while the supply price of the same wood to a small
retail buyer in an English country town is more than half
made up of the charges of the railways and middlemen who
have brought what he wants to his doors, and keep a stock of
it ready for him.   Again, the supply price of a certain kind of
labour may for some purposes be analysed into the expenses of
rearing, of general education and of special trade education.

It is to be taken for granted that as far as the knowledge
and business enterprise of the producers reach, they will in
each case choose those factors of production which are best
for their purpose; that is, which will attain the desired end
for the least outlay and trouble to themselves.   Whenever
it appears to the producers that this is not the case, they will,
Principle of as a rule, set to work to substitute the less
Substitution. expensive method.   We may call this for convenience of reference, *the Principle of Substitution.*

§ 4.   In our typical market then we assume that the
We assume forces of demand and supply have free play;
free play for that there is no combination among dealers on
demand and
supply in the either side; but each acts for himself, and there
market. is much *free competition;* that is, buyers generally
compete freely with buyers, and sellers compete freely with
sellers.   But though everyone acts for himself, his knowledge
of what others are doing is supposed to be generally sufficient
to prevent him from taking a lower or paying a higher price
than others are doing.

In such a market there is a definite demand price for each
amount of the commodity, that is, a definite price at which
each particular amount of the commodity can find purchasers
in a year, or whatever other period we choose as our unit of
time: the more of a thing is offered for sale in a market, the
lower is the price at which it will find purchasers; or in other
words, the demand price for each unit diminishes with every
increase in the amount offered.

In like way there is a supply price, that is, a price which may be expected to call forth a supply of each particular amount in a unit of time. To give precision to the ideas, let us suppose that a person well acquainted with the woollen trade sets himself to inquire what would be the normal supply price of a certain number of millions of yards annually of a particular kind of cloth. He would have to reckon (i) the price of the wool, coal, and other materials which would be used up in making it, (ii) wear-and-tear and depreciation of the buildings, machinery and other fixed capital, (iii) interest and insurance on all the capital, (iv) the wages of those who work in the factories, and (v) the gross earnings of management (including insurance against loss) of those who undertake the risks, who engineer and superintend the working. He would of course estimate the supply prices of all these different factors of production of the cloth with reference to the amounts of each of them that would be wanted; and he would suppose the conditions of supply to be normal, and the expenses of production to be those of a Representative Firm[1]. And he would add them all together to find the supply price of the cloth.

Construction of the supply schedule.

Let us suppose a list of supply prices (or a supply schedule) made on a similar plan to that of our list of demand prices (or demand schedule[2]): the supply price of each amount of the commodity in a year, or any other unit of time, being written against that amount. As the annual amount produced increases, the supply price increases, if nature is offering a sturdy resistance to man's efforts to wring from her a larger supply of raw material, and if there is no great room for introducing important new economies into the manufacture. But it might so happen that an increase in the volume of production would introduce new economies and enable the tendency to Increasing Return to prevail over that to Diminishing

---

[1] See Book IV. Ch. XIII. § 1.   [2] See Book III. Ch. III. § 2.

Return, so as ultimately to lessen the supply price of the commodity, and make it cheaper[1].

§ 5.   When therefore the amount produced (in a unit of time) is such that the demand price is greater than the supply price, then sellers receive more than is sufficient to make it worth their while to bring goods to market to that amount; and the amount brought forward for sale tends to increase. On the other hand, when the amount produced is such that the demand price is less than the supply price, sellers receive less than is sufficient to make it worth their while to bring goods to market on that scale; so that those, who were just on the margin of doubt as to whether to go on producing, are decided not to do so, and the amount brought forward for sale tends to diminish. When the demand price is equal to the supply price, the amount produced has no tendency either to be increased or to be diminished; it is in equilibrium.

What is meant by equilibrium.

Further, if any accident should move the scale of production from its equilibrium position (or position of rest), there will be instantly brought into play forces tending to bring it back to that position; just as, if a stone hanging by a string is displaced from its equilibrium position, the force of gravity will at once tend to bring it back to its equilibrium position[2].

[1] Compare above, p. 180.

[2] The following diagrams may help some readers. But they are not necessary for the argument, and may be omitted.

Measuring, as in the case of the demand curve, amounts of the commodity along Ox and prices parallel to Oy, we get for each point M along Ox a line MP drawn at right angles to it measuring the supply price for the amount OM, the extremity of which, P, may be called a *supply point*; this price MP being made up of the supply prices of the several factors of production for the amount OM. The locus of P may be called the *supply curve*. It is a curve such that, if from any point P on it a straight line PM be drawn perpendicular to Ox, PM represents the price at which sellers will be forthcoming for an amount OM.

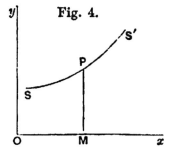

Fig. 4.

§ 6. But in real life such oscillations are seldom as rhythmical as those of a stone hanging freely from a string; the comparison would be more exact if the string were supposed to hang in the troubled waters of a mill-race, whose stream was at one time allowed to flow freely, *The problems* and at another partially cut off. The demand *of value in real life are* and supply schedules do not in practice remain *less simple.* unchanged for a long time together, but are constantly being changed; and every change in them gives new positions to the centres about which the amount and the price tend to oscillate.

These considerations point to the great importance of the element of time in relation to demand and supply, to some study of which we now proceed. We shall gradually discover a great many different limitations of the doctrine that the price at which a thing can be produced represents its real cost of production, that is, the efforts and sacrifices which have been directly and indirectly devoted to its production. That doctrine would indeed represent facts accurately enough in a stationary society, in which the habits of life, and the methods and volume of production remained unchanged from one generation to another; provided that people were tolerably free to choose those occupations for their capital and labour which seemed most advantageous.

This is the real drift of that much-quoted, and much-misunderstood doctrine of Adam Smith and other economists

To represent the equilibrium of demand and supply geometrically we may draw the demand and supply curves together as in Fig. 5. If then *OR* represents the rate at which production is being actually carried on, and *Rd* the demand price is greater than *Rs* the supply price, the production is exceptionally profitable, and will be increased; and *R* will move to the right. On the other hand, if *Rd* is less than *Rs*, *R* will move to the left. If *Rd* is equal to *Rs*, that is, if *R* is vertically under a point of intersection of the curves, demand and supply are in equilibrium.

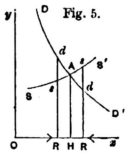

that the normal, or "natural," value of a commodity is that
which economic forces tend to bring about *in the long run.*
It is the average value which economic forces would bring
about if the general conditions of life were stationary for a
run of time long enough to enable them all to work out their
full effect.   The fact that the general conditions of life are
not stationary is the source of many of the difficulties that
are met with in applying economic doctrines to practical
problems.

§ 7.   Thus we see that utility and cost of production both
play a part in governing value.   And we might as reasonably
dispute whether it is the upper or the under blade of a pair
of scissors that cuts a piece of paper, as whether value is
governed by utility or cost of production.   It is true that
Influences of when one blade is held still, and the cutting is
utility and cost effected by moving the other, we may say with
of production
on value.   careless brevity that the cutting is done by the
second; but the statement is not strictly accurate, and
is to be excused only so long as it claims to be merely a
popular and not a strictly scientific account of what actually
happens.

In the same way, when a thing already made has to be
sold, the prices which people will be willing to pay for it will
be governed by their desire to have it, together with the
amount they can afford to spend on it.   Their desire to have
it depends partly on the chance that, if they do not buy it,
they will be able to get another thing like it at as low a price:
this depends on the causes that govern the supply of it, and
this again upon cost of production.   But it may so happen
that the stock to be sold is practically fixed.   This, for
instance, is the case with a fish-market, in which the value of
fish for the day is governed almost exclusively by the stock
on the slabs in relation to the demand.   And if a person
chooses to take the stock for granted; and say that the price
is governed by demand, his brevity may perhaps be excused

so long as he does not claim strict accuracy. So again it may be pardonable, but it is not strictly accurate to say that the varying prices which the same rare book fetches, when sold and resold at Christie's auction room, are governed exclusively by demand.

Taking a case at the opposite extreme, we find some commodities which conform pretty closely to the law of constant return; that is to say, their average cost of production will be very nearly the same whether they are produced in small quantities or in large. In such a case the normal level about which the market price fluctuates will be this definite and fixed money cost of production. If the demand happens to be great, the market price will rise for a time above the level; but as a result production will increase and the market price will fall. Conversely, if the demand falls for a time below its ordinary level, production will fall off, and the market price will be raised.

If, then, a person chooses to neglect market fluctuations; and takes it for granted that there will anyhow be enough demand for the commodity to insure that some of it, more or less, will find purchasers at a price equal to this cost of production, then he may be excused for ignoring the influence of demand, and speaking of normal price as governed by cost of production—provided only he does not claim scientific accuracy for the wording of his doctrine, and explains the influence of demand in its right place.

Thus we may say that, *as a general rule*, the shorter the period which we are considering, the greater must be the share of our attention which is given to the influence of demand on value; and the longer the period, the more important will be the influence of cost of production on value[1].

---

[1] For a discussion of further developments of this theory the reader is referred to *Principles*, V. III.

§ 8. There is one very difficult point, on which a few words must be said here. It is the relation in which money cost, or expenses, of production stands to rent.

The expenses of production of agricultural produce are estimated on the margin of cultivation. That is, they are estimated for a part of the produce which is raised either on land that pays no rent because it is poor or badly situated ; or, which is more probable, they are raised on land which does pay rent, but by applications of capital and labour which only just pay their way, and therefore can contribute nothing towards the rent [1]. It is these expenses which the demand price must just cover : for if it does not, the supply will fall off, and the price be raised till it does cover them. It is to these expenses therefore that the price conforms : and, as Ricardo pointed out, rent does not appear as an element of them.

Rent in relation to expenses of production.

Suppose for instance that, with an average harvest, ten million quarters of corn are raised in England, and that the expenses of production of the last million quarters are at the rate of 35s. a quarter. If the farmers had expected to get less than 35s. a quarter they would not have raised these last quarters. And since they find it worth their while to raise the whole ten million, we know that in an average year they get 35s. for each of the last million. And in the same market there can only be one price for one and the same commodity. Therefore they must have expected the average price of all the corn in the market to be 35s.

The Expenses of production of some of the corn may have been only 25s. a quarter. The 35s. got for a quarter of this corn is divided into 25s. which goes to the farmer, and 10s. which goes to the landlord as rent. And if a person looks at *this* corn he may argue that its whole expenses of production were 25s. to cover the farmer's outlay and 10s. to pay his rent,

---

[1] Compare above, Book IV. Ch. III. § 2.

and that therefore rent enters into the expenses of production of this corn. He would be right if he meant only that the expenses of production of this particular quarter of corn cannot be found by merely reckoning up the wages and profits of the labour and capital that were spent in raising it. But he would be wrong if he meant that the selling price of corn was *governed* by the rent that has to be paid for the use of land. He would then be mistaking cause for effect, and effect for cause. Rent is not the cause of a high price of corn, but its effect. The price of corn must be on the average just high enough to cover the expenses of production of that portion of it which is raised under the most unfavourable conditions. The amount that is raised, and the price at which it is sold, are thus governed by the numbers of the population which demand corn on the one hand, and by the amount of fertile land, which is the source of supply, on the other. A fertile land, which is specially suited for growing corn, is sure to be applied to that purpose; the rent obtained for that land does not therefore affect the supply of corn, and does not therefore affect its price. The price tends to equal the expenses of production of that which is raised under the most unfavourable conditions and which pays no rent. The rent is governed by the excess of this price over the expenses of production of the other produce that the farmer raises at less expense[1].

[1] This difficult doctrine is further discussed in Appendix C.

CHAPTER IV.

INVESTMENT OF RESOURCES FOR A DISTANT RETURN.
PRIME COST AND TOTAL COST.

§ 1. LET us suppose a man to build a house for himself on
Motives deter- land, and of materials, which nature supplies
mining the in- *gratis*, and to make his implements as he goes;
vestment of
capital.   the labour of making them being counted as part
of the labour of building the house. He would have to estimate
the efforts required for building on any proposed plan ; and to
allow almost instinctively an amount increasing in geometrical
proportion (a sort of compound interest) for the period that
would elapse between each effort and the time when the house
would be ready for his use. The utility of the house to him
when finished would have to compensate him not only for the
efforts, but for the waitings[1].

This case illustrates the way in which the efforts and
sacrifices which are the Real cost of production of a thing,
underlie the expenses which are its Money cost. But the
modern business man commonly takes the payments which he
has to make, whether for wages or raw material, as he finds
them ; without staying to inquire how far they are an accurate
measure of the efforts and sacrifices to which they correspond.
His expenditure is generally made piece-meal ; and the longer
he expects to wait for the fruit of any outlay, the richer must
that fruit be in order to compensate him. The anticipated
fruit may not be certain ; and in that case he will have to
allow for the risk of failure. After making that allowance,

---

[1] See above, Book IV. Ch. VIII. § 6.

the fruit of the outlay must be expected to exceed the outlay
itself by an amount which, independently of his own remuneration, increases at compound interest in proportion to the
time of waiting.

§ 2. ´At the beginning of his undertaking, and at every
successive stage, the business man is ceaselessly
striving so to modify his arrangements as to obtain better results with a given expenditure or
equal results with a less expenditure. He is continually studying
the advantages and disadvantages of different ways of obtaining his object. He is always looking for new suggestions,
watching the experiments of others and trying experiments
himself, so as to hit upon that combination which will yield
the largest incomings in proportion to any given outlay. In
other words, he ceaselessly applies the principle of substitution with the purpose of increasing his profits; ₐand in so
doing he seldom fails to increase the total efficiency of work,
the total power over nature which man derives from organization and knowledge.

The principle of substitution.

Every locality has incidents of its own which affect in
various ways the methods of arrangement of
every class of business that is carried on in it.
But even in the same place and the same trade
no two persons pursuing the same aims will adopt
exactly the same routes. The tendency to variation is a chief
cause of progress; and the abler are the undertakers in any
trade the greater will this tendency be. In some trades, as
for instance cotton-spinning, the possible variations are confined within narrow limits; no one can hold his own at all
who does not use machinery, and very nearly the latest
machinery, for every part of the work. But in others, as for
instance in some branches of the wood and metal trades, in
farming, and in shopkeeping, there can be great variations.
For instance, of two manufacturers in the same trade, one
will perhaps have a larger wages bill and the other heavier

Different routes are chosen to the same end.

charges on account of machinery; of two retail dealers one will have a larger capital locked up in stock and the other will spend more on advertisements and other means of building up the immaterial capital of a profitable trade connection. And in minor details the variations are numberless. Each man's actions are influenced by his special opportunities and resources, as well as by his temperament and his associations.

But each man, taking account of his own means, will push the investment of capital in his business in each several direction until what appears in his judgment to be the outer limit, or margin, of profitableness is reached; that is, until there seems to him no good reason for thinking that the gains resulting from any further investment in that particular direction would compensate him for his outlay. The margin of profitableness is not to be regarded as a mere point on any one fixed line of possible investment; but as a boundary line of irregular shape cutting one after another every possible line of investment.

§ 3. When investing his capital in providing the means of carrying on an undertaking, the business man looks to being recouped by the price obtained for its various products; and he expects to be able under normal conditions to charge for each of them a sufficient price; that is, one which will not **Prime or special cost.** only cover the *special, direct,* or *prime cost,* but also bear its proper share of the general expenses of the business; and these we may call its *supplementary cost.* These two elements together make its *total cost.*

There are great variations in the usage of the term Prime **Supplementary and total cost.** cost in business life. But it is taken here in a narrow sense. Supplementary . costs are here taken to include standing charges on account of the durable plant in which much of the capital of the business has been invested, and also the salaries of the upper employees: for the charges to which the business is put on account of their salaries cannot generally be adapted quickly to changes in the amount of work there is for them to do. There remains nothing but the (money) cost of the raw material used in making the commodity and the wages of that part of the labour spent on it which is paid by the hour or the piece, and the extra wear and tear of plant. This is the special cost which a manufacturer has in view, if he is calculating the lowest price at which it will be worth his while to accept an order, irrespectively of any effect that his action might have in spoiling the market for future orders, and trade being slack at the time. But in fact he must as a rule take account of this effect: the price at which it is just worth his while to produce, even when trade is slack, is in practice generally a good deal above this prime cost, as we shall see shortly[1].

[1] "There are many systems of Prime Cost in vogue...we take Prime Cost to mean, as in fact the words imply, only the original or direct cost of production; and while in some trades it may be a matter of convenience to include in the cost of production a proportion of indirect expenses, and a charge for depreciation on plant and buildings, in no case should it comprise interest on capital or profit." (Garcke and Fells, *Factory Accounts*, Ch. I.)

CHAPTER V.

EQUILIBRIUM OF NORMAL DEMAND AND SUPPLY, CON-
TINUED, WITH REFERENCE TO LONG AND SHORT
PERIODS.

§ 1.   THE present chapter is chiefly occupied with difficulties in the problem of value, resulting from differences between
the immediate and the later effects of the same causes.   In

**The term
Normal is
elastic.**

this case, as in others, the economist merely
brings to light difficulties that are latent in the
common discourse of life, so that by being frankly
faced they may be thoroughly overcome.   For in ordinary life
it is customary to use the word Normal in different senses,
with reference to different periods of time ; and to leave the
context to explain the transition from one to another.   The
economist follows this practice of every-day life : but, by
taking pains to indicate the transition, he sometimes seems
to have created a complication which in fact he has only
revealed.

Thus, for instance, when it is said that the price of wool
on a certain day was abnormally high though the average
price for the year was abnormally low, that the wages of coal-
miners were abnormally high in 1872 and abnormally low in
1879, that the (real) wages of labour were abnormally high
at the end of the fourteenth century and abnormally low in
the middle of the sixteenth ; everyone understands that the
scope of the term Normal is not the same in these various
cases.   Everyone takes the context as indicating the special
use of the term in each several case ; and a formal interpretation clause is seldom necessary, because in ordinary

conversation misunderstandings can be nipped in the bud by question and answer. But let us look at this matter more closely.

We have noticed[1] how a cloth manufacturer when calculating the expenses of producing all the different things required for making cloth would need to frame his estimates with reference to the amounts

Illustration from the cloth trade.

of each of them that would be wanted, and on the supposition in the first instance that the conditions of supply would be normal. But we have yet to take account of the fact that he must give to this term a wider or narrower range, according as he was looking more or less far ahead.

Thus in estimating the wages required to call forth an adequate supply of labour to work a certain class of looms, he might take the current wages of similar work in the neighbourhood: or he might argue that there was a scarcity of that particular class of labour in the neighbourhood, that its current wages there were higher than in other parts of England, and that looking forward over several years so as to allow for immigration, he might take the normal rate of wages at a rather lower rate than that prevailing there at the time. Or lastly, he might think that the wages of weavers all over the country were abnormally low relatively to others of the same grade, in consequence of a too sanguine view having been taken of the prospects of the trade half a generation ago. He might argue that this branch of work was overcrowded, that parents had already begun to choose other trades for their children which offered greater net advantages and yet were not more difficult; that in consequence a few years would see a falling-off in the supply of labour suited for his purpose; so that looking forward a long time he must take normal wages at a rate rather higher than the present average.

Again, in estimating the normal supply price of wool, he

---

[1] See above, Ch. III. § 4.

M.   14

would take the average of several past years. He would make allowance for any change that would be likely to affect the supply in the immediate future; and he would reckon for the effect of such droughts as from time to time occur in Australia and elsewhere; since their occurrence is too common to be regarded as abnormal. But he would not allow here for the chance of our being involved in a great war, by which the Australian supplies might be cut off; he would consider that any allowance for this should come under the head of extraordinary trade risks, and not enter into his estimate of the normal supply price of wool.

He would deal in the same way with the risk of civil tumult or any violent and long-continued disturbance of the labour market of an unusual character; but in his estimate of the amount of work that could be got out of the machinery, &c., under normal conditions, he would probably reckon for minor interruptions from trade disputes such as are continually occurring, and are therefore to be regarded as belonging to the regular course of events, that is, as not abnormal.

In all these calculations he would not concern himself specially to inquire how far mankind are under the exclusive influence of selfish or self-regarding motives. He might be aware that anger and vanity, jealousy and offended dignity are still almost as common causes of strikes and lockouts, as the desire for pecuniary gain: but that would not enter into his calculations. All that he would want to know about them would be whether they acted with sufficient regularity for him to be able to make a reasonably good allowance for their influence in interrupting work and raising the normal supply price of the goods.

In short, the practised business man simplifies his task by giving his attention to one set of difficulties at a time, making almost instinctively first one and then another provisional supposition to help him on his way.

§ 2. But though applications of the term Normal are thus elastic, and capable of being extended gradually from very short to very long periods; yet these periods may be divided roughly into two classes. In the first class there is time for the supply of those things which are used in producing the commodity (or in other words, its factors of production), to adapt itself to the demand; in the second class there is not.

Long and short period normal prices.

For instance, on the day following a large catch of mackerel the price in the market may settle down after a little manœuvring at as many pence as it had been at shillings on the previous day; and this change will in no way depend on the normal cost of catching mackerel, it will be governed by the volume of the past catch, with perhaps some slight reference to the chance that a similar catch may be had on the morrow. If we suppose the boat to be owned by a capitalist who pays the fisherman by the day, the net earnings of his boat for the day will be the excess of the price he gets for his fish over his outlay for wages and stores, together with allowance for the injury done to the boat and net by the day's work.

Illustration from fish markets.

Oscillations of market price.

For that particular day this excess may be either more or less than the normal supply price required to make it worth his while to provide the boat and its equipment and the business organization needed for managing it and selling its catch. But if, in the long run and on the average, it is more than this normal supply price, capital will drift into the fishing trade; if less, it will drift out; that is to say, old boats and nets, when worn out, will seldom be replaced. And therefore, if the general conditions of the fishing trade are stationary, the earnings of the boat will oscillate about this normal supply price.

But next suppose there to be great increase in the general demand for fish, such for instance as might arise from the

spreading of a disease through all kinds of farm stock simul-
taneously, by which meat was made a dear and

Oscillations of normal supply price for short periods. dangerous food. The increased demand for fish could not well be met without bringing into the
fishing trade some people from outside, who were
not fitted by training to do its work well, and to whom many
of its ordinary incidents would prove great hardships. Old and
unsuitable boats would be pressed into the service; while the
better class of boats would earn an excess above the expenses
of working them, that would amount in a year perhaps to
fifty per cent. or more on their total cost; and able fishermen,
whether paid by shares or by the day, might for a time get
twice their ordinary wages. Thus the normal price of fish
would be higher than before. Variations in the catch of fish
from day to day might make the market price oscillate at
least as violently as before about this normal level for an
increased amount, but this level would rise rapidly with every
such increase of demand.

Of course these high prices would tend to bring capital
and labour into the trade: but if it were expected that the
disease among live stock would not last very long, and that
therefore the unusual demand for fish would die away in a
few years, people would be cautious about investing capital
and skill in a trade that was in danger of being glutted. And
therefore, though when the demand slackened off, the price
would fall to, and probably below its old level; yet so long
as the demand was fully maintained the price would keep up.
And here we see an illustration of the almost universal law
that the term Normal, being taken to refer to a short period
of time, the normal supply price is likely to be raised by an
increase in demand.

§ 3. But if we turn to consider the normal supply price
with reference to a *long period* of time, we shall find that it is

Normal value in relation to long periods. governed by a different set of causes, and with
different results. For suppose that the disuse of
meat causes a permanent distaste for it, and that

an increased demand for fish continues long enough to enable the forces by which its supply is governed to work out their action fully. The source of supply in the sea might perhaps show signs of exhaustion, and the fishermen might have to resort to more distant coasts and to deeper waters, Nature giving a Diminishing Return to the increased application of capital and labour of a given order of efficiency. On the other hand, those might turn out to be right who think that man is responsible for but a very small part of the destruction of fish that is constantly going on ; and in that case a boat starting with equally good appliances and an equally efficient crew would be likely to get nearly as good a haul after the increase in the total volume of the fishing trade as before. In any case the normal cost of equipping a good boat with an efficient crew would certainly not be higher, and probably be a little lower after the trade had settled down to its now increased dimensions than before. For since fishermen require only trained aptitudes, and not any exceptional natural qualities, their number could be increased in less than a generation to almost any extent that was necessary to meet the demand ; while the industries connected with building boats, making nets, &c. being now on a larger scale would be organized more thoroughly and economically. If therefore the waters of the sea showed no signs of depletion of fish, an increased supply could be produced at a lower price after a time sufficiently long to enable the normal action of economic causes to work itself out : and, the term Normal being taken to refer to a long period of time, the normal price of fish would decrease with an increase in demand.

§ 4. To sum up first as regards short periods. The supply of specialized skill and ability, of suitable machinery and other material capital, and of the appropriate industrial organization, has not time to be fully adapted to demand ; but the producers have to adjust their supply to the demand as best they can with the

General conclusions as to short periods,

appliances already at their disposal. On the one hand there is not time materially to increase those appliances if the supply of them is deficient; and on the other, if the supply is excessive, some of them must remain imperfectly employed, since there is not time for the supply to be much reduced by gradual decay, and by conversion to other uses. The particular income derived from them does not *for the time* affect perceptibly the supply; and does not directly affect the price of the commodities produced by them. It is a surplus of total receipts over prime cost; but unless it is sufficient to cover in the long run a fair share of the general costs of the business, production will gradually fall off[1].

Next to sum up as to long periods. In them all investments of capital and effort in providing the material plant and the organization of a business, and in acquiring trade knowledge and specialized ability, *and as to long periods.* have time to be adjusted to the incomes which are expected to be earned by them: and the estimates of those incomes therefore directly govern supply, and are the true long-period normal supply price of the commodities produced. A great part of the capital invested in a business is generally spent on building up its internal organization and its external trade connections. If the business does not prosper all this capital is lost, even though its material plant may realize a considerable part of its original cost. And anyone proposing to start a new business in any trade must reckon for the chance of this loss. If himself a man of normal capacity for that class of work, he may look forward ere long to his business being a representative one, in the sense in which we have used this term, with its fair share of the economies of production on a large scale. If the net earnings of such a representative business seem likely to be greater than he could get by similar investments in other

---

[1] Thus it has something of the nature of a rent. Compare below, Ch. viii. § 1, and Appendix D.

trades to which he has access, he will choose this trade. Thus that investment of capital in a trade, on which the price of the commodity produced by it depends in the long run, is governed by estimates on the one hand of the outgoings required to build up and to work a representative firm, and on the other of the incomings, spread over a long period of time, to be got by such a price.

§ 5. To go over the ground in another way. Market values are governed by the relation of demand to stocks actually in the market; with more or less reference to 'future' supplies, and not without some influence of trade combinations. But the current supply is in itself the result of the action of producers in the past; this action has been mainly determined by their comparing the prices which they expect to get for their goods with the expenses to which they will be put in producing them. *The general drift of the term Normal Supply Price is the same for short and long periods.* The range of expenses of which they take account will depend on whether they are merely considering the extra expenses of certain extra production with their existing plant, or are considering whether to lay down new plant for the purpose. But in any case it will be the general rule that that portion of the supply which can be most easily produced will be produced, unless the price is expected to be very low. Every increase in the price expected will, as a rule, induce some people who would not otherwise have produced anything, to produce a little; while those who have produced something for the lower price, will probably produce more for the higher price.

The general drift of the term Normal Supply Price is always the same whether the period to which it refers is short or long; but there are great differences in detail. In every case it means the price the expectation of which is sufficient and only just sufficient to make it worth while for people to produce a certain aggregate amount yearly: in every case it is the marginal cost of production; that is, it is the cost of production of those goods which are on the margin of not being produced at all, and which would not be produced if the price to be got for them were expected to be at all lower. But the causes which determine this margin vary with the length of the period under consideration.

§ 6.   Of course there is no hard and sharp line of division
There is no sharp division between long and short periods. between "long" and "short" periods.   Nature has drawn no such lines in the economic conditions of actual life; and in dealing with practical problems they are not wanted.   Just as we contrast civilized with uncivilized races, and establish many general propositions about either group, though no hard and fast division can be drawn between the two; so we contrast long and short periods without attempting any rigid demarcation between them.   But four classes stand out.   In each, price is governed by the relations between demand and
Classification of problems of value by the periods to which they refer. supply.   But as regards *market* prices, Supply is taken to mean the stock of the commodity in question which is on hand, or at all events "in sight."   As regards *normal* prices, when the term Normal is taken to relate to *short* periods of a few months or a year, Supply means broadly what can be produced for the price in question with the existing stock of plant, personal and impersonal, in the given time.   As regards *normal* prices, when the term Normal is to refer to *long* periods of several years, Supply means what can be produced by plant, which itself can be remuneratively produced and applied within the given time; while lastly, there are very gradual or *Secular* movements of normal price, caused by the gradual growth of knowledge, of population and of capital, and the changing conditions of demand and supply from one generation to another.

The remainder of the present volume is chiefly concerned with the third of the above classes.   That is, it discusses the normal relations of wages, profits, prices, &c., for long periods of several years. But occasionally account has to be taken of gradual changes; and one chapter, Book VI. Ch. XII., is given up to "The Influence of Progress on Value," that is, to the study of very gradual, or secular, changes of value.

On the other hand the first two classes will come into prominence when we discuss, in the second volume, fluctuations of prices and wages arising from quickly passing changes in the state of commercial credit, and other causes. And the chapter on "Trade Unions" at the end of the present volume is partly concerned with these two classes.

CHAPTER VI.

JOINT AND COMPOSITE DEMAND: JOINT AND COMPOSITE SUPPLY.

§ 1. THE demand for the things used for making other

Derived demand and joint demand. things, and their factors of production, is indirect; it is *derived* from the demand for the things towards the production of which they contribute; or, in other words, the demands for all the various factors of production of a finished commodity are joined together in the *joint demand* for it. Thus the demand for beer is direct, and is a joint demand for hops, malt, brewers' labour, and the other factors of production of beer: and the demand for any one of them is an indirect demand derived from that for beer. Again there is a direct demand for new houses; and from this there arises a joint demand for the labour of all the various building trades, and for bricks, stone, wood, etc., which are factors of production of building work of all kinds, or as we may say for shortness, of new houses. But the demand for any one of these, as for instance the labour of plasterers, is only an indirect, or Derived, demand.

Let us take an illustration from a class of events that

Illustration taken from a labour dispute in the building trade. are of frequent occurrence in the labour market; and suppose that the supply and demand for building being in equilibrium, there is a strike on the part of one group of workers, say the plasterers, or that there is some other disturbance to the supply of plasterers' labour. In order to make a separate study of the demand for that factor, we suppose firstly that the general conditions of the demand for new houses remain unchanged (that is, that the demand schedule for new houses remains valid); and secondly we assume that there is no change in the general conditions of supply of the other factors, two of which are of course the business faculties and the business organizations of the master builders (that is, we assume that their supply schedules also remain valid). Then a temporary check to the supply of plasterers' labour will cause a proportionate check to the amount of building: the demand price for the diminished number of houses will be a little higher than before; and the supply prices for the other factors of production will not be greater than before. Thus new houses can now be sold at prices which exceed by a good margin the sum of the prices at which these other requisites for the production of houses can be bought; and that margin gives the limit to the possible rise of the price that will be offered for plasterers' labour, and on the supposition that plasterers' labour is indispensable[1].

§ 2. It is however important to remember that if the supply of one factor is disturbed, the supply of others is likely to be disturbed also. In particular, when the factor of which the supply is disturbed is one class of labour, as that of the plasterers, the employers' earnings generally act as a buffer. That is to say, the loss falls in the first instance on them; but by discharging some of their workmen and lowering the wages of others, they ultimately distribute a great part of it among the other factors of production.

We may note the general conditions, under which a check

---

[1] The different amounts of this margin, corresponding to different checks to the supply of plasterers' labour, are determined by the general rule that,—

The demand price for any thing used in producing a commodity is, for each separate amount of the commodity, limited by the excess of the price at which that amount of the commodity can find purchasers, over the sum of the prices at which the corresponding supplies of the other things needed for making it will be forthcoming.

This and several other results of the present chapter can be most clearly apprehended by the aid of diagrams. See *Principles* V. VI.

to the supply of a thing that is wanted not for direct use,

Conditions
under which
a check to
supply may
raise much the
price of a factor
of production. but as a factor of production, may cause a very great rise in its price. The first condition is that the factor itself should be essential, or nearly essential to the production of the commodity, no good substitute being available at a moderate price.

The second condition is that the commodity in the production of which it is a necessary factor, should be one for which the demand is stiff and inelastic; so that a check to its supply will cause consumers to offer a much increased price for it rather than go without it; and this of course includes the condition that no good substitutes for the commodity are available at a price but little higher than its equilibrium price. If the check to house building raises the price of houses very much, builders, anxious to secure the exceptional profits, will bid against one another for such plasterers' labour as there is in the market.

The third condition is that only a small part of the expenses of production of the commodity should consist of the price of this factor. Since the plasterers' wages are but a small part of the total expenses of building a house, a rise of even 50 per cent. in them would add but a very small percentage to the expenses of production of a house and would check demand but little.

The fourth condition is that even a small check to the amount demanded should cause a considerable fall in the supply prices of other factors of production; for that will increase the margin available for paying a high price for this one. If, for instance, bricklayers and other classes of workmen, or the employers themselves cannot easily find other things to do, and cannot afford to remain idle, they may be willing to work for much lower earnings than before, and this will increase the margin available for paying higher wages to plasterers.

The rise in plasterers' wages would be checked if it were possible either to avoid the use of plaster, or to get the work done tolerably well and at a moderate price by people outside the plasterers' trade. The Law of Substitution here as elsewhere exercises a subduing influence on forces which might otherwise lead to startling results.   The tyranny which one factor of production of a commodity might in some cases exercise over the other factors through the Law of Derived Demand is tempered by the Law of Substitution.

(margin note: Moderating influence of the Law of Substitution.)

The relations between plasterers, bricklayers, &c. are representative of much that is both instructive and romantic in the history of alliances and conflicts between trades unions in allied trades.   But the most numerous instances of Joint demand are those of the demand for a raw material and the operatives who work it up; as for instance cotton or jute or iron or copper, and those who work up these several materials. Again, the relative prices of different articles of food vary a good deal with the supply of skilled cooks' labour; thus for instance many kinds of meat and many parts of vegetables which are almost valueless in America, where skilled cooks are rare and expensive, have a good value in France where the art of cooking is widely diffused.

§ 3.   We have already[1] noticed how the demand for any commodity is made up or compounded of the composite demands of the different individuals who may need it.   But we now may extend this notion of *composite demand* to factors of production.   Nearly every raw material and nearly every kind of labour is applied in many different branches of industry, and contributes to the production of a great variety of commodities; and the total demand for it is the sum of the derived demands for it, in each of these several uses.

(margin note: Composite demand.)

[1] See Book III. Ch. III., IV.

§ 4. We may now pass to consider the case of *joint pro-*

Joint Supply.   *ducts :* i.e. of things which cannot easily be produced separately; but are joined in a common
origin, such as gas and coke, or beef and hides, or wheat and
straw. As there is a joint demand for things joined in a
common destination, so there is a *joint supply* of things which
have a common origin. The single supply of the common
origin is split up into the various derived supplies of the
things that proceed from it.

The prices of the gas and the coke, the joint products
that are got from a ton of coal, must together be enough
to cover their joint expenses of production. If the demand
for gas rises, more coke will be produced, and its price
must fall, so that the increased supply may be taken off
the market. The rise in the price of gas must be sufficient to
cover this fall in the price of coke, and also to cover the
increase, if there is any, in the joint expenses of production of
gas and coke. Again, since the repeal of the Corn Laws much
of the wheat consumed in England has been imported, of
course without any straw. This has caused a scarcity and a
consequent rise in the price of straw, and the farmer who
grows wheat looks to the straw for a great part of the value of
the crop. The value of straw then is high in countries which
import wheat, and low in those which export wheat. In the
same way the price of mutton in the wool-producing districts
of Australia was at one time very low. The wool was exported, the meat had to be consumed at home; and as there
was no great demand for it, the price of the wool had to
defray almost the whole of the joint expenses of production of
the wool and the meat. Afterwards the low price of meat
gave a stimulus to the trade of preserving meat for exporta-
tion, and now its price in Australia is higher.

There are very few cases of joint products the cost of production of both of which together is exactly the same as that

of one of them alone.   So long as any product of a business has a market value, it is almost sure to have devoted to it some special care and expense, which would be dimin- *The proportions of joint products can generally be modified.* ished, or dispensed with if the demand for that product were to fall very much. Thus, for instance, if straw were valueless, farmers would exert them- selves more than they do to make the ear bear as large a proportion as possible to the stalk.   Again, the importation of foreign wool has caused English sheep to be adapted by judicious crossing and selection so as to develop heavy weights of good meat at an early age, even at the expense of some deterioration of their wool.   It is only when one of two things produced by the same process is valueless, unsaleable, and yet does not involve any expense for its removal, that there is no inducement to attempt to alter its amount.

§ 5.   We may pass to the problem of *composite supply*, which is analogous to that of composite demand. *Composite Supply.* When a thing has several sources of production, its total supply is made up, or compounded, of the supplies from all the several sources; and these supplies are *rival* and *competitive* to one another.   Each is likely to be applied in "substitution" for the others: for the principle of substitu- tion leads every business man to select those means to his end that are most efficient in proportion to their cost; unless indeed he is negligent, or has some independent reason for preferring the more costly one.

If the causes which govern the production of two of these rivals are nearly the same, they may for many purposes be treated as one commodity.   For instance, beef and mutton may be treated as varieties of one commodity for many pur- poses; but they must be treated as separate for others, as for instance for those in which the question of the supply of wool enters.

Rival things are however often not finished commodities,

but factors of production: for instance, there are many rival fibres which are used in making ordinary printing paper. We have just noticed how the fierce action of derived demand for one of several complementary supplies, as e.g. for the supply of plasterers' labour, was liable to be moderated, when the demand was met by the competitive supply of a rival thing which could be "substituted" for it.

§ 6.   All the four chief problems, which have been discussed in this chapter, have some bearing on the causes that govern the value of almost every commodity: and many of the most important cross connections between the values of different commodities are not obvious at first sight.

Thus when charcoal was generally used in making iron, the price of leather depended in some measure on that of iron; and the tanners petitioned for the exclusion of foreign iron in order that the demand on the part of English iron smelters for oak charcoal might cause the production of English oak to be kept up, and thus prevent oak bark from becoming dear.

Instances of intricate relations between the values of different things.

Again, the development of railways and other means of communication for the benefit of one trade, as for instance for wheat growing in some parts of America and for silver mining in others, greatly lowers some of the chief expenses of production of nearly every other product of those districts. Again, the prices of soda, and bleaching materials, and other products of industries the chief raw material of which is salt, move up and down relatively to one another with almost every improvement in the various processes which are used in those industries. And every change in those prices affects the prices of many other goods; for the various products of the salt industries are more or less important factors in many branches of manufacture.

Again, cotton and cotton-seed oil are joint products, and

the recent fall in the price of cotton is largely due to the improved manufacture and uses of cotton-seed oil: and further,
as the history of the cotton famine shows, the price of cotton
largely affects that of wool, linen and other things of its own
class.

CHAPTER VII.

PRIME AND TOTAL COST IN RELATION TO JOINT PRO-
DUCTS. COST OF MARKETING. INSURANCE AGAINST
RISK.

§ 1. WE may now return to the consideration of Prime
and Supplementary Costs, with special reference
to the proper distribution of the latter between
the Joint products of a business. For instance
the shipowner has to apportion the expenses of
his ship between heavy goods and goods that are bulky but
not heavy. He tries, as far as may be, to get a mixed cargo
of both kinds; and an important element in the struggle for
existence of rival ports is the disadvantage under which those
ports lie which are able to offer a cargo only of bulky or only
of heavy goods: while a port whose chief exports are weighty
but not bulky, attracts to its neighbourhood industries which
make for export goods that can be shipped from it at low
freights.

Difficulties as to the joint products of the same business.

From the expenses of transport we pass easily to those of
marketing. Some kinds of goods are easily mar-
keted; there is a steady demand for them, and
it is always safe to make them for stock. But
for that very reason competition cuts their price "very fine,"
and does not allow a large margin above the direct cost of
making them. Sometimes the tasks of making and selling
them can be rendered almost automatic, so as to require very
little to be charged on their account under the heads of the
expenses of management and marketing. But in practice it is

Difficulties as to the expenses of marketing.

not uncommon to charge such goods with even less than the small share that would properly fall to them, and to use them as a means of obtaining and maintaining a business connection, that will facilitate the marketing of other classes of goods, the production of which cannot so well be reduced to routine; for as to these there is not so close a competition. Manufacturers, especially in trades connected with furniture and dress, and retailers in almost all trades, frequently find it best to use certain of their goods as a means of advertising others, and to charge the first with less and the second with more than their proportionate share of Supplementary expenses. In the former class they put those goods which are so uniform in character and so largely consumed that nearly all purchasers know their value well, in the second those with regard to which purchasers think more of consulting their fancy than of buying at the lowest possible price.

Economic progress is constantly offering new facilities for marketing goods at a distance: it not only lowers cost of carriage, but what is often more important, it enables producers and consumers in distant places to get in touch with one another. In spite of this, the advantages of the producer who lives on the spot are very great in many trades; they often enable him to hold his own against competitors at a distance whose methods of production are more economical. He can sell in his own neighbourhood as cheaply as they can, because though the cost of making is greater for his goods than for theirs, he escapes much of the cost which they incur for marketing. But time is on the side of the more economic methods of production; and his distant competitors will gradually get a stronger footing in the place, unless he or some new man adopts their improved methods.

Local facilities for marketing.

A great part of these expenses of marketing results from the risk that a thing preparing for a certain market will not find the expected sale there. But it still remains to make a

15—2

closer study of the relation in which Insurance against the risks of a business stands to the supply price of any particular commodity produced in it.

§ 2.   The manufacturer and the trader commonly insure

Insurance against risk. against injury by fire and loss at sea; and the premiums which they pay are among the general expenses, a share of which has to be added to the Prime cost in order to determine the Total cost of their goods.   But the greater part of business risks are so inseparably connected with the general management of the business that an insurance company which undertook them would really make itself responsible for the business: and in consequence every firm has to act as its own insurance office with regard to them. The charges to which it is put under this head are part of its general expenses, and a share of them has to be added to the Prime cost of each of its products.

But there is a danger of allowing for these risks more than once.   When a farmer has calculated the expenses of raising any particular crop with reference to an average year, he must not count in addition insurance against the risk that the season may be bad, and the crop a failure: for in taking an average year, he has already set off the chances of exceptionally good and bad seasons against one another. When the earnings of a ferryman have been calculated on the average of a year, allowance has already been made for the risk that he may sometimes have to cross the stream with an empty boat.

When a manufacturer has taken the average of his sales of dress materials over a long time, and based his future action on the results of his past experience, he has already allowed for the risks that the machinery will be depreciated by new inventions that will render it nearly obsolete and that his goods will be depreciated by changes in fashion.   If he were to allow separately for insurance against these risks, he would be counting the same thing twice over.

This discussion of the risks of trade has again brought before us the fact that the value of a thing, though it tends to equal its normal (money) cost of production, does not coincide with it at any particular time, save by accident. The value in use of a bell with a flaw in it is very little; it can be used only as old metal and therefore its price is only that of the old metal in it. When it was being cast the same trouble and expense were incurred for it as for other bells which turned out sound. Its Expenses of production were the same as those of sound bells: but they have great value in use and are therefore sold at a high price. The price of each particular bell is limited by its value in use: what the Law of Normal Value states is that the price of cracked bells and sound bells together must in the long run cover the expenses of making bells.

CHAPTER VIII.

SHORT NOTES ON SEVERAL PROBLEMS.

§ 1. WE are now at the end of that part of the general theory of value which can be presented in an easy form. But a word or two may be said here as to the general drift of a few doctrines, the investigation of which belongs to an advanced course of study.

In Appendix D it is shortly argued that the so-called "rent" of a house, after deducting for the value
Quasi-rents. of the land on which it is built, is really profits on capital invested in building: but that such profits, and also the profits earned by machinery and other appliances for production, have something in them of the nature of rent; and that when short periods of time are under consideration they may properly be regarded as *Quasi-rents*.

The average income earned by the machinery in normal times is pretty sure to be about enough to give a moderate return of net profits. For if it gave but a very poor profit, capital would leave the trade; and if it gave a very high profit, capital would flow into the trade, and by its competition bring the rate of profits down to the normal level. But this argument assumes that the trade is open. It is not applicable to a monopoly.

§ 2. A monopolist may be, and often is, influenced by many other motives than the immediate desire
Monopolies. for gain. But in so far as he is governed by this motive, he will endeavour to keep the price of his commodity

at the level which will give him the greatest net revenue. If, for instance, a steam-ferry company with a practical monopoly of a short cut between a town and its suburb could get 2,000 passengers weekly at a fare of 3$d.$, 4,000 at 2$d.$, or 10,000 at 1$d.$; and if it calculated that its working expenses would be at the rate of 2$d.$ for the first number, 1$\frac{1}{4}d.$ for the second, and $\frac{3}{4}d.$ for the third, it would be likely to fix the fare at 2$d.$ For the figures would stand thus:

Fare.	Number carried.	Cost per head.	Net revenue.
3$d.$	2,000	2$d.$	2,000$d.$
2$d.$	4,000	1$\frac{1}{4}d.$	3,000$d.$
1$d.$	10,000	$\frac{3}{4}d.$	2,500$d.$

It would thus get a higher revenue with a fare of 2$d.$, than with either 3$d.$ or 1$d.$

If, however, it could be induced to lower its fare to 1$d.$, the 4,000 people who had paid the 2$d.$ would gain 4,000$d.$ net: and the 6,000 people who would walk round rather than pay 2$d.$, but would pay 1$d.$ rather than walk, would also derive a benefit from the change. If we put the aggregate value of this benefit to them at 2,000$d.$, we find that a change which took but 500$d.$ from the net income of the ferry company would confer 6,000$d.$ worth of benefit, or consumers' surplus as we have called it, on the public. This case illustrates the starting point of many interesting problems[1].

§ 3. The striking features of the case of the ferry are derived from the fact that a great number of passengers can be carried at a lower cost per head to the company than a small number. And it may be observed that in any branch of production which is free from monopoly and in which this rule holds (or in technical terms which shows a tendency to Increasing Return), an

Indirect results of variations in demand.

[1] The practical applications of such lines of reasoning belong to a later stage of economic study: but their leading outlines are shown by aid of diagrams in *Principles*, V. XIII.

increased demand is sure to be followed by a fall in supply price under the direct influence of competition; and thus every additional purchaser confers a benefit on others. Books, for instance are made cheaper, to the benefit of all concerned, by an increase in the demand for them. But oats are made dearer by an increase in the demand for them. If rich men kept many superfluous horses, they would make food dearer. If instead they bought many books, they would enable other people to buy more books for a given outlay than before. This case also points to many interesting problems[1].

---

[1] The leading outlines of some of these are shown by aid of diagrams in *Principles*, V. XI. and XII.

BOOK VI.

VALUE,

OR

DISTRIBUTION AND EXCHANGE.

CHAPTER I.

PRELIMINARY SURVEY OF DISTRIBUTION AND EXCHANGE.

§ 1. THE keynote of this Book is in the fact that free human beings are not brought up to their work on the same principles as a machine, a horse, or a slave. If they were there would be very little difference between the distribution and the exchange side of value; for then the return to each agent of production would only just suffice on the average to cover its expenses of production with wear and tear, etc. :—on the average; *i.e.* after allowance had been made for casual failures to adjust supply to demand. But as it is, our growing power over nature makes her yield an ever larger surplus above necessaries; and, though this might be absorbed by a very rapid increase of population, yet in fact population in a modern civilized country does not increase rapidly up to the means of subsistence; and all save the poorest do in fact enjoy a growing surplus above mere necessaries. There remain therefore the questions:—What are the general causes which govern the distribution of this surplus among the people? What part is played by conventional necessaries, *i.e.* the Standard of

Drift of Book VI. as a whole.

Comfort? What by the influence which methods of consumption and habits of life exert on efficiency; by wants in relation to activities, *i.e.* by the Standard of Life? What by the many-sided action of the principle of substitution, and by the struggle for survival between hand-workers and brain-workers of different classes and grades? What by the power which the use of capital gives to those in whose hands it is? What share of the general flow is turned to remunerate those who work and "wait," as contrasted with those who work and consume at once the fruits of their endeavours? An attempt is made to give a broad answer to these and some similar questions.

The problem of distribution is difficult: no solution of it,

The problem difficult: simple illustrations needed.

which is simple, can be true. Closer study has shown that what professed to be easy answers to it, were really partial answers to imaginary questions that might have arisen in other worlds than ours in which the conditions of life were very simple[1]. But yet the work done in answering these questions was not wasted: for a very difficult problem can best be solved by being broken up into pieces; and each of these simple questions contained a part of the great and difficult problem which we have to solve. Let us profit by this experience and work our way by successive steps.

§ 2. Let us begin by studying the influence of demand on

First, all supposed industrially equal and interchangeable: population stationary.

the earnings of labour, drawn from an imaginary world in which everyone owns the capital that aids him in his labour; so that the problem of the relations of capital and labour does not arise in it. That is, let us suppose that but little capital is used; while everyone owns whatever capital he does use, and the gifts of nature are so abundant that they are free and unappropriated. Let us suppose, further, that everyone is not only of equal capacity, but of equal willingness to work,

[1] Compare Appendix E. § 1.

and does in fact work equally hard : also that all work is un-skilled,—or rather unspecialized in this sense, that if any two people were to change occupations, each would do as much and as good work as the other had done.   Lastly, let us suppose that everyone produces things ready for sale without aid, and that he himself disposes of them to their ultimate consumers : so that the demand for everything is direct.

In this case the problem of value is very simple.   Things exchange for one another in proportion to the labour spent in producing them.   If any one thing runs short in supply, it may for a short time sell for more than its normal price : it may exchange for things the production of which had required more labour than it had; but, if so, people will at once leave other work to produce it, and in a very short time its value will fall to the normal level.   Therefore, though there may be slight temporary disturbances, yet as a rule everyone's earnings will be equal to those of everyone else.   In other words, each will have an equal share in the net sum total of things and services produced ; or, as we may say, the real *National Income* or *Dividend*.   This will constitute the demand for labour ; and may be called the common Wages-Fund or Earnings-Fund, or better still Earnings-stream ; since a Fund fails to suggest the constant flow of new goods into the world through supply, which flow out again through demand and consumption.

If a new invention should double the efficiency of work in any trade, so that a man can make twice as many things of a certain kind in a year without requiring additional appliances, then those things will fall to half their old exchange value. The effective demand for everyone's labour will be a little increased ; and the share which he can draw from the common earnings-stream will be a little larger than before.   He may if he chooses take twice as many things of this particular kind, together with his old allowance of other things : or he may. take somewhat more than before of everything.   If there be an increase in the efficiency of production in many trades, the common earnings-stream or dividend will be considerably larger; the commodities produced by those trades will be given more largely in exchange for those produced by other trades; and this will of course increase the purchasing power of everyone's earnings.

§ 3. Nor will the position be greatly changed if we suppose that some specialized skill is required in each trade, provided other things remain as before: that is, provided the workers are still supposed to be all of equal capacity and *Next sup-* industry, and all trades to be equally agreeable *pose that* *each has his* and equally easy to be learnt. The normal rate *own trade.* of earnings will still be the same in all trades; for if a day's labour in one trade produces things that sell for more than a day's labour in others, and this inequality shows any signs of lasting, people will bring up their children by preference to the favoured trade. The productive power of the community will have been increased by the division of labour; the common National Dividend or Earnings-stream will be larger; and as, putting aside passing disturbances, all will share alike in it, each will be able to buy with the fruits of his own labour things more serviceable to him than he could have produced for himself.

In this stage, as in those considered before, it is still true that the value of each thing corresponds closely to the amount of labour spent upon it; and that the earnings of everyone are governed simply by the bounty of nature and the progress of the arts of production.

§ 4. Next, let us look at the influence of changes in the numbers of the population on their earnings[1]. We *Next, allow* *for a growth of* are still supposing all labour to be of the same *population.* grade; so that, as in the last section, the normal rate of earnings will still be the same in all trades: because,

---

[1] It will be recollected that the reciprocal influence of earnings upon population is to be reckoned with in the following chapter. The reasonings of this

if a day's labour in one trade produced things that sold for more than a day's labour in others, and this inequality showed any signs of lasting, people would bring up their children by preference to the favoured trade. In this case then, as before, the national income will be divided out equally to each family, save for some slight passing inequalities; and, therefore, every improvement in the arts of production or transport, every new discovery, every new victory over nature will increase equally the comforts and luxuries at the command of each family.

But this case differs from the last; because in this case, the increase of population, if maintained long enough, must ultimately outgrow the improvements in the arts of production, and cause the law of diminishing return to assert itself in agriculture. That is to say, those who work on the land will get less wheat and other produce in return for their labour and capital. An hour's labour will represent a less quantity of wheat than before throughout the agricultural trades, and therefore throughout all other trades; since all labour is of the same grade, and earnings are therefore as a rule equal in all trades.

Further we must note that the surplus or rental value of land will tend to rise. For the value of any kind of produce must equal that of the labour, aided on our supposition by a uniform quantity of capital throughout, which is required to produce it on the margin of cultivation[1]. More labour and capital than before will be needed to raise a quarter of wheat &c. on the margin; and therefore the wheat &c., which is returned by nature to the labour applied under advantageous circumstances, will have a higher value relatively to

section apply to any growth of population however caused, for instance to one caused by advance of medical science, and a consequent lessening of the death rate.

[1] The marginal application of labour may be on land that will barely repay any labour at all; or it may be that cultivation of fertile land which is only just remunerative. See Book IV. Ch. III. §·2.

that labour and capital than before: or, in other words, it will yield a larger surplus value over that of the labour and capital used in raising it.

This surplus will go to the private owner of the land, if there is one: though of course it might conceivably be appropriated to public uses: or conceivably everyone might have an equal share of land.

§ 5. Let us now drop the supposition that labour is so mobile as to ensure equal remuneration for equal efforts, throughout the whole of society; and let us approach much nearer to the actual condition of life by supposing that labour is not all of one industrial grade, but of several. Let us suppose that parents always bring up their children to an occupation in their own grade; that they have a free choice within that grade, but not outside it. In the next chapter we shall have to consider what causes are likely to govern the increase of numbers in each grade; but whatever be those causes, it is clear that the share of each of the members of any grade, or other industrial compartment, will be the higher, the fewer the number of those members and the greater the need for their services on the part of the community and especially of rich people.

Next allow for differences in grade.

Suppose for instance artists to form a grade or caste by themselves; then their earnings will be governed, partly by their own numbers, partly by the resources which the population have available for spending on such gratifications as artists can supply for them, and partly by their desire for such gratifications.

§ 6. We may now leave the imaginary world, in which every one owns the capital that aids him in his work; and return to our own, where the relations of labour and capital play a great part in the problem of distribution; and where the action of economic forces is largely directed by a set of men who specialize themselves in the organization of business.

We return to real life, but consider only demand.

It is chiefly their agency in the modern world which justifies the common sayings of every-day life, that "every thing tends to find its own level," that "most men earn just about what they are worth," and "if one man can earn twice as much as another, that shows that his work is worth twice as much," that "machinery will displace manual labour whenever it can do the work cheaper." If there are two methods of obtaining the same result, one by skilled and the other by unskilled labour, that one will be adopted which is more efficient in proportion to its cost. There will be a margin on which either will be indifferently applied, and on that margin the efficiency of each will be in proportion to its cost.

Again, there will be a rivalry between hand-power and machine-power similar to that between two different kinds of hand-power or two different kinds of machine-power. Thus hand-power has the advantage for some operations, as, for instance, for weeding out valuable crops that have an irregular growth; horse-power in its turn has a clear advantage for weeding an ordinary turnip-field; and the application of each of them will be pushed till any further use of it would bring no net advantage.   On the margin of indifference as between hand-power and horse-power their prices must be proportionate to their efficiency; and thus the principle of Substitution will have established a direct relation between the wages of labour and the price that has to be paid for horse-power[1].

---

[1] See above, Book v. Ch. iii. and iv. It will be remembered that, so far as the knowledge and business enterprise of the producers reach, they will in each case choose those factors of production which are best for their purpose: the sum of the prices which they pay for those factors which are used is, as a rule, less than the sum of the prices which they would have to pay for any other set of factors which could be substituted for them: whenever it appears to the producers that this is not the case, they will, as a rule, set to work to substitute the less expensive method. The margin of profitableness is not to be regarded as a mere point on any one fixed line of possible investment; but as a boundary line of irregular shape cutting one after another every possible line of investment. See especially pp. 195, 196, 205, 206.

As a rule many kinds of labour, of raw material, of machinery and other plant, and of business organization both internal and external, go to the production of a commodity: and the advantages of economic freedom are never more strikingly manifest than when a business man endowed with genius is trying experiments, at his own risk, to see whether some new method, or combination of old methods, will be more efficient than the old.

Every business man indeed is constantly endeavouring to obtain a notion of the relative efficiency of every agent of production that he employs; as well as of others that might possibly be substituted for some of them. He

Net product.

estimates as best he can how much net product will be caused by a certain extra use of any one agent. By *net* product is meant net addition to the total value of his product, after deducting for any extra expenses that may be indirectly caused by the change, and adding for any incidental savings. He endeavours to employ each agent up to that margin at which its net product would no longer exceed the price he would have to pay for it; he works generally by trained instinct rather than formal calculation; and it would be too long a task here to write out in slow reasonings the quick thoughts that pass through his mind. But all his reckonings are substantially similar to those which he makes in the case in which he is in doubt whether he has enough labour to turn his stock, machinery and other trade appliances to good account; and whether he could not, by hiring one more man, increase the production by more than the equivalent of his wages, without having to supply additional capital in any other way[1].

§ 7. So far we have considered chiefly the demand for labour. But it may be well to push a little further our illustration of the nature of the demand for capital for any use; and to observe the way in which the aggregate demand for it is made up of the demands for many different uses.

[1] Compare *Principles*, VI. I. 8.

To fix the ideas, let us take some particular trade, say that of hat-making, and inquire what determines the amount of capital which it absorbs. Suppose that the rate of interest is 3 per cent. per annum on perfectly good security; and that the hat-making trade absorbs a capital of one million pounds. This implies that there is a million pounds' worth of capital which the hat-making trade can turn to so good account that they would pay 3 per cent. per annum *net* for the use of it rather than go without it.

Illustration of the demand for capital in a particular trade.

Some things are necessary to those engaged in the trade; they must have not only some food, clothing, and house-room, but also some Circulating capital, such as raw material, and some Fixed capital, such as tools and perhaps a little machinery. And though competition prevents anything more than the ordinary trade profit being got by the use of this necessary capital; yet the loss of it would be so injurious that those in the trade would have been willing to pay 50 per cent. on the capital, if they could not have got the use of it on easier terms. There may be other machinery which the trade would have refused to dispense with if the rate of interest had been 20 per cent. per annum, but not if it had been higher. If the rate had been 10 per cent., still more would have been used; if it had been 6 per cent., still more; if 4 per cent., still more; and finally the rate being 3 per cent. they use more still. When they have this amount, the marginal utility of the machinery, *i.e.* the utility of that machinery which it is only just worth their while to employ, is measured by 3 per cent.

A rise in the rate of interest would diminish their use of machinery; for they would avoid the use of all that did not give a net annual surplus of more than 3 per cent. on its value. And a fall in the rate of interest would lead them to demand the aid of more capital, and to introduce machinery which gave a net annual surplus of something less than 3 per

M.   16

cent. on its value.   Again, the lower the rate of interest, the
more substantial will be the style of building used for the
hat-making factories and the homes of the hat-makers ; and
a fall in the rate of interest will lead to the employment of
more capital in the hat-making trade in the form of larger
stocks of raw material, and of the finished commodity in the
hands of retail dealers[1].

The methods in which capital will be applied may vary

Variety in
the forms of
demand for
capital.
much even within the same trade.   Each undertaker having regard to his own means, will push
the investment of capital in his business in each
several direction until what appears in his judgment to be the
margin of profitableness is reached ; and that margin is, as we
have said, a boundary line cutting one after another every
possible line of investment, and moving irregularly outwards
in all directions whenever there is a fall in the rate of interest
at which extra capital can be obtained.   Thus the demand for
the loan of capital is the aggregate of the demands of all
individuals in all trades; and it obeys a law similar to that
which holds for the sale of commodities; just as there is a
certain amount of a commodity which can find purchasers
at any given price, and when the price rises the amount
that can be sold diminishes, so it is with regard to the use
of capital.

And as with borrowings for productive purposes, so with
those of spendthrifts or Governments who mortgage their future
resources in order to obtain the means of immediate expenditure.   It is true that their actions are often but little governed
by cool calculation, and that they frequently decide how much
they want to borrow with but little reference to the price they
will have to pay for the loan; but still the rate of interest
exercises a perceptible influence on borrowings even of this
kind.

---

[1] On Jevons' doctrine of the "Advantage of Capital to Industry," see
Principles, Ed. III. p. 487.

§ 8.   To sum up the whole in a comprehensive, if difficult, statement:—Every agent of production, land, machinery, skilled labour, unskilled labour, &c., tends to be applied in production as far as it profitably can be.   If employers, and other business men, think that they can get a better result by using a little more of any one agent they will do so.   In this they do on a large scale just what we have seen the housewife doing on a small scale : they estimate the net product (that is the net increase of their total output after allowing for incidental expenses) that will be got by a little more outlay in this direction, or a little more outlay in that ; and if they can gain by shifting a little of their outlay from one direction to another, they do so'.

Provisional conclusion.

Thus then the uses of each agent of production are governed by the general conditions of demand in relation to supply : that is, on the one hand by the urgency of all the uses to which the agent can be put, taken together with the means at the command of those who need it ; and, on the other hand, by the available stocks of it.   And equality is maintained between its values for each use by the constant tendency to shift it from uses, in which its services are of less value

Marginal uses do not govern value, but are governed together with value by the conditions of demand in relation to supply.

¹ It may be well to compare step by step the case of the housewife, distributing her wool between its various uses for direct domestic consumption, and the capitalist employers distributing the general resources of the community in production, and for ease of comparison the opening paragraph of Book III. Ch. v. is reproduced here:—The primitive housewife finding that she has a limited number of hanks of yarn from the year's shearing, considers all the domestic wants for clothing and tries to distribute the yarn between them in such a way as to contribute as much as possible to the family well-being. She will think she has failed if, when it is done, she has reason to regret that she did not apply more to making, say socks, and less to vests.   That would mean that she had miscalculated the points at which to suspend the making of socks and vests respectively ; that she had gone too far in the case of vests, and not far enough in that of socks ; and that therefore at the points at which she actually did stop, the utility of yarn turned into socks was greater than that of yarn turned into vests.   But if, on the other hand, she hit on the right points to stop at, then she made just so many socks and vests that she

to others in which they are of greater value, in accordance with the principle of substitution.

If less use is made of unskilled labour or any agent, the reason will be that at some point at which people were on the margin of doubt whether it was worth while to use that agent, they have decided that it is not worth their while. That is what is meant by saying that we must watch the *marginal* uses, and the *marginal* efficiency of each agent. We must do so, simply because it is only at the margin that any of those shiftings can occur by which changed relations of supply and demand manifest themselves[1].

got an equal amount of good out of the last bundle of yarn that she applied to socks, and the last she applied to vests.

[1] Some critics of the modern doctrine of value have misunderstood its character and supposed that it represents the marginal use of a thing as *governing* the value of the whole. It is not so; the modern doctrine says we must *go to the margin to study the action of those forces which govern* the value of the whole: and that is a very different affair. Of course the withdrawal of iron from any of its necessary uses would have just the same influence on its value as its withdrawal from its marginal uses; in the same way as, in the case of a boiler for cooking under high pressure, the pressure in the boiler would be affected by the escape of any other steam just as it would by the escape of the steam in one of the safety valves. But in fact the steam does not escape except through the safety valves; and iron, or any other agent of production, is not thrown out of use except at points on its marginal uses.

CHAPTER II.

PRELIMINARY SURVEY OF DISTRIBUTION AND EXCHANGE,
CONTINUED.

§ 1. In the last chapter we confined our attention to the manner in which the national income is distributed among the various agents of production, in accordance with the quantity of each agent, and the services which it renders. We have now to consider the other side of the problem, viz. the influence which the remuneration of each agent exerts on the supply of that agent.

When a man is fresh and eager, and doing work of his own choice, it really costs him nothing. For as some socialists have urged with pardonable ex- aggeration, few people know how much they enjoy moderate work, till something occurs to prevent them from working altogether. But rightly or wrongly, most persons believe that the greater part of the work which they do, when earning their living, yields them no surplus of pleasure; but on the contrary costs them something. They are glad when the hour for stopping arrives: perhaps they forget that the earlier hours of their work have not cost them as much as the last.

Work often yields pleasure.

The longer a man works, or even is on duty, the greater is his desire for a respite, unless indeed he has become

numbed by his work; while every hour's additional work
gives him more pay, and brings him nearer to
the stage at which his most urgent wants are
satisfied; and the higher the pay, the sooner
this stage is reached. It depends then on the
individual, whether with growing pay new wants
arise, and new desires to provide comforts for others or for
himself in after years; or he is soon satiated with those
enjoyments that can be gained only by work, and then craves
more rest, and more opportunities for activities that are themselves pleasurable. No universal rule can be laid down; but
experience seems to show that the more ignorant and phleg-
matic of races and of individuals, especially if they live in a
southern clime, will stay at their work a shorter time, and
will exert themselves less while at it, if the rate of pay rises
so as to give them their accustomed enjoyments in return for
less work than before. But those whose mental horizon is
wider, and who have more firmness and elasticity of character,
will work the harder and the longer the higher the rate of
pay which is open to them; unless indeed they prefer to
divert their activities to higher aims than work for material
gain. But this point will need to be discussed more fully
under the head of the influence of progress on value. On the
whole then we may conclude that increased remuneration
causes an immediate increase in the supply of efficient work,
as a rule; and that the exceptions to this rule, though
significant, are seldom on a large scale.

§ 2. When however we turn from the immediate influence
exerted by a rise in wages on the work done by an individual
to its ultimate effect after a generation or two, the result is
less uncertain. It is indeed true that, though a
temporary improvement will give a good many
young people the opportunity to marry and set
up house, for which they have been waiting; yet
a permanent increase of prosperity is quite as

Increased remuneration generally stimulates to increased exertions.

Supply of efficient labour dependent mainly on earnings.

likely to lower as to raise the birth-rate. But on the other hand, an increase of wages is almost certain to diminish the death-rate, unless it has been obtained at the price of the neglect by mothers of their duties to their children. And the case is much stronger when we look at the influence of high wages on the physical and mental vigour of the coming generation.

For there is a certain consumption which is strictly necessary for each grade of work in this sense, that if any of it is curtailed the work cannot be done efficiently: the adults might indeed take good care of themselves at the expense of their children, but that would only defer the decay of efficiency for one generation. Further, there are conventional necessaries, which are so strictly demanded by custom and habit, that in fact people generally would give up much of their necessaries, strictly so called, rather than go without the greater part of these. Thirdly, there are habitual comforts, which some, though not all, would not entirely relinquish even when hardly pressed. Many of these conventional necessaries and customary comforts are the embodiment of material and moral progress, and their extent varies from age to age and from place to place. The greater they are, the less economical is man as an agent of production. But, if they are wisely chosen, the greater they are the better for man: and that is the important matter. For man himself is always the sole end of production.

Any increase in consumption that is strictly necessary to efficiency pays its own way and adds to, as much as it draws from, the national dividend. But an increase of consumption, that is not thus necessary, can be afforded only through an increase in man's command over nature: and that can come about through advance in knowledge and the arts of production, through improved organization and access to larger and richer sources of raw material, and lastly through the growth of capital

Influence of modes of expenditure of earnings.

and the material means of attaining desired ends in any form.

Thus the question how closely the supply of labour responds to the demand for it, is in a great measure resolved into the question how great a part of the present consumption of the people at large consists of necessaries, strictly so called, for the life and efficiency of young and old; how much consists of conventional necessaries which theoretically could be dispensed with, but practically would be preferred by the majority of the people to some of those things that were really necessary for efficiency; and how much is really superfluous regarded as a means towards production, though of course part of it may be of supreme importance regarded as an end in itself.

The earlier French and English economists classed nearly all the consumption of the working classes under the first head[1]. They did so, partly for simplicity, and partly because those classes were then poor in England and very poor in France; and they inferred that the supply of labour would correspond to changes in the effective demand for it in the same way, though of course not quite as fast as that of machinery would. And an answer not very different from theirs must be given to the question with regard to the less advanced countries even now. For throughout the greater part of the world the working classes can afford but few luxuries and not even many conventional necessaries; and any increase in their earnings would result in so great an increase of their numbers as to bring down their earnings quickly to nearly the old level at their mere expenses of rearing. Over a great part of the world wages are governed, nearly after the so-called *iron* or *brazen* law, which ties them close to the cost of rearing and sustaining a rather inefficient class of labourers.

As regards the modern western world the answer is

---

[1] Compare Appendix E. § 1.

materially different; so great has been the recent advance in knowledge and freedom, in vigour and wealth, and in the easy access to rich distant fields for the supply of food and raw material. But it is still true even in England to-day that much the greater part of the consumption of the main body of the population conduces to sustain life and vigour; not perhaps in the most economical manner, but yet without any great waste. Doubtless some indulgences are positively harmful; but these are diminishing relatively to the rest; the chief exception perhaps being that of gambling. Most of that expenditure which is not strictly economical as a means towards efficiency, yet helps to form habits of ready resourceful enterprise, and gives that variety to life without which men become dull and stagnant, and achieve little though they may plod much ; and it is well recognized that even in western countries skilled labour is generally the cheapest where wages are the highest. It may be admitted that the industrial development of Japan is tending to show that some of the more expensive conventional necessaries might conceivably be given up without a corresponding diminution of efficiency : but, though this experience may be fruitful of far-reaching results in the future, yet it has little bearing on the past and the present. It remains true that, taking man as he is, and has been hitherto, in the western world the earnings that are got by efficient labour are not much above the lowest that are needed to cover the expenses of rearing and training efficient workers, and of sustaining and bringing into activity their full energies[1].

---

[1] On all locomotives there is some brass or copper work designed partly for ornament, and which could be omitted or displaced without any loss to the efficiency of the steam-engine. Its amount does in fact vary with the taste of the officials who select the patterns for the engines of different railways. But it might happen that custom required such expenditure; that the custom would not yield to argument, and that the railway companies could not venture to offend against it. In that case, when dealing with periods during which the custom ruled, we should have to include the cost of that ornamental metal

We conclude then that an increase of wages, unless earned under unwholesome conditions, almost always increases the strength, physical, mental and even moral of the coming generation; and that, other things being equal, an increase in the earnings that are to be got by labour increases its rate of growth; or, in other words, a rise in its demand price increases the supply of it. If the state of knowledge, and of social and domestic habits be given; then the vigour of the people as a whole if not their numbers, and both the numbers and vigour of any trade in particular, may be said to have a supply price in this sense, that there is a certain level of the demand price which will keep them stationary; that a higher price would cause them to increase, and that a lower price would cause them to decrease.

Thus again we see that demand and supply exert equally important influences on wages; neither has a claim to pre-

Twofold influences of demand and supply on wages. dominance; any more than has either blade of a pair of scissors, or either pier of an arch. Wages tend to equal the net product of labour; its marginal productivity rules the demand price for it; and, on the other side, wages tend to retain a close though indirect relation with the cost of rearing, training and sustaining the energy of efficient labour. Thus the supply-price and the demand-price of labour tend to be equal: wages are not governed by demand-price nor by supply-price, but by the whole set of causes which govern demand and supply.

§ 3. To pass to the material agents of production:—We have seen how the accumulation of capital is governed by a great variety of causes: 'by custom, by habits of self-control

The supply of capital. and of realizing the future, and above all by the power of family affection: security is a necessary condition for it, and the progress of knowledge and intelligence

work in the cost of producing a certain amount of locomotive horse-power, on the same level with the cost of the piston itself. And there are many practical problems, especially such as relate to periods of but moderate length, in which conventional and real necessaries may be placed on nearly the same footing.

furthers it in many ways. But though affected by many causes other than the rate of interest; and though the rate of saving of many people is but little affected by the rate of interest, while a few who have determined to secure an income of a certain fixed amount for themselves or their family will save less with a high rate than with a low rate of interest; yet a strong balance of evidence seems to rest with the opinion that a rise in the rate of interest, or demand-price for saving, tends to increase the volume of saving[1].

Thus then interest, being the price paid for the use of capital in any market, tends towards a level such that the aggregate demand for capital in that market, at that rate of interest, is equal to the aggregate stock forthcoming there at that rate. If the market, which we are considering, is a small one—say a single town, or a single trade in a progressive country—an increased demand for capital in it will be promptly met by an increased supply drawn from surrounding districts or trades. But if we are considering the whole world, or even the whole of a large country as one market for capital, we cannot regard the aggregate supply of it as altered quickly and to a considerable extent by a change in the rate of interest. For the general fund of capital is the product of labour and waiting; and the extra work, and the extra waiting, to which a rise in the rate of interest would act as an incentive, would not quickly amount to much as compared with the work and waiting, of which the total existing stock of capital is the result. An extensive increase in the demand for capital in general will therefore be met for a time not so much by an increase of supply, as by a rise in the rate of interest; which will cause capital to withdraw itself partially from those uses in which the need for it is least urgent. It is only slowly and gradually that the

Interest governed by the forces of supply and demand.

---

[1] See Book IV. Ch. VII. summarized in § 6.

rise in the rate of interest will increase the total stock of capital.

§ 4.   We here take "Land" to include all those agents of production which are supplied freely by nature in quantities less than man needs[1]. And land is on a different footing from man himself and those agents of production which are made by man ; among which are included improvements made by him on the land itself[2].   For while the supplies of all other agents of production respond in various degrees and various ways to the demand for their services, land makes no such response. Thus an exceptional rise in the earnings of any class of labour, tends to increase its numbers, or efficiency, or both ; and the increase in the supply of efficient work of that class tends to cheapen the services which it renders to the community.   If the increase is in their numbers then the rate of earnings of each will tend downwards towards the old level. But if the increase is in their efficiency ; then, though they will probably earn more per head than before, the gain to them will come from an increased national dividend, and will not be at the expense of other agents of production.   And the same is true as regards capital : but it is not true as regards land.   While therefore the value of land, in common with the values of other agents of production, is subject to those influences which were discussed towards the end of the preceding chapter ; it is not subject to those which have been brought into the reckoning in the present discussion.

Land is on a different footing from other agents of production.

§ 5.   To conclude this stage of our argument :—The net aggregate of all the commodities produced is itself the true source from which flow the demand prices for all these commodities, and therefore for the agents of production used in making them.   Or, to put the same thing in another way,

---

[1] See Book IV. Chapter II. § 1.

[2] For a further discussion of this subject see *Principles*, VI. II. 5.   Compare also Appendices C and D below.

this national dividend is at once the aggregate net product of, and the sole source of payment for, all the *The earnings of the several agents of production within the country: it is agents of divided up into earnings of labour; interest of production, capital; and lastly the producer's surplus, or rent, according to their marginal of land. It constitutes the whole of them, and services, the whole of it is distributed among them; and exhaust the national the larger it is, the larger, other things being dividend.* equal, will be the share of each of them. Any addition to the share of any one, the stock of which can be increased · by human effort, will cause the stock of it to be increased. But the increase may be slow: for it may be checked by habit and custom, and in the case of labour by the growth of new conventional necessaries. And, if there is no very violent change in the arts of production or the general economic condition of society, the stock of each agent will stand always in a close relation to its cost of production: account being taken of those conventional necessaries, which constantly expand as the growing richness of the national income yields to one class after another an increasing surplus above the mere necessaries for efficiency.

The national income is distributed among these several agents in proportion to the need which people have for their several services—*i.e.* not the *total* need, but the *marginal* need. By this is meant the need at that point, at which people are indifferent whether they purchase a little more of the services (or the fruits of the services) of one agent, or devote their further resources to purchasing the services (or the fruits of the services) of other agents.

§ 6. There remain some points on which a little more needs to be said here.

In studying the influence which increased efficiency and increased earnings in one trade exert on the condition of others we may start from the general fact that, other things being equal, the larger the supply of any agent of production, the further will it have to push its way into uses for which

Increase of any agent benefits most others.
it is not specially fitted; the lower will be the demand price with which it will have to be contented in those uses in which its employment is on the verge or margin of not being found profitable; and, in so far as competition equalizes the price which it gets in all uses, this price will be its price for all uses. The extra production resulting from the increase in that agent of production will go to swell the national dividend, and other agents of production will benefit thereby: but that agent itself will have to submit to a lower rate of pay.

For instance, if without any other change, capital increases fast, the rate of interest must fall; if without any other change, the number of those ready to do any particular kind of labour increases, their wages must fall. In either case there will result an increased production, and an increased national dividend: in either case the loss of one agent of production must result in a gain to others; but not necessarily to all others. Thus an opening up of rich quarries of slate or an increase in numbers or efficiency of quarrymen, would tend to improve the houses of all classes; and it would tend to increase the demand for bricklayers' and carpenters' labour, and raise their wages. But it would injure the makers of roofing tiles as producers of building materials, more than it benefited them as consumers. The increase in the supply of this one agent increases the demand for many others by a little, and for some others by much; but for some it lessens the demand.

§ 7. Now we know that the wages of any worker, say for instance a shoemaker, tend to be equal to the net product of his labour: and that since the wages of all workers in the

Dependence of wages on the efficiency of labour.
same grade tend to be equal to one another, therefore in a state of equilibrium every worker will be able with the earnings of a hundred days' labour to buy the net products of a hundred days' labour

of other workers in the same grade with himself: he may select them in whatever way he chooses, so as to make up that aggregate sum.

If the normal earnings of workers in another grade are half as high again as his own, the shoemaker must spend three days' wages in order to get the net product of two days' labour of a worker in that grade; and so in proportion.

Thus, other things being equal, every increase in the net efficiency of labour in any trade, including his own, will raise in the same proportion the real value of that part of his wages which the shoemaker spends on the products of that trade; and other things being equal, the level of the real wages of the shoemaker depends directly on the average increase in the efficiency of the trades, including his own, which produce those things on which he spends his wages. If any trade rejects an improvement by which its efficiency could be increased ten per cent., it inflicts on the shoemaker an injury measured by ten per cent. of that part of his wages which he spends on the products of that trade. But an increased efficiency on the part of workers, whose products compete with his own, may injure him temporarily at least, especially if he is not himself a consumer of those products.

Again, the shoemaker will gain by anything that changes the relative positions of different grades in such a way as to raise his grade relatively to others. He will gain by an increase of medical men whose aid he occasionally needs. And he will gain more if those grades which are occupied chiefly with the tasks of managing business, whether manufacturing, trading, or any other, receive a great influx from other grades: for then the earnings of management will be lowered permanently relatively to the earnings of manual work, there will be a rise in the net product of every kind of manual labour; and, other things being equal, the shoemaker will get more of every commodity on which he spends those wages that represent his own net product.

§ 8.   The process of substitution, of which we have been discussing the tendencies, is one form of competition ; and it may be well to insist again* that we do not assume that competition is perfect.   Perfect competition requires a perfect

Knowledge and freedom of competition are not assumed to be perfect.
knowledge of the state of the market ; and though no great departure from the actual facts of life is involved in assuming this knowledge on the part of dealers when we are considering the course of business in Lombard Street, the Stock Exchange, or in a wholesale Produce Market ; it would be altogether unreasonable to make this assumption when we are examining the causes that govern the supply of labour in any of the lower grades of industry.   For if a man had sufficient ability to know everything about the market for his labour, he would have too much to remain long in a low grade.   The older economists, in constant contact as they were with the actual facts of business life, must have known this well enough ; but they sometimes seemed to imply that they did assume this perfect knowledge.

It is therefore specially important to insist that we do not assume the members of any industrial group to be endowed with more ability and forethought, or to be governed by motives other than those which are in fact normal to, and would be attributed by every well-informed person to, the members of that group ; account being taken of the general conditions of time and place.   There may be a good deal of wayward and impulsive action, sordid and noble motives may mingle their threads together ; but there is a constant tendency for each man to select such occupations for himself and his children as seem to him on the whole the most advantageous of those which are within the range of his resources, and of the efforts which he is able and willing to make in order to reach them.

§ 9.   The last group of questions, which still remain to be discussed, is concerned with the relation of capital in general to wages in general. It is obvious that though capital in general is constantly competing with labour for the field of employment in particular trades; yet since capital itself is the embodiment of labour as well as of waiting, the competition is really between some kinds of labour aided by a good deal of waiting, and other kinds of labour aided by less waiting. On the one side, for instance, are many who make shoes by hand, and a very few who make awls and other simple implements, aided by a little waiting; on the other are a relatively small number who work powerful sewing-machines which were made by engineers, aided by a good deal of waiting. There is a real and effective competition between labour in general and waiting in general. But it covers a small part of the whole field, and is of small importance relatively to the benefits which labour derives from obtaining cheaply the aid of capital, and therefore of efficient methods in the production of things that it needs.

Relations of capital and labour in general.

For speaking generally, an increase in the power and the willingness to save will cause the services of waiting to be pushed constantly further; and will prevent it from obtaining employment at as high a rate of interest as before. That is, the rate of interest will constantly fall, unless indeed invention opens new advantageous uses of roundabout methods of production. But this growth of capital will increase the national dividend; open out new and rich fields for the employment of labour in other directions; and will thus more than compensate for the partial displacement of the services of labour by those of waiting.

§ 10. It is to be understood that the share of the national dividend, which any particular industrial class receives during the year, consists either of things that were made during the year, or of the equivalents of those things. For many of the things made, or partly made, during the year will remain

Earnings of labour in relation to advances made by capital.

in the possession of employers and other capitalists, and be
added to the stock of capital; while in return the employers,
directly or indirectly, hand over to the working classes some
things that had been made in previous years[1].

Thus finally, capital in general and labour in general
co-operate in the production of the national dividend, and
draw from it their earnings in the measure of their respective
(marginal) efficiencies. Their mutual dependence is of the
closest; capital without labour is dead; the labourer without
the aid of his own or someone else's capital would not long be
alive. Where labour is energetic, capital reaps a high reward
and grows apace; and, thanks to capital and knowledge, the
ordinary labourer in the western world is in many respects
better fed, clothed and even housed than were princes in
earlier times. The co-operation of capital and labour is as
essential as that of the spinner of yarn and the weaver of
cloth : there is a little priority on the part of the spinner;
but that gives him no preeminence. The prosperity of each
is bound up with the strength and activity of the other;
though each may gain temporarily, if not permanently, a
somewhat larger share of the national dividend at the expense
of the other.

In the modern world, the employer, who may have but
little capital of his own, acts as the boss of the great
industrial wheel. The interests of owners of capital and
of workers radiate towards him and from him : and he
holds them all together in a firm grip. He will therefore
take a predominant place in those discussions of fluctuations
of employment and of wages, which are deferred to the
second volume of this treatise; and a prominent, though
not predominant, place in those discussions of the secondary
features in the mode of action of demand and supply peculiar
to labour, capital and land respectively, which will occupy the
next eight chapters.

[1] As to the so-called Wages-Fund doctrine, see Appendix E § 2.

CHAPTER III.

EARNINGS OF LABOUR.

§ 1. WE have now to apply the general reasonings of Book V. and of the first two chapters of the present Book to the special problems of Earnings, Profits, and Rent; and to examine in more detail how different kinds of Labour, Capital, and Natural Agents earn their several shares of the national dividend. The present chapter is devoted to methods of reckoning earnings. It is mainly a question of arithmetic or book-keeping: but it is not unimportant[1].

Scope of the present and the following seven Chapters.

When watching the action of demand and supply with regard to a material commodity, we are constantly met by the difficulty that two things which are being sold under the same name in the same market, are really not of the same quality and not of the same value to the purchasers. Or, if the things are really alike, they may be sold even in the face of the keenest competition at prices which are nominally different, because the conditions of sale are not the same: for instance, a part of the expense or risk of delivery which is borne in the one case by the seller may in the other be transferred to the buyer. But difficulties of this kind are much greater in the case of labour than of material commodities: the true price that is paid for labour often differs widely, and in ways that are not easily traced, from that which is nominally paid.

---

[1] On the subject of this chapter compare Schloss' *Methods of Industrial Remuneration.*

The earnings (or wages) which a person gets in any given time, such as a day, a week, or a year, may be called his
Time-earnings. *Time-earnings* (or *Time-wages*) : and we may then regard competition, or to speak more exactly, economic freedom and enterprise, as tending to make Time-earnings in occupations of equal difficulty and in neighbouring places (not equal, but) proportionate to the efficiency of the workers.

But this phrase, "the efficiency of the workers," has some
Payment by Piece-work. ambiguity. When the payment for work of any kind is apportioned to the quantity and quality of the work turned out, it is said that uniform rates of PIECE-WORK wages are being paid ; and if two persons work under the same conditions and with equally good appliances, they are paid in proportion to their efficiencies when they receive piece-work wages calculated by the same lists of prices for each several kind of work. If however the appliances are not equally good, a uniform rate of piece-work wages gives results disproportionate to the efficiency of the workers. If, for instance, the same lists of piece-work wages were used in Lancashire Cotton Mills supplied with old-fashioned machinery, as in those which have the latest improvements, the apparent equality would represent a real inequality. The more effective competition is, and the more perfectly economic freedom and enterprise are developed, the more surely will the lists be higher in the mills that have old-fashioned machinery than in the others.

In order therefore to give its right meaning to the statement that economic freedom and enterprise tend to equalize wages in occupations of the same difficulty and in the same neighbourhood, we require the use of a new term ; and we may find it in *Efficiency-wages*, or more broadly *Efficiency-*
Efficiency-earnings. *earnings ;* that is, earnings measured, not as Time-earnings are with reference to the time spent in earning them ; and not as piece-work earnings are

with reference to the amount of output resulting from the work by which they are earned; but with reference to the severity of the *task* which was imposed on the worker; or, to get at the same result by another route, the exertion of ability and *efficiency* required of him. For competition tends to make the earnings got by two individuals of unequal efficiency in any given time, say, a day or a year, not equal, but unequal; and, in like manner, it tends not to equalise, but to render unequal the average weekly wages in two districts in which the average standards of efficiency are unequal. Given that the average strength and energy of the working-classes are higher in the North of England than in the South, it then follows that the more completely "competition makes things find their own level," the more certain is it that average weekly wages will be higher in the North than in the South.

The tendency then of economic freedom and enterprise (or in more common phrase, of competition) to cause every one's earnings to find their own level, is a tendency to *equality of Efficiency-earnings* in the same district. This tendency will be the stronger, the greater is the mobility of labour, the less strictly specialised it is, the more keenly parents are on the look out for the most advantageous occupations for their children, the more rapidly they are able to adapt themselves to changes in economic conditions, and lastly the slower and the less violent these changes are.

This statement of the law is, however, still subject to a slight correction. For we have hitherto supposed that it is a matter of indifference to the employer whether he employs few or many people to do a piece of work provided his total wages-bill for the work is the same. But that is not the case. Those workers who earn most in a week when paid at a given rate for their work, are those who are cheapest to their employers (and ultimately to the community, unless indeed they over-

Low-waged labour is generally dear, if working with expensive machinery.

strain themselves, and work themselves out prematurely). For they use only the same amount of fixed capital as their slower fellow workers; and, since they turn out more work, each part of it has to bear a less charge on this account. The Prime costs are equal in the two cases; but the Total cost of that done by those who are more efficient, and get the higher Time-wages, is lower than that done by those who get the lower Time-wages at the same rate of piece-work payment.

This point is seldom of much importance in out-of-door work, where there is abundance of room, and comparatively little use of expensive machinery; for then, except in the matter of superintendence, it makes very little difference to the employer, whose wages-bill for a certain piece of work is £100, whether that sum is divided between twenty efficient or thirty inefficient workers. But when expensive machinery is used which has to be proportioned to the number of workers, the employer would often find the total cost of his goods lowered if he could get twenty men to turn out for a wages-bill of £50 as much work as he had previously got done by thirty men for a wages-bill of £40. In all matters of this kind the leadership of the world lies with America, and it is not an uncommon saying there that he is the best business man who contrives to pay the highest wages.

The corrected law then stands that the tendency of economic freedom and enterprise is generally to equalize efficiency-earnings in the same district: but where much expensive fixed capital is used, it would be to the advantage of the employer to raise the Time-earnings of the more efficient workers more than in proportion to their efficiency.

Of course this tendency is liable to be opposed by special customs and institutions, and, in some cases, by trades-union regulations.

§ 2. Thus much with regard to estimates of the work for which the earnings are given: but next we have to consider more carefully the facts, that in estimating the real earnings of an occupation account must be taken of many things besides its money receipts, and that on the other side of the account we must reckon for many incidental disadvantages besides those directly involved in the strain and stress of the work.

As Adam Smith says, "the *Real wages* of labour may be said to consist in the quantity of the necessaries and conveniences of life that are given for it; its *Nominal wages* in the quantity of money...... The labourer is rich or poor, is well or ill rewarded, in proportion to the real, not to the nominal, wages of his labour[1]." But the words "that are given for it" must not be taken to apply only to the necessaries and conveniences that are directly provided by the purchaser of the labour or its products; for account must be taken also of the advantages which are attached to the occupation, and require no special outlay on his part.

Real wages and Nominal wages.

In endeavouring to ascertain the Real wages of an occupation at any place or time, the first step is to allow for variations in the purchasing power of the money in which Nominal wages are returned; and especially we must take account of those things on which the class of labour in question spends most of its wages. For instance, the prices of velvet, of operatic entertainments and scientific books are not very important to the lower ranks of industry: but a fall in the price of bread or of shoe leather affects them much more than it does the higher ranks.

Next, allowance must be made for all trade expenses. Thus from the barrister's gross income we must deduct the rent of his office and the salary of his clerk: from the carpenter's gross income we must deduct the expenses which he incurs for tools; and when estimating the earnings of quarrymen in any district we must find out whether local custom assigns the

---

[1] *Wealth of Nations*, Book i. Ch. v.

expenses of tools and blasting powder to them or their employers. And on the other hand we must reckon in all the allowances, and privileges, such as those of a cottage rent free or at a low rent, and of course free board and lodging when they are given[1].

§ 3. Next we have to take account of the influences

Uncertainty of success. exerted on the real rate of earnings in an occupation by the uncertainty of success and the inconstancy of occupation in it.

We should obviously start by taking the earnings of an occupation as the average between those of the successful and unsuccessful members of it; taking care to get the true average[2]. We thus obviate the necessity of making any separate allowance for insurance against risk; but account remains to be taken of the evil of uncertainty. For there are many people of a sober steady-going temper, who like to know what is before them, and who would far rather have an appointment which offered a certain income of say £400 a year than one which was not unlikely to yield £600, but had an equal chance of affording only £200. Uncertainty, therefore, which does not appeal to great ambitions and lofty aspirations, has special attractions for very few; while it acts as a deterrent to many of those who are making their choice of a career. And as a rule the certainty of moderate success attracts more than an expectation of an uncertain success that has an equal actuarial value.

But on the other hand, if an occupation offers a few

---

[1] They should be counted at their value to those who receive them, not at their cost to those who give them. This point and the evils of the Truck system are dwelt on in *Principles* VI. III. 5.

[2] If the average earnings of those who are successful are £2000 a year, and of those who are unsuccessful are £400 a year, the average of the whole will be £1200 a year if the former group is as large as the latter; but if, as is perhaps the case with barristers, the unsuccessful are ten times as numerous as the successful, the true average is but £550. And further, many of those who have failed most completely, are likely to have left the occupation altogether, and thus to escape being counted.

extremely high prizes, its attractiveness is increased out of all proportion to their aggregate value. For this there are two reasons. The first is that young men of an adventurous disposition are more attracted by the prospects of great success than they are deterred by the fear of failure; and the second is that the social rank of an occupation depends more on the highest dignity and the best position which can be attained through it than on the average good fortune of those engaged in it.

We may next consider the influence which inconstancy of employment exerts on wages. It is obvious that in those occupations, in which employment is irregular, the pay must be high in proportion to the work done: the medical man and the shoeblack must each receive when at work a pay which covers a sort of retaining fee for the time when he has nothing to do. If the advantages of their occupations are in other respects equal, and their work equally difficult, the bricklayer when at work must be paid a higher rate than the joiner, and the joiner than the railway guard. For work on the railways is nearly constant all the year round; while the joiner and the bricklayer are always in danger of being made idle by slackness of trade, and the bricklayer's work is further interrupted by frost and rain. The ordinary method of allowing for such interruptions is to add up the earnings for a long period of time and to take the average of them; but this is not quite satisfactory unless we assume that the rest and leisure, which a man gets when out of employment, are of no service to him directly or indirectly.

Irregularity of employment.

Next we must take account of the opportunities which a man's surroundings may afford of supplementing the earnings which he gets in his chief occupation, by doing work of other kinds. And account may need to be taken also of the opportunities which these surroundings offer for the work of other members of his family.

Supplementary earnings.

§ 4.   Thus then the attractiveness of a trade depends on
many other causes besides the difficulty and
strain of the work to be done in it on the one
hand, and the money-earnings to be got in it on
the other.   And when the earnings in any occupation are regarded as acting on the supply of
labour in it, or when they are spoken of as being
its supply price, we must understand that the term Earnings
is only used as a short expression for its *Net Advantages*. We
must take account of the facts that one trade is healthier or
cleanlier than another, that it is carried on in a more wholesome or pleasant locality, or that it involves a better social
position; as is instanced by Adam Smith's well-known remark
that the aversion which many people have for the work of a
butcher, and to some extent for the butcher himself, raises
the earnings of butchers above those of bakers.

Of course individual character will always assert itself in
estimating particular advantages at a high or a
low rate.   Some persons for instance are so fond
of having a cottage to themselves that they prefer
living on very low wages in the country to
getting much higher wages in the town; while others are indifferent as to the amount of house-room they get, and are
willing to go without the comforts of life provided they can
procure what they regard as its luxuries.   Personal peculiarities, such as these, prevent us from predicting with certainty the conduct of particular individuals.   But if each
advantage and disadvantage is reckoned at the average of the
money values it has for the class of people who would be
likely to enter an occupation, or to bring up their children to
it, we shall have the means of estimating roughly the relative
strengths of the forces that tend to increase or diminish the
supply of labour in that occupation *at the time and place* which
we are considering.   For it cannot be too often repeated that
grave errors are likely to result from taking over an estimate

of this kind based on the circumstances of one time and place, and applying it without proper precaution to those of another time or another place.

Lastly, the disagreeableness of work seems to have very little effect in raising wages, if it is of such a kind that it can be done by those whose indus- industrial trial abilities are of a very low order. For the grades. progress of sanitary science has kept alive many people who are unfit for any but the lowest grade of work. They compete eagerly for the comparatively small quantity of work for which they are fitted, and in their urgent need they think almost exclusively of the wages they can earn: they cannot afford to pay much attention to incidental discomforts and indeed the influence of their surroundings has prepared many of them to regard the dirtiness of an occupation as an evil of but minor importance.

And from this arises the strange and paradoxical result that the dirtiness of some occupations is a cause An evil of the lowness of the wages earned in them. For paradox. employers find that this dirtiness adds much to the wages they would have to pay to get the work done by skilled men of high character working with improved appliances; and so they often adhere to old methods which require only unskilled workers of but indifferent character, and who can be hired for low (Time-) wages, because they are not worth much to any employer. There is no more urgent social need than that labour of this kind should be made scarce and dear.

CHAPTER IV.

EARNINGS OF LABOUR, CONTINUED.

§ 1. In the last chapter we discussed the difficulties of as-

Many peculiarities in the action of demand and supply with regard to labour are cumulative in their effects. certaining the real as opposed to the nominal price of labour. But now we have to study some peculiarities in the action of the forces of demand and supply with regard to labour which are of a more vital character; since they affect not merely the form, but also the substance of that action.

We shall find that the influence of many of these peculiarities is not at all to be measured by their first and most obvious effects. For flaws in the industrial arrangements of society may be divided into two classes according as their effects are, or are not *cumulative;* that is as they do or do not end with the evil by which they were caused, and do or do not have the indirect effect of lowering the character of the workers or of hindering it from becoming stronger. For these last cause further weakness and further suffering, which again in their turn cause yet further weakness and further suffering, and so on cumulatively; and conversely, high earnings, and a strong character, lead to greater strength and higher earnings, which again lead to still greater strength and still higher earnings, and so on cumulatively[1].

---

[1] There is a similar distinction between the cumulative and non-cumulative effects of custom. See *Principles* VI. iv. 1.

§ 2. The first point to which we have to direct our attention is the fact that human agents of pro- *First peculiarity: the worker sells his work, but retains property in himself.* duction are not bought and sold as machinery and other material agents of production are. The worker sells his work, but he himself remains his own property : those who bear the expenses of rearing and educating him receive but very little of the price that is paid for his services in later years.

Whatever deficiencies the modern methods of business may have, they have at least this virtue, that he *Consequently the investment of capital in him is limited by the means, the forethought, and the unselfishness of his parents.* who bears the expenses of production of material goods, receives the price that is paid for them. He who builds factories or steam-engines or houses, or rears slaves, reaps the benefit of all net services which they render so long as he keeps them for himself ; and when he sells them he gets a price which is the estimated net value of their future services. The stronger and the more efficient he makes them, the better his reward ; and therefore he extends his outlay until there seems to him no good reason for thinking that the gains resulting from any further investment would compensate him. But the investment of capital in the rearing and early training of the workers of England is limited by the resources of parents in the various grades of society, by their power of forecasting the future, and by their willingness to sacrifice themselves for the sake of their children.

This evil is indeed of comparatively small importance with regard to the higher industrial grades. For in those grades most people distinctly realize the future, and "discount it at a low rate of interest." They exert themselves much to select the best careers for their sons, and the best trainings for those careers ; and they are generally willing and able to incur a considerable expense for the purpose. The professional classes especially, while generally eager to save some

capital *for* their children, are even more on the alert for
opportunities of investing it *in* them.   And whenever there
occurs in the upper grades of industry a new opening for
which an extra and special education is required, the future
gains need not be very high relatively to the present outlay,
in order to secure a keen competition for the post.

But in the lower ranks of society the evil is great.   For
Disadvantages the slender means and education of the parents,
of children
of poor   and the comparative weakness of their power of
parents.   distinctly realizing the future, prevent them from
investing capital in the education and training of their
children with the same free and bold enterprise with which
capital is applied to improving the machinery of any well-
managed factory. Many of the children of the working-
classes are imperfectly fed and clothed ; they are housed in a
way that promotes neither physical nor moral health ; they
receive a school education which, though in modern England
it may not be very bad so far as it goes, yet goes only a little
way ; they have few opportunities of getting a broader view
of life or an insight into the nature of the higher work of
business, of science or of art ; they meet hard and exhausting
toil early on the way, and for the greater part keep to it all
their lives.   At last they go to the grave carrying with them
undeveloped abilities and faculties ; which, if they could have
borne full fruit, would have added to the material wealth of
the country—to say nothing of higher considerations—many
times as much as would have covered the expense of providing
adequate opportunities for their development.

But the point on which we have specially to insist now is
This evil is   that this evil is cumulative.   The worse fed are
cumulative.   the children of one generation, the less will they
earn when they grow up, and the less will be their power of
providing adequately for the material wants of their children ;
and so on : and again, the less fully their own faculties are

developed, the less will they realize the importance of developing the best faculties of their children, and the less will be their power of doing so. And conversely any change that awards to the workers of one generation better earnings, together with better opportunities of developing their best qualities, will increase the material and moral advantages which they have the power to offer to their children : while by increasing their own intelligence, wisdom and forethought, it will also to some extent increase their willingness to sacrifice their own pleasures for the well-being of their children ; though there is much of that willingness now even among the poorest classes, so far as their means and the limits of their knowledge will allow.

§ 3. The advantages which those born in one of the higher grades of society have over those born in a lower, consist in a great measure of the *Start in life.* better introductions and the better start in life which they receive from their parents. But the importance of this good start in life is nowhere seen more clearly than in a comparison of the fortunes of the sons of artisans and of unskilled labourers.

There are not many skilled trades to which the son of an unskilled labourer can get easy access; and in *The sons of* the large majority of cases the son follows the *artisans and* father's calling. In the old-fashioned domestic *of labourers.* industries this was almost a universal rule; and, even under modern conditions, the father has often great facilities for introducing his son to his own trade.

But the son of the artisan has further advantages. He generally lives in a better and cleaner house, and under material surroundings that are more consistent with refinement than those with which the ordinary labourer is familiar. His parents are likely to be better educated, and to have a higher notion of their duties to their children; and, last but not least, his mother is likely to be able to give more of her time to the care of her family.

If we compare one country of the civilized world with another, or one part of England with another, or one trade in England with another, we find that the degradation of the working-classes varies almost uniformly with the amount of rough work done by women. The most valuable of all capital is that invested in human beings; and of that capital the most precious part is the result of the care and influence of the mother, so long as she retains her tender and unselfish instincts, and has not been hardened by the strain and stress of unfeminine work.

§ 4. As the youth grows up, the influence of his parents and his schoolmaster declines; and thenceforward to the end of his life his character is moulded chiefly by the nature of his work and the influence of those with whom he associates for business, for pleasure and for religious worship.

Something has already been said of the technical training of adults, of the decadence of the old apprenticeship system, and of the difficulty of finding anything to take its place. Here again we meet the difficulty that whoever may incur the expense of investing capital in developing the abilities of the workman, those abilities will be the property of the workman himself: and thus the virtue of those who have aided him must remain for the greater part its own reward.

The technical training of the workshop depends in a great measure on the unselfishness of the employer.

It is true that high-paid labour is really cheap to those employers who are aiming at leading the race, and whose ambition it is to turn out the best work by the most advanced methods. They are likely to give their men high wages and to train them carefully; partly because it pays them to do so, and partly because the character that fits them to take the lead in the arts of production is likely also to make them take a generous interest in the well-being of those who work for them. But though the number of such employers is increasing, they are still comparatively few.

Again, in paying his workpeople high wages and in caring

for their happiness and culture, the liberal employer confers benefits which do not end with his own genera- *Its benefits are* tion. For the children of his workpeople share *cumulative,* in them, and grow up stronger in body and *but accrue only in part to him* in character than otherwise they would have *or his heirs.* done. The price which he has paid for labour will have borne the expenses of production of an increased supply of high industrial faculties in the next generation : but these faculties will be the property of others, who will have the right to hire them out for the best price they will fetch : neither he nor even his heirs can reckon on reaping much material reward for this part of the good that he has done.

§ 5. The next of those characteristics of the action of demand and supply peculiar to labour, which we *Second* have to study, lies in the fact that when a person *peculiarity.* sells his services, he has to present himself where *The seller of labour must* they are delivered. It matters nothing to the *deliver it him-* seller of bricks whether they are to be used in *self.* building a palace or a sewer : but it matters a great deal to the seller of labour, who undertakes to perform a task of given difficulty, whether or not the place in which it is to be done is a wholesome and a pleasant one, and whether or not his associates will be such as he cares to have. In those yearly hirings which still remain in some parts of England, the labourer inquires what sort of a temper his new employer has, quite as carefully as what rate of wages he pays.

This peculiarity of labour is of great importance in many individual cases, but it does not often exert a *The effects of* broad and deep influence of the same nature as *this are not* that last discussed. The more disagreeable the *cumulative.* incidents of an occupation, the higher of course are the wages required to attract people into it : but whether these incidents do lasting and wide-spreading harm depends on whether they are such as to undermine men's physical health and strength or to lower their character. When they are not of this sort,

M. 18

they are indeed evils in themselves, but they do not generally cause other evils beyond themselves; their effects are seldom cumulative.

Since however no one can deliver his labour in a market in which he is not himself present, it follows that the mobility of labour and the mobility of the labourer are convertible terms: and the unwillingness to quit home, and to leave old associations, including perhaps some loved cottage and burial-ground, will often turn the scale against a proposal to seek better wages in a new place. And when the different members of a family are engaged in different trades, and a migration, which would be advantageous to one member, would be injurious to others, the inseparability of the worker from his work considerably hinders the adjustment of the supply of labour to the demand for it.

§ 6. Again, labour is often sold under special disadvantages, arising from the closely connected group of facts that labour power is "perishable," that the sellers of it are commonly poor and have no reserve fund, and that they cannot easily withhold it from the market. Perishableness is an attribute common to the labour of all grades: the time lost when a worker is thrown out of employment cannot be recovered, though in some cases his energies may be refreshed by rest[1].

Third and fourth peculiarities. Labour is perishable and the sellers of it are often at a disadvantage in bargaining.

The want of reserve funds and of the power of long withholding their labour from the market is common to nearly all grades of those whose work is chiefly with their hands. But it is especially true of unskilled labourers, partly because their wages leave very little margin for saving, partly because when any group of them suspends work, there are large numbers who are capable of filling their places. And, as we shall see presently when we come to discuss trade combinations, it is more difficult for them than for skilled artisans to

[1] See above, Ch. III. § 3.

form themselves into strong and lasting combinations; and so to put themselves on something like terms of equality in bargaining with their employers. For it must be remembered that a man who employs a thousand others, is in himself an absolutely rigid combination to the extent of one thousand units among buyers in the labour market. But these statements do not apply to all kinds of labour. Domestic servants though they have not large reserve funds, and seldom any formal trades-union, are sometimes better able than their employers to act in concert[1].

Turning next to the highest grades of industry, we find that as a rule they have the advantage in bargaining over the purchaser of their labour. Many of the professional classes are richer, have larger reserve funds, more knowledge and resolution, and much greater power of concerted action, with regard to the terms on which they sell their services, than the greater number of their clients and customers[2].

It is however certain that manual labourers as a class are at a disadvantage in bargaining; and that the disadvantage wherever it exists is likely to be This last evil is cumulative.

[1] The total real wages of the domestic servants of fashionable London are very high in comparison with those of other trades in which equal skill and ability are required. But those domestic servants who have no specialized skill, and who hire themselves to persons with very narrow means, have not been able to make even tolerably good terms for themselves: they work very hard for very low wages.

[2] If further evidence were wanted that the disadvantages of bargaining under which the vendor of labour commonly suffers, depend on his own circumstances and qualities, and not on the fact that the particular thing which he has to sell is labour; such evidence could be found by comparing the successful barrister or solicitor or physician, or opera singer or jockey with the poorer independent producers of vendible goods. Those, for instance, who in remote places collect shell-fish to be sold in the large central markets, have little reserve funds or knowledge of the world, and of what other producers are doing in other parts of the country: while those to whom they sell, are a small and compact body of wholesale dealers with wide knowledge and large reserve funds; and in consequence the sellers are at a great disadvantage in bargaining. And much the same is true of the women and children who sell hand-made lace, and of the garret masters of East London who sell furniture to large and powerful dealers.

18—2

cumulative in its effects.   For though, so long as there is any
competition among employers at all, they are likely to bid for
labour something not very much less than its real value to
them, that is, something not very much less than the highest
price they would pay rather than go on without it; yet anything that lowers wages tends to lower the efficiency of the
labourer's work, and therefore to lower the price which the
employer would rather pay than go without that work.   The
effects of the labourer's disadvantage in bargaining are therefore cumulative in two ways.   It lowers his wages; and as we
have seen, this lowers his efficiency as a worker, and thereby
lowers the normal value of his labour.   And in addition it
diminishes his efficiency as a bargainer, and thus increases the
chance that he will sell his labour for less than its normal
value.

CHAPTER V.

EARNINGS OF LABOUR, CONTINUED.

§ 1. THE next peculiarity in the action of demand and supply with regard to labour, which we have to consider, is closely connected with some of those we have already discussed: It consists in the length of time that is required to prepare and train labour for its work, and in the slowness of the returns which result from this training.

Fifth peculiarity. Slowness of growth of new supplies of labour.

Not much less than a generation elapses between the choice by parents of a skilled trade for one of their children, and his reaping the full results of their choice. And meanwhile the character of the trade may have been almost revolutionized by changes, of which some probably threw long shadows before them, but others were such as could not have been foreseen even by the shrewdest persons and those best acquainted with the circumstances of the trade.

Difficulty of forecasting the future of trades.

The working classes in nearly all parts of England are constantly on the look-out for advantageous openings for the labour of themselves and their children ; and they are eager to learn from friends and relations who have settled in other districts everything that they can as to the wages that are to be got in other trades. It is astonishing with what assiduity and sagacity many of them pursue their inquiries, not only as to the money wages to be obtained in a trade, but also as to all those incidental advantages and disadvantages which have been discussed in the last chapter but one. But it is very difficult to ascertain the causes that are likely to determine the distant future of the trades which they are selecting for their children; and there are not many who enter on this abstruse inquiry. The majority assume without a further thought that the condition of each trade in their own time sufficiently indicates what it will be in the future; and, so far as the influence of this habit extends, the supply of labour in a trade in any one generation tends to conform to its earnings not in that but in the preceding generation.

Again, some parents, observing that the earnings in one trade have been for some years rising relatively to others in the same grade, assume that the course of change is likely to continue in the same direction. But it often happens that the previous rise was due to temporary causes, and that, even if there had been no exceptional influx of labour into the trade, the rise would have been followed by a fall instead of a further rise: and, if there is such an exceptional influx, the consequence may be a supply of labour so excessive, that its earnings remain below their normal level for many years.

§ 2. But we must not omit to notice those adjustments of the supply of labour to the demand for it, which are effected by movements of adults from one trade to another, one grade to another, and one place to another. The movements from one grade to another can seldom be on a very large scale; although it is true that exceptional opportunities may sometimes develop rapidly a great deal of latent ability among the lower grades. Thus, for instance, the sudden opening out of a new country, or such an event as the American War, will raise from the lower ranks of labour many men who bear themselves well in difficult and responsible posts.

The movements of adult labour,

And the movements of adult labour from trade to trade and from place to place can in some cases be so large and so rapid as to reduce within a very short compass the period which is required to

are however of increasing importance.

enable the supply of labour to adjust itself to the demand. That general ability which is easily transferable from one trade to another, is every year rising in importance relatively to that manual skill and technical knowledge which are specialized to one branch of industry[1]. And thus economic progress brings with it on the one hand a constantly increasing changefulness in the methods of industry, and therefore a constantly increasing difficulty in predicting the demand for labour of any kind a generation ahead; but on the other hand it brings also an increasing power of remedying such errors of adjustment as have been made.

§ 3. Thus these market variations in the price of a commodity are governed by the temporary relations between demand and the stock that is in the market or within easy access of it. When the market price so determined is above its normal level, those who are able to bring new supplies into the market in time to take advantage of the high price receive an abnormally high reward. If they are small handicraftsmen working on their own account, the whole of this rise in price goes to increase their earnings.

Fluctuations of earnings are governed chiefly by fluctuations of demand.

In the modern industrial world, however, those who undertake the risks of production and to whom the benefits of any rise in price, and the evils of any fall come in the first instance, are employers and other business men. But the force of competition among the employers themselves, each desiring to extend his business, and to get for himself as much as possible of the rich harvest that is to be reaped when their trade is prosperous, makes them consent to pay higher wages to their employees in order to obtain their services. Even if they act in combination, they are not likely to endeavour to deprive the workman of all share of the harvest of good times : nor if they did make the attempt, would it be at all likely to succeed.

Thus the high wages of coal-miners during the inflation which culminated in 1873, were determined for the time by

[1] See Book IV. Ch. VI. § 1.

the relation in which the demand for their services stood to the amount of skilled mining labour available, the unskilled labour imported into the trade being counted as equivalent to an amount of skilled labour of equal efficiency. Had it been impossible to import any such labour at all, the earnings of miners would have been limited only by the elasticity of the demand for coal on the one hand, and the gradual coming to age of the rising generation of miners on the other. As it was, men were drawn from other occupations which they were not eager to leave; for they could have got high wages by staying where they were, since the prosperity of the coal and iron trades was but the highest crest of a swelling tide of credit. These new men were unaccustomed to underground work; its discomforts told heavily on them, while its dangers were increased by their want of technical knowledge, and their want of skill caused them to waste much of their strength. The limits therefore which their competition imposed on the rise of the temporary wages of miners' skill were not narrow.

Illustration from the history of the coal trade.

When the tide turned, those of the new-comers who were least adapted for the work, left the mines; but even then the miners who remained were too many for the work to be done, and their wage fell, till it reached that limit at which they could get more by selling their labour in other trades. And that limit was a low one; for the swollen tide of credit, which culminated in 1873, had undermined solid business, impaired the true foundations of prosperity, and left nearly every trade in a more or less unhealthy and depressed condition. The miners had therefore to sell their skilled labour in markets which were already over full, and in which their special .skill counted for nothing.

§ 4. To conclude this part of our argument. The market price of everything, *i.e.* its price for short periods, is determined mainly by the relations in which the demand for it stands to the available stocks of it; and in the case of labour or any other agent of production this demand is "derived" from the demand for those things which the agent is used in making. In these relatively short periods fluctuations in wages follow, and do not precede, fluctuations in the selling prices of the goods produced.

But the incomes which are being earned by all agents of production, human as well as material, and those which appear likely to be earned by them in the future, exercise a ceaseless influence on those persons by whose action the future supplies of these agents are determined. There is a constant tendency towards a position of normal equilibrium, in which the supply of each of these agents shall stand in such a relation to the demand for its services, as to give to those who have provided the supply a sufficient reward for their efforts and sacrifices. If the economic conditions of the country remained stationary sufficiently long, this tendency would realize itself in such an adjustment of supply to demand, that both machines and human beings would earn generally an amount that corresponded fairly with their cost of rearing and training, conventional necessaries as well as those things which are strictly necessary being reckoned for. But conventional necessaries might change under the influence of non-economic causes, even while economic conditions themselves were stationary : and this change would affect the supply of labour, and thus modify the national dividend and slightly alter its distribution. As it is, the economic conditions of the country are constantly changing, and the point of adjustment of normal demand and supply in relation to labour is constantly being shifted [1].

---

[1] In *Principles* VI. v., the argument of this last Section is pursued more at length, and with reference to several difficulties that are ignored here. In particular it is argued that the extra income earned by some natural abilities may be regarded as a Rent sometimes, but not when we are considering the normal earnings of a trade. This analogy is valid so long as we are merely analysing the source of the incomes of individuals, and it might even be carried further if persons were born with rare abilities specialised to particular branches of production.

CHAPTER VI.

INTEREST OF CAPITAL.

§ 1. THE main principles of the action of demand and supply with regard to capital have been discussed in the first two chapters of this Book. We there looked back at the results of our earlier studies, and endeavoured to bring together and study in their mutual relations a number of separate doctrines as to capital, each of which is familiar to every intelligent man; though he may not be able, without some special study, to see their bearings on one another and the part they severally play in the great central problem of distribution.

But in earlier times even great thinkers failed not only to understand the part which capital plays in this great problem, but even to recognise clearly many of the separate truths which are now regarded as common-place. They were impressed by observing that most borrowers were poor, that most lenders were rich; that the lenders very often suffered no material loss through making a loan, and that they often wrung exorbitant usury out of the needs of the poor. These facts enlisted their sympathies; and, aided by some specious metaphysical reasoning, prevented them from perceiving that he who lends to another hands over to him the power of using temporarily some desirable thing, and that this action has as much right to payment, as the act of handing to him absolutely some other thing of smaller value.

If the first man be rich it may be his duty in either case to confer a benefit freely on his poorer neighbour without expecting anything in return. But if a person can use £100 so as to produce, after allowing for his trouble, things worth £103 net at the end of a year, there is no reason for his lending the £100 free of interest to another, which would not require him to make to that other a free present of £3.[1]

§ 2. We have seen that interest is the reward of waiting in the same sense that wages are the reward of labour. Much work is pleasurable; but every one claims his full pay for all the work he does for others as a matter of ordinary business, however pleasurable it may be to himself. Similarly many people would wish to defer some of their enjoyments, even if they had to put by the money, which gives command over them, without hope of interest: but yet those who have the means of lending, will not lend gratis as a rule; because, even if they have not themselves some good use to which to turn the capital or its equivalent, they are sure to be able to find others to whom its use would be of benefit, and who would pay for the loan of it: and they stand out for the best market. And there always is a market, because though the stock of loanable wealth is increasing fast, new openings for its profitable use are ever being made by the progress of the mechanical arts and the opening up of new countries.

But now we may leave these general considerations, and make a more detailed study of this notion of Interest. For the interest of which we speak when we say that interest is the earnings of capital simply, or the

Net and Gross interest.

---

[1] This line of argument is pursued in some detail in *Principles* VI. vi. It is argued that the modern theories of Carl Marx and some others as to capital, repeat this old error in a disguised form, and without the excuse which there was for it in earlier times: but that with this exception, the history of the theory of interest has been one of almost continuous progress during the last three centuries: every generation has done something to forward it, none has been able to make any fundamental change. Reasons are also given for dissenting from Prof. Böhm-Bawerk's doctrines on the subject.

reward of waiting simply, is *Net* interest ; but what commonly passes by the name of Interest, includes other elements besides this, and may be called *Gross* interest.

These additional elements are the more important, the lower **Gross interest** and more rudimentary the state of commercial **includes some** **Insurance** security and of the organization of credit. Thus, **against risk,** for instance, in mediæval times, when a prince wanted to forestall some of his future revenues, he borrowed perhaps a thousand ounces of silver, and undertook to pay back fifteen hundred at the end of a year. There was how- ever no perfect security that he would fulfil the promise; and perhaps the lender would have been willing to exchange that promise for an absolute certainty of receiving thirteen hundred at the end of the year. In that case, while the nominal rate at which the loan was made, was fifty per cent., the real rate was thirty.

The necessity for making this allowance for insurance **and also Earn-** against risk is so obvious, that it is not often **ings of Man-** overlooked. But it is less obvious that every **agement.** loan causes some trouble to the lender; that when, from the nature of the case, the loan involves considerable risk, a great deal of trouble has often to be taken to keep these risks as small as possible ; and that then a great part of what appears to the borrower as interest, is, from the point of view of the lender, Earnings of Management of a troublesome business.

At the present time the net interest on capital in England is a little under three per cent. per annum ; for no more than that can be obtained by investing in such first-rate Stock Exchange securities as yield to the owner a secure income without appreciable trouble or expense on his part. And when we find capable business men borrowing on perfectly secure mortgages, at (say) four per cent., we may regard that gross interest of four per cent. as consisting of net interest, or interest proper, to the extent of a little under three per cent., and of Earnings of Management by the lenders to the extent of rather less than one per cent.

Again, a pawnbroker's business involves next to no risk; but his loans are generally made at the rate of 25 per cent. per annum, or more; the greater part of which is really Earnings of Management of a troublesome business. Or to take a more extreme case, there are men in London and Paris and probably elsewhere, who make a living by lending money to costermongers: the money is often lent at the beginning of the day for the purchase of fruit, &c., and returned at the end of the day, when the sales are over, at a profit of ten per cent.; there is little risk in the trade, and the money is seldom lost. Now a farthing invested at ten per cent. a day would amount to a billion pounds at the end of a year. But no one can become rich by lending to costermongers; because no one can lend much in this way. The so-called interest on the loans really consists almost entirely of earnings of a kind of work for which few capitalists have a taste.

§ 3. It is then necessary to analyse a little more carefully the extra risks which are introduced into business when much of the capital used in it has been borrowed. Let us suppose that two men are carrying on similar businesses, the one working with his own, the other chiefly with borrowed capital.

Further analysis of Gross interest.

There is one set of risks which is common to both; which may be described as the *Trade Risks* of the particular business in which they are engaged. They arise from fluctuations in the markets for their raw materials and finished goods, from unforeseen changes of fashion, from new inventions, from the incursion of new and powerful rivals into their respective neighbourhoods, and so on. But there is another set of risks, the burden of which has to be borne by the man working with borrowed capital, and not by the other; and we may call them *Personal*

Trade Risks.

Risks.   For he who lends capital to be used by   Personal
another for trade purposes, has to charge a high   Risks.
interest as insurance against the chances of some flaw or
deficiency in the borrower's personal character or ability.

The price then that the borrower has to pay for the loan
of capital, and which he regards as interest, is
from the point of view of the lender more   Gross interest
does not tend
properly to be regarded as profits : for it includes   to equality.
insurance against risks which are often very heavy, and
Earnings of Management for the task, which is often very
arduous, of keeping those risks as small as possible. Variations in the nature of these risks and of the task of management will of course occasion corresponding variations in the
Gross interest, so called, that is paid for the use of money.
The tendency of competition is therefore not towards equaliz-
ing this Gross interest : on the contrary, the more thoroughly
lenders and borrowers understand their business, the more
certainly will some classes of borrowers obtain loans at a
lower rate than others.

We must defer to a later stage our study of the marvel-
lously efficient organization of the modern Money Market by
which capital is transferred from one place where it is super-
abundant to another where it is wanted ; or from one trade
that is in the process of contraction to another which is being
expanded : and at present we must be contented to take it
for granted that a very small difference between the rates of
Net interest to be got on the loan of capital in two different
modes of investment in the same Western country will cause
capital to flow, though perhaps by indirect channels, from the
one to the other.

CHAPTER VII.

PROFITS OF CAPITAL AND BUSINESS POWER.

§ 1. IN the concluding Chapters of Book IV. we made some study of the various forms of business management, and the faculties required for them; and we saw how the supply of business power in command of capital may be regarded as consisting of three elements, the supply of capital, the supply of the business power to manage it, and the supply of the organization by which the two are brought together and made effective for production. We have now to carry this study further; and to inquire more closely into the nature of the services rendered to society by those who undertake and manage business enterprises, and the rewards of this work. We shall find that the causes which govern the earnings of business men are less arbitrary, and present closer analogies to those which govern other kinds of earnings than is commonly supposed.

We must however make a distinction at starting[1]. The Struggle for Survival tends to make those methods of organization prevail, which are best fitted to *thrive in* their environment; but not necessarily those best fitted to *benefit* their environment, unless it happens that they are duly rewarded for all the benefits which they confer, whether direct or indirect. And in fact this is not so. For as a general rule the Law of Substitution—which is nothing more than a special and limited application of the Law of Survival of the Fittest—tends to

This Chapter in relation to the latter part of Book IV.

Action of the Struggle for Survival.

[1] See Book IV. Ch. VIII.

make one method of industrial organization supplant another when it offers a direct and immediate service at a lower price. The indirect and ultimate services which either will render have, as a general rule, little or no weight in the balance; and as a result many businesses languish and die, which might in the long run have done good work for society if only they could have obtained a fair start. This is especially true of some forms of co-operative associations.

In this connection we may divide employers and other undertakers into two classes, those who open out new and improved methods of business, and those who follow beaten tracks. The services which the latter perform for society are chiefly direct and seldom miss their full reward: but it is otherwise with the former class.

For instance, economies have lately been introduced into some branches of iron manufacture by diminishing the number of times which the metal is heated in passing from pig iron to its final form; and some of these new inventions have been of such a nature that they could neither be patented nor kept secret. Let us suppose then that a manufacturer with a capital of £50,000 is getting in normal times a net profit of £4,000 a year, £1,500 of which we may regard as his Earnings of Management, leaving £2,500 for the other two elements of profits. We assume that he has been working so far in the same way as his neighbours, and showing an amount of ability which, though great, is no more than the normal or average ability of the people who fill such exceptionally difficult posts; that is, we assume that £1,500 a year is the normal earnings for the kind of work he has been doing. But as time goes on, he thinks out a way of dispensing with one of the heatings that have hitherto been customary; and in consequence, without increasing his expenses, he is able to increase his annual output by things which can be sold for £2,000 net. So long, therefore, as he can sell his wares at the old price, his Earnings of Management will be £2,000 a year above the average; and he will earn the full reward of his services to society. His neighbours however will copy his plan, and probably make more than average profits for a time. But soon competition will increase the supply, and lower the price of their wares, until their profits fall to about their old level; for no one could get extra high wages for making eggs stand on their ends after Columbus' plan had become public property.

Many business men whose inventions have in the long run been of almost priceless value to the world, have died in poverty; and while many men have amassed great wealth by good fortune, rather than by exceptional ability in the performance of public services of high importance, it is probable that those business men who have pioneered new paths have often conferred on society benefits out of all proportion to their own gains, even though they have died millionaires.

§ 2. We will now begin by tracing the action of the Law of Substitution in adjusting the rewards of the services rendered to society by ordinary workmen, by foremen, and by employers of different grades. We have already noticed that a great part of the work done by the head of a small business himself, is relegated in a large business to salaried heads of departments, managers, foremen and others. And this thread will guide us to much that is useful for our present inquiry. The simplest case is that of the earnings of the ordinary foreman; with which we may begin.

The action of the Law of Substitution in controlling Earnings of Management.

Let us suppose, for instance, that a railway contractor or a dockyard manager finds that it answers best to have one foreman to every twenty labourers, and to pay him twice the wages of one of them. This means that, if he found himself with 500 labourers and 24 foremen, he would expect to get just a little more work done at the same expense by adding one more foreman, than by adding two more ordinary labourers: while if he had had 490 labourers and 25 foremen,

M.   19

he would have found it better to add two more labourers. If
he could have got his foreman for one and a half times the
wages of a labourer, perhaps he would have employed one
foreman to every fifteen labourers. But, as it is, the number
of foremen employed is determined at one-twentieth of that
of the labourers, and their demand price at twice the
labourers' wages.

In exceptional cases the foremen may earn their wages
by over-driving those whose work they superintend. But we
may now suppose them to contribute to the success of the
undertaking in a legitimate way, by securing a better organization of its details; so that fewer things are done amiss
and need to be undone; so that everyone finds the help that
he wants in moving heavy weights, &c., ready for him just
when he wants it; so that all machinery and implements are
kept in good working order, and no one has to waste his time
and strength by working with inadequate appliances, and so
on. The wages of foremen who do work of this kind may
be taken as typical of a great part of the Earnings of Management: society, acting through the individual employer,
offers an effective demand for their services until that margin
is reached at which the aggregate efficiency of industry would
be increased by adding workers of some other grade more
than by adding the foremen whose wages would add an equal
amount to the expenses of production.

§ 3. So far the Employer has been regarded as the agent

The Law of
Substitution
acts through
the employer
and also on
him.

through whom the Law of Substitution acts in
contriving and arranging the factors of production so that the maximum of direct services
(estimated by their money measure) should be
performed at a minimum money cost. But now
we have to look at the work of the employers themselves
being contrived and arranged for them, though of course in
a more haphazard fashion, by the immediate action of their
own competition.

In the first place we find the small employer, who does the whole work of management and superintendence in his business competing with the large employer who retains in his own hands only the supreme work of controlling the higher policy of the business. And in this way as the earnings and services of foremen are weighed on the one side against those of ordinary labourers, so on the other the earnings and services of the foremen and managers who in the large business are hired to do much that the small employer does himself, are weighed against his[1].

It is true that the small employer needs capital of his own; but as we have already noticed[2] there is a constant increase in the ease with which a man who has the faculties for managing a business, can borrow the requisite capital.

It is true that the new man with but little capital of his own is at a disadvantage in trades which move slowly and in which it is necessary to sow a long time before one reaps. But in all those industries in which bold and restless enterprise *The business- man working with borrowed capital* can reap a quick harvest; and in particular wherever high profits are to be made for a time by cheaper reproductions of costly wares, there the new man is in his element : it is he who by his quick resolution and dexterous contrivances, and perhaps also a little by his natural recklessness, "forces the pace."

And he often holds his own with great tenacity even under considerable disadvantages; for the freedom and dignity of his position are very attractive to him. Thus the peasant proprietor whose little *will work hard for a small re- ward.* plot is heavily mortgaged, the small so-called "sweater" or "garret master" who takes out a sub-contract at a low price, will often work harder than the ordinary workman, and for a lower net income. And the manufacturer who is doing a large business with comparatively little capital of his own

[1] This point is worked out at some length in *Principles* VI. vii. 3, 4.
[2] Comp. Book iv. Ch. xii.§ 7.

19—2

will reckon his labour and anxiety almost as nothing, for he knows that he must anyhow work for his living, and he is unwilling to go into service to another: he will therefore work feverishly for a gain that would not count much in the balance with a wealthier rival, who, being able to retire and live in comfort on the interest of his capital, may be doubting whether it is worth while to endure any longer the wear-and-tear of business life[1].

§ 4. But the weighing in the balance of the services, and
Joint stock companies. therefore the earnings, of employees against the Earnings of Management of employers is in some ways best illustrated by reference to Joint-stock companies. For in them most of the work of management is divided between salaried directors (who indeed hold a few shares themselves) and salaried managers and other subordinate officials, most of whom have little or no capital of any kind; and their earnings, being almost the pure earnings of labour, are governed in the long run by those general causes which rule the earnings of labour of equal difficulty and disagreeableness in ordinary occupations.

Joint-stock companies seldom have the enterprise, the energy, the unity of purpose and the quickness of action of a private business. But these disadvantages are of relatively small importance in some trades. That publicity, which is one of the chief drawbacks of public companies in many branches of manufacture and of speculative commerce, is a positive advantage in ordinary Banking and Insurance and kindred businesses; while in these, as well as in most of the Transport industries (railways, tramways, canals, and the supply of gas, water and electricity), their unbounded command over capital gives them almost undisputed sway.

On the whole they exert a steadying influence on the demand for capital, and on the demand for labour of all kinds,

[1] The advantages and disadvantages of the undertaker with borrowed capital are further discussed in *Principles* VI. VII. 5.

and especially for the services of those who, having business ability but no capital of their own, desire to reap some Earnings of Management as salaried officials of a great undertaking. And as has already been observed, Co-operation promises, more than any other form of *Co-operation.* business association, to turn to good account the capabilities of the working man for the higher posts of business management.

Thus then each of the many modern methods of business has its own advantages and disadvantages: and its application is extended under the action of the Law of Substitution in every direction until that limit or margin is reached, at which its special advantages for that use no longer exceed its disadvantages.

§ 5. The supply of business power is large and elastic, since the area from which it is drawn is wide. Every-one has the business of his own life to conduct; *The supply of business ability is drawn from a wide area,* this, if done well, affords to some extent training for business management; and there is therefore no other kind of highly paid ability which depends so little on labour and expense applied specially to obtaining it, and which depends so much on so-called "natural qualities." And, secondly, business power is *and is non-specialized.* highly non-specialized; because in the large majority of trades, technical knowledge and skill become every day less important relatively to the broad and non-specialized faculties of judgment, promptness, resource, carefulness and steadfastness of purpose.

And we may conclude that the rarity of the natural abilities and the expensiveness of the special *The adjustment of Earnings to the difficulty and importance of the work done is fairly accurate.* training required for the work affect normal Earnings of Management in much the same way as they do the normal wages of skilled labour. In either case a rise in the income to be earned sets in operation forces tending to increase the supply of those capable of earning it; and in either case the extent to which the supply will be increased by a given rise of income, depends upon the social and economic condition of those from whom the supply is drawn. For though it is true that an able business man who starts in life with a great deal of capital and a good business connection is likely to obtain higher Earnings of Management than an equally able man who starts without these advantages; yet there are similar, though smaller, inequalities between the earnings of professional men of equal abilities who start with unequal social advantages; and the wages even of a working man depend on the start he has had in life almost as much as on the expense which his father has been able to afford for his education[1].

[1] Some difficulties in obtaining accurate knowledge of the true Earnings of Management in different trades are indicated in *Principles* VI. VII. 7.

CHAPTER VIII.

PROFITS OF CAPITAL AND BUSINESS POWER, CONTINUED.

§ 1. THE *profits* of a business are the excess of its receipts over its outgoings, and the *annual rate of profits* is the ratio which the yearly profits bear to the capital in- We have next vested. We have next to inquire whether there to examine the tendency of the is any general tendency of the rate of profits to rate of profits to equality. equality.

Adam Smith said :—"The whole drugs which the best employed apothecary in a large market-town will sell in a year may not perhaps cost him above thirty or forty pounds. Though he should sell them, therefore, for three Variations in or four hundred or a thousand per cent. profit nominal profits between large this may frequently be no more than the reason- and small able wages of his labour in the only way in businesses. which he can charge them, upon the price of the drugs. The greater part of the apparent profit is real wages disguised in the garb of profit."

But it is important to distinguish between the *annual* rate of profits on the capital invested in a Profits per business, and the rate of profits that are made annum and on every time the capital of the business is turned the turnover. over ; that is every time sales are made equal to that capital, or the rate of profits *on the turnover*. At present we are concerned with profits *per annum*.

The greater part of the nominal inequality between the normal rates of profit in small businesses and in large would disappear, if the scope of the term profits were narrowed in the former case or widened in the latter, so that it included

Correction of an anomaly of language. in both cases the remuneration of the same classes of services. There are even reasons for thinking that the rate of profit, rightly estimated, on large capitals tends to be higher than on small. For of two businesses competing in the same trade, that with the larger capital can nearly always buy at the cheaper rate, and can avail itself of many economies in the specialization of skill and machinery and in other ways, which are out of the reach of the smaller business: while at most the only important advantage, which the latter is likely to have, consists of its greater facilities for getting near its customers and consulting their individual wants. In trades in which this last advantage is not important, and especially in some manufacturing trades in which the large firm can sell at a better price than the small one, the outgoings of the former are proportionately less and the incomings larger; and therefore, if the profits be reckoned in the same way in both cases, the rate of profits in the former case must be higher than in the latter.

But these are the very businesses in which it most frequently happens that large firms after first crushing out small ones, either combine with one another and thus secure for themselves the gains of a limited monopoly, or by keen competition among themselves reduce the rate of profit very low. There are many branches of the textile, the metal, and the transport trades in which no business can be started at all except with a large capital; while those that are begun on a moderate scale struggle through great difficulties, in the hope that, after a time, it may be possible to find employment for a large capital, which will yield Earnings of Management high in the aggregate though low in proportion to the capital.

There are some trades which require a very high order of ability, but in which it is nearly as easy to manage a very large business as one of moderate size. In rolling mills, for instance, there is little detail which cannot be reduced to routine, and a capital of £1,000,000 invested in them can be controlled by one able man. A rate of profits of 20 per cent., which is not a very high average rate for some parts of the iron trade, would give the owner of such works Earnings of Management amounting to more than £150,000 a year. And since iron-masters can with so little additional effort get the Earnings of Management on an increased capital, wealthy men remain in the trade longer than in most others; and the competition of the great iron-masters with one another is said to have reduced the average rate of profits in the trade below the ordinary level.

The rate of profits is low in nearly all those trades which require very little ability of the highest order, and in which a public or private firm with a good connection and a large capital can hold its own against new-comers, so long as it is managed by men of industrious habits with sound common sense and a moderate share of enterprise. And men of this kind are seldom wanting either to a well-established public company or to a private firm which is ready to take the ablest of its servants into partnership.

We may then conclude, firstly that the true rate of profits in large businesses is higher than at first sight appears, because much that is commonly counted as profits in the small business ought to be classed under another head before the rate of profits in it is compared with that in a large business: and secondly that, even when this correction has been made, the rate of profits declines generally as the size of the business increases. *General result of the comparison between large businesses and small.*

§ 2. The normal Earnings of Management are of course high in proportion to the capital, and therefore the rate of profits per annum on the capital is high, when the work of management is heavy in proportion to the capital. Individual trades have indeed peculiarities of their own; and all rules on the subject are liable to great exceptions. But gene- *Profits are high where the Circulating capital is large relatively to the Fixed.*

rally it may be said that the extent of the work of management needed in a business depends more on the amount
of Circulating capital used than on that of the Fixed. The
rate of profit tends therefore to be low in trades in which
there is a disproportionately large amount of durable plant
that requires but little trouble and attention when once
it has been laid down. As we have seen, these trades are
likely to get into the hands of joint-stock companies : and the
aggregate salaries of the directors and higher officials bear a
very small proportion to the capital employed in the case of
railway and water companies, and, even in a more marked
degree, of companies that own canals and docks and bridges[1].

§ 3. Our inquiry may now pass away from the annual
rate of profits on the capital invested in a business, to the
The rate of profits on the turnover. rate of profits that are made every time sales
equal to the capital of the business are made, or,
as is commonly said, the rate of profits "on the
turnover." It is clear that if the average net profits in two
businesses are twelve per cent. per annum, and the first turns
over its capital 4 times in the year and the other only once,
the profits on the turnover must be twelve per cent. in the
latter case, and only about three per cent. in the former.
And we are thus brought to consider the causes which determine the rate of profits on the "turnover;" or, which comes
to the same thing, the percentage of the supply price of a
commodity which has to be classed as profits.

It is obvious that wholesale dealers, who buy and sell
large quantities of produce in single transactions, and who are
able to turn over their capital very rapidly, may make large

---

[1] Profits are exceptionally high where the wages-bill is very large relatively to the capital. This subject is treated in *Principles* VI, VIII. 2 where
it is argued that the least inaccurate of all the broad statements that can be
made with regard to a general tendency of profits to equality in different
trades, is that where equal capitals are employed, profits tend to be a certain
percentage per annum on the total capital, together with a certain percentage
on the wages-bill.

fortunes though their average profits on the turnover are less than one per cent.; and, in the extreme case of large stock exchange dealings, even when they are only a small fraction of one per cent.   But a shipbuilder who has to put labour and material into the ship, and to provide a berth for it, a long while before it is ready for sale, and who has to take care for every detail connected with it, must add a very high percentage to his direct and indirect outlay in order to remunerate him for his labour, and the locking up of his capital.

It varies more widely than the annual rate of profits on capital. Illustrative instances.

Again, in the textile industries some firms buy raw material and turn out finished goods, while others confine themselves to spinning, to weaving, or to finishing: and it is obvious that the rate of profit on the turnover of one of the first class must be equal to the sum of the rates of profit of one of each of the three other classes.   Again, the retail dealers' profit on the turnover is often only five or ten per cent. for commodities which are in general demand, and which are not subject to changes of fashion; so that while the sales are large, the necessary stocks are small, and the capital invested in them can be turned over very rapidly, with very little trouble and no risk.   But a profit on the turnover of nearly a hundred per.cent. is required to remunerate the retailer of some kinds of fancy goods which can be sold but slowly, of which varied stocks must be kept, which require a large space for their display, and which a change of fashion may render unsaleable except at a loss; and even this high rate is often exceeded in the case of fish, fruit, flowers and vegetables.

We see then that there is no general tendency of profits on the turnover to equality; but there may be, and as a matter of fact there is in each trade and in every branch of each trade, a more or less definite rate of profits on the turnover which is regarded as a "fair" or normal rate.   Of course these rates are always changing in consequence of changes in the methods of trade; which are generally begun by individuals

who desire to do a larger trade at a lower rate of profit on
the turnover than has been customary, but at a larger rate
of profit per annum on their capital. If however there
happens to be no great change of this kind going on, the
traditions of the trade that a certain rate of profit on the
turnover should be charged for a particular class of work are
of great practical service to those in the trade. Such traditions
are the outcome of much experience tending to show that, if
that rate is charged, a proper allowance will be made for all
the costs incurred for that particular purpose, and in addition
the normal rate of profits per annum in that class of business
will be afforded. If they charge a price which gives much
less than this rate of profit on the turnover they can hardly
prosper; and if they charge much more they are in danger
of losing their custom, since others can afford to undersell
them. This is the "fair" rate of profit on the turnover which
an honest man is expected to charge for making goods to
order, when no price has been agreed on beforehand; and it is
the rate which a court of law will allow, in case a dispute
should arise between buyer and seller.

§ 4.   During all this inquiry we have had in view chiefly
the ultimate, or long-period or true normal results
of economic forces; we have considered the way
in which the supply of business ability in command
of capital tends in the long run to adjust itself to
the demand; we have seen how under the action of the Law
of Substitution it seeks constantly every business and every
method of conducting every business in which it can render
services that are so highly valued by persons who are able to
pay good prices for the satisfaction of their wants, that those
services will in the long run earn a high reward. The motive
force is the competition of undertakers: each one tries every
opening, forecasting probable future events, reducing them to
their true relative proportions, and considering what surplus
is likely to be afforded by the receipts of any undertaking over

Profits are a constituent element of normal supply-price.

the outlay required for it. All his prospective gains enter into the profits which draw him towards the undertaking; all the investments of his capital and energies in making the appliances for future production, and in building up the "Immaterial" capital of a business connection, have to show themselves to him as likely to be profitable, before he will enter on them: the whole of the profits which he expects from them enter into the reward, which he expects in the long run for his venture.

Much of the argument of Chapter V. as to the earnings of industrial skill is applicable to the earnings of business power. There are, however, some differences between the two cases, which call for our study.

§ 5. In the first place the undertaker's profits bear the first brunt of any change in the price of those *Profits fluctu-* things which are the product of his capital *ate with prices* (including his business organization), of his *and in even* labour and of the labour of his employés; and as a result *greater ratio:* fluctuations of his profits generally precede fluctuations of their wages, and are much more extensive. For, other things being equal, a comparatively small rise in the price for which he can sell his product is not unlikely to increase his profit manyfold, or perhaps to substitute a profit for a loss. That rise will make him eager to reap the harvest of good prices while he can; he will be in fear that his employés will leave his employment or refuse to work. He will be more able and more willing to pay high wages; and wages *but the wages* will rise. But experience shows that (whether *of employés lag* they are governed by sliding scales or not) they *behind, and* *their fluctua-* seldom rise as much in proportion as prices; and *tions are less.* therefore they do not rise nearly as much in proportion as profits.

Another aspect of the same fact is that when trade is bad, the employé at worst is earning nothing towards the support of himself and his family; but the employer's out-goings are likely to exceed his incomings, particularly if he

is using much borrowed capital. In that case his Gross
Earnings of Management are a negative quantity; that is, he
is losing his capital. In very bad times this happens to a
great number, perhaps the majority of undertakers; and it
happens almost constantly to those who are less fortunate, or
less able, or less well fitted for their special trade than others.

The profits of individuals differ more widely than ordinary earnings do. § 6. To pass to another point, the number of those who
succeed in business is but a small per-centage of
the whole; and in their hands are concentrated
the fortunes of others several times as numerous
as themselves, who have made savings of their
own, or who have inherited the savings of others
and lost them all, together with the fruits of their own efforts,
in unsuccessful business. In order therefore to find the
average profits of a trade we must not divide the aggregate
profits made in it by the number of those who are reaping
them, nor even by that number added to the number who
have failed: but from the aggregate profits of the successful
we must subtract the aggregate losses of those who have
failed, and perhaps disappeared from the trade; and we must
then divide the remainder by the sum of the numbers of those
who have succeeded and those who have failed. It is probable
that the true Gross Earnings of Management, that is, the
excess of profits over interest, is not on the average more than
a half, and in some risky trades not more than a tenth part,
of what it appears to be to persons who form their estimate
of the profitableness of a trade by observation only of those
who have secured its prizes. There are however reasons for
thinking that the risks of trade are on the whole diminishing
rather than increasing[1].

---

[1] There are other differences between the earnings of business power and
of ordinary earnings, for a study of which, as well as of the relation in which
earnings of management stand to the rent of exceptional ability, and of the
conditions under which Profits are to be regarded as a Quasi-rent, the reader
is referred to *Principles*, VI, VIII.

CHAPTER IX.

RENT OF LAND.

§ 1. WE may call to mind that the land has an "inherent" income of heat and light and air and rain, which man cannot appreciably affect; and advantages of situation, of which many are beyond man's control, while but few of the remainder are the direct result of the investment of capital and effort in the land by its individual owners. The supply of these properties is not dependent on human effort, and would therefore not be increased by extra rewards to that effort. On the other hand those chemical or mechanical properties of the soil, on which its fertility largely depends, can be modified, and in extreme cases entirely changed by man's action.

Income attributed to inherent properties of land.

Now let us revert to our study of the tendency to diminishing return in agriculture; still supposing that the owner of the land undertakes its cultivation, so that our reasoning may be general, and independent of the incidents of particular forms of land tenure. We saw how the return to successive "doses," or applications of capital and labour, though it may increase for the first few doses, will begin to diminish when the land is already well cultivated. The cultivator continues to apply additional capital and labour, till he reaches a point at which the return is only just sufficient to repay his outlay and

Résumé of Book IV. Ch. II. III.

reward him for his own work. That will be the dose on the margin of cultivation, whether it happens to be applied to rich or to poor land. An amount equal to the return to it will be required, and will be sufficient to repay him for each of his previous doses; and the excess of the gross produce over this amount is his producer's surplus. Supposing him to be a man of ordinary ability and enterprise and to farm fairly well, this will be what is commonly called the rental value of the land.

This surplus or rental value depends on, firstly, the richness of the land, and secondly, the relative values of those things which he has to sell and of those things which he needs to buy. And the prices at which the various requisites of the farm can be bought, and its various products sold, depend on his surroundings; and changes in that are continually changing the relative values of different crops and therefore the relative values of land in different situations.

Thus it is important to remember that inequalities of situation relatively to the best markets are just as powerful causes of inequalities of producer's surplus as are inequalities of absolute productiveness. But England is so small and so thickly peopled, that the cultivator can get nearly the same net price in whatever part of England he is; and English economists have ascribed to fertility the first rank among the causes which determine the value of agricultural land, and have treated situation as of secondary importance. They have therefore often regarded the producer's surplus, or rental value, of land as the excess of the produce which it yields, over what is returned to equal capital and labour (applied with equal skill) to land that is so barren as to be on the margin of cultivation; without taking the trouble to state that separate allowance must be made for differences in the expense of marketing. But economists in new countries, observing that the richest land may lie uncultivated if it has not good access to markets think of situation at least equally important with fertility in determining the value of land. In their view land on the margin of cultivation is land far from markets; and the producer's surplus presents itself to them as the excess value of the produce from well-situated land over that which equal labour, capital (and skill), would get on the worst situated land; allowance being of course made for differences of fertility, if necessary.

§ 2. The argument of this chapter so far is applicable to all systems of land tenure, which recognize private ownership of land in any form; for it is concerned _Argument_ with that producer's surplus, which accrues to _applicable to all systems_ the owner if he cultivates his land himself; or, _of tenure._ if he does not, then accrues to him and his tenants, regarded as a firm engaged in the business of cultivation. Thus it holds true, whatever be the division which custom or law or contract may have arranged between them with regard to their several shares of the cost of cultivation on the one hand, and the fruits of the cultivation on the other. Petty's memorable statement of the law of rent is so worded as to apply to all forms of tenure and to all stages of civilization:—"Suppose a man could with his own hands plant a certain scope of Land with Corn, that is, could Digg, or Plough; Harrow, Weed, Reap, Carry home, Thresh, and Winnow so much as the Husbandry of this Land requires; and had withal Seed wherewith to sow the same. I say, that when this man hath subducted his seed out of the proceed of his Harvest, and also what himself hath both eaten and given to others in exchange for Clothes, and other Natural necessaries; that the Remainder of Corn, is the natural and true Rent of the Land for that year; and the _medium_ of seven years, or rather of so many years as make up the Cycle, within which Dearths and Plenties make their revolution, doth give the ordinary Rent of the Land in Corn[1]."

[1] _Taxes and Contributions_, IV. 13.

M. 20

At the present day, in those parts of England where custom and sentiment count for least, and free competition and enterprise for most in the bargaining for the use of land, it is commonly understood that the landlord supplies, and in some measure maintains, those improvements which are slowly made and slowly worn out. That being done, he requires of his tenant the whole producer's surplus which the land thus equipped is estimated to afford in a year of normal harvests and normal prices; after deducting enough to replace the farmer's capital with normal profits; so that the farmer stands to lose in bad years and gain in good years. In this estimate it is implicitly assumed that the farmer is a man of normal ability and enterprise for that class of holding; and therefore, if he rises above that standard, he will himself reap the benefit; and if he falls below it will himself bear the loss, and perhaps ultimately leave the farm[1].

The so-called English system has some disadvantages; but when we come to compare it with other systems, we shall see that it afforded great advantages to a country, which pioneered the way for the world in the development of free enterprise; and which therefore was impelled early to adopt all such changes as give freedom and vigour, elasticity and strength.

---

[1] In other words, that part of the income derived from the land which the landlord obtains, is governed, for all periods of moderate length, mainly by the market for the produce, with but little reference to the cost of providing the various agents employed in raising it; and it therefore is of the nature of a rent. And that part which the tenant retains, is to be regarded, even for short periods, as profits entering directly into the normal price of the produce; because the produce would not be raised unless it were expected to yield those profits. The more fully therefore the distinctively English features of land tenure are developed, the more nearly is it true that the line of division between the tenant's and the landlord's share coincides with the deepest and most important line of cleavage in economic theory.

CHAPTER X.

LAND TENURE.

§ 1. In early times, and in some backward countries even in our own age, all rights to property depend on general understandings rather than on precise laws and documents. In so far as these under- standings can be reduced to definite terms and expressed in the language of modern business, they are generally to the following effect:—The ownership of land is vested, not in an individual, but in a firm of which one member or group of members is the sleeping partner, while another member or group of members (it may be a whole family) is the working partner.

Early forms of Land-tenure have generally been based on partnerships.

The sleeping partner is sometimes the ruler of the State, sometimes he is an individual who inherits what was once the duty of collecting the payments due to this ruler from the cultivators of a certain part of the soil; but what, in the course of silent time, has become a right of ownership, more or less definite, more or less absolute. The sleeping partner, or one of them, is generally called the proprietor, or landholder or landlord, or even the landowner; though this is an incorrect way of speaking, when he is restrained by law or custom from turning the cultivator out of his holding, either by an arbitrary increase of the payments exacted from him or by any other means[1].

---

[1] Custom is however really more elastic than at first sight appears, as is shown even by recent English history. Caution is therefore needed in applying Ricardian analysis to modern English land problems as well as to those arising out of more primitive systems of land tenure. See *Principles* VI. x. 2, 3.

§ 2.　In a great part of Latin Europe the land is divided into holdings, which the tenant cultivates by the labour of himself and his family, and sometimes, though rarely, that of a few hired labourers, and for which the landlord supplies buildings, cattle and, sometimes even, farm implements. This system is called *Metayage*. Its advantages are considerable when the holdings are very small, the tenants poor, and the landlords not averse to taking much trouble about small things: but it is not suitable for holdings large enough to give scope to the enterprise of an able and responsible tenant. It is commonly associated with the system of peasant proprietorship; and we may consider that next[1].

Metayage or rental by shares.

The position of a peasant proprietor has great attractions. He is free to do what he likes, he is not worried by the interference of a landlord, and the anxiety lest another should reap the fruits of his work and self-denial. His feeling of ownership gives him self-respect, and stability of character, and makes him provident and temperate in his habits. He is scarcely ever idle,' and seldom regards his work as mere drudgery; it is all for the land that he loves so well.

The peasant proprietor

"The magic of property turns sand into gold," said Arthur Young. It undoubtedly has done so in many cases in which the proprietors have been men of exceptional energy. But such men might perhaps have done as well or better if their horizon had not been limited to the narrow hopes of a peasant proprietor. For indeed there is another side to the picture. "Land," we are told, "is the best savings-bank for the working man." Sometimes it is the second best. But the very best is the energy of himself and his children; and the peasant pro-

is generally an industrious but seldom an efficient worker

---

[1] Metayage enables a poor man to get the use of capital at a low charge, and to have more freedom and responsibility than a hired labourer, though less than an English farmer. It is a form of Co-operation.

prietors' thoughts are so full of the one that they often starve the other. Many even of the richest of them stint the food of themselves and their families: they pride themselves on the respectability of their houses and furniture; but they live in their kitchens for economy, and are practically worse housed and far worse fed than the better class of English cottagers. And the poorest of them work hard during very long hours, but do not really get through much work, because they feed themselves worse than the poorest English labourers. They do not understand that wealth is useful only as the means towards a real income of happiness; they sacrifice the end to the means.

And it must be recollected that the English labourers represent the failures rather than the successes of the English system. They are the descendants of those who for many successive generations have not availed themselves of the opportunities by which their abler and more adventurous neighbours were rising to leading posts at home, and, what is far more important, were acquiring the fee simple of a great part of the surface of the globe. Of the causes which have contributed to make the English race the chief owners of the New World, the most important is that bold enterprise which has made a man, who is rich enough to be a peasant proprietor, generally refuse to be content with the humdrum life and the narrow income of a peasant. And among the causes which have fostered this enterprise, none is more important than the absence of the temptations to wait about for a petty inheritance, and to marry for the sake of property rather than in the free exercise of individual choice—temptations which have often dulled the energy of youth in places in which peasant properties have predominated.

It is partly in consequence of the absence of these temptations that the "farmers" of America, though they are men of the working class cultivating *The American farmer.*

and he is not so well represented in the New World as the English labourer.

their own land with their own hands, do not resemble "peasant proprietors[1]." They invest their income freely and wisely in developing the energies of themselves and their children; and these energies constitute the chief part of their capital, for their land generally is as yet of but little value. Their minds are always active, and though many of them have little technical knowledge of agriculture, their acuteness and versatility enable them to find out almost unerringly the best solution of the problem immediately before them.

That problem is generally to obtain a produce large in proportion to the labour spent on it, though small in proportion to the abundant land at their disposal. In some parts of America however, in which land is beginning to get a scarcity value, and in which the immediate neighbourhood of good markets is making an intensive cultivation profitable, the methods of farming and of tenure are rearranging themselves on the English model. And within the last few years there have been signs of a tendency on the part of native Americans to hand over to persons of recent European origin the farms of the West, as they have already done the farms of the East, and as they did long ago the textile industries.

American methods of cultivation.

§ 3. Let us then turn to the English system of tenure. Faulty and harsh as it has been in many respects, it yet had a great power of stimulating and economizing that enterprise and energy, which, aided by England's geographical advantages and freedom from devastating wars, gave her the leadership of the world in Manufacture and Colonization and, though in a less marked degree, in Agriculture. England has learnt lessons in agriculture from

The English system

---

[1] Three-fourths of the farms in the United States are cultivated by their owners; and only one-third of the remainder is held by tenants under the English plan, while two-thirds are in a position somewhat similar to that of Metayers, except that they hold under definite contracts which are but little influenced by custom.

many countries and especially the Netherlands; but on the whole she has taught far more than she has learnt. And there is now no country except the Netherlands, which can compare with her in the amount of produce per acre of fertile land; and no country in Europe which obtains nearly so high returns in proportion to the labour expended in getting them.

The chief merit of the system is that it enables the landlord to keep in his own hands the responsibility for that part and only that part of the property which he can look after with but little trouble to himself, and little vexation to his tenant. His part consists of land, buildings and permanent *enables the landlord to supply that capital over which he can keep control;* improvements; and averages in England five times that which the farmer has to supply himself. The landlord is willing to supply this five-sixths of the necessary capital at a net rent, which seldom gives as much as three per cent. interest on its cost; and there is no other business in which the enterprising undertaker can borrow what capital he wants at so low a rate, or can often borrow so large a part of his capital at any rate at all.

The second merit of the English system, which partly follows from the first, is that it gives the landlord considerable freedom in the selection of an able and responsible tenant. But it is true that *and it gives considerable freedom of selection.* his good and bad qualities alike often tend to prevent his selecting tenants on strictly commercial principles. He seldom goes far afield for a new tenant: and until quite recently, he has seldom given facilities for an able working man, similar in character to the American farmer, to make a start on a small farm which he can cultivate with his own hands and those of his family and a few hired men[1].

§ 4. We may next inquire how far those general ten-

[1] The English system on the whole tends to promote the discovery and the diffusion of improved methods: but even in England progress in agriculture is slower than in manufactures. See *Principles* VI. x. 7.

dencies towards production on a large scale, which we studied
in Book IV., are applicable to agriculture under modern
English conditions.

Firstly, agriculture must be spread over the broad land:
Special con-
ditions of agri-
culture.
raw material can be brought to the manufacturer
for him to work on; but the agriculturist must
seek his work.   Again, the workers on the land
must adapt their work to the seasons, and can seldom confine
themselves entirely to one class of work; and in consequence
agriculture, even under the English system, cannot move fast
in the direction of the methods of manufacture.

But yet there are considerable forces tending to push it
in that direction. The progress of invention is constantly
increasing the number of serviceable, but expensive machines,
for most of which a small farmer can find employment during
only a very short time. He may hire some of them from
people who make it their business to undertake steam ploughing and thrashing; but there are many, the use of which can
be got only by co-operation with his neighbours; and the
uncertainties of the weather prevent this plan from working
very smoothly in practice.

Again, the farmer must go beyond the results of his own
It affords an
increasing
scope for high
business
ability.
and his father's experience in order to keep
abreast of the changes of the day. He should be
able to follow the movements of agricultural
science and practice closely enough to see their
chief practical applications to his own farm. To do all this
properly requires a trained and versatile mind; and a farmer
who has these qualities could find time to direct the general
course of the management of several hundred, or even of
several thousand acres; and the mere superintendence of his
men's work in matters of detail is not a task fitting for him.
The work which he ought to do is as difficult as that of a
large manufacturer; and he would never dream of spending
his own strength on minute supervision which he can easily

hire subordinates to do. A farmer who can do this higher work, must be wasting his strength on work that is beneath him, unless he employs many gangs of workmen, each of them under a responsible foreman. But there are not many farms which give scope for this, and there is therefore very little inducement for really able men to enter the business of farming; the best enterprise and ability of the country generally avoid agriculture and go to trades in which there is room for a man of first-rate ability to do nothing but high class work, to do a great deal of it, and therefore to get high Earnings of Management.

The experiment of working farms on a very large scale is difficult and expensive; because, to be tried properly, it would require farm buildings and means of communication specially adapted to it; and it would have to overcome a good deal of resistance from custom and sentiment not altogether of an unhealthy kind. The risk also would be great; for in such cases those who pioneer often fail, though their route when well trodden may be found to be the easiest and best.

If a farm is not very large, and if, as is often the case, the farmer has no greater ability and activity of mind than is commonly to be found among the better class of working foremen in manufactures, *The farmer who works with his men.* then it would be best for others, and in the long run for himself, that he should return to the old plan of working among his men. Perhaps also his wife might return to some of those lighter tasks in and near the farmhouse which tradition ascribes to her. They require discretion and judgment, they are not inconsistent with education and culture; and combined with it they would raise and not lower the tone of her life, and her real claims to a good social position. There is some reason for thinking that the stern action of the principle of natural selection is now displacing those farmers, who have not the faculty to do difficult head-work, and yet decline to do hand-work. Their places are being taken by men of more than average natural ability who, with the help of modern education, are rising from the ranks of labourers; who are quite able to manage the ordinary routine work of a model farm; and who are giving to it a new life and spirit by calling their men to come and work, instead of telling them to go and work. Very large farms being left out of view, it is with rather small farms worked on these principles that the immediate future of English agriculture seems to lie.

Very small holdings. Very small holdings however have great advantages wherever so much care has to be given to individual plants, that machinery is out of place; and there is reason for hoping that they will continue to hold their own in raising vegetables, flowers and fruit.

§ 5. We may next consider how far landlords will in their own interest adjust the size of holdings to the real needs of the people. Small holdings often require more expensive buildings, roads and fences, and involve greater trouble and incidental expenses of management to the landlord in proportion to their acreage than do large holdings; and while a large farmer who has some rich land can turn poor soils to good account, small holdings will not flourish generally except on good soil[1]. Their gross rental per acre must therefore always be at a higher rate than that of large farms. But it is contended that, especially when land is heavily burdened by settlements, landlords are unwilling to incur the expense of subdividing farms, unless they see their way to rents for small holdings that will give them, in addition to high profits on their outlay, a heavy insurance

The interests of landlords and of the public as regards small holdings.

---

[1] The interpretation of this term varies with local conditions and individual wants. On permanent pasture land near a town or an industrial district the advantages of small holdings are perhaps at their maximum, and the disadvantages at their minimum. If the land is arable, it must not be light, but strong, and the richer the better; and this is especially the case with holdings so small as to make much use of the spade. If the land is hilly and broken the small cultivator loses but little from his want of command of machinery.

fund against the chance of having to throw the holdings together again; and that the rental for small holdings, and especially for those of only a few acres, is extravagantly high in many parts of the country. Sometimes the prejudices of the landlord and his desire for undisputed authority make him positively refuse to sell or let land to persons who are not in harmony with him on social, political or religious questions; but it seems certain that evils of this kind have always been confined to a few districts, and that they are rapidly diminishing.

But they rightly attract much attention. For there is a public need for small holdings, as well as large, in every district. They increase the number of people who are working in the open air with their heads and their hands: and by giving the agricultural labourer a stepping-stone upwards, they tend to prevent him from being compelled to leave agriculture to find some scope for his ambition, and thus check the great evil of the continued flow of the ablest and bravest farm lads to the towns.

Moreover very small holdings, which can be worked by people who have some other occupation, and also allotments and large gardens, render great services *Allotments.* to the State, as well as to those who cultivate them. They break the monotony of existence, they give a healthy change from indoor life, they offer scope for variety of character and for the play of fancy and imagination in the arrangement of individual life; they afford a counter attraction to the grosser and baser pleasures; they often enable a family to hold together that would otherwise have to separate; under favourable conditions they improve considerably the material condition of the worker; and they diminish the fretting as well as the positive loss caused by the inevitable interruptions of their ordinary work.

And lastly though peasant proprietorship, as a system, is unsuited to the economic conditions of England, to her soil,

her climate and the temper of her people, yet there are a few
There should be no artificial hindrances to peasants' properties. peasant proprietors in England who are perfectly happy in this condition; and there are a few others who would buy small plots of land and would live happily on them, if they could get just what they wanted where they wanted it. Their temper is such that they do not mind working hard and living sparely, provided they need call no one master; they love quiet and dislike excitement; and they have a great capacity for growing fond of land[1]. Reasonable opportunity should be given to such people to invest their savings in small plots of land, on which they may raise suitable crops with their own hands; and at the very least the present grievous legal charges on the transfer of small plots should be diminished.

Co-operation might seem likely to flourish in agriculture
Co-operation in agriculture. and to combine the economies of production on a large scale with many of the joys and the social gains of small properties. But it requires habits of mutual trust and confidence; and unfortunately the bravest and the boldest, and therefore the most trustful, of the countrymen have always moved to the towns, and agriculturists are a suspicious race. Co-operative movements in agriculture therefore must needs be very cautious, until the way has been well prepared for them by the less ambitious but safer system of profit-sharing.

As co-operation might combine more of the advantages of all systems of tenure, so the cottier system of Ireland often combined the disadvantages of all; but its worst evils and their causes are rapidly disappearing, and the economic elements of the problem are just now overshadowed by the political. We must therefore pass it by[2].

[1] The number of holdings under 50 acres in Great Britain in 1885 was over three hundred thousand.
[2] The English system of tenure is competitive in its essence, but agriculture offers great obstacles to the full and free action of competition. These

§ 6. Finally a word may be said as to private and public interests with regard to open spaces in towns.

Wakefield and the American economists have taught us how a sparsely inhabited new district is enriched by the advent of every new settler. The converse truth is that a closely peopled district is impoverished by everyone who adds a new building or raises an old one higher. The want of air and light, of peaceful repose out-of-doors for all ages and of healthy play for children, exhausts the energies of the best blood of England which is constantly flowing towards our large towns. By allowing vacant spaces to be built on recklessly we are committing a great blunder from a business point of view, since for the sake of a little material wealth we are wasting those energies which are the factors of production of all wealth; and we are sacrificing those ends towards which material wealth is only a means. It is a difficult question to decide how far the expense of clearing open spaces in land already built on should fall on the neighbouring owners; but it seems right that for the future every new building erected, save in the open country, should be required to contribute in money or in kind towards the expenses of open places in its neighbourhood.

Conflict between public and private interests in the matter of building on open spaces.

arise partly from the difficulty of deciding what are normal prices and harvests; partly from local variations in the standard of normal farming skill and enterprise. On this and some allied questions relating to compensation for improvements, see *Principles* VI. x. 10.

CHAPTER XI.

GENERAL VIEW OF DISTRIBUTION.

§ 1. THE argument of the preceding ten chapters may now be brought to a head. It falls far short of a complete solution of the problem before us: for that involves questions relating to foreign trade, to fluctuations of credit and employment, and to the influences of associated and collective action in its many forms. But yet it extends to the broadest and deepest influences which govern distribution and exchange.

To begin with, we have seen that there is a general correspondence between the causes that govern the supply prices of material and of personal capital: the motives which induce a man to accumulate personal capital *in* his son's education, are similar to those which control his accumulation of material capital *for* his son. There is a continuous transition from the father who works and waits in order that he may bequeath to his son a rich and firmly-established manufacturing or trading business, to one who works and waits in order to support his son while he is slowly acquiring a thorough medical education, and ultimately to buy for him a lucrative practice. Again, there is the same continuous transition from him to one who works and waits in order that his son may stay long at school; and may afterwards work for some time almost without pay while

[margin: Comparison of conditions of normal supply of material, capital, and industrial training.]

learning a skilled trade, instead of being forced to support himself early in an unskilled occupation, such as that of an errand-boy. For such occupations, because they lead the way to no future advance, sometimes offer comparatively high wages to young lads.

It is indeed true that as society is now constituted, the only persons, who are very likely to invest much in developing the personal capital of a youth's abilities are his parents: and that many first-rate abilities go for ever uncultivated because no one, who can develop them, has had any special interest in doing so. This fact is very important practically, for its effects are cumulative; that is, the deficiency in education of one generation is likely to impair the education of the next, and that again of the generation which follows it, and so on, cumulatively. But it does not give rise, as has been supposed, to a fundamental difference between material and human agents of production: for it is analogous to the fact that much good land is poorly cultivated because those who would cultivate it well have not access to it.

Again, since human beings grow up slowly and are slowly worn out, and parents in choosing an occupation for their children must as a rule look forward a whole generation, changes in demand take a longer time to work out their full effects on supply in the case of human agents than of most kinds of material appliances for production; and a specially long period is required in the case of labour to give full play to the economic forces which tend to bring about a normal adjustment between demand and supply[1].

§ 2. The efficiency of human agents of production on the one hand, and that of material agents on the other, are weighed against one another and compared with their costs; and each tends to be applied as far as it is more efficient than the other in proportion to its cost. A chief function of

Business men weigh the services of the different industrial classes;

[1] Comp. IV. v. vi. vii. and xii.; and VI. iv. v. and vii.

business enterprise is to facilitate the free action of this great principle of substitution. Generally to the public benefit, but sometimes in opposition to it, business men are constantly comparing the services of machinery, and of labour, and again of unskilled and skilled labour, and of extra foremen and managers; they are constantly devising and experimenting with new arrangements which involve the use of different factors of production, and selecting those most profitable to themselves[1].

The efficiency as compared with the cost of almost every class of labour, is thus continually being weighed in the balance in one or more branches of production against some other classes of labour: and each of these in its turn against others. This competition is primarily "vertical:" it is a struggle for the field of employment between groups of labour belonging to different grades, but engaged in the same branch of production, and inclosed, as it were, between the same vertical walls. But meanwhile "horizontal" competition is always at work, and by simpler methods: for, firstly, there is great freedom of movement of adults from one business to another within each trade; and secondly, parents can generally introduce their children into almost any other trade of the same grade with their own in their neighbourhood. By means of this combined vertical and horizontal competition there is an effective and closely adjusted balance of payments to services as between labour in different grades; in spite of the fact that the labour in any one grade is mostly recruited even now from the children of those in the same grade[2].

The working of the principle of substitution is thus chiefly indirect. When two tanks containing fluid are joined by a pipe, the fluid, which is near the pipe in the tank with the higher level, will flow into the other, even though it be rather

and give effect to the principle of substitution.

---

[1] Compare VI. i. 6, and vii. 2.
[2] Compare IV. vi. 5; and VI. v. 2.

viscous; and thus the general levels of the tanks will tend to be brought together, though no fluid may flow from the further end of the one to the further end of the other; and if several tanks are connected by pipes, the fluid in all will tend to the same level, though some tanks have no direct connection with others. And similarly the principle of substitution is constantly tending by indirect routes to apportion earnings to efficiency between trades, and even between grades, which are not directly in contact with one another, and which appear at first sight to have no way of competing with one another.

§ 3. There is no breach of continuity as we ascend from the unskilled labourer to the skilled, thence to the foreman, to the head of a department, to the general **But as regards** manager of a large business paid partly by a **the work of business men** share of the profits, to the junior partner, and **themselves** lastly to the head partner of a large private **substitution is less highly** business: and in a joint-stock company there is **organized.** even somewhat of an anti-climax when we pass from the directors to the ordinary shareholders, who undertake the chief ultimate risks of the business. Nevertheless business men, those who undertake business enterprises, are to a certain extent a class apart.

For while it is through their conscious agency that the principle of substitution chiefly works in balancing one factor of production against another; with regard to them it has no other agency than the indirect influence of their own competition. So it works blindly, or rather wastefully; it forces many to succumb who might have done excellent work if they had been favoured at first: and, in conjunction with the law of increasing return, it strengthens those who are strong, and hands over the businesses of the weak to those who have already obtained a partial monopoly.

But on the other hand there is also a constant increase in the forces which tend to break up old monopolies, and

M.

to offer to men, who have but little capital of their own, openings both for starting new businesses and for rising into posts of command in large public and private concerns; and these forces tend to put business ability in command of the capital required to give it scope.

On the whole the work of business management is done cheaply—not indeed as cheaply as it may be in the future when men's collective instincts, their sense of duty and their public spirit are more fully developed; when society exerts itself more to develop the latent faculties of those who are born in a humble station of life, and to diminish the secrecy of business; and when the more wasteful forms of speculation and of competition are held in check. But yet it is done so cheaply as to contribute to production more than the equivalent of its pay. For the business undertaker, like the skilled artisan, renders services which society needs, and which it would probably have to get done at a higher cost if he were not there to do them[1].

The ablest business men are generally those who get the highest profits, and at the same time do their work most cheaply; and it would be as wasteful if society were to give their work to inferior people who would undertake to do it more cheaply, as it would be to give a valuable diamond to be cut by a low waged but unskilled cutter.

The similarity between the causes that determine the normal rewards of ordinary ability on the one hand, and of business power in command of capital on the other, does not extend to the fluctuations of their current earnings. For the employer stands as a buffer between the buyer of goods and all the various classes of labour by which they are

Contrasts between fluctuations of current profits and wages.

[1] We postpone a criticism of the contention of the socialists that it would be better for the State to take the work into its own hands and hire business managers to conduct it: and we postpone a study of those forms of speculation and commercial competition which are not beneficial to society, and perhaps are even harmful.

made. He receives the whole price of the one and pays the whole price of the others. The fluctuations of his profits go with fluctuations of the prices of the things he sells, and are more extensive: while those of the wages of his employees come later and are less extensive. The earnings at any particular time of his capital and ability are sometimes large, but sometimes also a negative quantity: whereas those of the ability of his employees are never very large, and are never a negative quantity. The wage-receiver is likely to suffer much when out of work; but that is because he has no reserve, not because he is a wage-receiver[1].

§ 4. Returning to the point of view of the second chapter of this Book, we may call to mind the double relation in which the various agents of production stand to one another. On the one hand they are often rivals for employment; any one that is more efficient than another in proportion to its cost tending to be substituted for it, and thus limiting the demand price for the other. And on the other hand they all constitute the field of employment for each other: there is no field of employment for any one, except in so far as it is provided by the others: the national dividend which is the joint product of all, and which increases with the supply of each of them, is also the sole source of demand for each of them.

The agents of production are the sole source of employment for one another.

Thus an increase of material capital causes it to push its way into new uses; and though in so doing it may occasionally diminish the field of employment for manual labour in a few trades, yet on the whole it will very much increase the demand for manual labour and all other agents of production. For it will much increase the national dividend, which is the common source of the demand for all; and since

How an increase of capital enriches the field for the employment of labour.

[1] Compare VI. iv. 6.

21—2

by its increased competition for employment it will have forced down the rate of interest, therefore the joint product of a dose of capital and labour will now be divided more in favour of labour than before. Thus, the chief benefit which capital confers upon labour is not by opening out to it new employments, but by increasing the joint product of land, labour and capital (or of land, labour and waiting), and by reducing the share of that product which any given amount of capital (or of waiting) can claim as its reward[1].

§ 5. In discussing the influence which a change in the supply of work of any one industrial group exerts on the field of employment for other kinds of labour, there was no

Increase in number or efficiency of any group of workers in relation to wages of themselves and others. need to raise the question whether the increase of work came from an increase in the numbers or in the efficiency of those in the group: for that question is of no direct concern to the others. In either case there is the same addition to the national dividend: in either case competition will compel them to force themselves to the same extent into uses in which their marginal utility is lower; and will thus lessen to the same extent the share of the joint product which they are able to claim in return for a given amount of work of a given kind.

---

[1] The new demand for labour will partly take the form of the opening-out of new undertakings which hitherto could not have paid their way. It will, for instance, lead to the making of railways and waterworks in districts which are not very rich, and which would have continued to drag their goods along rough roads, and draw up their water from wells, if people had not been able and willing to support labour while making railway embankments and water conduits, and to wait for the fruits of their investment long and for a relatively low reward.

Another part of this new demand for labour will come from the makers of new and more expensive machinery in all branches of production. For when it is said that machinery is substituted for labour, this means that one class of labour combined with much waiting is substituted for another combined with less waiting: and for this reason alone, it would be impossible to substitute capital for labour in general, except indeed locally by the importation of capital from other places.

But the question is of vital importance to the members of that group. For, if the change is an increase of one-tenth in their average efficiency, then each ten of them will have as high an aggregate income as each eleven of them would have if their numbers had increased by one-tenth, their efficiency remaining unchanged.

We shall have to look at some other aspects of this question in the next chapter while discussing the relative merits of increased leisure and increased material production as aims of progress.

CHAPTER XII.

THE INFLUENCE OF PROGRESS ON VALUE.

§ 1. THE field of employment which any place offers for labour and capital depends firstly on its natural resources; secondly, on the power of turning them to good account, derived from its progress in knowledge and in social and industrial organization; and thirdly, on the access that it has to markets in which it can sell those things of which it has a superfluity. The importance of this last condition is often underrated; but it stands out prominently when we look at the history of new countries.

The field of employment for capital and labour

It is commonly said that wherever there is abundance of good land to be had free of rent, and the climate is not unhealthy, the real earnings of labour and the interest on capital must both be high. But this is only partially true. The early colonists of America lived very hardly. Nature gave them wood and meat almost free: but they had very few of the comforts and luxuries of life. And even now there are, especially in South America and Africa, many places to which Nature has been abundantly generous, which are nevertheless shunned by labour and capital, because they have no ready communications with the rest of the world. On the other hand high rewards may be offered to capital and labour by a mining district in the midst of an alkaline desert, when once communications have been opened up with the outer world, or again by a trading centre on a barren sea-coast; though, if limited to their own resources, they could support

is not always rich in new countries which have no good access to the markets of the Old World.

but a scanty population, and that in abject poverty. And the splendid markets which the Old World has offered to the products of the New, since the growth of steam-communication, have rendered North America and Australia the richest large fields for the employment of capital and labour that there have ever been.

But after all the chief cause of the modern prosperity of new countries lies in the markets that the old world offers, not for goods delivered on the spot, but for promises to deliver goods at a distant date. A handful of colonists having assumed rights of perpetual property in vast tracts of rich land, are anxious to reap in their own generation its future fruits; and as they cannot do this directly, they do it indirectly, by selling in return for the ready goods of the old world promises to pay much larger quantities of the goods that their own soil will produce in a future generation. In one form or another they mortgage their new property to the old world at a very high rate of interest. Englishmen and others, who have accumulated the means of present enjoyment, hasten to barter them for larger promises in the future than they can get at home: a vast stream of capital flows to the new country, and its arrival there raises the rate of wages very high. The new capital filters but slowly towards the outlying districts: it is so scarce there, and so many persons are eager to have it, that it has often commanded for a long time two per cent. a month, from which it has fallen by gradual stages down to six, or perhaps even five per cent., a year.

Old countries offer a market for mortgages of the future incomes of a new country,

and the consequent influx of capital into the latter

For the settlers being full of enterprise, and seeing their way to acquiring private title-deeds to property that will shortly be of great value, are eager to become independent undertakers, and if possible employers of others; so wage-earners have to be attracted by

raises nominal wages very high.

high wages, which are paid in a great measure out of the commodities borrowed from the old world on mortgages, or in other ways. It is, however, difficult to estimate exactly the real rate of wages in outlying parts of new countries. The workers are picked men with a natural bias towards adventure; hardy, resolute, and enterprising; men in the prime of life, who do not know what illness is; and the strain of one kind and another which they go through, is more than the average English, and much more than the average European labourer could sustain. There are no poor among them, because there are none who are weak : if anyone becomes ailing, he is forced to retire to some more thickly-peopled place where there is less to be earned, but where also a quieter and less straining life is possible. Their earnings are very high if reckoned in money; but they have to buy at very high prices, or altogether dispense with, many of the comforts and luxuries which they would have obtained freely, or at low prices, if they had lived in more settled places. It is however true that many of these things are of but little real utility, and can be easily foregone, where no one has them and no one expects them.

As population increases, the best situations being already occupied, nature gives generally less return of raw produce to the marginal effort of the cultivators; and this tends a little to lower wages. But even in agriculture the Law of Increasing Return is constantly contending with that of Diminishing Return, and many of the lands which were neglected at first, give a generous response to careful cultivation; and meanwhile the development of roads and railroads, and the growth of varied markets and varied industries, render possible innumerable economies in production. Thus the actions of the Laws of Increasing and Diminishing Return appear pretty well balanced, sometimes the one, sometimes the other being the stronger. There is no reason so far why the wages of labour (of a given effici-

As time goes on though the Law of Diminishing Return may not be acting very strongly,

ency) should fall.   For if, taking one thing with another, the Law of Production is that of Constant Return, there will be no change in the reward to be divided between a dose of capital and labour ; that is, between capital and labour working together in the same proportions as before.   And, since the rate of interest has fallen, the share which capital takes of this stationary joint reward is less than before ; and therefore the amount of it remaining for labour is greater[1].

But whether the Law of production of commodities be one of Constant Return or not, that of the production of new title-deeds to land is one of rapidly Diminishing Return.   The influx of foreign capital, though perhaps as great as ever, becomes less in proportion to the population ; *the influx of capital becomes relatively slower and wages tend to fall.* wages are no longer paid largely with commodities borrowed from the old world : and this is the chief reason of the subsequent fall in Real Efficiency wages ; that is, in the necessaries, comforts and luxuries of life which can be earned by work of a given efficiency.   But there are two other causes tending to lower average daily wages measured in money. The first is, that as the comforts and luxuries of civilization increase, the average efficiency of labour is lowered by the influx of immigrants of a less sturdy character than the earlier settlers.   And the second is, that many of these new comforts and luxuries do not enter directly into money wage, but are an addition to it[2].

---

[1] Of course the aggregate share of capital may have increased. For instance, while labour has doubled capital may have quadrupled, and the rate of interest may be two-thirds of what it was: and then, though each dose of capital gets a lower reward by one-third, and leaves for labour a larger share of the joint product of a dose of capital and labour, the aggregate share of capital will have risen in the ratio of eight to three. Much of the argument of Mr Henry George's *Progress and Poverty* is vitiated by his having over-looked this distinction.

[2] We took account of them when arriving at the conclusion that the action of the Law of Increasing Return would on the whole countervail that of Diminishing Return : and we ought to count them in at their full value when

§ 2.   The influence which access to distant markets exerts on the growth of the National Dividend has been conspicuous in the history of England also.

For more than a hundred years she has pursued with energy those manufacturing industries which give an Increasing Return to increasing capital and labour. She has exported goods that are made the more easily, the larger the scale on which they are produced, in exchange for some raw produce that could not be easily raised in her own climate, and for some grain and meat which she could not have produced for herself, except by a cultivation of her land so intensive as to call the Law of Diminishing Return strongly into operation. For a long time her exports met with little effective competition. But as the century wore on, other nations developed their manufactures, and Englishmen are no longer able to get in return for, say, a bale of calico as much of the products of backward countries as before. At one time they could get for the calico nearly as much as the same cost of production in that backward country as a similar bale ; and every improvement in England's arts of manufacture would have increased considerably the amount of foreign goods she could have brought back in return for the product of a given quantity of her own labour and capital. But now every improvement in manufacture spreads itself quickly over the Western World, and causes additional bales of cotton to be offered to backward countries at a cheaper and still cheaper rate.   Those

England has exchanged manufactures for goods that obey the Law of Diminishing Return.

She has gradually lost her partial monopoly

and now gains but little so far as foreign trade is concerned from improvements in manufacture.

tracing the changes in Real wages. Many historians have compared wages at different epochs with exclusive reference to those things which have always been in common consumption. But from the nature of the case, it is just these things to which the Law of Diminishing Return applies; and which tend to become scarce as population increases. The view thus got is one-sided and misleading in its general effect.

countries gain much, while England herself gains but little from the improvement and the cheapening of the manufacture of the goods that she sends them.

And she fares even worse with the goods that she sends to other manufacturing countries and especially to America. The amount of wheat which can be bought in Illinois with a ton of steel cannot be more than the produce of as much capital and labour as would make a ton of steel in Illinois by the new processes; and therefore it has fallen in the same proportion as the efficiency of English and American labour in making steel has increased. It is for this reason, as well as because of the heavy tariffs levied on her goods by many countries, that in spite of England's large trade, the progress of invention in the manufacturing arts has added less than might have been otherwise expected to her real National Income or Dividend.

It is no slight gain that she can make cheaply clothes and furniture and other commodities for her own use: but those improvements in the arts of manufacture which she has shared with other nations, have not directly increased the amount of raw produce which she can obtain from other countries with the product of a given quantity of her own capital and labour. Probably more than three-fourths of the whole benefit she has derived from the progress of manufacture during the present century has been *But she gains much from the cheapening of transport of various kinds* through its indirect influences in lowering the cost of transport of men and goods, of water and light, of electricity and news; for the dominant economic fact of our own age is the development not of the Manufacturing, but of the Transport industries. It is these that are growing most rapidly in aggregate volume and in individual power, and which are giving rise to most anxious questions as to the tendencies of large capitals to turn the forces of economic freedom to the destruction of that freedom: but, on the other hand, it is they also which have done by far the most towards increasing England's wealth.

One effect of this cheapening of transport has been that, while a century ago the goods which England gained by foreign trade were chiefly the luxuries of the well-to-do, they now consist largely of bulky commodities and especially wheat and other kinds of simple food. And thus although England's gains from her foreign trade may not have been increasing quite in proportion to the great increase in its volume, the additions which it has made to the real purchasing power of the wages of the working classes have been very great and constantly increasing.

which have told especially on the prices of common food.

§ 3. The influence, which the improvement of the means and the arts of transport has exerted in this direction, has been aided by two great changes. The first is the adoption of Free Trade in the middle of this century; and the second is the subsequent development of the Mississippi valley and the Far West of America, which are especially suited for growing the grain and the meat, that constitute the chief food of the English working man.

Influence of progress on the labour values of some leading commodities: viz. grain,

The only parts of America that were thickly peopled fifty years ago were ill-suited for growing wheat; and the cost of carrying it great distances by land was prohibitive. The labour value of wheat—that is the amount of labour which will purchase a peck of wheat—was then at its highest point, and now is at its lowest. It would appear that agricultural wages have been generally below a peck of wheat a day; but that in the first half of the eighteenth century they were about a peck, in the fifteenth a peck and a half or perhaps a little more, while now they are two or three pecks[1].

---

[1] Rogers' estimates for the Middle Ages are higher: but he seems to have taken the wages of the more favoured part of the population as representative of the whole. In the Middle Ages, even after a fairly good harvest, the

It is true that, where population is very sparse, nature supplies grass and therefore animal food almost *gratis;* and in South America beggars pursue their calling on horseback.   During the Middle Ages however the population of England was always dense enough to give a considerable labour value to meat, though it was of poor quality [1].   A century ago very little meat was eaten by the working classes ; while now, though its price is a little higher than it was then, they probably consume more of it, on the average, than at any other time in English history.

meat,

Turning next to the rent of house room, we find that ground-rents in towns have risen, both extensively and intensively.   For an increasing part of the population is living in houses on which ground-rents at an urban scale have to be paid, and that scale is rising.   But house rent proper, that is what remains of the total rent after deducting the full rental value of the ground, is probably little, if at all, higher than at any previous time for similar accommodation ; for the rate of profits on the turnover which is earned by capital engaged in building is now low, and the labour cost of building materials has not much altered.   And it must be remembered that those who pay the high town rents get in return the amusements and other advantages of modern town life, which many of them would not be willing to forego for the sake of a much greater gain than their total rent.

house room,

wheat was of a lower quality than the ordinary wheat of to-day ; while after a bad harvest much of it was so musty that now-a-days it would not be eaten at all ; and the wheat seldom became bread without paying a high monopoly charge to the mill belonging to the lord of the manor.

[1] For cattle, though only about a fifth as heavy as now, had very large frames : their flesh was chiefly in those parts from which the coarsest joints come ; and since they were nearly starved in the winter and fed up quickly on the summer grass, the meat contained a large percentage of water, and lost a great part of its weight in cooking.   At the end of the summer they were slaughtered and salted : and salt was dear.   Even the well-to-do scarcely tasted fresh meat during the winter.

The labour value of wood, though lower than at the beginning of the century, is higher than in the Middle Ages: but that of mud, brick or stone walls has not much changed; while that of iron—to say nothing of glass—has fallen much.

And indeed the popular belief that house rent proper has risen, appears to be due to an imperfect acquaintance with the way in which our forefathers were really housed. The modern suburban artisan's cottage contains sleeping accommodation far superior to that of the gentry in the Middle Ages; and the working classes had then no other beds than loose straw, reeking with vermin, and resting on damp mud floors. But even these were probably less unwholesome, when bare and shared between human beings and live stock, than when an attempt at respectability covered them with rushes, which were nearly always vile with long accumulated refuse. It is undeniable that the housing of the very poorest classes in our towns now is destructive both of body and soul: and that with our present knowledge and resources we have neither cause nor excuse for allowing it to continue. And it is true that in earlier times bad housing was in so far a less evil than now, as those who were badly housed by night had abundant fresh air by day. But a long series of records, ending with the evidence of Lord Shaftesbury and others before the recent Commission on the Housing of the Poor, establishes the fact that all the horrors of the worst dens of modern London had their counterpart in worse horrors of the lairs of the lowest stratum of society in every previous age.

Fuel, like grass, is often a free gift of nature to a sparse population; and during the Middle Ages the cottagers could generally, though not always, get the little brushwood fire needed to keep them warm as they huddled together round it in huts which had no chimney through which the heat could go to waste. But as population increased the scarcity of fuel pressed heavily on the working classes, and would have arrested England's progress altogether, had not coal been ready to take the place of wood as fuel for domestic purposes, as well as for smelting iron. It is now so cheap that even the comparatively poor can keep themselves warm indoors without living in an unwholesome and stupefying atmosphere.

This is one of the great services that coal has wrought for modern civilization. Another is to provide cheap under-clothing, without which cleanliness *clothing,* is impossible for the masses of the people in a cold climate: and that is perhaps the chief of the benefits that England has gained from the direct application of machinery to making commodities for her own use. Another, and not less important service, is to provide abundant water, even in large towns[1]; and another to supply, *water,* with the aid of mineral oil, that cheap and artificial light which is needed not only for some of man's work, but, what is of higher moment, for the good use of *light,* his evening leisure. To this group of requisites for a civilized life, derived from coal on the one hand, and modern means of transport on the other, we must add, as has just been noticed, the cheap and thorough means of communication *news and* of news and thought by steam-presses, by steam- *travel.* carried letters and steam-made facilities for travel.

§ 4. We have seen that the National Dividend is at once the aggregate net product of, and the sole *The influence* source of payment for, all the agents of pro- *of progress on* duction within the country; that the larger it is, *the values of the chief a-* the larger, other things being equal, will be the *gents of pro-* *duction:* share of each agent of production, and that an increase in the supply of any agent will generally lower its price, to the benefit of other agents.

---

[1] Primitive appliances will bring water from high ground to a few public fountains: but the omnipresent water supply which both in its coming and its going performs essential services for cleanliness and sanitation, would be impossible without coal-driven steam-pumps and coal-made iron pipes.

This general principle is specially applicable to the case

it has some-
times lowered
the value of
English agri-
cultural land,

of land. An increase in the amount or productiveness of the land that supplies any market
redounds in the first instance to the benefit of
those capitalists and workers who are in possession of other agents of production for the same market.
And the influence on values which has been exerted in the
modern age by the new means of transport is nowhere so
conspicuous as in the history of land; its value rises with
every improvement in its communications with markets in
which its produce can be sold, and its value falls with every
new access to its own markets of produce from more distant
places.

But anything that promotes the prosperity of the people

but not of agri-
cultural and
urban land
taken together.

promotes also in the long run that of the landlords of the soil. It is true that English rents
rose very fast when, at the beginning of this
century, a series of bad harvests struck down a
people that could not import their food; but a rise so caused
could not from the nature of the case have gone very much
further. And the adoption of free trade in corn in the middle
of the century, followed by the expansion of American wheat-
fields, is rapidly raising the real value of the land urban and
rural taken together; that is, it is raising the amount of the
necessaries, comforts and luxuries of life which can be purchased by the aggregate rental of all the landowners urban
and rural taken together[1].

[1] It seems that the agricultural (money) rent of England doubled between
1795 and 1815, and then fell by a third till 1822; after that time it has been
alternately rising and falling; and it is now about 45 or 50 millions as against
50 or 55 millions about the year 1873, when it was at its highest. It was
about 30 millions in 1810, 16 millions in 1770, and 6 millions in 1600. But the
rental of urban land in England is now rather greater than the rent of
agricultural land: and in order to estimate the full gain of the landlords from
the expansion of population and general progress, we must reckon in the
values of the land on which there are now railroads, mines, docks, &c. Taken
all together, the money rental of England's soil is probably twice as high, and

§ 5. Political Arithmetic may be said to have begun in England in the seventeenth century; and from that time onwards we find a constant and nearly steady increase in the amount of accumulated wealth per head of the population.

It has greatly increased the supply of capital,

This increase of capital per head tended to diminish its marginal utility, and therefore the rate of interest on new investments; but not uniformly, because there were meanwhile great variations in the demand for capital, both for political and military and for industrial purposes.

and has lowered its proportionate though not its total income.

Thus the rate of interest which was vaguely reported to be 10 per cent. during a great part of the Middle Ages, had sunk to 3 per cent. in the earlier half of the eighteenth century; but the immense industrial and political demand for capital raised it again, and it was relatively high during the great war. It fell as soon as the political drain had ceased; but it rose again in the middle of this century, when railways and the development of the Western States of America and of Australia made a great new demand for capital. These new demands have not slackened; but the rate of interest is again falling fast, in consequence of the great recent accumulations of wealth in England, on the Continent, and above all in America.

§ 6. The growth of general enlightenment and of a sense of responsibility towards the young has turned a great deal of the increasing wealth of the nation from investment as Material capital to investment as Personal capital.

There is a relative fall in the earnings of trained ability.

There has resulted a largely increased supply of trained abilities, which has much increased the National Dividend, and raised the average income of the whole people : but it has taken away from these

its Real rental three or four times as high, as it was when the corn laws were repealed.

Progress may lower the value of the appliances of production, when this can be separated from that of their sites; but not of such things as railways, when the value of their sites is reckoned in. See *Principles* VI. XII. 7.

M. 22

trained abilities much of that scarcity value which they used to possess, and has lowered their earnings not indeed absolutely, but relatively to the general advance; and it has caused many occupations, which not long ago were accounted skilled, and which are still spoken of as skilled, to rank with unskilled labour as regards wages.

A striking instance is that of writing. It is true that many kinds of office work require a rare combination of high mental and moral qualities; but almost any one can be easily taught to do the work of a copying clerk, and probably there will soon be few men or women in England who cannot write fairly well. When all can write, the work of copying, which used to earn higher wages than almost any kind of manual labour, will rank among unskilled trades[1].

Again, a new branch of industry is often difficult simply because it is unfamiliar; and men of great force and skill are required to do work, which can be done by men of ordinary capacity or even by women and children, when the track has once been well beaten: its wages are high at first, but they fall as it becomes familiar. And this has caused the rise of average wages to be underrated, because it so happens that many of the statistics, which seem typical of general movements of wages, are taken from trades which were comparatively new a generation or two ago, and are now within the grasp of men of much less real ability than those who pioneered the way for them[2].

Earnings in old and familiar skilled occupations tend to fall relatively to those in new.

---

[1] In fact the better kinds of artisan work educate a man more, and will be better paid than those kinds of clerk's work which call for neither judgment nor responsibility. And, as a rule, the best thing that an artisan can do for his son is to bring him up to do thoroughly the work that lies at his hand, so that he may understand the mechanical, chemical or other scientific principles that bear upon it; and may enter into the spirit of any new improvement that may be made in it. If his son should prove to have good natural abilities, he is far more likely to rise to a high position in the world from the bench of an artisan than from the desk of a clerk.

[2] Comp. Book IV. Ch. VI. §§ 1, 2; and Ch. IX. especially § 3. As the trade

The consequence of such changes as these is to increase the number of those employed in occupations which are called skilled, whether the term is now properly applied or not: and this constant increase in the numbers of workers in the higher classes of trades has caused the average of all labour to rise much faster than the average of representative wages in each trade[1].

In the middle ages, though some men of great ability remained artisans all their lives, and became artists; yet as a class the artisans ranked more nearly with the unskilled labourers than they do now. At the beginning of the new industrial era a hundred years ago the artisans had lost much of their old artistic traditions and had not yet acquired that technical command over their instruments, that certainty and facility in the exact performance of difficult tasks which belong to the modern skilled artisan; and observers early in this century were struck by the social gulf that was being opened out in their

Artisans' wages

progresses, improvements in machinery are sure to lighten the strain of accomplishing any given task; and therefore to lower task wages rapidly. But meanwhile the pace of the machinery, and the quantity of it put under the charge of each worker, may be increased so much that the total strain involved in the day's work is greater than before. On this subject employers and employed frequently differ. It is for instance certain that Time wages have risen in the textile trades; but the employés aver, in contradiction to the employers, that the strain imposed on them has increased more than in proportion; that is, that Efficiency-wages have fallen. In this controversy wages have been estimated in money; but when account is taken of the increase in the purchasing power of money there is no doubt that Real Efficiency-wages have risen.

[1] This may be made clearer by an example. If there are 500 men in grade A earning 12s. a week, 400 in grade B earning 25s. and 100 in grade C earning 40s. the average wages of the 1000 men are 20s. If after a time 300 from grade A have passed on to grade B, and 300 from grade B to grade C, the wages in each grade remaining stationary, then the average wages of the whole thousand men will be about 28s. 6d. And even if the rate of wages in each grade had meanwhile fallen 10 per cent., the average wages of all would still be about 25s. 6d., that is would have risen more than 25 per cent. Neglect of such facts as these, as Mr Giffen has pointed out, is apt to cause great errors.

own generation between the artisan and the unskilled labourer.

rose relatively to those of un- skilled labour at the begin- ning of the century:

This social change was a consequence partly of the increase of the wages of the artisan, which rose to about double those of the unskilled labourer; and partly of the same cause that secured him his high wages, that is the great increase in the demand for highly skilled labour, especially in the metal trades, and the consequent rapid absorption of the strongest characters among the labourers and their children into the ranks of the artisans; for the breaking down, just at that time, of the old exclusiveness of the artisans, had made them less than before an aristocracy by birth and more than

but now that tendency is re- versed.

before an aristocracy by worth. But about a generation ago, as has just been explained, some of the simpler forms of skilled trades began to lose their scarcity value, as their novelty wore off; and at the same time continually increasing demands began to be made on the ability of those in some trades, that are traditionally ranked as unskilled. The navvy for instance, and even the agricultural labourer, have often to be trusted with expensive and complicated machinery, which a little while ago was thought to belong only to the skilled trades, and the Real wages of these two representative occupations are rising fast[1].

Again, there are some skilled and responsible occupations, such as those of the head heaters and rollers in iron works, which require great physical strength, and involve much discomfort: and in them wages are very high. For the

---

[1] The rise of wages of agricultural labourers would be more striking than it is, did not the spread of modern notions to agricultural districts cause many of the ablest children born there to leave the fields for the railway or the workshop, to become policemen, or to act as carters or porters in towns. Perhaps there is no stronger evidence of the benefits of modern education and economic progress than the fact that those who are left behind in the fields, though having less than an average share of natural abilities, are yet able to earn much higher Real wages than their fathers.

temper of the age makes those who can do high class work, and can earn good wages easily, refuse to undergo hardship, except for a very high reward.

§ 7. We may next consider the changes in the relative wages of old and young men, of women and children.

The conditions of industry change so fast that long experience is in some trades almost a disadvantage, and in many it is of far less value than a quickness in taking hold of new ideas and adapting one's habits to new conditions. In these trades *There is a relative fall in the wages of elderly men;* an elderly man finds it difficult to get employment except when trade is brisk, at all events if he is a member of a union which will not allow him to work for less than the full wages of the district. In any case he is likely to earn less after he is fifty years old than before he is thirty; and the knowledge of this is tempting artisans to follow the example of unskilled labourers, whose natural inclination to marry early has always been encouraged by the desire that their family expenses may begin to fall off before their own wages begin to shrink. Trades-unions are afraid that abuses might creep in if they allowed men "with grey hairs" to compete for employment at less than full wages; but many of them are coming to see that it is to their own interest, as it certainly is to that of the community, that such men should not be forced to be idle.

A second and even more injurious tendency of the same kind is that of the wages of children to rise relatively to those of their parents. Machinery has displaced many men, but not many boys; *and a rise in the wages of boys and girls,* the customary restrictions which excluded them from some trades are giving way; and these changes, together with the spread of education, while doing good in almost every other direction, are doing harm in this that they are enabling boys, and even girls, to set their parents at defiance and start in life on their own account.

The wages of women are for similar reasons rising fast

and of women. relatively to those of men. And this is a great gain in so far as it tends to develop their faculties; but an injury in so far as it tempts them to neglect their duty of building up a true home, and of investing their efforts in the Personal capital of their children's character and abilities.

§ 8. The relative fall in the incomes to be earned by moderate ability, however carefully trained, is

The earnings of exceptional genius are rising, accentuated by the rise in those that are obtained by many men of extraordinary ability. There never was a time at which moderately good oil paintings sold more cheaply than now, and there never was a time at which first-rate paintings sold so dearly. A business man of average ability and average good fortune gets now a lower rate of profits on his capital than at any previous time; while yet the operations, in which a man exceptionally favoured by genius and good luck can take part, are so extensive as to enable him to amass a huge fortune with a rapidity hitherto unknown.

The causes of this change are chiefly two; firstly, the general growth of wealth; and secondly, the

as a result of two causes development of new facilities for communication, by which men, who have once attained a commanding position, are enabled to apply their constructive or speculative genius to undertakings vaster, and extending over a wider area, than ever before.

It is the first cause, almost alone, that enables some bar-

of which one acts almost alone on professional incomes, risters to command very high fees; for a rich client whose reputation, or fortune, or both, are at stake will scarcely count any price too high to secure the services of the best man he can get: and it is this again that enables jockeys and painters and musicians of exceptional ability to get very high prices. In all these occupations the highest incomes earned in our own generation are the highest that the world has yet seen. But so long as the number of persons who can be reached by a human voice is strictly limited, it is not very likely that any singer will make an advance on the £10,000, said to have been earned in a season by Mrs Billington at the beginning of this century, nearly as great as that which the business leaders of the present generation have made on those of the last.

For the two causes have co-operated to put enormous power and wealth in the hands of those business men of our own generation who have had first-rate genius, and have been favoured by fortune. *while both act fully with regard to business incomes.* This is most conspicuous in America, where several men who began life poor, have amassed more than £10,000,000 each. It is true that a great part of these gains have come, in some cases, from the wrecks of the rival speculators who had been worsted in the race. But in others, as for instance, that of the late Mr Vanderbilt, they were earned mainly by the supreme economizing force of a great constructive genius working at a new and large problem with a free hand : and Mr Vanderbilt probably saved to the people of the United States more than he accumulated himself.

§ 9. But these fortunes are exceptional. The diffusion of knowledge, the improvement of education, the growth of prudent habits among the masses of the people, and the opportunities which the new methods of business offer for the safe investment of small capitals :—all these forces are telling on *Progress is fast improving the condition of the great body of the working classes.* the side of the poorer classes as a whole relatively to the richer. The returns of the income tax and the house tax, the statistics of consumption of commodities, the records of salaries paid to the higher and the lower ranks of servants of Government and public companies, tend in the same direction, and indicate that middle class incomes are increasing faster than those of the rich ; that the earnings of artisans are increasing faster than those of the professional classes, and that the wages of healthy and vigorous unskilled labourers are increasing faster even than those of the average artisan[1].

It must be admitted that a rise in wages would lose part of its benefit, if it were accompanied by an increase in the time spent in enforced idleness. Inconstancy of employment is a great evil, and rightly attracts public attention. But several causes combine to make it appear to be greater than it really is.

The inconstancy of employment in modern industry is apt to be exaggerated.

When a large factory goes on half time, rumour bruits the news over the whole neighbourhood, and perhaps the newspapers spread it all over the country. But few people know when an independent workman, or even a small employer, gets only a few days' work in a month; and in consequence whatever suspensions of industry there are in modern times, are apt to seem more important than they are relatively to those of earlier times. In earlier times some labourers were hired by the year: but they were not free, and were kept to their work by personal chastisement. There is no good cause for thinking that the mediæval artisan had constant employment. And the most persistently inconstant employment now to be found in Europe is in those non-agricultural industries of the West which are most nearly mediæval in their methods, and in those industries of Eastern and Southern Europe in which mediæval traditions are strongest.

In many directions there is a steady increase in the proportion of employés who are practically hired by the year.

---

[1] A great body of statistics relating to nearly all civilized countries, and uniformly tending in this direction is contained in M. Leroy Beaulieu's *Essai sur la répartition des Richesses, et sur la tendance à une moindre inégalité des conditions*, 1881. Mr Goschen's Address to the Royal Statistical Society in 1887 on *The increase of moderate incomes* points the same way; and above all so do the very careful and instructive studies of wage statistics made by Mr Giffen in his private and in his official capacity.

This is for instance the general rule in many of those trades connected with Transport which are growing fastest, and are the representative industries of the second half of the nineteenth century, as the manufacturing trades were of the first half. And though the rapidity of invention, the fickleness of fashion, and above all the instability of Credit, do certainly introduce disturbing elements into modern industry; yet, as we shall see presently, other influences are working strongly in the opposite direction, and there seems to be no good reason for thinking that inconstancy of employment is increasing on the whole.

Progress then has done much: but there still remains a great, and—in consequence of improved sanitation—perhaps a growing Residuum of persons **But not of those who are unfit for hard work.** who are physically, mentally or morally incapable of doing a good day's work with which to earn a good day's wage; and some of those who are called artisans, together with many unskilled labourers, work hard for over long hours, and provide for others the means of refinement and luxury, but obtain neither for themselves nor their children the means of living a life that is worthy of man.

There is a strong temptation to over-state the economic evils of our own age, and to ignore the existence of similar and worse evils in earlier ages; for by **The temptation to understate the benefits of progress.** so doing we may for the time stimulate others, as well as ourselves, to a more intense resolve that the present evils shall no longer be allowed to exist. But it is not less wrong, and generally it is much more foolish, to palter with truth for a good than for a selfish cause. And the pessimist descriptions of our own age, combined with romantic exaggerations of the happiness of past ages, must tend to the setting aside of methods of progress, the work of which if slow is yet solid; and to the hasty adoption of others of greater promise, but which resemble the potent medicines of a charlatan, and while quickly effecting a little good, sow the seeds of widespread and lasting decay. This impatient insincerity is an evil only less great than that moral torpor which can endure that we, with our modern resources and knowledge, should look on contentedly at the continued destruction of all that is worth having in multitudes of human lives, and solace ourselves with the reflection that anyhow the evils of our own age are less than those of the past.

§ 10. We have not yet reached the stage at which we can profitably examine the general effects of economic progress on human well being. But it will be well, before ending this Book, to pursue a little further the line of thought on which we started in Book III., when considering Wants in relation to Activities. We there saw reasons for thinking that the true key-note of economic progress is the development of new activities rather than of new wants; and we may now make some study of a question that is of special urgency in our own generation; viz.—what is the connection between changes in the manner of living and the rate of earnings; how far is either to be regarded as the cause of the other, and how far as the effect.

The broader influences of progress.

Let us take the term the STANDARD OF LIFE to mean the Standard of Activities and of Wants. Thus a rise in the Standard of Living implies an increase of intelligence, and energy and self-respect; leading to more care and judgment in expenditure, and to an avoidance of food and drink that gratify the appetite but afford no strength, and of ways of living that are unwholesome physically and morally. A rise in the Standard of Life for the whole population will much increase the National Dividend, and the share of it which accrues to each grade and to each trade; and a rise in the Standard of Life for any one trade or grade will raise their efficiency and their own real wages; while it will at the same time enable others to obtain their assistance at a cost somewhat less in proportion to its

Standard of Life.

efficiency; and of course it will increase the National Dividend a little.

But many writers have spoken of the influence exerted on wages by a rise not in the Standard of *Life*, but in that of *Comfort;*—a term that may suggest a mere increase of artificial wants, among which perhaps the grosser wants may predominate. It is true that every broad improvement in the Standard of Comfort is sure to bring with it a better manner of living, and to open the way to new and higher activities; while those who have hitherto had neither the necessaries nor the decencies of life can hardly fail to get some increase of vitality and energy from an increase of comfort, however gross and material the view which they may take of it. Thus a rise in the Standard of Comfort does to some extent involve a rise in the Standard of Life; and in so far as this is the case it does tend to increase the National Dividend and to improve the condition of the people.

A rise in the Standard of Comfort raises wages chiefly through its indirect influence in raising the Standard of Activities.

Some writers however of our own and of earlier times have gone further than this, and have implied that a mere increase of wants tends to raise wages. But the only direct effect of an increase of wants is to make people more miserable than before. And if we put aside its probable indirect effect in increasing activities, and otherwise raising the Standard of Life, it can raise wages only by another indirect effect, viz. by diminishing the supply of labour.

Limitations of the influence on wages exerted by a rise in the Standard of Wants causing a diminished supply of labour.

The doctrine that, merely through its action in diminishing the supply of labour, a rise in the Standard of Comfort raises wages, and is one of the most effective means for that purpose, has been consistently held by those who believe that population is pressing on the means of subsistence so hardly, that the rate of growth of population exercises a predominating influence on the rate of wages. For if that be true,

then it is also true that at least one of the most efficient means
of raising wages is to induce people to adopt a higher Standard
of Comfort, in however mean and sordid a sense the term
Comfort is used : since in order to indulge the new desires
rising out of their extended desire for comfort they may
probably marry late, or otherwise limit the number of their
children.

But this cannot be maintained by those who hold, as most
writers of the present generation do, that the new facilities
of transport have much lessened for the present the influence which the Law of Diminishing Return exercises on
production; and that the countervailing influences of the
Law of Increasing Return are so strong that an increase of
numbers does not at present tend greatly to reduce the
average income of the people.

It is indeed still possible to contend that a mere diminution in the supply of manual labourers as a whole, or of any
one class of them in particular, will increase the competition
for their aid on the part of the higher grades of labour, and
the owners of material capital; and that in consequence their
wages will rise.   This argument is no doubt valid so far as it
goes : but the rise of wages that can be got by any class of
labour simply by making itself scarce, and independently of
any improvement in its Standard of Activities, is generally not
very great, except in the case of the lowest grades.   We will
consider this problem in some detail with reference to that
particular change in the Standard of Living which takes the
form of shortening the hours of labour, and of wise uses of
leisure.

§ 11.   The earnings of a human being are commonly
counted *gross ;* no special reckoning being made
for his wear-and-tear, of which indeed he is himself often rather careless ; and, on the whole,
but little account is taken of the evil effects of the overwork
of men on the well-being of the next generation, although

*The wasteful-
ness of exces-
sive work.*

the hours of labour of children are regulated by law in their own interests and those of women in the interests of their families.

When the hours and the general conditions of labour are such as to cause great wear-and-tear of body or mind or both, and to lead to a low standard of living; when there has been a want of that leisure, rest and repose, which is one of the necessaries for efficiency; then the labour has been extravagant from the point of view of society at large, just as it would be extravagant on the part of the individual capitalist to keep his horses or slaves overworked or underfed. In such a case a moderate diminution of the hours of labour would diminish the National Dividend only temporarily; for as soon as the improved Standard of Life had had time to have its full effect on the efficiency of the workers, their increased energy, intelligence and force of character would enable them to do as much as before in less time; and thus, even from the point of view of material production, there would be no more ultimate loss than is involved by sending a sick worker into hospital to get his strength renovated. And, since material wealth exists for the sake of man, and not man for the sake of material wealth, the fact that inefficient and stunted human lives had been replaced by more efficient and fuller lives would be a gain of a higher order than any temporary material loss that might have been occasioned on the way. This argument assumes that the new rest and leisure raises the Standard of Life. And such a result is almost certain to follow in the extreme cases of overwork which we have been now considering; for in them a mere lessening of tension is a necessary condition for taking the first step upwards.

This brings us to consider the lowest grade of honest workers. Few of them work very hard; but they have little stamina; and many of them are so overstrained that they might probably, after a time, do as much in a shorter day as they now do

Exceptional conditions of the lowest grade of workers.

in a long one. Moreover they are the one class of workers, whose wages might be raised considerably at the expense of other classes by a mere diminution in the supply of their labour. Some of them indeed are in occupations that are closely pressed by the competition of skilled workers using machinery; and their wages are controlled by the Law of Substitution. But many of them do work for which no substitute can be found; they might raise the price of their labour considerably by stinting its supply; and they might have been able to raise it a very great deal in this way, were not any rise sure to bring into their occupation other workers of their own grade from occupations in which wages are controlled by the Law of Substitution[1].

§ 12. Again there are some branches of industry which at present turn to account expensive plant during only ten hours a day; and in which the gradual introduction of two shifts of eight hours would be an unmixed gain. The change would need to be introduced gradually; for there is not enough skilled labour in existence to allow such a plan to be adopted at once in all the workshops and factories for which it is suited. But some kinds of machinery, when worn out or antiquated, might be replaced on a smaller scale; and, on the other hand, much new machinery that cannot be profitably introduced for a ten hours' day, would be introduced for a sixteen hours' day; and when once introduced it would be improved on. Thus the arts of production would progress more rapidly; the National Dividend would increase; working men would be able to earn higher wages without tempting capital to migrate to countries where wages were lower, and all classes of society would reap benefit from the change.

In some trades shorter hours combined with double shifts would be an almost unmixed gain.

The importance of this consideration is more apparent every year, since the growing expensiveness of machinery,

[1] See end of Book VI. Ch. III.

and the quickness with which it is rendered obsolete, are constantly increasing the wastefulness of keeping the untiring iron and steel resting in idleness during sixteen hours out of the twenty-four. In any country, such a change would increase the Net produce, and therefore the wages of each worker; because much less than before would have to be deducted from his total output on account of charges for machinery, plant, factory-rent, &c. But the Anglo-Saxon artisans, unsurpassed in accuracy of touch, and surpassing all in sustained energy, would more than any others increase their Net produce, if they would keep their machinery going at its full speed for sixteen hours a day, even though they themselves worked only eight.

It must however be remembered that this particular plea for a reduction of the hours of labour applies only to those trades which use, or can use, expensive plant; and that in some cases, as for instance in some mines and branches of railway work, the system of shifts is already applied so as to keep the plant almost constantly at work.

§ 13. There remain therefore many trades in which a reduction of the hours of labour would certainly lessen the output in the immediate present, and would not certainly bring about at all quickly any such increase of efficiency as would raise the average work done per head up to the old level. In such cases the change would diminish the National Dividend; and the greater part of the resulting material loss would fall on the workers whose hours of labour were diminished. It is true that in some trades a scarcity of labour would raise its price for a good long while at the expense of the rest of the community. But as a rule a rise in the real price of labour would cause a diminished demand for the product, partly through the increased use of substitutes; and would also cause an inrush of new labour from less favoured trades.

This leads us to consider the origin of the common belief

that a reduction of the hours of labour would raise wages generally by merely making labour scarce, and independently of any effect it might have in keeping machinery longer at work and therefore making it more efficient, or in preventing people from being stunted and prematurely worn out by excessive work. This opinion is an instance of those misunderstandings as to the ways in which a rise in the Standard of Comfort can raise wages, to which we referred a little while back.

§ 14. It appears to rest on two fallacies. The first of these is that the immediate and permanent effects of a change will be the same. People see that when there are competent men waiting for work outside the offices of a tramway company, those already at work think more of keeping their posts than of striving for a rise of wages: and that if these men were away, the employers could not resist a demand for higher wages unless they were prepared to stop work altogether. They dwell on the fact that if tramway men work very short hours, more men must for the time be employed, at higher wages per hour and perhaps at higher wages per day. But they overlook the more important fact that as a result tramway extensions will be checked, there will be less demand for the work of those who make tramway plant; fewer men in the future will find employment on the tramways; many workpeople and others will walk to work who might have ridden; and many will live in closely packed cities, who otherwise might have had pleasant gardens in the suburbs. If it were true that the aggregate amount of wages could be increased by causing every person to work one fifth less than now, then it could be increased as much by diminishing the population by one fifth. Nay more it would follow that, had the population at last census been one fifth less than it was, the aggregate wages would have been actually higher, and therefore the average wages more than

The fallacy that a general lessening of the hours of labour would cause a permanent increase in the demand for labour:

a fifth higher than they are now—propositions which go beyond the doctrines of the extremest Malthusians.

Thus their error lies in assuming that there is a fixed Work-Fund, a certain amount of work which has to be done, whatever the price of labour. On the contrary, the demand for work comes from the National Dividend; that is, it comes from work : the less work there is of one kind, the less demand there is for work of other kinds ; and if labour were scarce, fewer enterprises would be undertaken. Again, the constancy of employment depends on the organization of industry and trade, and on the success with which those who arrange supply are able to forecast coming movements of demand and of price, and to adjust their actions accordingly. But this would not be better done with a short day's work than with a long one ; and indeed the adoption of a short day, not accompanied by double shifts, would discourage the use of that expensive plant, the presence of which makes employers very unwilling to close their works ; and it would therefore probably tend, not to lessen, but to increase the inconstancy of employment.

and that there is a fixed Work-Fund.

It would be at least as likely to increase as to diminish the inconstancy of employment.

§ 15. The second fallacy is allied to the first. It is that all trades will gain by the general adoption of a mode of action which has been proved to enable one trade, under certain conditions, to gain at the expense of others. It is undoubtedly true that, if they could exclude external competition, plasterers or shoemakers would have a fair chance of raising their wages by a mere diminution of the amount of work done by each. But these gains can be got only at the cost of a greater aggregate loss to other sharers in the National Dividend[1].

The fallacy of arguing that all trades can gain by making their labour scarce.

It is a fact—and, so far as it goes, an important fact—that some of these shares will not belong to the working classes ;

---

[1] See Book v. Ch. vi. § 2, and Book vi. Ch. ii. § 6.

part of the loss will certainly fall on employers and capitalists whose Personal and Material capital is sunk in building or shoemaking, and part on the well-to-do users or consumers of houses or shoes. But a part of the loss will fall on the working classes as users or consumers of houses or shoes ; and part of the loss resulting from the plasterers' gain will fall on bricklayers, carpenters, &c., and a little of it on brickmakers, seamen employed in importing wood for building, and others.

If then all workers reduce their output there will be a great loss of National Dividend; capitalists and employers may indeed bear a large share of the burden; but they are sure not to bear all. For—to say nothing of the chance that they may emigrate and take or send their free capital for investment abroad—a great and general diminution of Earnings of Management and of interest on capital, would lead on the one hand to some substitution of the higher grades of labour for the lower throughout the whole continuous descending scale of employment[1], and perhaps to some falling-off in the energy and assiduity of the leading minds of industry; while, on the other hand, it would check the saving of capital[2]. And in so far as it had this last result it would diminish that abundance of capital relatively to labour which alone would enable labour to throw on capital a part of its share of the loss of the National Dividend[3].

Lessening of general output lowers wages generally.

[1] See Book VI. Ch. VII. §§ 2—4.
[2] See Book IV. Ch. VII § 6, and Book VI. Ch. VI. § 1.
[3] To take an illustration, let us suppose that shoemakers and hatters are in the same grade, working equal hours, and receiving equal wages, before and after a general reduction in the hours of labour. Then both before and after the change, the hatter could buy, with a month's wages, as many shoes as were the Net product of the shoemaker's work for a month (see Book VI. Ch. I. § 6). If the shoemaker worked less hours than before, and in consequence did less work, the Net product of his labour for a month would have diminished, unless either by a system of working double shifts the employer and his capital had earned profits on two sets of workers, or his profits could be cut down by the full amount of the diminution in output. The last supposition is inconsistent with what we know of the causes which govern the

But we must be careful not to confuse the two questions whether a cause tends to produce a certain effect and whether that cause is sure to be followed by that effect. Opening the sluice of a reservoir tends to lower the level of the water in it; but if meanwhile larger supplies of water are flowing in at the other end, the opening of the sluice may be followed by a rising of the level of the water in the cistern. And so although a shortening of the hours of labour would tend to diminish output in those trades which are not already overworked, and in which there is no room for double shifts; yet it might very likely be accompanied by an increase of production arising from the general progress of wealth and knowledge[1].

Caution against crude arguments from facts: the fallacy post hoc ergo propter hoc.

supply of capital and business power. And therefore the hatter's wages would go less far than before in buying shoes; and so all round for other trades.

A small part of the loss might be thrown on rent: but it is not necessary to allow for much under this head. Also our argument assumed, what would be sure to be approximately true, that, taken one with another, the values relatively to shoes of the things that the employer had to buy remain unchanged.

[1] We must distrust all attempts to solve the question, whether a reduction of the hours of labour reduces production and wages, by a simple appeal to facts. For whether we watch the statistics of wages and production immediately after the change or for a long period following it, the facts which we observe are likely to be due chiefly to causes other than that which we are wishing to study. Firstly, the effects which immediately follow are likely to be misleading for many reasons. If the reduction was made as a result of a successful strike, the chances are that the occasion chosen for the strike was one when the strategical position of the workmen was good, and when the general conditions of trade would have enabled them to obtain a rise of wages if there had been no change in the hours of labour: and therefore the immediate effects of the change on wages are likely to appear more favourable than they really were. And again many employers, having entered into contracts which they are bound to fulfil, may for the time offer higher wages for a short day than before for a long day: but this is a result of the suddenness of the change, and is a mere flash in the pan. On the other hand, if men have been overworked, the shortening of the hours of labour will not at once make them strong: the physical and moral improvement of the condition of the workers, with its consequent increase of efficiency and therefore of wages, cannot show itself at once.

And secondly, the statistics of production and wages several years after the

§ 16. All this tends to show that a general reduction of the hours of labour is likely to cause a little net material loss and much moral good : that it is not adapted for treatment by a rigid cast-iron system, and that the conditions of each class of trades must be studied separately.

General con-clusion as to the hours of labour.

Perhaps £100,000,000 annually are spent even by the working classes, and £400,000,000 by the rest of the population of England in ways that do little or nothing towards making life nobler or truly happier. And it would certainly be well that all should work less, if we could secure that the new leisure be spent well, and the consequent loss of material income be met exclusively by the abandonment by all classes of the least worthy methods of consumption. But this result is not easy to be attained: for human nature changes slowly, and in nothing more slowly than in the hard task of learning to use leisure well. In every age, in every nation, and in every rank of society, those who have known how to work well have been far more numerous than those who have known how to use leisure well; but on the other hand it is only through freedom to use leisure as they will that people can learn to use leisure well: and it is true that no class of workers who are devoid of leisure can have much self-respect and become full citizens: some time free from fatigue and free from work are necessary conditions of a high Standard of Life.

Leisure is a good, but only if it is well-spent.

A person can seldom exert himself to the utmost for more

reduction of hours are likely to reflect changes in the prosperity of the country, or of the trade in question, or of the methods of production, or lastly of the purchasing power of money: and it may be as difficult to isolate the effects of reduction of the hours of labour as it is to isolate the effects on the waves of a noisy sea caused by throwing a stone among them.

It must be remembered that a reduction of the hours of labour has often been a form and a good form, in which the workers have chosen to take out a part of that rise in real wages which the economic changes of the time put at their command.

than eight hours a day with advantage to any one; but he may do light work for longer, and he may be "on duty," ready to act when called on, for much longer. And since adults, whose habits are Those who are not over-worked. already formed, are not likely to adapt themselves quickly to long hours of leisure, it would seem more conducive to the well-being of the nation as a whole, to take measures for increasing the material means of a noble and refined life for all classes, and especially the poorest, than to secure a sudden and very great diminution in the hours of labour of those who are not now weighed down by their work.

In this, as in all similar cases, it is the young whose faculties and activities are of the highest im- Leisure for the young. portance both to the moralist and the economist. The most imperative duty of this generation is to provide for the young the best education for the work they have to do as producers and as men or women, together with long-continued freedom from mechanical toil, and abundant leisure for school and for such kinds of play as strengthen and develop the character.

And, even if we took account only of the injury done to the rising generation by living in homes in which the father and the mother lead joyless lives, it The interest of the rising generation in the hours of labour of their parents. would be in the interest of society to afford them some relief. Able workers and good citizens are not likely to come from homes from which the mother is absent during the great part of the day, nor from homes to which the father seldom returns till his children are asleep. And therefore not only the individuals immediately concerned, but society as a whole, has a direct interest in the curtailment of extravagantly long hours of duty away from home even for mineral-train-guards and others, whose work is not in itself very hard.

CHAPTER XIII.

TRADE UNIONS.

§ 1. In considering the recent progress of the working **Trade Unions** classes, but little has yet been said of the growth **in relation to** of Trade-unions; but the two movements have **progress.** certainly kept pace with one another; and there is a *primâ facie* probability that they are connected, each being at once partly a cause and partly a consequence of the other. We may now proceed to inquire into the matter more closely.

We have already noticed[1] how the first endeavours of the **Early action of** new workmen's associations or Unions at the **Unions.** beginning of this century were directed to securing the enforcement of mediæval labour laws. But these, no less than the ordinances of the old gilds, were unsuited to the modern age of mechanical invention, and of production on a large scale for markets beyond the seas; and early in this century the Unions set themselves to win the right of managing their own affairs, free from the tyranny of the Combination Laws.

These laws had made a crime of what was no crime, the **Repeal of the** agreement to refuse to work in order to obtain **Combination** higher wages; and "men who know that they **Laws.** are criminals by the mere object which they have in view, care little for the additional criminality involved in the means they adopt." They knew that the law was full

[1] Book I. Ch. II. § 5.

of class injustice: destruction of life and property, when it was wrought for the purpose of enforcing what they thought justice, seemed to them to have a higher sanction than that of the law; and their moral sense became in a measure reconciled to crimes of brutal violence. But step by step the Combination Laws have been repealed: until now nothing is illegal if done by a workman, which would not be illegal if done by anyone else; nothing is illegal when done by a combination of workmen, which would not be illegal when done by a combination of other people; and the law no longer refuses to protect the property of the Unions.

With freedom came responsibility. Violence and the intimidation of Non-Unionists, which had lost all excuse, soon went out of favour; and workmen generally chose for their leaders able and far-seeing men, and under their guidance the modern organization of Unions has been rapidly developed[1].

A modern Union is generally an Association of workers in the same or allied trades, which collects funds from all its members and applies them firstly to support those of its members who cannot obtain employment except on terms which it is contrary to the general trade policy of the Union for them to accept, and secondly to grant certain Provident Benefits to members in need. The policy of the Unions varies in detail with time and circumstances; but its chief aims are generally the increase of wages, the reduction of the hours of labour, the securing healthy, safe and pleasant conditions of work, and the defending individual workers from arbitrary and unjust treatment by their employers. Most of their regulations are framed either for the direct attainment of some of these aims; or for securing conditions of hiring which will enable the employed to deal as a body with their employers, conditions

Twofold functions of Unions.

[1] The various stages through which the chief aims and the plan of organization of the Unions have passed are explained in *The History of Trade Unionism* by Sidney and Beatrice Webb.

which they regard as generally needed for the attainment of all their aims.

§ 2. A large Union is often an amalgamation of numerous smaller associations, originally local or confined to a subdivision of the trade. But whatever its origin, nearly every important Union has many branches, each of which, while managing its own affairs in details, is bound to conform to the general rules of the whole body. These rules are very explicit; and in particular they prescribe rigidly the ways in which each branch may spend the funds in its charge: for the power of the purse is retained strictly in the hands of the central body. The branch dispenses Provident Benefits according to rule; but except on emergency and for a short time it may not spend the corporate funds on a trade dispute, without the sanction of the central council or *Executive* representing the whole body, who are generally selected from the branch-officials that have deserved best of their Society.

Local responsibility and central authority.

The character and ability of the branch-officials are tested in action as well as in speech. For they have important business to manage, and those who neglect their duties, who prove themselves lax financiers, or give advice that is not justified by the event, are not promoted, however eloquent they may be; and consequently the Executive of the best Unions are shrewd, far-seeing men, resolute but with great self-control.

It is these men whose sanction has to be obtained by any branch that wishes to use the corporate funds in a trade dispute. They come to the question with tempers unruffled by any personal vexations. Their vanity is not enlisted in the continuance of the struggle; they can decide without loss of prestige that it is inopportune, or even wrong in principle; and they have nothing to gain, but much to lose, by becoming responsible for an expensive strike that ultimately fails. The decisions of the Executive are generally binding till the next annual general meeting

Precautions against unwise disputes.

of the representative delegates of the whole body; but in certain emergencies a special meeting of the delegates is called, or a plébiscite of the whole body is taken by voting papers.

The administration of the funds with regard to Provident Benefits is more a matter of routine, and is governed strictly by rule. These Benefits vary.

Provident Benefits.

The "New" Unions that have sprung up in recent times, chiefly in unskilled trades, generally regard Provident Funds as an encumbrance, hindering freedom in fight, and tending to an over-cautious and unenterprising policy in trade matters. And the list of Benefits afforded by many even of the older Unions is a meagre one. But the best Unions pride themselves on rendering their members independent of all charitable aid, public or private, during any of the more common misfortunes of life. They provide Sick, Accident, Superannuation and Funeral Benefits; and above all, they give out-of-work pay for a long (though of course not unlimited) time to any member, who needs it through no fault of his own—a Benefit which none but a trade Society could undertake. For only the members of his own trade can judge whether his want of work is due to his idleness or other fault, and whether he is putting too high an estimate on the value of his work: and they alone have an interest in supporting him in the refusal to sell his work for less than they think it is really worth. And at the same time the expense of managing the whole business of the Union is less than would be that of managing its Provident business alone by any other Society: for the local officers get good information without trouble, they spend nothing on advertising, and they receive but trifling salaries[1].

[1] The reader is referred to the excellent Reports of Mr Burnett to the Board of Trade, which give details of the expenditure of all the chief Unions for each successive year of their history. It is instructive to note that all the Benefits increase and the Funds diminish during periods of commercial depression. But the burden of Superannuation Benefit increases steadily with

§ 3. Such being the general plan of Trade-unions, we may pass to examine the influence which they can exert on wages.

We have already incidentally inquired whether wages can be raised permanently by diminishing the supply of labour; and we may begin by recapitulating the results obtained. If the workers in any trade are able to limit artificially the supply of their labour, they can certainly secure a considerable increase of wages, which will be the greater, the more fully four conditions are satisfied[1]. They are: *Firstly,* that there is no easy alternative method of obtaining the commodity which their trade helps to produce; and this generally requires (*a*) that they have control over the supply of labour in their trade and district; (*b*) that the commodity cannot easily be brought from some other district, in which the conditions of labour are beyond their control; and (*c*) that there is no available mechanical or other contrivance by which the commodity can be produced independently of them: *Secondly,* that the commodity is one the price of which will be raised considerably by a stinting of supply, or in other words the demand for it is not very elastic: *Thirdly,* that the share of the total expenses of production of the commodity which consists of their wages is small, so that a great proportionate rise in them will not greatly raise its

An artificial scarcity of labour in a trade can raise wages much if four conditions are satisfied.

the lapse of years; for the average age of the Unionists has not yet reached its maximum. Less than a tenth of the total expenditure comes under the head of strike pay in an average year's budget of the first class Unions. But many of the differences between individual workpeople and their employers, which result in their ceasing to be employed, are of the nature of trade "disputes," though not technically so called. And some Unions do not even attempt to make any distinction in their accounts between "out-of-work" pay and strike pay: though the former, when given at all, is at a lower rate than the latter. It seems however that not more than a fifth of the total expenditure can be ascribed to "disputes" in the broadest use of the term.

The accumulated Funds of the chief Old Unions average about two weeks' wages of their members.

[1] Comp. Book V. Ch. VI. § 2.

price and diminish the demand for it. And, *Fourthly*, that the other classes of workers, and the employers, in the trade are squeezable, or at least are not in a position to secure for themselves an increased share of the price of the joint product by limiting artificially the supply of their labour and capital.

The effect on the wages paid for doing a given piece of work would be just the same whether the number of workers in a trade were diminished by a tenth, or the amount of work done by each were diminished by a tenth (other things being equal)[1]: but on the latter plan the same aggregate wages would be divided among more people, and the rate of wages per head would be a tenth lower.

Different effects of limiting the number of workers and the work done by each.

If the amount of work done per head is diminished by lessening the hours or the severity of work, there is some compensating gain in increased leisure, or freedom from strain: but if it is diminished by insisting on uneconomical methods of work, there is no such compensation.

When the Net Advantages of a trade are abnormally high relatively to others in the same grade, there will be a strong drift into the trade, both of adult workers and of children, by routes direct and indirect; and this drift can be resisted only by hard and harsh measures which interfere much with the free course of business. Human nature being what it is, the drift from outside will be stronger into a trade with very high money wages than into one with rather high wages, and considerable other Net advantages. And partly for this reason the Unions of the skilled trades are aiming rather at the latter than the former end.

High money wages versus other Net Advantages.

---

[1] Other things would indeed not be equal: for the larger number of men would want more superintendence, more space, and more machinery (unless they worked double shifts instead of single); and therefore their aggregate wages would be less, and their wages per head more than a tenth less than if the supply of labour were lessened by a mere diminution of numbers.

The recent extension of Trade-unionism to unskilled

Permanent limitations of the work done in all trades must lower wages generally. labour has been confronted by the fact that an artificial restriction of the numbers in any unskilled trade is difficult, and in all trades together impossible, unless multitudes are to be supported in idleness. But it is not impossible to make labour scarce in all trades by shortening the hours of labour sufficiently. The movement in this direction, is, as we saw in the last chapter, the composite product of a genuine desire for more leisure for its own sake, and of a fallacious belief that there is a fixed Work-Fund. We concluded that, if there is a general diminution in the amount of work done, the National Dividend will shrink and the share of it that goes to the working classes, or in other words the aggregate of weekly (real) wages will shrink also, though not perhaps quite in the same proportion. And since there would be no diminution in the number among whom this aggregate was divided, average (real) wages would fall very nearly in proportion to the diminution of the work done.

§ 4. Leaving then this recapitulation of the results of

We pass to attempts to secure higher wages for labour by threatening to withhold its supply temporarily. permanently lessening the supply of labour, we will pass to the main task of this Chapter. That is to inquire whether, by a judicious use of the threat of temporarily withholding the supply of labour, Unions can force employers, and through them the community at large, to pay higher wages temporarily. It is clear that this question is not decided by the argument of the last Section. For if two men are rowing in the same boat and one pulls all the time with only half his strength, his progress will be slow: but if he thinks the other is doing less than a fair share of work, he may possibly find it a good policy to refuse to row till the other exerts himself more; he may conceivably reach his journey's end quicker than if he rowed on steadily without demur. Here then is the true centre of this contest as to the efficacy of Unions to raise wages.

We may start from the indisputable fact that the wage of labour of any kind tends, like the value of a material commodity, to a position of equilibrium at which the amount which will be normally demanded is equal to that which will be normally supplied. But this tendency does not always operate freely : it may even be suspended for the time, if either the buyers or the sellers have no reserve price[1].

The normal forces of supply and demand do not always act freely on wages of labour.

A working man who is not a member of a Trade-union can seldom stand out long for a reserved price for his labour; and thus he may fail to get much benefit from the fact that, other things being equal, it will be to the interest of employers to pay wages equal to the net value of his work, if they cannot get a sufficient supply of labour on cheaper terms.

Take for instance the case of a farmer who calculates that the work of an additional labourer would add to the produce of his farm enough to repay with profits the outlay of 14s. a week in wages. No doubt it will then be to his interest, other things being equal, to offer these wages rather than go without the extra assistance. But other things are very likely not to be equal. If the current rate in the parish is 12s. a week, he could not bid 14s. without incurring odium among his brother farmers, and perhaps tempting the labourers already in his employ to demand 14s. So he will probably offer only 12s., and complain of the scarcity of labour. The price of 12s. will be maintained because competition is not perfectly free; because the labourers have not much choice as to the market in which they sell their labour; and because they cannot hold back their labour at a reserve price equal to the highest wage which the employer can afford to pay[2].

Case of local combinations of employers.

---

[1] The general theory bearing on this point is indicated in Book V. Ch. II., and is worked out more fully in the corresponding chapter of the *Principles*.

[2] The disadvantage under which labourers lie in such a case as this, may

And even where employers are not in any combination, tacit or avowed, to regulate wages, each large employer is in his own person a perfectly firm combination of employing power. A combination of a thousand workers has a very weak and uncertain force in comparison with that of a single resolute employer of a thousand men: and though such an employer sees his profits in hiring a few more men at the current or even rather higher wages, he may yet think it the better policy not to bid for them lest he should suggest to those already in his employment that they should raise their demands.

A single large employer is a combination in himself.

be seen by considering the position of a shopkeeper in like circumstances. As a rule a shopkeeper fixes the price of his goods; and if the customers who come into his shop on one day refuse to pay that price, he waits till others come who will pay it. But if at any time he were compelled to sell off his goods quickly, taking whatever offers he could get, and not holding back for any reserve price, he might have to sell them at much less than their real value, at all events if he had access to only a few buyers. For these few might not happen to have much occasion for his goods, so that it might not be worth their while to pay him a good price; and they might even combine to take advantage of his necessity, and force him to sell at a lower price than it would have been worth their while to pay. Of course the fishmonger or fruiterer who has to sell off at very low prices on Saturday night, is able to recoup himself by charging high prices at other times; otherwise he would not stay in the trade. But the labourer is often wanting in these means of defence, though perhaps not to as great an exent as is often supposed (See Book VI. Ch. iv. § 6 and Ch. v. §§ 1, 2; or the corresponding parts of the *Principles*).

Thornton in his book *On Labour*, which caused Mill considerably to modify his views as to the influence of Trade-unions, illustrated the indeterminateness of equilibrium price in a small market, by showing that in such a market Dutch auction might sometimes yield a higher price than English. Mr J. S. Cree in his vigorous and suggestive *Criticism of the Theory of Trade-unions* has shown that under ordinary conditions it is a disadvantage, and not as Thornton supposed an advantage, to have the initiative even in a small market. But this does not impair the substance of Thornton's main argument; which is that where there is little competition, price is indeterminate; and then those are at a disadvantage who are known to be bound to sell without reserve. It is true, as Mr Cree urges, that the price would be even more indeterminate if it were settled between two combinations of employers and employed, than if employers and employed bargain freely with one another: but in the former case the employed are not at the same disadvantage in bargaining as they are in the latter.

In such cases as these the special disadvantages of the workman in bargaining certainly put his wages for a time below the position at which they would find their level under the free action of demand and supply: and Unionists need not deny that those forces are always at work. It is enough for their argument that, whenever these special disadvantages put the current rate of wages below the normal rate, the force of economic friction is exerted against the workman. And they contend that by organization they can frequently make that force act in his favour. A viscous fluid in a vessel tends to form a level surface: but if from time to time an artificial force pushes down the left side, which we may take to correspond to wages, it may reasonably be maintained that the average position of the left side is lower than it would have been without such interference, in spite of the indisputable fact that the force of gravitation is constantly tending to reinstate the position of equilibrium. What Unions claim to be able to do, corresponds to applying frequent and stronger pressure on the right-hand side, thus causing profits to yield the higher level to wages; so that the average level of wages, partially sustained by friction which will now act for them, will be higher instead of lower than if the forces of demand and supply acted with perfect freedom.

Unions claim to make economic friction side with the workman instead of against him.

§ 5. The chief means at the disposal of Unions for this purpose—putting aside for the present the modern "boycott,"—are threats of withholding for a time the labour which employers need in order to turn to account the investments of capital (material and personal) made in expectation of getting that labour. They have learnt that this threat has but little power when business is slack. But when the time has come for the trade to reap the harvest for which it has been waiting, the employers will be very unwilling to let it slip; and even if an agree-

Manner in which Unions apply threats to withhold the supply of labour.

ment to resist the demands of the men is made, it will
not easily be maintained, especially if the fruits that they
might have gathered are being snatched up by rivals outside
of their combination. Unions further hold that the threat of
a strike, though less powerful when the tide of prosperity is
falling than when it is rising, may yet avail for the comparatively easy task of slackening the fall in the high wages they
have gained. They claim thus to secure an earlier rise, a
greater rise, and a more prolonged rise than they could get
without combination.

The questions at issue are then—Can Unions really make
economic friction act for the workman instead of against him?
Are the means which they take for this purpose injurious
to production and therefore indirectly to the workman? If
the answers to both these questions are affirmative, is the
good on the whole greater or less than the evil?

§ 6. Let us then look at the answers to these ques-

Rejoinder by opponents of Unions. tions given by those who dispute the power of
Unions thus to raise wages.

They take a preliminary objection to the common assumption of Unionists that cases, such as that of agri-

Preliminary objection to the assumption that friction is strong in the labour market. cultural labourers quoted above, represent the
actual condition of any considerable part of
England's industries. They say that there are
but few trades in which the employers really act
in concert, even though they undertake to do so;
and that when an employer sees his way to making a profit
by hiring more labour at the current wages or even a little
higher, he generally finds means of doing so; and that he
would almost invariably do so were it not for the influence of
Trade-unions. For they insist that the very means which
Unions take to prevent an employer from paying individual
workers less than a standard rate, make him often hesitate to
raise the wages of individual men, when he would do so, if
free from the restrictions and demands of the Union. Thus,

so far as this count goes, they maintain that competition is much more effective, at all events in the industrial districts of modern England, than the arguments of Unionists generally imply ; or, to revert to our previous simile, that the action of competition corresponds to that of a fluid that is only very slightly viscous. And they go on to assert that that slight viscosity is partly due to the influence of Unions.

It is difficult to decide how far this answer is valid. On the one hand it is in agriculture, where Unions are weak, that we find the most grounds for the complaint that efficient and inefficient workers are paid so nearly alike as to give but small encouragement to energy. But, on the other hand, while this evil is diminishing in agriculture under the influence of the growing mobility and independence of the labourer, it is increasing in some other industries in which employers fear that a concession to their best men will be followed by further demand of a strong Union on behalf of inferior men. This is however a side issue : let us pass to the main issue.

§ 7. Let us look first at the influence of strikes and threats of strikes in a single trade. It is clear that, if in any trade the employer is to be harassed at all times, and especially when he sees his way to profitable business, then business men generally will shun that trade ; unless indeed, taking one time with another, they are able to get from it a rate of profits not merely as high as, but rather higher than is to be got in other trades. For the extra worry and fatigue of the work to be done will require some compensation ; and until they get it, the undertakers will seize every convenient opportunity of diminishing the stakes which they hold in the trade.

Rejoinder by opponents of Unions to their main claim so far as a single trade is concerned.

The relative strategic strength of employer and employed may determine for the time the shares in which the aggregate net income of the trade is divided ; but the terms of the division will soon react on the amount of capital in the trade, and therefore on the amount of that income which is available for division[1].

It may be impossible to force the consumer to pay a price that will cover these charges: in that case employment in the trade must decline; and then, in spite of the Unions, there will be many men running after one employer and wages will fall.

It is true that if the wares produced by the trade have even a partial local monopoly and are in strong demand, the employés may be able, by well-timed strikes and threats of strikes, to obtain a rise of wages at the expense of the consumer, and to retain it for a considerable time. But they cannot retain long a much higher wage than can be earned in similar and neighbouring trades, except by permanently limiting the numbers in their trade—a case which we have already considered.

Next the claim of a Union to obtain a rise of wages by striking or threatening a strike, when the employers are becoming very busy, is compared by opponents of Unions to the claim of those, who have prematurely shaken down unripe apples, to have produced the apples. They insist that, as the orchard would have yielded better apples and with less injury to the trees that have to bear next year's crop, if nature had been left to run her course; so the rise in wages that belongs to a period of trade prosperity, though it might not have come so soon or have been so sharp, would have lasted much longer. The Unions boast of resisting the tendency to a subsequent fall: but really that tendency, it is argued, is in a great measure of their own creation; and it need not have been felt for a long while, if employers

[1] That is, the income is not a Rent proper fixed by external conditions, and permanently available for division among the parties interested: but it is a Quasi-rent which will be lessened by every diminution in the inducements to keep up the supplies of capital in the trade. Comp. Appendix D.

had been able to give their minds to their work untroubled by strikes and the rumours of them, and if plans could have been made far ahead with confidence that they could be carried out, and therefore with but a narrow margin of profit.

So far the rejoinder relates to the effects of a Union in a single trade; and it appears to have much force, on the assumption that the net effect of Trade-union action is to worry and fret the undertaker, to make his work more difficult and uncertain, and thus to narrow his enterprise.

Assumption involved in this rejoinder.

§ 8. Leaving this assumption for discussion later on, we may follow the course of the argument when Trade-unionism is supposed to be extended to all the chief trades of the country. Capital and business power cannot then take refuge from the injuries of Trade-unions by the comparatively easy means of drifting into adjoining trades.

Rejoinder by opponents of Unions to their main claim as to wages in general.

But it is still true that a rise in wages, if obtained at the expense of profits, is likely to diminish the accumulation and to promote the emigration of capital; and that it may diminish the enterprise of business men, or at least of such of them as do not emigrate with their capital. It will thus tend both to diminish the National Dividend, which is the source of all wages, and to lessen the competition of capital for the aid of wages. In both these ways the rise of wages is in danger of bringing about its own destruction.

This old argument has both gained and lost strength in recent times. On the one hand migration from one country to another is becoming less difficult both for capital and for the employing class; and, if England should ever cease to be an eminently desirable country to live in, a small fall in the rate of profits below that obtainable elsewhere with equal trouble and worry, would cause so great a lack of capital and business power, that

This rejoinder is partly stronger partly weaker than it was.

24—2

the working-classes would be compelled either to provide these requisites of production for themselves, or to submit to such low wages that they would soon want to emigrate in pursuit of the capital and business power. But on the other hand every country has industrial troubles of its own; and, so long as Englishmen meet theirs in as brave and conciliatory a spirit as any other people, the owners of capital and business power will have no strong inducement to seek other lands.

Again, though the dependence of industry on a large supply of capital is constantly increasing, yet the influence which the fall in the rate of interest exerts in checking the accumulation of capital is a little less important than was formerly supposed.

And again though progress depends ever more and more on the energies of business men, and though some of them might slacken their efforts a little if the Earnings of Management were lessened; yet the growth of wealth and intelligence are constantly increasing the numbers of those who would do the work of business management with great vigour for a moderate reward, so long as they could retain their full freedom and responsibility, and all the excitements of the chase.

The rejoinder of the opponents of Unions proceeds :—If it be conceded that the National Dividend would not be much lessened at once by a general rise of wages obtained at the expense of profits; and that labour, getting a larger share of a Dividend but little diminished, would be a little better off for the time; even then it has still to be considered that this diminution would be progressive and *cumulative*, unless the rise in wages exercises some compensatory effect. Thus if in one year the diminution of profits causes the stock of capital to be one per cent. less than it otherwise would have been, this loss will have increased to about two per cent. at the end of the second year, to about three per cent. at the end of the third year, to about ten per cent. at the end of the tenth

But there remains a powerful argument in the background.

year, and so on. But this cannot go on for long. For while the loss increases steadily year by year, there will be no corresponding increase in the advantage which combination gives to labourers in their bargaining; and sooner or later the competition of capital for the aid of labour in production will be lessened; wages will fall, and will probably go on falling until the removal of the causes which lessened the supply of capital, and therefore the National Dividend[1].

It is then clear that if a rise of wages is obtained simply at the expense of profits, if it lowers profits without exerting any compensatory effect on the National Dividend, it must be self-destructive in the long run. It must lead in time to such a scarcity of capital and of business power that the National Dividend will be insufficient to afford high wages to labour, even while capital is getting a low rate of interest, and business power is receiving low Earnings of Management.

§ 9. Thus the main issue between those who do and those who do not think that Unions can permanently raise wages, resolves itself almost entirely into the narrower question whether the latter are right in assuming that there is no important compensatory effect to the injuries which some forms of Trade-union action inflict on production; that the net effect of the action of Unions is to hamper business

The main issue resolves itself into the question whether Union action on the whole lessens production.

---

[1] A fall in the rate of interest from say three to two per cent. would cut off a good deal from the savings of some people. But those of others would be very little affected by it (see Book IV. Ch. VII. § 6), and therefore the percentage, which this lowering of the rate of interest from three to two, took from the stock of capital in successive years would slightly diminish. In fact however this correction is much less important than one tending in the opposite direction. For wages could not be kept at their raised level without throwing a continually increasing burden on profits; and therefore the diminution (or check to the growth) of the National Dividend would be greater in the second year than in the first, greater in the third year than in the second, and so on. Further, a fall in the rate of interest promotes the use of machinery, and tends to increase Auxiliary-capital at the expense of Wage-capital, and thus slightly to lower wages.

and lessen production.   Let us then address ourselves to this narrower question.

On the side of Unions it is contended : (i) that the ablest Unionists recognize the general solidarity of their interests with those of the employer, and so far from needlessly hindering him in his business, do all that they can to make it work easily, smoothly and certainly by every means that is compatible with their retaining their strategic advantages in bargaining; and (ii) that their action as a whole tends to improve the character and increase the efficiency of labour, that this influence is *cumulative,* and that its benefits outweigh any harm Unions can do in checking the growth of the material means of production.   Let us investigate these pleas.

§ 10.   Firstly as to the evils caused by strikes.   Strikes

Strikes are generally discouraged by the best Unions.

are often regarded as peculiarly the results of Trade-unionism.   But, as has already been shown, the better organized a Union is, the smaller is the chance that a local quarrel will mature into a strike.   And though when a strong Union does strike, the contest is likely to be a long one; yet the unwillingness of employers to try conclusions with it, and the prudence of the officials of such a Union, together with the form of its government, tend to diminish the number of strikes.

Strikes are of course expensive.   But too much attention

The direct expenses of strikes are of small importance

has been paid to the direct expense which they cause to both sides, and perhaps even to the occasional privation which they occasion to the families of the employed.   These evils obtrude themselves on the notice of every one : and no doubt they are great.   But they are not great relatively to the immense issues at stake.   They are not even great relatively to the uncer-

relatively to the policy which they support.

tainty and friction which strikes bring into business.   It is therefore the general policy of the Unions, more than the direct expenses of the occasional strikes by which they enforce that policy, to which we must turn our attention[1].

§ 11. We may then pass to that part of Union policy which consists of fixing a minimum (local) rate of wage, and making it so high that it practically becomes the ordinary rate. Unionists contend that this, while essential to enable them to bargain as a body with the employer, is not an unmixed evil to him. It saves him trouble and anxiety to be able to buy his labour, just as it does to buy his raw material, at wholesale prices: for then he can be sure that no neighbouring competitor is buying them at a lower price and thus preparing to sell the finished commodity more cheaply than he can afford to. What public markets do for the fair-dealing employer as regards raw material, Unions do for him, it is maintained, as regards labour.

A fixed minimum wage is not an unmixed evil to the fair-dealing employer;

But unfortunately this is not quite true of labour when hired by time, because the labour is not sufficiently *graded*[2]. At present, no doubt, the most incompetent people of all are excluded from Unions by the rule that a candidate for admission must prove that he is capable of earning the local minimum rate of wages[3]. But to begin with, that is

its evil arises chiefly from the fact that men differ much in ability and industry.

[1] There is of course no advantage in comparing the expense of any particular strike with the total direct gain to wages of any that follow after it: partly because the events that follow the strike, may have been due to other causes, and partly because a strike is a mere incident in a campaign, and the policy of keeping up an army and entering on a campaign has to be judged as a whole. The gain of any particular battle is not to be measured by the booty got in it; and even defeat is no proof that the General was wrong in not submitting without a battle. The cost of strikes is discussed with full statistical detail in Mr Burnett's excellent reports on the subject to the Board of Trade, and in several Reports of American Labour Bureaux.

[2] Compare Book v. Ch. i. § 3.

[3] Some weight must be allowed to the claim of the Unions that young men are stimulated to exertions by knowing that they must work up to this standard. But it is not always a very high one; and, no doubt, some men, when they have attained it, exert themselves but little to get beyond it; being not unwilling to draw largely on the out-of-work funds of their Union.

only at the date of his admission: and for this very reason admissions to Unions are most numerous when trade is good, and when men rather below the average are for the time worth the standard wages. And further men vary as much in their willingness, as in their power, to exert themselves to do a good day's work for their wages[1].

. A conceivable remedy for this could be found by the classi-

This could be lessened if the Unions favour-ed more classi-fication;

fication of the workers in each trade into several grades, with a minimum (local) rate for each. Of course learners always have special rates, and a few Unions allow old men to work below the regular rate. But most Unions are opposed to carrying the classification further than this in the same branch of work; partly because they fear it might enable the employer to bargain with his men as individuals under the cover of offering them work in a lower grade.

The difficulty is a real one; but perhaps Unionists would make greater efforts to overcome it, if they realized fully how

which would diminish in-constancy of employment in the trade con-cerned and therefore in others.

much it diminishes the National Dividend, and therefore in the long run the average wages throughout the country. For even when trade is brisk, there are some men who need a stimulus to exertion closer at hand than the fear of being left out of employment when trade declines; and when it does decline, the employers have to dismiss more men, and to dismiss them earlier, than would be necessary if their wages were graded according to their efficiency. The full extent of this evil is not readily perceived: for men look chiefly at their own trade; and they think that, if there is less done by one set of men, there will remain more to be done by others. While some fall into the ever-recurring fallacy that there is a fixed Work-Fund, many forget that the

---

[1] It is commonly said by employers that ordinary men will do more than half as much again when they have a direct interest in their work as when they are paid by time.

demand for the goods and services of each trade and pro-
fession comes solely from the products of other trades and
professions, and depends solely upon their activity; and that
therefore by cutting short the period of activity of one trade,
they tend to throw others out of full work sooner than would
otherwise have been necessary; that thus trade depression
spreads and causes further interruptions of work, which again
act and react on other trades. In fact, while the growing
expensiveness of machinery and the growing breadth of
markets give rise to strong forces constantly tending towards
increased regularity of employment, the haste of some Unions
to put their minimum rate of wages a little too high for those
men whom the employer is not very anxious to have except
in prosperous times, is one of the chief modern hindrances to
settled conditions of work[1].

§ 12. The system of piece-work is seldom found in the
finest and best of industrial relations. The most careful

[1] It should however be noticed that many Unions admit of classification to
this extent that the variations in the minimum wages demanded by the
different local branches are very great. There is no universal rule; but the
general rule is that the minima are highest in and near London, and next
in the manufacturing districts; and that they gradually decrease with the
distance from any great centre of the trade where a high standard of work
is needed and paid for. Thus the Amalgamated Society of Carpenters and
Joiners reported in 1888 minima of 20s. in Penzance, 22s. in Barnstaple, 25s. in
Taunton, 28s. in Bath and Worcester, 31s. in Bristol, 36s. in Birmingham and
Manchester, and 42s. in some London suburbs.

Where the wages are high, the standard of efficiency which a man must
attain in order to earn the current wages of the district is high. If then a
member of the Union at Bristol cannot get 31s. a week, he will be forbidden to
work for less there, but the Union will pay the expense of his going, say, to
Taunton where he will be able to get employment at the current wages. On
the other hand an exceptionally able carpenter in Taunton is likely to migrate
to Bristol or London to get higher wages. By thus sending inefficient men to
places where the standard of efficiency is low, and indirectly at least helping
efficient men to go to places where it is high, Unions tend to perpetuate
local inequalities of efficiency and therefore local inequalities of Time-wages.

A proposal is now under consideration in some Unions representing large
trades to admit a little more classification even with regard to members of the
same Branch, in order that a larger percentage of workers may be eligible for
admission to the Unions of their several trades.

and artistic work can seldom be measured by it; and in

Piece-work is not suited to all trades.

many trades, especially small trades, the work varies so much from bench to bench and from day to day that no regular tariff can be devised; and piece-work degenerates into contract work, in which the individual workman has to bargain alone with his employer.

But in others it has great advantages.

But in the majority of trades, the various tasks can be graded accurately; and when a list of prices for them is agreed on, the employés grade themselves, and yet present an unbroken phalanx in bargaining with their employers. Piece-work adds to the wages of the industrious workers; and it checks those habits of half-hearted work, which flourish in every rank of life where the soil is favourable. In many trades however for which it is apparently well suited the Unions either prohibit it, or at least avow dislike to it.

Causes of dislike to it.

In some cases this is caused by an undue eagerness of certain employers to reduce piece-work rates when they have thought their men were taking too much money home. Some workmen oppose it because they desire to take things easily, and have perhaps a latent dislike to be graded according to their merits. And some oppose it because they think it makes work scarce, by inducing men to get through more of it than they otherwise would; and here again come in the combined effects of a little trade-selfishness, and the fallacy of the fixed Work-Fund. Perhaps these imperfections of human nature, rather than

Unions not specially responsible for this.

Unionism, are further to be held responsible for whatever ground there may be for the complaint that some Unionists urge their fellows not to exert themselves over-much and absorb work that others might be glad to do[1].

[1] This is not effected by general regulations; but in some workshops Unionist and Non-unionist alike, social pressure is brought to bear on any one

§ 13. The old doctrine that where there is a will there is a way, is well illustrated by the success with which those trades, that are much subject to the bracing action of foreign competition, have grappled with the difficulty of making Union action effective on behalf of the employed, and yet neither generally vexatious to the employer nor expensive to the consumer. The trades which make largely for foreign markets are more uniform in their methods of organization than many others. They not only buy their materials but they sell their products very much in open markets; and special trade connections and trade secrets are, as a rule, of comparatively small importance in them: and these conditions have of course facilitated the minute classification and grading of different tasks. But there have been more powerful causes tending in the same direction. For a quick nemesis has followed on any quarrelsome or obstructive tendencies that have hindered in

Trades that are much subject to foreign competition

generally adopt an enlightened policy;

who works so hard as to set a standard of work higher than the others like; and no doubt the presence of a Union element may increase this pressure. Again a foreman, if a member of the Union, is sometimes apt to conceal the faults of Unionists, and to give them an undue preference over abler Non-unionists. The control of a branch of a Union has occasionally got into the hands of men who have used its machinery to obtain full wages for very little work; and though such cases are rare, the mischief which they cause is perhaps greater than that due to other kinds of Union action which have attracted a larger share of public attention.

There are general rules against working overtime; but as was indicated in the last Chapter, if moderate in character, they promote the efficiency of the worker, and are not injurious to production in the long run. Overtime is sometimes forced on an unwilling employer by the resolve of some strong and able men to get very high wages at any cost. They are just the men on whom he can depend most in a difficulty; so he is anxious to retain them; and their individual demand for overtime overrides the collective opposition of the Union to it.

Some Unions have hard and selfish rules limiting very narrowly indeed the number of apprentices, and other learners. The effects of such limitations have already been discussed. But it should be added that in some cases they are prompted, though not justified, by the action of some employers who get bad work done at low wages almost exclusively by learners, for whom they do not endeavour to make any provision at the end of their time.

any way, direct or indirect, the full efficiency of the human energies and the material capital invested in the trade; and any injury that a union may cause to the employers, not being capable of being passed on to the consumers, acts quickly on the supply of capital in the trade; and therefore reacts quickly on the wages of the employed.

In trades that are largely subject to foreign competition,

and employers and employed co-operate;

therefore, those union officials who most fully realize the fundamental solidarity between the interests of employers and employed, and who oppose all demands which would needlessly hamper production or inflict loss on the employers, are those whose advice is found to bear the test of experience best: their influence generally increases, and their character spreads itself over the Union. Meanwhile similar causes tend generally to bring to the front those employers who give the most moderate and prudent counsels, and whose relations with their employés are most cordial.

The workmen in these trades were the first to welcome

and form Boards of Conciliation.

machinery, and to accept payment by the piece. And the employers in these trades were the first to welcome Trade-unions, to enter into negotiations with them, and to arrange conjointly with them Boards of Conciliation. In these Boards an equal number of representatives of employers and employed meet on equal terms; they discuss now the minor details and now the broader principles of wage-arrangements with reference to the current condition of trade; and when they can agree, as they generally can, their decision is in effect binding on the whole of their trade in their district.

The character of their agreement varies with the nature of the trade; but in all cases they aim at graduating the payment to the difficulty of each particular task, taking account in some cases of differences in the character of the raw material supplied, and in others of the delays caused by working with machinery that has not the very latest improvements. And in some trades they arrange lists of the prices to be paid for each of many thousand different tasks[1].

Arrangements of this kind, and even the much less satisfactory expedient of occasional appeals to Arbitration, do not work easily without the aid of strong organization on either side. Little but mischief indeed comes from a weak Union, always

In such trades Unions often greatly facilitate business.

ready to interfere, but seldom able to secure the faithful carrying out of an agreement, to which its own officers have been a party. But a strong Union, guided by able and far-seeing men who have a grave sense of responsibility, is found to enable a few minutes' quiet conversation to settle innumerable petty disputes that in old times would have caused much delay and worry and loss of mutual good feeling. And, when the time comes for great changes in wages either way, the case is argued out by those who know exactly what are the real points of difficulty; and who, though there must be in the background an appeal to force, will yet have recourse to

---

[1] In the coal and iron trades these payments are sometimes made to vary by a *Sliding Scale* with the price of the product. The standard price and the standard wage are usually taken as those prevailing at a date at which the condition of trade is recognized by both sides to have been normal; and it is agreed that for every rise or fall of the price above or below its standard level, wages should rise or fall above or below their standard level by a corresponding but generally smaller percentage. The percentage is generally smaller to correspond to the natural and beneficent tendency of fluctuations of wages to be less in extent than those of prices (See Book vi. Ch. viii. § 5). The Sliding Scale, when working at its best, arranges that those influences which short-period fluctuations in the price of a commodity are bound to exercise on the current wages of the labour by which they are made, shall work themselves out smoothly and easily. But the basis of the Scale needs to be changed from time to time to correspond with altered conditions of trade, of production, and of the labour market generally. These changes at rare intervals give effect to the influence which the supply price of labour exercises in long periods on the price of the commodities raised by it. There are however special difficulties connected with Sliding Scales, some of which arise from the fact that in many of the trades to which they apply, foreign competition is only a partial regulator, and something approaching a local monopoly is not rare.

industrial war only as a last resource. In such trades we may conclude confidently that Trade-unions on the whole facilitate business[1].

§ 14.   Other trades in which many able employers are not

A strong Union is often on the whole helpful in a trade in which it cannot become too strong.

sorry to be confronted by a fairly strong Union, are those in which the labour is not highly skilled or specialized; and the employers, knowing that in case of need they can bring in fresh labour from a distance, have no fear of losing the effective control of their own businesses.   In such cases the able and prudent Union leaders, having the confidence of their followers, and being able to make practically binding contracts on their behalf, may save more trouble and worry to the employer in small questions than they cause in large ones; and they are more likely to hinder than promote such aggressive action as would force the employer to extreme measures.   Many of the firms engaged in these trades are large, and use much fixed capital; they buy and sell everything in large quantities, and would be willing to pay a little extra for anything, labour included, to save themselves the time and expense of making many detailed bargains.   But while the employers in such cases may welcome the presence of a Union so long as it remains of moderate strength; their attitude would quickly be changed if any great measure of success should attend the endeavours that

Trade Federations.

are now being made in these very trades to revive and extend old projects of Federation of Unions, and to make them irresistible by the use of the modern weapons of sympathetic strikes and boycotts[2].

---

[1] In some trades an employer having ground of complaint against one of his employés not unfrequently appeals to the Union secretary; and he having investigated the matter compels the workman to make good his default under penalty of losing the support of the Union.

[2] An interesting history of earlier attempts at Federation as well as of Trade Councils and Trade-union Congresses is given in Mr Howell's *Conflicts of Capital and Labour*, Ch. x.   Throughout it all we find evidence of the high

§ 15. The disturbing effects of Trade-union action are probably seen at their maximum in trades which have a

education that Unionists are deriving from all these various forms of association. They help different trades to enter into one another's difficulties; to bring to bear on one another the force of a public opinion, which, though often one-sided, is on the whole beneficial; and lastly to smooth away any quarrels which may arise between different trades, especially with regard to apparent encroachments by one on another's province. For such quarrels are as frequent among modern Unions as they were among mediaeval Gilds. The chief discussions at Trade-union Congresses have however related to Industrial Legislation; on which they have exerted a great, and on the whole a beneficial influence.

It is too early to form a sound judgment of the more ambitious new schemes for Federation. Under the guidance of able and resolute men they change their shapes rapidly to avoid first one difficulty and then another: it is possible they may attain a power, that would at present appear fraught with some danger to the State, and yet use that power with moderation. If so, they will do much towards changing the course of industrial history. For they aim at little less than controlling the general conduct of business in the interest of the workers, just as much being allowed to the employers (that is to capital and business power) as is needed to avoid greatly checking the supply of capital and the activity of business.

The method by which they propose to attain this result is generally to submit every dispute to the supreme Council of the Federation, who are empowered—in some cases subject to the explicit consent of the several Unions —to declare war against the firms which resist their decrees. The council may, for instance, order that the Federated trades shall not handle any goods coming from or going to those firms or even that they shall not work at all for any employer who refuses to cease dealing with those firms. The policy which they propose is one requiring great judgment and self-control; qualities that have not been shown in some of the recent ventures of such Federations in America, Australia and England. But men learn by experience.

In some recent schemes for an alliance between Co-operators and Trade-unionists in England, it has been proposed that co-operators should buy no goods that did not bear a Trade-union mark. It is certain that at present the worst conditions of labour are generally found among those who are making goods for the consumption of the working classes themselves; and it is quite right that they, and other people, should as far as possible avoid purchasing goods made under these conditions. But it is a strong measure to put it in the power of a Union to destroy the trade of an employer on the ground that he does not conform to their requirements, without making sure that those requirements are such as it is to the public interest to enforce. Errors of this kind will however correct themselves in time. And meanwhile, together with some little harm and perhaps injustice, good will be done by an attempt that calls the attention of the working classes as consumers to the ultimate effect of a policy, of which they are apt to see only one side when they approach it as Trade-unionists.

monopoly of some special skill, and are not much influenced by the fear of foreign competition. It is in some of these trades that a bad use of Trade-union forces is most likely to show itself, a use that injures employers in the first instance, but in the long run is chiefly at the expense of the general public.

And indeed it is true now, as it was in the time of the old Gilds, that in a trade which has any sort of monopoly, natural or artificial, the interests of the public are apt to be sacrificed most, when peace reigns in the trade, and employers and employed are agreeing in a policy, which makes access to the trade difficult, stints production, and keeps prices artificially high.

§ 16. So far we have discussed the influence of Union action on general wages, with reference to the question whether on the balance it renders business more difficult and uncertain, diminishes profits, and lessens the supply of capital and the energy of business men. But we have not yet considered the strongest grounds of the claim made by Unions that they do not on the whole lessen the National Dividend, and thereby bring into action forces which will render futile their efforts to raise wages. We have still to consider that the strongest claim of Unions to sustain wages depends on the influence they exert on the character of the workers themselves; though their position is not so strong as it might be made by the abandonment of all regulations and practices which needlessly limit the number of learners in skilled trades, or tend to deprive the workers of a good opportunity and a strong motive for exerting their best abilities to the full extent that is compatible with a due amount of rest and leisure.

But Unionism must be judged mainly by its influence on the character of the workers.

It is true that Trade-unionism has already done much of its work in this direction. It found even the artisan with but little independence and self-respect, incensed against his employers, but with no well-considered policy for compelling them to

Unions found many workers oppressed, and gave them self-respect.

treat him as an equal who had something to sell that they wanted to buy. This state of things would in any case have been much modified by the increase of wealth and of knowledge; which, together with the cessation of great wars and the opening of our markets freely for the workman's food, would have taken away much of that want and fear of hunger which depressed the physique and the moral character of the working classes. Unions have been at once a chief product and a chief cause of this constant elevation of the Standard of Life: where that Standard is high, Unions have sprung up naturally; where Unions have been strong, the Standard of Life has generally risen; and in England to-day few skilled workers are depressed and oppressed[1].

But there still remain trades in which special causes have lowered the independence of the workers and induced them to submit to conditions of hire and conditions of work, which constantly press them downwards. Selling their labour without any effective reserve to employers among whom there is but little effective competition, they have not partaken in the general progress. Relatively, if not absolutely, the price of their labour has fallen: and yet it is not always cheap to the employer; for long years and in some cases long generations of poverty and dependence, without knowledge and without self-respect, have left them weak and unprofitable workers: and it is in relation to these classes that Trade-unionism is doing its most important work among the present generation of Englishmen.

And there are still a few trades in which such help is needed.

Its work has been successful in proportion as it has resisted the temptation to go counter to the economic forces of the time; and has directed its chief efforts to giving men a new spirit and a trust in and care for one another; and

---

[1] Till recently workmen suffered much hardship and wrong from some bad masters. Unions have checked this partly by explaining the law to the workman and putting it in force for him.

M.   25

inciting them to avail themselves of those economic forces that can be made to work on their side.

Thus for instance under the old régime at some of the London Docks, the inevitable uncertainty of employment was increased through lack of due consideration; men were kept waiting about needlessly for the chances of an odd job, till their spirit was gone; they turned their little earnings to very bad account, and they were at once among the most miserable, and the dearest workers in the country. A Trade-union giving them some confidence in themselves and their fellows, insisting on the removal of conditions which were very injurious, and finally appealing to public sympathy for funds which enabled them to put a reserve price on their labour, was able to give them a wonderful start: and though they have not in every case known how to use their victory with moderation and wisdom, they are now on a higher level than before.

Labour at the Docks under the old régime.

There is an almost equal waste of human life, though of another kind in some other industries, such as nail-making, and hand-sewing, in which old-fashioned methods vainly struggle for life. These are the industries in which the evils of the so-called sweating system are greatest, and the workers are most helpless. The forces of the time are moving them slowly on to better methods of work, and therefore higher wages: but, if they could take combined action, the movement would be hastened; and the growth of Trade-unions among them would be partly a result and partly a cause of their rise from their present low state to a higher one.

So called "Sweated" trades.

§ 17. Though there is no longer room for Unionism to render services of this order to skilled workmen, there is still much that it can do even for them. Unions all can, and most of them in fact do, exercise an elevating influence by punishing

There is much aid that Unions can still render to the moral character of the workers,

any member who conducts himself badly, or who is frequently out of employment from excessive drinking. There is much moral strength in the *esprit de corps* that makes a man anxious not to bring disgrace on his Union, and in the just pride with which he contemplates the provision that its Benefit and Provident Funds make to secure him from needing the aid of public or private charity.

The better the influences which Unions exert in these respects the more likely is any increase of wages that they may obtain, to be turned to account in promoting the industrial efficiency of the present and the coming generation of workers. In so far as they do this, the Unions have an effective *and in so far as they do this they are likely to raise wages permanently.* answer to the argument, recently given, that any check to the growth of capital caused by a rise of wages at the expense of profits is likely to be cumulative. If they do what they can to make labour honest and hearty, they can reply that an addition to the wages of their trade is as likely to be invested in the Personal Capital of themselves and their children, as an increase in profits is to be invested in Material Capital : that from the national point of view persons are at least as remunerative a field of investment as things : and that investments in persons are cumulative in their effects from year to year and from generation to generation[1]. But this answer is not open to those Unions, or branches of Unions, that in effect foster dull and unenergetic habits of work.

§ 18. It would be a great gain if the net influence of Unions on wages could be clearly traced in history. But this cannot be done. For many of the most important effects of Trade-union action are so remote from their causes as to escape notice, unless they are carefully sought out ; and even then they are so intermingled with the effects *Difficulty of ascertaining the influence of Unions by direct observation.*

---

[1] See above Ch. IV. §§ 1, 6. In England, and to an even greater extent in America, the material savings of working men are themselves considerable.

of other and, in some cases, more powerful causes, that their true meaning is not easily read[1].

Let us however consider the relation of Trade-unions to some of the broad movements of wages noticed in the first half of the preceding Chapter. Trade-unions have been stronger in England than on the Continent, and in America; and wages have been higher in England than on the Continent, but lower than in America. Their strength in England was partly due to that force of character, which was the chief cause of the excess of English over Continental wages. Their weakness in America was partly due to the very causes that made the wages of the American working man so high; viz. his restless enterprise, his constant opportunities of bettering himself by changing his abode and his occupation, and the abundance of land on which he could settle as an independent owner. The highest wages of all that the world has known have been in some parts of California and Australia; but they were due to causes which excluded the action of Unions. Gradually real wages in those places have fallen—perhaps not absolutely, but —relatively to the rest of the Western world; and in their desire to retard that fall, men have betaken themselves to Unionism of a specially active and adventurous character. But it is not easy to decide whether in so doing they have not checked the growth of wages by retarding the influx of capital, as much as they have increased it by modifying in their own favour the distribution of the joint product of labour and capital. Again, not long ago wages were very low in Scotland; but they have already risen nearly up to the English level, as a result of the general tendency of local inequalities of wages to diminish, and in spite of the fact that Unions are weaker in Scotland than in England. Unionism is however growing fast in Scotland; and in shipbuilding, for

Unions and wages in different countries.

[1] Compare the footnote on pages 355, 356.

which the Clyde has great natural advantages, Unionism is as strong and wages as high as in England.

Again, those occupations in which wages have risen most in England happen to be those in which there are no Unions: they are those kinds of domestic service and those employments for women and children in which there has been a great increase of demand, while the increase of supply has been checked by the growing unpopularity of domestic service, and the unwillingness of the better grades of working men to let their wives leave home and their children leave school early. Again, few of those branches of skilled labour which have had strong Unions for the last fifty years, can show as great a rise in wages as has been secured in most unskilled occupations in which physical strength is required, even though they have had no effective Unions.

It is true that Unions claim to have made life more pleasant in manufacturing and other industries, and thus to have increased the inducements needed to keep people in domestic service. And it is further true that, in so far as Unionist action may have raised the general level of life of some classes of workers, it has helped to raise the intelligence and character, and therefore the wage-earning power of their children, among whom are many domestic servants. But, even if we take an optimist estimate of these influences, such facts as those just quoted prove that the direct influence of Unions on wages is small relatively to the great economic forces of the age. They prove this, but they prove no more than this.

And on the other hand the advocates of Unionism can bring forward a long series of facts to prove that when a comparison is made of wages in two similar trades, or in two branches of the same trade, or in the same branch of the same trade in two places; if it so happens that neither of them is favoured relatively to the other by the

[marginal notes:]

Unions and wages in different occupations.

Inference that the influence of Unions on wages is limited.

Inference that other things being equal Unions do raise wages in the trades in which they are relatively to others.

economic changes of the age, then that one which has the stronger Unions has almost invariably the higher wages; and that one in which the strength of Unions is increasing most rapidly is that in which wages are rising fastest[1].

Such facts prove that, other things being equal, wages in trades in which there are strong Unions are likely to be higher than in those in which there are not. But they do not afford a conclusive answer to those who hold that a Union can obtain a relative rise in wages in its trade only by means which indirectly cause a greater loss in other trades; and that therefore the effect of Unionism is to lower general wages.

It should also be noted that all such facts lose some of their significance, when it is remembered that a rise of wages, even when caused by a general increase in the prosperity of a trade, is nearly always followed, as statistics show, by an

---

[1] There are several cases of trades with strong Unions, in which the rise of wages has been retarded by causes which may easily escape observation. For instance, the rise of the wages of compositors has been hindered by the diffusion of education which, while it much increases the demand for their work, prevents the power of reading and writing from having any longer a monopoly value: their wages have however risen relatively to the incomes of clerks who are affected by the same cause but have no Union. Again, skilled iron-founders were heavily struck by the invention of machinery, the use of which required mere physical strength, and enabled many navvies to earn 10s. a day at iron-founding at the very time when the Unemployed List of the Ironfounders' Union was quoted before the Commission on the Depression of Trade, as strong evidence of a growing dearth of employment. And again, the engineers have suffered, nominally at least, from the fact that—to say nothing of those who are below the Union standard—there is a constant increase in the number of men who confine themselves to comparatively simple work in the management of machines, and are not highly skilled all-round men. The average incomes to-day of those who entered the engineers' trade thirty years ago are very high indeed. Not a few are employers, many more are foremen and in positions of trust in all kinds of industries; and many are earning exceptionally high wages for delicate and varied work in small, but high class businesses. A great many of these however are not members of the Union at all; and those who are, owe very little at present (whatever they may have done in the past) to the aid of the Union. All these three trades have to do with branches of production for which the demand is increasing much faster than in proportion to the population. They all have very strong and well-managed Unions; and yet all have to contend with strong and not very obvious hindrances to a rapid rise in their minimum wage.

increase in the strength of the Union. For the rise, however caused, increases the men's confidence in their leaders, and makes them more willing as well as more able to pay their entrance fees and subscriptions; and further it increases the numbers of those who are qualified for admission by earning the standard wages.

§ 19. The direct evidence of wage statistics is then inconclusive. But, on the whole, they tend to confirm the conclusions to which our general reasonings seemed to point; and we may now sum them up.

General conclusions.

In trades which have any sort of monopoly the workers, by limiting their numbers, may secure very high wages at the expense partly of the employers, but chiefly of the general community. But such action generally diminishes the number of skilled workers and in this and other ways takes more in the aggregate from the real wages of workers outside, than it adds to those of workers inside: and thus on the balance it lowers average wages. Passing from selfish and exclusive action of this sort, we find that Unions generally can so arrange their bargaining with employers as to remove the special disadvantages under which workmen would lie if bargaining as individuals and without reserve; and in consequence employers may sometimes find the path of least resistance in paying somewhat higher wages than they would otherwise have done. In trades which use much fixed capital a strong Union may for a time divert a great part of the aggregate net income (which is really a Quasi-rent) to the workers; but this injury to capital will be partly transmitted to consumers; and partly, by its rebound, reduce employment and lower wages. Some of those, who have caused this result, may escape it themselves by changing their occupation or their abode. But in trades in which competition from a distance is effective, the nemesis follows quickly: and, in these trades more than others, Unions direct their energies to

Influence of Unions on wages in particular trades.

maintaining a moderate level of wages by means that do not hamper production. Other things being equal, the presence of a Union in a trade raises wages relatively to other trades.

But the influence which Unions exert on the average level

Influence of Union action on wages in general. Its drawbacks and limitations. of wages is less than would be inferred by looking at the influence which they exert on wages in each particular trade. When the measures which they take to raise wages in one trade have the effect of rendering business more difficult, or anxious, or impeding it in any other way; they are likely to diminish employment in other trades, and thus to cause a greater aggregate loss of wages to other trades than they gain for themselves, and to lower and not raise, the average level of wages. For a fall in the rate of profits exerts an influence that is real, though less than used to be once supposed, in causing capital to emigrate or even to be consumed, and in causing men of business ability to emigrate or slacken their energies; and this influence is cumulative.

The power of Unions to raise general wages by direct means is never great; it is never sufficient to contend successfully with the general economic forces of the age, when their drift is against a rise of wages. But yet it is sufficient materially to benefit the worker, when it is so directed as to co-operate with and to strengthen those general agencies, which are tending to improve his position morally and economically. And it will be so directed if the following conditions are

Conditions under which Unions may permanently raise general wages. satisfied. Firstly, Unions must aim at making business easy and certain: this is already done by formal and informal Boards of Conciliation in some trades, especially such as produce largely for foreign markets. Secondly, they must aim at raising the Standard of Life among the workers of the present and the coming generation by fostering habits of sobriety and honesty, independence and self-respect: this is done in different degrees by all Unions; and whatever influence they exert in this direction is cumulative. Thirdly, they must aid as many as possible of the rising generation to acquire industrial skill, and to join the higher paid ranks of labour: this calls for some self-sacrifice, and is inconsistent with any attempt to raise very high the wages in skilled trades by making the entrance to them artificially difficult. Fourthly, they must strive to develop the great stores of business power and inventive resource that lie latent among the working classes, so that, production being economical and efficient, the National Dividend may be large; and that, business power being cheap, and the share going as Earnings of Management being relatively small, that which remains for wages may be high. The training which Unionists get from the management of Union affairs, though highly beneficial to them as men and as citizens, is yet not exactly what is wanted for this end. But Unions might do much towards it, by undertaking particular contracts and even general business on their own accounts; and by aiding and promoting all forms of co-operative enterprise, and especially such as open the greatest number of opportunities to men of natural business ability to find free scope for their constructive and originating faculties[1]. (Fifthly, they must be always specially careful to avoid action by which one class of workers inflict a direct injury on others. (Contests between Unions contending for the same field of employment)—as for instance between Unions of

---

[1] Thus sacrificing the shadow for the substance, they should where necessary, relax the rigid forms of some of their own rules in favour of small genuine co-operative productive societies in the few trades in which such societies can successfully contend with the great natural difficulties by which they are opposed. And in particular they should encourage productive branches of distributive stores in which responsibility for risks and power of experiment are very nearly in the same hands; and in which the business energies of men of the working class can be vivified and prepared for taking an important part in increasing the National Dividend and diminishing the share of it which goes as Earnings of Management. (Some aspects of this question are further considered in an address by the present writer to the Co-operative Congress in 1889.)

shipwrights and carpenters, or plumbers and fitters—attract their full meed of attention; but more importance really attaches to the injuries which one trade inflicts on others by stinting the output of the raw material which they have to use, or by throwing them out of work through a strike in which they have no concern.

§ 20.   As Mill says: "Except on matters of mere detail,

Connection between the moral and the economic aspects of the problem.

there are perhaps no practical questions even among those which approach nearest to the character of pure economic questions which admit of being decided on economic premises alone;" and it is alike unscientific and injurious to the public welfare to attempt to discuss men's conduct in industrial conflicts without taking account of other motives beside the desire for pecuniary gain.   The world is not ready to apply in practice principles of so lofty a morality, as that implied in many socialistic schemes, which assumes that no one will desire to gain at the expense of an equal loss of happiness to others.   But it is ready, and working men among others are ready, to endeavour to act up to the principle, that no one should desire a gain which would involve a very much greater loss of happiness to others.   Of course the loss of £1 involves much less loss of happiness to a rich man than to a poor man. And it would not be reasonable to ask working-men to abstain from a measure which would give them a net gain of £1 at the expense of a loss of 30s. to profits, unless it could be shown that this loss would react on wages in the long run.   But many of them are willing to admit that no Union should adopt a course which will raise its own wages at the expense of a much greater total loss of wages to others; and if this principle be generally adopted as a basis of action, then nearly all the evil that still remains in the policy of Unions can be removed by such a study of economic science, as will enable them to discern those remote effects of their action "which are not seen," as well as those immediate results "which are seen."

Thus Union policy as a whole is likely to be economically successful provided Unionists as individuals and in their corporate capacity follow the dictates of morality directed by sound knowledge. In this respect Unions derive an ever-increasing assistance from public sympathy and public criticism; and the more they extend the sphere of their undertakings by Federation and International alliances, the more dependent do they become on that sympathy and the more amenable to that criticism; the larger the questions at issue, the greater is the force of public opinion. Public opinion, based on sound economics and just morality, will, it may be hoped, become ever more and more the arbiter of the conditions of industry[1].

Power and responsibility of public opinion.

[1] The strength and the responsibility of public opinion as regard the modern developments of trade combinations of all kinds are discussed in an address by the present writer to the Economic Section of the British Association, which is republished in the *Statistical Journal* for Dec. 1890. And something further is said on the meaning of the phrase "a fair rate of wages" with special reference to Conciliation and Arbitration in an Introduction by him to Mr L. L. Price's *Industrial Peace*, a book which, supplemented by Prof. Munro's papers on *Sliding Scales*, throws much light on an important class of problems. The general history of Unions is told in the writings of Mr and Mrs Webb, Mr Howell and Mr Burnett, also in the Reports of a Committee of the National Association for Promoting Social Science in 1860, and of the Royal Commission on Trades Unions in 1866—9. A great deal of information bearing on these and other questions discussed in this Chapter is published by the Commission on Labour.

Among the many aspects of Unionism with which it has not been possible to deal at present are the subtler and more indirect influences of foreign competition; and the claim of Unions to aid, or sometimes even to compel the action of employers in *Regulating Trade*. No doubt there are occasions on which a trade cannot continue to produce at its full strength without forcing the sales of its wares on an inelastic market at prices disastrous to itself. But since every check to the production of one trade tends to throw others out of employment, what is called the Regulation of trade often tends to increase instability of prices, of wages and of employment in some directions more than it diminishes them in others; and its general adoption would probably increase the uncertainties of trade and of work. If we assume however that it is reasonable for those in a trade to try to regulate it, it seems to follow that the employed should have their say in the matter; and some slight weight must be conceded to that objection to Sliding Scales, which urges that under them wages are reduced when the employers accept lower prices, without the workers being consulted as to whether they would prefer to produce less, so that higher prices could be got and higher wages paid.

APPENDIX A¹.

METHODS OF STUDY.

§ 1. IT is the business of economics, as of almost every other science, to collect facts, to arrange and interpret them, and to draw inferences from them. All the devices for the discovery of the relations between cause and effect, which are described in treatises on scientific method, have to be used in their turn by the economist: there is not any one method of investigation which can properly be called the method of economics; but every method must be made serviceable in its proper place, either singly or in combination with others. And as the number of combinations that can be made on the chess-board is so great that probably no two games exactly alike were ever played; so no two games which the student plays with nature to wrest from her her hidden truths, which were worth playing at all, ever made use of quite the same methods in quite the same way.

Induction and deduction inseparable.

But in some branches of economic inquiry and for some purposes, it is more urgent to ascertain new facts, than to trouble ourselves with the explanations of those which we already have. While in other branches there is still much uncertainty as to whether those causes of any event, which lie on the surface and suggest themselves at first, are both *true* causes of it and the *only* causes of it; and in these branches it is even more urgently needed to scrutinize our reasonings about facts which we already know, than to seek for more facts.

The reasoning from particular facts to general principles is called induction; the reasoning from general principles to particular facts is called deduction. Prof. Schmoller, an eminent German historian and economist, says well: "Induction and deduction are both needed for scientific thought as the right and left foot are both needed for walking. ...They rest on the same tendencies, the same beliefs, the same needs of our reason."

¹ See above, p. 28.

§ 2. There is however no scope in economics for long chains of deductive reasoning; that is for chains in which each link is supported, wholly or mainly, by that which went before, and without obtaining further support and guidance from observation and the direct study of real life. Such chains can be made in astronomy and in some other branches of physical science, in which the character and strength of all the chief causes at work are known so exactly that we can predict beforehand the effect of each singly, and thence infer the combined effect of all. But it cannot be done as yet in chemistry; for we cannot be quite sure how a new combination of chemical elements will work until we have tried. And when drugs are used medicinally, it is often found that they affect different people in different ways: it is not always safe to give a large dose of a new drug to one patient, trusting to the fact that it has worked well in an apparently similar case. And economics has as various and uncertain a subject-matter to deal with as has medical science.

Long chains of reasoning not profitable.

Thus if we look at the history of such strictly economic relations as those of credit and banking, of trade-unionism or co-operation, we find that modes of working, that have been generally successful at some times and places, have uniformly failed at others. The difference may sometimes be explained simply as the result of variations in general enlightenment, or of moral strength of character and habits of mutual trust; but sometimes the explanation is more difficult.

§ 3. On the other hand, there is need at every stage for analysis, that is, for taking to pieces each complex part and studying the relations of the several parts to one another and to the whole: and in doing this we are constantly making inferences, that is, short steps of reasoning both inductive and deductive. The process is substantially the same whether we are explaining what has happened or predicting what is likely to happen. Explanation and prediction are really the same mental operation; though they are worked in opposite directions, the one from effect to cause, the other from cause to effect.

Explanation of observed facts involves reasoning.

Observation may tell us that one event happened with or after another, but only by the aid of analysis and reason can we decide whether one was the cause of the other, and if we reason hastily we are likely to reason wrong. Wider experience, more careful inquiry, may show that the causes to which the event is attributed could not have produced it unaided; perhaps even that they hindered the event, which was brought about in spite of them by other causes that have escaped notice.

If we are dealing with the facts of remote times we must allow for the

changes that have meanwhile come over the whole character of economic
life : however closely a problem of to-day may resemble in its outward
incidents another recorded in history, it is probable that a thorough
scientific examination will detect a fundamental difference between their
real characters. Till this examination has been made, no valid argument can be drawn from one case to the other.

§ 4. The part which systematic scientific reasoning plays in the
production of knowledge resembles that which machinery plays in the

Further
observations
on the nature
of economic
laws.

production of goods. For when the same operation has
to be performed over and over again in the same way,
it generally pays to make a machine to do the work;
and where there is so much changing variety of detail
that it is unprofitable to use machines the goods must be
made by hand. Similarly in knowledge, when there are any processes of
investigation or reasoning in which the same kind of work has to be done
over and over again in the same kind of way, then it is worth while to
reduce the processes to system, to organize methods of reasoning and to
formulate general Laws.

It is true that there is so much variety in economic problems,
economic causes are intermingled with others in so many different ways,
that exact scientific reasoning will seldom bring us very far on the way
to the conclusion for which we are seeking. But it would be foolish to
refuse to avail ourselves of its aid, so far as it will reach :—just as foolish
as would be the opposite extreme of supposing that science alone can
do all the work, and that nothing will remain to be done by practical
instinct and trained common sense.

Natural instinct will select rapidly and combine justly considerations
which are relevant to the issue in hand ; but it will select chiefly from
those which are familiar ; it will seldom lead a man far below the surface,
or far beyond the limits of his personal experience. And we shall find
that in economics, neither those effects of known causes, nor those causes
of known effects which are most patent, are generally the most important.
"That which is not seen" is often better worth studying than that
"which is seen." Especially is this the case when we are trying to go
behind the immediate causes of events and trying to discover the
causes of those causes (causæ causantes).

It is sometimes said that physical laws are more universally true and
less changeable than economic laws. It would be better to say that an
economic law is often applicable only to a very narrow range of circumstances which may exist together at one particular place and time, but
which quickly pass away. When they are gone, the law, though still true
as an abstract proposition, has no longer any practical bearing ; because

the particular set of causes with which it deals are nowhere to be found acting together without important disturbance from other causes. Though economic reasoning is of wide application, we cannot insist too urgently that every age and every country has its own problems; and that every change in social conditions is likely to require a new development of economic doctrines.

It is true also that human effort may alter the conditions under which people live, and their characters, and thus may affect the economic laws that will be valid in the next generation. It may for instance destroy the conditions under which the most helpless of our match-box makers have been formed; in the same way as it has substituted sheep whose law of life it is to mature early, for the older breeds which did not attain nearly to their full weight till their third year.

The "normal" conditions with which economics deals are constantly being changed, partly through the unconscious influence of general social progress, partly through conscious and deliberate endeavour. And while with advancing knowledge we are constantly finding that economic analysis and general reasoning have wider and wider applications, and are learning in unexpected ways to see the One in the Many and the Many in the One; we are also getting to understand more fully how every age and every country has its own problems, and how every change in social conditions is likely to require a new development of economic doctrines.

APPENDIX B[1].

CONSUMERS' SURPLUS.

§ 1. THE benefit, which a person gets from purchasing at a low price things which he would rather pay a high price for than go without, has already been called his consumers' surplus. Our aim now is to apply the notion of consumers' surplus as an aid in estimating roughly some of the benefits which a person derives from his environment or his conjuncture.

In order to give definiteness to our notions, let us consider the case of tea purchased for domestic consumption. Let us take the case of a man

Consumers' surplus in relation to the demand of an individual.

who, if the price of tea were 20*s.* a pound, would just be induced to buy one pound annually; who would just be induced to buy two pounds if the price were 14*s.*, three pounds if the price were 10*s.*, four pounds if the price were 6*s.*, five pounds if the price were 4*s.*, six pounds if the price were 3*s.*, and who, the price being actually 2*s.*, does purchase seven pounds. We have to investigate the consumers' surplus which he derives from his power of purchasing tea at 2*s.* a pound.

The fact that he would just be induced to purchase one pound if the price were 20*s.*, proves that the total enjoyment or satisfaction which he derives from that pound is as great as that which he could obtain by spending 20*s.* on other things. When the price falls to 14*s.*, he could, if he chose, continue to buy only one pound. He would then get for 14*s.* what was worth to him at least 20*s.*; and he will obtain a surplus satisfaction worth to him at least 6*s.*, or in other words a consumers' surplus of at least 6*s.* But in fact he buys a second pound of his own free choice, thus showing that he regards it as worth to him at least 14*s.* He obtains for 28*s.* what is worth to him at least 20*s.* + 14*s.*; i.e. 34*s.* His surplus satisfaction is at all events not diminished by buying it, but remains

worth at least 6s. to him.   The total utility of the two pounds is worth
at least 34s., his consumers' surplus is at least 6s.

When the price falls to 10s., he might, if he chose, continue to buy
only two pounds ; and obtain for 20s. what was worth to him at least
34s., and derive a surplus satisfaction worth at least 14s.   But in fact he
prefers to buy a third pound : and as he does this freely, we know that
he does not diminish his surplus satisfaction by doing it.   He now gets
for 30s. three pounds ; of which the first is worth to him at least 20s.,
the second at least 14s., and the third at least 10s.   The total utility of
the three is worth at least 44s., his consumers' surplus is at least 14s.,
and so on.

When at last the price has fallen to 2s. he buys seven pounds, which
are severally worth to him not less than 20, 14, 10, 6, 4, 3, and 2s. or
59s. in all.   This sum measures their total utility to him, and his
consumers' surplus is (at least) the excess of this sum over the 14s.
he actually does pay for them, i.e. 45s.   This is the excess value of the
satisfaction he gets from buying the tea over that which he could have
got by spending the 14s. in extending a little his purchase of other
commodities, of which he had just not thought it worth while to buy
more at their current prices ; and any further purchases of which at
those prices would not yield him any consumers' surplus.   In other
words, he derives this 45s. worth of surplus enjoyment from his conjuncture, from the adaptation of the environment to his wants in the
particular matter of tea.   If that adaptation ceased, and tea could not
be had at any price, he would have incurred a loss of satisfaction at least
equal to that which he could have got by spending 45s. more on extra
supplies of things that were worth to him only just what he paid for
them.

The first pound was probably worth to him more than 20s.   All that
we know is that it was not worth less to him.   He probably got some
small surplus even on that.   Again, the second pound was probably
worth more than 14s. to him.   All that we know is that it was worth at
least 14s. and not worth 20s. to him.   He would get therefore at this
stage a surplus satisfaction of at least 6s., probably a little more.

The significance of the condition that he buys the second pound of
his own free choice is shown by the consideration that if the price of 14s.
had been offered to him on the condition that he took two pounds, he
would then have to elect between taking one pound for 20s. or two
pounds for 28s. : and then his taking two pounds would not have proved
that he thought the second pound worth more than 8s. to him.   But as it
is, he takes a second pound paying 14s. unconditionally for it ; and that
proves that it is worth at least 14s. to him.

It is sometimes objected that as he increases his purchases, the urgency of his need for his earlier purchases is diminished, and their utility falls; therefore we ought to continually redraw the earlier parts of our list of demand prices at a lower level, as we pass along it towards lower prices (i.e. to redraw at a lower level our demand curve as we pass along it to the right). But this misconceives the plan on which the list of prices is made out. The objection would have been valid, if the demand price set against each number of pounds of tea represented the *average* utility of that number. For it is true that, if he would pay just 20*s.* for one pound, and just 14*s.* for a second, then he would pay just 34*s.* for the two; i.e. 17*s.* each on the average. And if our list had had reference to the *average* prices he would pay, and had set 17*s.* against the second pound; then no doubt we should have had to redraw the list as we passed on. For when he has bought a third pound the average utility to him of each of the three will be less than that of 17*s.*; being in fact 14*s.* 8*d.* if, as we go on to assume, he would pay just 10*s.* for a third pound. But this difficulty is entirely avoided on the plan of making out demand prices which is here adopted; according to which his second pound is credited, not with the 17*s.* which represents the average value per pound of the two pounds; but with the 14*s.*, which represents the *additional* utility which a second pound has for him. For that remains unchanged when he has bought a third pound, of which the additional utility is measured by 10*s.*[1]

§ 2. We may now pass from the demand of an individual to that of a market. If we neglect for the moment the fact that the same sum of money represents different amounts of pleasure to different people, we may measure the surplus satisfaction which the sale of tea affords, say, in the London market, by the aggregate of the sums by which the prices shown in a complete list of demand prices for tea exceeds its selling price.

The demand of a market.

Let us then consider the demand curve *DD'* for tea in any large market.

[1] Again it has been objected:—"Of what avail is it to say that the utility of an income of (say) £100 a year is worth (say) £1000 a year?" There would be no avail in saying that. But there might be use, when comparing life in Central Africa with life in England, in saying that, though the things which money will buy in Central Africa may on the average be as cheap there as here, yet there are so many things which cannot be bought there at all, that a person with a thousand a year there is not so well off as a person with three or four hundred a year here. If a man pays 1*d.* toll on a bridge, which saves him an additional drive that would cost a shilling, we do not say that the penny is worth a shilling, but that the penny together with the advantage offered him by the bridge (the part it plays in his conjuncture) is worth a shilling for that day. Were the bridge swept away on a day on which he needed it, he would be in at least as bad a position as if he had been deprived of eleven pence.

Let *OH* be the amount which is sold there at the price *HA* annually, a year being taken as our unit of time. Taking any point *M* in *OH* let us draw *MP* vertically upwards to meet the curve in *P* and cut a horizontal line through *A* in *R*. We will suppose the several lbs. numbered in the order of the eagerness of the several purchasers: the eagerness of the purchaser of any lb. being measured by the price he is just willing to pay for that lb. The figure informs us that *OM* can be sold at the price *PM*; but that at any higher price not quite so many lbs. can be

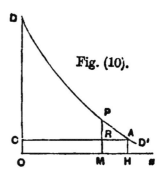

Fig. (10).

sold. There must be then some individual who will buy more at the price *PM*, than he will at any higher price; and we are to regard the *OM*th lb. as sold to this individual. Suppose for instance that *PM* represents 4s., and that *OM* represents a million lbs. The purchaser described above is just willing to buy his fifth lb. of tea at the price 4s., and the *OM*th or millionth lb. may be said to be sold to him. If *AH* and therefore *RM* represent 2s., the consumers' surplus derived from the *OM*th lb. is the excess of *PM* or 4s. which the purchaser of that lb. would have been willing to pay for it over *RM* the 2s. which he actually does pay for it. Let us suppose that a very thin vertical parallelogram is drawn of which the height is *PM* and of which the base is the distance along *Ox* that measures the single unit or lb. of tea. It will be convenient henceforward to regard price as measured not by a mathematical straight line without thickness, as *PM*; but by a very thin parallelogram, or as it may be called a thick straight line, of which the breadth is in every case equal to the distance along *Ox* which measures a unit or lb. of tea. Thus we should say that the total satisfaction derived from the *OM*th lb. of tea is represented (or, on the assumption made in the last paragraph above is measured) by the thick straight line *MP*; that the price paid for this lb. is represented by the thick straight line *MR* and the consumers' surplus derived from this lb. by the thick straight line *RP*. Now let us suppose that such thin parallelograms, or thick straight lines, are drawn for all positions of *M* between *O* and *H*, one for each lb. of tea. The thick straight lines thus drawn, as *MP* is, from *Ox* up to the demand curve will each represent the aggregate of the satisfaction derived from a lb. of tea; and taken together thus occupy and exactly fill up the whole area *DOHA*. Therefore we may say that the area *DOHA* represents the aggregate of the satisfaction derived from the consumption of tea. Again, each of the straight lines drawn, as *MR* is, from *Ox* upwards as far as *AC* represents the price that actually is paid for a lb. of tea.

These straight lines together make up the area $COHA$; and therefore this area represents the total price paid for tea. Finally each of the straight lines drawn as RP is from AC upwards as far as the demand curve, represents the consumers' surplus derived from the corresponding lb. of tea. These straight lines together make up the area DCA; and therefore this area represents the total consumers' surplus that is derived from tea when the price is AH. But it must be repeated that this geometrical measurement is only an aggregate of the measures of benefits which are not all measured on the same scale except on the assumption just made above. Unless that assumption is made the area only represents an aggregate of satisfactions, the several amounts of which are not exactly measured. On that assumption only, its area measures the volume of the total *net* satisfaction derived from the tea by its various purchasers.

APPENDIX C[1].

RENT, OR INCOME FROM AN APPLIANCE FOR PRODUCTION NOT
MADE BY MAN, IN RELATION TO THE VALUE OF ITS PRODUCE.

§ 1. THE relations between rent and cost of production are obscure, and intricate. But the following statement sets forth the central, and comparatively simple, idea which underlies them all.

We start from the position that, when a thing is produced for sale in a free market, its price must in the long run be enough to remunerate the producers for every part of their output. The price must cover the cost of that part of the produce which is raised at the greatest disadvantage; and therefore every other part must yield a surplus above its direct cost. These facts have been indicated in two classical doc-trines; viz.:—that the price of the whole produce is *determined by* the expenses, or money cost, of production on the margin of cultivation; and that rent does not *enter into* cost of production. These phrases are true in the senses in which they were meant; but they are frequently misinterpreted.

It is certainly true that the expenses of raising agricultural produce are best estimated on the margin of cultivation. That is, they are best estimated for a part of the produce which either is raised on land that pays no rent because it is poor or badly situated; or, is raised on land that does pay rent, but by applications of capital and labour which only just pay their way, and therefore can contribute nothing towards the rent. It is these expenses which the demand must just cover: for if it does not, the supply will fall off, and the price will be raised till it does cover them. Those parts of the produce which yield a surplus will generally be produced even if that price is not maintained; there-fore their surplus can not govern the price: and since no surplus is

Classical doctrines as to rent in relation to cost.

[1] See above, p. 203.

yielded by that portion of the produce, the expenses of production of

Cautions
needed in
interpreting
them.

which do take direct part in governing the price, therefore no surplus enters into *that* (money) cost of production, which gives the level at which the price of the whole supply is fixed. Thus we see that there are three cautions to be observed in interpreting these classical doctrines :—

In the first place, Rent is here taken as another name for the *surplus produce* which is in excess of what is required to remunerate the cultivator for his capital and labour; and if the cultivator owns the land himself, he of course retains this surplus.

Next, the *marginal* application of capital and labour, by the return to which we estimate the amount required to remunerate the farmer, is not necessarily applied to inferior land; it is on the *margin of profitable expenditure* on land of any quality.

Lastly, the doctrines do not mean that a tenant farmer need not take his rent into account when making up his year's balance-sheet. When he is doing that, he must count his rent just in the same way as he does any other expense. What they do mean is that, when the farmer is doubting whether it is worth his while to apply more capital and labour to the land, *then* he need not think of his rent; for he will have to pay this same rent whether he applies this extra capital and labour, or not. Therefore if the marginal produce due to this additional outlay seems likely to give him normal profits, he applies it: and his rent does not *then* enter into his calculations.

The classical doctrines may then be restated thus :—(1) The amount

Restatement
of the classical
doctrines.

of produce raised, and therefore the position of the margin of cultivation (i.e. the margin of the profitable application of capital and labour to good and bad land alike) are both governed by the general conditions of demand and supply. They are governed on the one hand by demand; that is, by the numbers of the population who consume the produce, the intensity of their need for it, and their means of paying for it; and on the other hand by supply; that is, by the extent and fertility of the available land, and the numbers and resources of those ready to cultivate it. Thus cost of production, eagerness of demand, margin of production, and price of the produce mutually govern one another. (2) But rent takes no part in controlling the general conditions of demand and supply or their relations to one another. It is governed by the fertility of land, the price of the produce, and the position of the margin: it is the excess of the value of the total returns which capital and labour applied to land do obtain, over those which they would have obtained under circumstances as unfavourable as those on the margin of cultivation. (3) If the cost of production were estimated for parts of the produce which do not come from the margin, a charge on account of rent would of course need to be entered in this estimate; and if this estimate were used in an account of the causes which govern the price of the produce, then the reasoning would be circular. For that which is wholly an effect would be reckoned up as part of the cause of those things of which it is an effect. (4) *The cost of production of the marginal produce can be ascertained without reasoning in a circle. The cost of production of other parts of the produce cannot. The cost of production on the margin of the profitable application of capital and labour is that to which the price of the whole produce tends, under the control of the general conditions of demand and supply.*

Thus differences in the rent (or producer's surplus) of land result from differences in its *net advantages*, account being taken both of its situation and its fertility: but all that is required for the existence of rent is that the demand for produce should be sufficient to cause some of it to be raised under conditions which call into play the tendency to diminishing return. Rent would exist even if all land were equally advantageous, provided only that the population were just a little more than sufficient to bring it under cultivation. On the outskirts of a new country, where some of the best land still remains uncultivated and free to the first comer, there is no rent.

This argument refers to the price of agricultural produce as a whole. The case is somewhat different if we confine our attention to one particular crop, as for instance oats[1].

---

[1] The argument is continued in *Principles*, V. viii., where it is shown that when the doctrine is so modified as to be applicable to one particular crop, it is then applicable also to the rent of building land in relation to the price of the goods manufactured or warehoused on it: and so on.

APPENDIX D[1].

QUASI-RENT, OR INCOME FROM AN APPLIANCE FOR PRODUCTION ALREADY MADE BY MAN, IN RELATION TO THE VALUE OF ITS PRODUCE.

The farmer's "rent." § 1. THE farmer pays "rent" to his landlord without troubling himself to distinguish how much of the annual net value of his land is due to the free gift of nature, and how much to the investment of capital by his landlord in the improvement of the land, and in erecting buildings on it. Now the income derived from farm buildings, or houses, is clearly of the same character as the income derived from durable machines; and that income is popularly classed with profits more often than with rent. But yet the farmer's habit of speaking has much justification. For the incomes derived from appliances for production made by man have really something analogous to true rents.

Quasi-rent. The net incomes derived from appliances for production already made, may be called their *quasi-rents:* partly because we shall find that, when we are considering periods of time too short to enable the supply of such appliances to respond to a change in the demand for them, the stock of them has to be regarded as *temporarily* fixed. For the time they hold nearly the same relation to the price of the things which they take part in producing, as is held by land, or any other free gift of nature, of which the stock is *permanently* fixed; and whose net income is a true rent. Let us take an illustration from manufacture.

Illustration relating to manufacture. § 2. Let us suppose that an exceptional demand for a certain kind of textile fabrics is caused by, say, a sudden movement of the fashions. The special machinery required for making that fabric will yield for the time a high income, governed by the price that can be got for the produce, and consisting of the excess of the aggregate price of that produce over the direct outlay (including wear-and-tear) incurred in its production; and the quasi-rent, or net income, from the machinery will be for the time greater than normal profits on the original investment.

If later on the tide turns, and the demand is less than had been expected; the factories with the most imperfect appliances, and the

[1] See above, p. 214.

worst machinery in other factories will be thrown out of work; while those machines, which it is just worth while to keep in work, will just pay the actual expenses of working them, but will yield no surplus. But the excess of the price got for the goods made by the better appliances over their wear-and-tear, together with the actual expenses of working them, will be the income which these appliances yield during the short period of depression. This quasi-rent or net income derived from the machinery will in this second period be less than normal profits on the original investment.

These remarks may be extended. Appliances for production are of many different kinds: they include not only land, factories and machines, but also business ability and manual skill. The owner of any one of those will not generally apply it to produce anything, unless he expects to gain in return at least enough to compensate him for the immediate and special trouble, sacrifice and outlay involved in this particular operation, and which he could escape by declining to undertake it.

In short periods the supply of these various appliances for production—whether machinery and other material plant, or specialized skill and ability—has not time to be fully adapted to demand; and the producers have to adjust their supply to the demand as best they can with the appliances already at their disposal. On the one hand there is not time materially to increase those appliances if the supply of them is deficient; and on the other, if the supply is excessive, some of them must remain imperfectly employed, since there is not time for the supply to be much reduced by gradual decay, and by conversion to other uses. The particular income derived from them during those times, does not *for the time* affect perceptibly the supply, nor therefore the price, of the commodities produced by them: it is a surplus of total receipts over Prime (money) cost, governed by the more or less accidental relations of demand and supply for that time. And this excess has enough resemblance to that excess value of the produce of land over the direct cost of raising it, which is the basis of rent as ordinarily understood, to justify us in calling it a Quasi-rent.

A Quasi-rent differs however from a true Rent in this way. If true Rent ceased, those gifts of nature which are free and imperishable would remain undiminished, and be ready to contribute their part to production as before. But if the Quasi-rent from any class of appliances for production not made by man fell so low that it did not amount in the long run to normal profits on the investment of capital and effort required to sustain the supply of those appliances; then those appliances would dwindle, and would *not* contribute their part to production as before. In long periods, on

Rent proper and Quasi-rent.

the other hand, there is time to adjust the resources of supply to demand.

§ 3.   The general principle under discussion may then be put thus.

Restatement of the main principle.

The price of anything and the amount of it that is produced are together governed by the general relations of demand and supply: the price just covers the expenses of production of that part of this amount which is raised at the greatest disadvantage; every other part yields a surplus above its direct cost; and this surplus is a result and not a cause of the selling price.   For the price is governed by the relations of supply and demand; and while, of course, the surplus does not affect the demand, so neither does it affect the supply, since it is yielded only by a part of the produce which would be produced even at a lower price.

When we are taking a broad view of normal value extending over a very long period of time, when we are investigating the causes which determine normal value " in the long run," when we are tracing the "ultimate" effects of economic causes, then the income that is derived from capital in these forms enters into the payments by which the expenses of production of the commodity in question have to be covered, and it directly controls the action of the producers who are on the margin of doubt as to whether to increase the means of production or not.   But, on the other hand, when we are considering the causes which determine normal prices for a period which is short relatively to that required for largely increasing the supply of those appliances for production, then the stock of these appliances has to be taken as fixed, almost as though they were free gifts of nature.   The shorter the period which we are considering, and the slower the process of production of those appliances, the less part will variations in the income derived from them play in checking or increasing the supply of the commodity produced by them, and in raising or lowering its supply price; and the more nearly true will it be that, for the period under discussion, the net income to be derived from them is to be regarded as a producer's surplus or quasi-rent.

This doctrine is however difficult, and easily misunderstood.   Further study is required before it can be safely applied to complex issues[1].

---

[1] Some further study will be found in *Principles*, V. IX., part of which is reproduced in this Appendix.

APPENDIX E[1].

DEVELOPMENT OF THE DOCTRINE OF WAGES.

§ 1. THE simplest account of the causes which determine the distribution of the national income is that given by the French economists who just preceded Adam Smith; and it is based upon the peculiar circumstances of France in the latter half of last century. The taxes, and other exactions levied from the French peasant, were then limited only by his ability to pay; and few of the labouring classes were far from starvation; and therefore the Physiocrats, as the French economists of the time were called, assumed for the sake of simplicity, that there was a natural law of population according to which the wages of labour were kept at starvation limit. They did not suppose that this was true of the whole working population, but the exceptions were so few, that they thought that the general impression given by their assumption was true.

Origin of the opinion that wages are fixed by the price of necessaries.

Again, they knew that the rate of interest in Europe had fallen during the five preceding centuries, in consequence of the fact that "economy had in general prevailed over luxury." But they were impressed very much by the sensitiveness of capital, and the quickness with which it evaded the oppressions of the tax-gatherer by retiring from his grasp; and they therefore concluded that there was no great violence in the supposition that if its profits were reduced below what they then were, capital would speedily be consumed or migrate. Accordingly they assumed, again for the sake of simplicity, that there was something like a natural, or necessary rate of profit, corresponding in some measure to the natural rate of wages; that if the current rate exceeded this necessary level, capital would grow rapidly, till it forced down the rate of profit to that level; and that, if the current rate went below that level, capital would shrink quickly, and the rate would be forced upwards again. They thought that, wages and profits being thus fixed by natural laws, the natural value of everything was governed simply as the sum of wages and profits required to remunerate the producers.

[1] See above, p. 258.

Adam Smith saw that labour and capital were not at the verge of

The western
world has out-
grown the
facts on which
that opinion
was based.

starvation in England, as they were in France. In England the wages of a great part of the working classes were sufficient to allow much more than the mere necessaries of existence; and capital had too rich and safe a field of employment there to be likely to go out of existence, or to emigrate. So when he is carefully weighing his words, his use of the terms "the natural rate of wages," and "the natural rate of profit," has not that sharp definition and fixedness which it had in the mouths of the Physiocrats; and he goes a good way towards explaining how they are determined by the ever-fluctuating conditions of demand and supply. He even insists that the liberal reward of labour "increases the industry of the common people"; that "a plentiful subsistence increases the bodily strength of the labourer; and the comfortable hope of bettering his condition, and of ending his days perhaps in ease and plenty, animates him to exert that strength to the utmost. Where wages are high, accordingly, we shall always find the workman more active, diligent and expeditious, than where they are low; in England, for example, than in Scotland; in the neighbourhood of great towns than in remote country places[1]." And yet Adam Smith sometimes falls back into the old way of speaking, and thus makes careless readers suppose that he believes the mean level of the wages of labour to be fixed by an iron law at the bare necessaries of life.

Malthus[2] again, in his admirable survey of the course of wages in England from the thirteenth to the eighteenth centuries, shows how their mean level oscillated from century to century, falling sometimes down to about half a peck of corn a day, and rising sometimes up to a peck and a half or even, in the fifteenth century, to about two pecks: a height beyond which they have never passed except in our own day. But although he observes that "an inferior mode of living may be a cause as well as a consequence of poverty," he traces this effect almost exclusively to the consequent increase of numbers; he does not anticipate the stress which economists of our own generation lay on the influence which habits of living exercise on the efficiency, and therefore on the earning power of the labourer.

Ricardo's language is even more unguarded than that of Adam Smith and Malthus; his whole treatment of wages is in some respects less satisfactory than theirs. It is true, indeed, that he says distinctly[3]:— "It is not to be understood that the natural price of labour, estimated in

---

[1] *Wealth of Nations*, Bk. I. ch. VIII.   [2] *Political Economy*, IV. 2.
[3] Ricardo's *Principles*, V.

food and necessaries is absolutely fixed and constant. It essentially depends on the habits and customs of the people." But, having said this once, he does not take the trouble to repeat it constantly; and in consequence many readers forget that he says it; and suppose him to believe that the population always increases very rapidly as soon as wages rise above the bare necessaries of life, and thus causes wages to be fixed by "a natural law" to the level of these bare necessaries. This law has been called, especially in Germany, Ricardo's "iron" or "brazen" law: many German socialists believe that this law is in operation now even in the western world; and that it will continue to be so, as long as the plan on which production is organized remains "capitalistic" or "individualistic"; and they erroneously claim Ricardo as on their side.

Mill followed Malthus in dwelling on those lessons of history which show that, if a fall of wages caused the labouring classes to lower their standard of comfort "the injury done to them will be permanent, and their deteriorated condition will become a new minimum tending to perpetuate itself as the more ample minimum did before."

But it is only in our own generation that a careful study has begun to be made of the effects that high wages have in increasing the efficiency not only of those who receive them, but also of their children and grandchildren. In this matter the lead has been taken by Walker and other American economists; and the application of the comparative method of study to the industrial problems of different countries of the old and new worlds is forcing constantly more and more attention to the fact that highly paid labour is generally efficient and therefore not dear labour; a fact which, though it is more full of hope for the future of the human race than any other that is known to us, will be found to exercise a very complicating influence on the theory of distribution.

§ 2. At the beginning of this century, great as was the poverty of the English people, the peoples of the Continent were poorer still. In most of them population was sparse, and therefore food was cheap; but for all that they were underfed, and could not provide themselves with the sinews of war. France, after her first victories, helped herself along by the forced contributions of others. But the countries of Central Europe could not support their own armies without England's aid. Even America, with all her energy and national resources, was not rich; she could not have subsidised Continental armies. The economists found the explanation chiefly in England's capital, which was much greater than that of any other country. Other nations were envious of England, and wanted to follow in her steps; but they were unable to do so, partly indeed for other reasons, but chiefly because they had not

Origin of extreme prominence given to dependence of wages on capital.

capital enough. Their annual income was required for immediate consumption. There was not in them a large class of people who had a good store of wealth set by, which they did not need to consume at once, and which they could devote to making machines and other things that would aid labour, and would enable it to produce a larger store of things for future consumption. A special tone was given to their arguments by the scarcity of capital everywhere, even in England; that the growing dependence of labour on the aid of machinery; and lastly, by the folly of some followers of Rousseau, who were telling the working classes that they would be better off without any capital at all.

In consequence, the economists gave extreme prominence to the statements; first, that labour requires the support of capital, *i.e.* of good clothes, &c., that have been already produced; and secondly, that labour requires the aid of capital in the form of factories, stores of raw material, &c. Of course the workman might have supplied his own capital, but in fact he seldom had more than a little store of clothes and furniture, and perhaps a few simple tools of his own—he was dependent for everything else on the savings of others. The labourer received clothes ready to wear, bread ready to eat, or the money with which he could purchase them. The capitalist received a spinning of wool into yarn, a weaving of yarn into cloth, or a ploughing of land, and only in a few cases commodities ready for use, coats ready to be worn, or bread ready to be eaten. There are, no doubt, important exceptions, but the ordinary bargain between employers and employed is that the wage-receiver gets command over commodities in a form ready for immediate consumption, and in exchange carries his employer's goods a stage further towards being ready for immediate consumption. But while this is true of most employees, it is not true of those who finish the processes of production. For instance, those who put together and finish watches, give to their employers far more commodities in a form ready for immediate consumption, than they obtain as wages. And if we take one season of the year with another, so as to allow for seed and harvest time, we find that workmen as a whole hand over to their employers more finished commodities than they receive as wages. There is, however, a rather forced sense in which we may perhaps be justified in saying that the earnings of labour depend upon advances made to labour by capital. For—not to take account of machinery and factories, of ships and railroads—the houses loaned to workmen, and even the raw materials in various stages which will be worked up into commodities consumed by them, represent a far greater provision of capital for their use than the equivalent of the advances which they make to the capitalist, even when they work for a month for him before getting any wages.

Such are the facts which economists of the present as well as of earlier times have wished to express by saying that all labour requires the support of capital, whether owned by the labourer or by someone else; and that when anyone works for hire, his wages are, as a rule, advanced to him out of his employer's capital—advanced, that is, without waiting till the things which he is engaged in making are ready for use. These simple statements have been a good deal criticized, but they have never been denied by anyone who has taken them in the sense in which they were meant.

Unfortunately, however, some of the older economists were not content to leave the matter there. They went further and said that the amount of wages was limited by the amount of capital; and this statement cannot be defended; at best it is but a slovenly way of talking. It has suggested to some people the notion that the total amount of wages that could be paid in a country in the course of, say a year, was a fixed sum. If by the threat of a strike, or in any other way, one body of workmen got an increase of wages, they would be told that in consequence other bodies of workmen must lose an amount exactly equal in the aggregate to what they had gained. Those who have said this have perhaps thought of agricultural produce, which has but one harvest in the year. If all the wheat raised at one harvest is sure to be eaten before the next, and if none can be imported, then it is true that if anyone's share of the wheat is increased, there will be just so much less for others to have. But this does not justify the statement that the amount of wages payable in a country is fixed by the capital in it, a doctrine which has been called 'the vulgar form of the Wages-Fund theory.'

§ 3. The doctrine of the Wages-Fund received countenance from some careless expressions into which Mill was betrayed by his desire to treat the problem of Distribution in his second Book before that of Exchange in his third. The attempt was necessarily a failure. But he collects all the various elements of the problem in the third chapter of his fourth Book: and there the relations of labour and capital are presented symmetrically, and the Wages-Fund does not appear.

Some of Mill's propositions are badly worded.

The proposition that *Industry is limited by capital*, was often interpreted so as to make it practically convertible with the Wages-Fund theory. It can be explained so as to be true: but a similar explanation would make the statement that "capital is limited by industry" equally true. It was however used by Mill chiefly in connection with the argument that the aggregate employment of labour cannot generally be increased by preventing people, by Protective duties or in other ways, from satisfying their wants in that manner which they would prefer.

The effects of protective duties are very complex and cannot be discussed here; but Mill is clearly right in saying that in general the capital, that is applied to support and aid labour in any new industry created by such duties, "must have been withdrawn or withheld from some other, in which it gave, or would have given, employment to probably about the same quantity of labour which it employs in its new occupation." Or, to put the argument in a more modern form, such legislation does not *primâ facie* increase either the national dividend or the share of that dividend which goes to labour. For it does not increase the supply of capital; nor does it, in any other way, cause the marginal efficiency of labour to rise relatively to that of capital. The rate that has to be paid for the use of capital is therefore not lowered; the national dividend is not increased (in fact it is almost sure to be diminished); and as neither labour nor capital gets any new advantage over the other in bargaining for the distribution of the dividend, neither can benefit by such legislation.

The first Fundamental Proposition of Mill's is closely connected with his fourth, viz. that *Demand for commodities is not demand for labour*: and this again expresses his meaning badly. It is true that those, who purchase any particular commodities, do not generally supply the capital that is required to aid and support the labour which produces those commodities: they merely divert capital and employment from other trades to that for the products of which they make increased demand. But Mill, not contented with proving this, seems to imply that, to spend money on the direct hire of labour is more beneficial to the labourer than to spend it on buying commodities. Now there is a sense in which this contains a little truth. For the price of the commodities includes profits of manufacturer and middleman; and if the purchaser acts as employer, he slightly diminishes the demand for the services of the employing class, and increases the demand for labour as he might have done by buying, say, hand-made lace instead of machine-made lace. But this argument assumes that the wages of labour will be paid, as in practice they commonly are, while the work is proceeding; and that the price of the commodities will be paid, as in practice it commonly is, after the commodities are made: and it will be found that in every case which Mill has chosen to illustrate the doctrine, his arguments imply, though he does not seem to be aware of it, that the consumer when passing from purchasing commodities to hiring labour, postpones the date of his own consumption of the fruits of labour. And the same postponement would have resulted in the same benefit to labour if the purchaser had made no change in the mode of his expenditure[1].

[1] A fuller discussion of the Wages-Fund is given in *Principles*, VI. II. 12.

INDEX.

Words printed in Italics are technical terms; and the numbers immediately following them are those of the pages on which they are defined.

CAMBRIDGE: PRINTED BY J. AND C. F. CLAY, AT THE UNIVERSITY PRESS.

CPSIA information can be obtained at www.ICGtesting.com
Printed in the USA
BVOW051138130512

290088BV00004B/82/P